Marxism
Queer Theory
Gender

Marxism
Queer Theory
Gender

Edited by

Mas'ud Zavarzadeh
Teresa L. Ebert
Donald Morton

2

Transformation
Marxist Boundary Work in Theory, Economics, Politics, and Culture

---

Published by
The Red Factory, 2001

ISBN 0-9674545-0-6

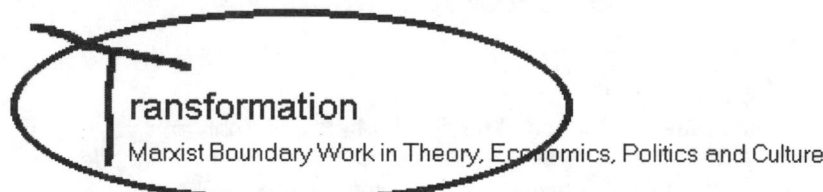

ransformation

Marxist Boundary Work in Theory, Economics, Politics and Culture

2. *Marxism, Queer Theory, Gender*

Pataphysics of the Closet	Donald Morton	1
Queer Theory and 'Family Values'	Dana Cloud	71
Post-Marxist Queer Theory and the 'Politics of AIDS'	Bob Nowlan	115
Sexual Harassment as/and (Self) Invention: Class, Sexuality, Pedagogy and (Creative) Writing	Jennifer Cotter	155
'Women's Oppression' and Property Relations	Huei-Ju Wang	217
Cyberpedagogy and Class-as-Life-Style	Rob Wilkie	251
The Spectral Concrete: Bodies, Sex Word and (some notes on) Citizenship	Teresa L. Ebert	275
Books Received		304
Announcements		306
Notes to Contributors		331
Notes on Contributors		333

On *Transformation*

These are not friendly times for a Marxist journal, and yet these are exactly the times in which a Marxist journal is urgently needed to provide transformative knowledges for social change. *Transformation: Marxist Boundary Work in Theory, Economics, Politics and Culture* is a response to the crisis of revolutionary theory and praxis. The contemporary "left" has abandoned the project of revolution in favor of radical (bourgeois) democracy and "third way" reformism; marginalized problems of labor, class and exploitation; and elided the centrality of "need." Left theory has deserted economic and labor issues at a time of increasing class differences between North and South, the poor and the rich; a time when the workers of the world are increasingly subjected to exploitation by more innovative technologies and subtle forms of management to keep the rate of profit high for transnational cartels.

Transformation is a journal of historical materialist analyses of economic, political and cultural practices, their history and consequences. The goal of *Transformation* is to produce effective knowledges for understanding the world in order to change it.

There are, of course, many journals publishing texts on the contemporary situation from neomarxist, postmarxist, social democratic, feminist, postcolonialist, anarchist, anti-racist, lesbigay, and ecological perspectives. The underlying assumption of most "left" readings of the world is that capitalism is here to stay and it is only one of the many modes of "oppression" anyway. By dehistoricizing capitalism and substituting "oppression" for "exploitation," they not only naturalize the "multiple oppression" theory of social inequality but capitalism itself. They further assume that capitalism has changed from a regime of "production" to a culture of "consumption," that "labor" has been displaced by "knowledge," and that we have entered a moment in history which is post-class, post-production, post-theory, post-ideology and post-dialectical, and post-capitalist--in short a "post-al" phase in which history has come to an end. History is, in these journals, a spectral (re)writing. The post-al, as spectral history, has, in effect, put an end to politics based on "need," "class struggle," "use-value," "collectivity" and the fight against "exploitation," and, in its place, has instituted a politics based on "desire," "difference," "aesthetics," "conversation," "consensus," and "coalition." In post-al left journals, the agent of social change, which is actually a euphemism for bourgeois accommodationism and reformism, is the radical middle not the proletariat. Social analysis, in these journals, is therefore shifted from the political economy of material practices and class struggle to cultural politics and poetics, from the laws of motion of capital to the strategies and tactics of consumption, the problematics of representation, and (deconstructed) "identity politics."

ii >> *Transformation*

Materiality in the post-al left is not the materiality of class struggle, the mode of production, and "need"--the structure of contradictions and antagonisms in history. Rather, it is the post-conceptual "matterism" of the "body," "language," and "desire."

In opposition to this spectral cultural matterism and its ludic politics of difference, *Transformation* deploys classical Marxist theory to provide boundary explanations of contemporary capitalism-without-borders and the world order it has legitimated. By boundary work, we mean producing historical materialist analyses that move beyond the limits of bourgeois divisions of knowledge and directly engage the most advanced modes of bourgeois knowledges and supersede them to provide guidelines for revolutionary praxis. It places classical Marxist theory in new terrain and brings it to bear on understanding the emerging contradictions in global capitalism--from labor relations to sexuality; from markets to the cyberspaces of virtual reality; from health care to "crime" and "family values"; from post-al forms of racism to hypercolonialism and "welfare". . . .

Transformation is committed to constantly bringing classical Marxist theories into zones in which they have not often been situated before. At the moment, some classical Marxist writers, in their encounter with the new post-al and cyber discourses of global capitalism, seem to think that they have offered an effective intervention when, for instance, they denounce bourgeois theory and science for their opaque, elitist language and mystifying "jargon," or when they substitute moral outrage for an explanatory materialist critique of the dominant practices. *Transformation* will go beyond such commonsense criticism and, in the tradition of Marx, Engels, Lenin, Luxemburg, Trotsky and other classical Marxist theorists, will not turn away from the "new" and the post-al. It will confront and historicize them in order to develop class consciousness for transformative praxis. In confronting global capitalism, *Transformation* will, if necessary, deploy the unfamiliar languages and opaque concepts and will unpack their class politics. The vanguard cannot turn away from difficult texts and retreat into the smug comfort of common sense and its seemingly clear language.

Transformation is a vanguard journal opposing both nostalgia and utopia and insisting on developing rigorous materialist boundary understandings of the social totality--boundary analyses, in short, that are necessary for a sustained intervention by revolutionary praxis towards ending the private ownership of the means of production and establishing international socialism. The agent of this historical change is neither the singular individual--who spontaneously rebels against the regime of wage labor and capital through the sheer experience of the violence of exploitation--nor the radical middle and its reformist practices but the collectivity of workers: what Lenin calls workers as "socialist theorists" whose revolutionary praxis is founded upon a coherent historical materialist theory of the social relations of production and the international division of labor.

We are, of course, aware that the specific political conditions of the present moment put our goal to make *Transformation* the site of active classical Marxist knowledges beyond our immediate reach. Classical Marxism has been so violently and systematically excluded from the scene of social struggle and analytical contestations that it will take some time for *Transformation* to become a place for living revolutionary Marxism. But *Transformation* will energetically work towards this goal by activating classical Marxist knowledges among already practicing Marxists and, perhaps more importantly, among younger Marxists, both of whom are forced into silence because their work is marked in the bourgeois knowledge industry as, among other things, "dogmatic" and thus dismissed and blacklisted

To change these unequal conditions, *Transformation* will provide a place for the articulation of lost and suppressed revolutionary knowledges and praxis. Thus we will publish only those texts that advance classical Marxist theory (or significantly move in this direction). We believe that under unequal conditions (that allow anti-Marxist texts a free reign but impose all sorts of constraints and restrictions on Marxist writings) to provide "equal" space for the texts of right-wing writers or their "third way" allies or the practitioners of the reformist left, in the name of an open debate and discussion, is not an open debate but rather a travesty of free inquiry and a mockery of "equality"--it is an instance of cynical performativity. The dominant bourgeois knowledge industry has successfully marginalized and silenced many radical thinkers and workers, either by false promise of an "open debate" (which always turns out to be staged event, to limit their practices) or by accusing them of being undemocratic and authoritarian if they do not give equal space to their opponents (who use that space to suppress them). In a society that has been anything but open to revolutionary knowledges and practices, such cynical arguments are aimed simply at further restricting and appropriating the limited space available for radical praxis. The entire capitalist knowledge industry is freely available to the opponents of Marxism. To give space to bourgeois left writers, in the name of open debate, is to fall for the liberal myths of equal and free debate when that formal openness is severely restricted by the actual unequal economic and material resources available to the two sides of the debate. To give room, then, in the pages of *Transformation*, to the opponents of classical Marxism is to further expand the space already abundantly available to them in all sites of culture--from the ludic academy and post-al left journals to the corporate spaces of publishing houses and communications, radio and television cartels to cybertexts. One of the projects of *Transformation* is to demystify the deceptive liberal theology of ecumenicism and coalition and to open up a space for emancipatory praxis and knowledges. Since *Transformation* is in contestation with the entire bourgeois knowledge industry, the space of this debate should be understood globally and not locally: those who wish to criticize our praxis can easily do so in the pages of practically all the available publications of the left, right and the center.

Donald Morton

Pataphysics of the Closet:

Queer Theory as the Art of Imaginary

Solutions for Unimaginary Problems

"Democracy does *not* abolish class oppression. It only makes the class struggle more direct, wider, more open and pronounced, and that is what we need . . . The fuller . . . equality . . . , the clearer will the workers . . . see that the cause of their oppression is capitalism not lack of rights."

--Lenin

The closet is an annex of the system of wage-labor--a place in which inequalities in the exchange of labor power for wages are justified by pathologising resistant sexualities. By drawing on the discourses of poststructuralism, postmodernism, postcapitalism, . . . , through such concepts as "reparative reading," "the sublime," "claustrophiliac ecstasy," "(self)addiction," . . . , Queer Theory--in a notable reversal--now affirms the closet as the site of the singular; of excess-ive and non-representable desires; of (melancholic) self-reflexivity; and of the jouissance of the nomadic subject of post-socialism. In this essay, I will argue that the closet is not an autonomous place of self-enraptured ecstasy but part of the political economy of capitalism. It is a space constituted by the laws of motion of capital.

The queer left's new quietistic affirmation of the closet converges with the reformist left's homophobic tactics: the practices of both groups are part of ongoing mainstream cultural strategies for normalizing wage-labor. In other words, today's queer left texts celebrating the ecstasies of claustrophilia (Casarino, "The Sublime of the Closet") ultimately serve the same interests as the writings of such leftists as Cary Nelson who deploy homophobia and homophobic representations to marginalize--as a perversion--any anti-capitalist critique-al practice. In his popular *Academic Key Words: A Devil's Dictionary for Higher Education* co-authored with Stephen Watt, for instance, Nelson attacks--with all the violence of a police raid--those who refuse to go along with the "normal" left's agenda of reform and collaboration. In the language of surveillance and punishment, he demonizes and brackets as "pseudo-Marxists" (12) revolutionary Marxists who fight for "nothing less than 'radical' transformations" (126). In emerging global capitalism, when wage-labor is facing new contradictions, such left collaborators as Nelson are deploying more and more violent tactics to suppress oppositional practices that foreground these contradictions and thereby mark the crisis of wage-labor. For Nelson such "ruthless critiques" of wage-labor are the perverse acts of a "Red Sphincter" (12). Nelson can unleash such homophobic violence from the "left" knowing that--contrary to popular representation--the queer left will not only support but in fact relish his homophobic attack against revolutionaries. Nelson and the queer left share the same pro-capitalist agenda: the only revolution they support is, in Nelson's entrepreneurial rhetoric, a "revolution in how we do business" (12). The alliance between the pro-capitalist homophobic left and the pro-capitalist queer left shows the objective truth of the underlying argument of this essay: under the wage-labor system, objective class interests always take priority over cultural differences. In the struggle against capitalism, both side with big business: they want not the end of wage-labor itself but capitalism with a smile, better benefits, better pay, and blurring of the difference between exploiter and exploited (Graham-Gibson, *The End of Capitalism [As We Knew It]*; Nelson, *Manifesto of a Tenured Radical*; Delaney, *Times Square Red, Times Square Blue*).[1] Homophobia is the cultural legitimization of the inequalities of wage-labor; to end homophobia one must first end capitalism. Nelson's concept "Red Sphincter"--by relying on the homophobic structure of feeling under capitalism--abnormalizes as deviant all who struggle against wage-labor and thus makes sure that capitalism itself remains immune from "ruthless critique" and consequently continues as the "normal." In the end what Nelson's strategy amounts to is this: now that queers ("in" or "out") have joined the mainstream, it is revolutionaries who have to be quarantined to the closet.[2] In the defense of wage-labor, in other words, "the closet" is a necessary space both for the queer left and the homophobic right.

One

It is a cliché that "coming out" and "the closet" are categories special to discussions of the sexual margins because—as the classic 1970s Gay Liberation text, *With Downcast Gays*, once put it—those groups "are unlike any other oppressed group in that their identity is almost always invisible to others" (Hodges and Hutter, 15).[3] Twenty-five years later the queer left went even further to insist on the closet's absolute centrality not just for understanding sexuality but "virtually any aspect of modern Western culture" (Sedgwick *Epistemology* 1). Until very recently (and recent developments are the main focus of this essay), the imperative carried by these discourses has been an unequivocal call for homosexuals to "come out" of "the closet" in order to achieve not only "personal" and "psychological" wholeness (freeing themselves from the burden of the repression that marks them as "sinful" or "sick" as the beginning of the formation of a healed identity), but also "public" and "political" goals (finding strength in numbers as the basis for developing an effective political presence to demand "democratic rights"). As merely a shift from invisibility to visibility, however, the moment of "coming out" as such says nothing about the ultimate aims of this gesture (I set aside here the fact that the absolute "invisibility" of homosexuality in any culture is a questionable thesis).[4] This essay, which critiques the prevailing understandings of "coming out" and "the closet," is written at a time when the public discussion of homosexuality is being monopolized by the pro-capitalist "queer left"[5] which erases class as the determinate factor in homosexual oppression and exploitation. Setting class aside, the queer left mystifies public discussion by proposing that the problem of homosexuality can be solved (like the problem of race, the problem of gender, the problem of . . .) by extending so-called "democratic rights" to the various social margins under the prevailing economic system and attacks Marxism for supposedly neglecting these rights.[6] By labeling it as "economic reductionism," the queer left (mis)represents Marxism as an opponent of democracy and democratic rights, when history clearly records its vigorous commitment to what Marx called--discussing the Jewish question--"*political* emancipation" as "a big step forward" (Marx, "On the Jewish Question" 155). When, however, Marx adds that "*political* emancipation" is by no means "the final form of human emancipation" (Marx, "On the Jewish Question" 155), we find suddenly and sharply clarified the differences between the queer left's defense of "coming out" under capitalist democracy and the Red left's defense of "coming out" under socialist democracy. Marxism insists that "the final form of human emancipation" is NOT "political emancipation" at the level of the superstructure (capitalist democracy) but "economic emancipation" (equal access to society's resources) at the level of the material base (socialist democracy). In other words, "coming out" for the sake of "political emancipation" will prove insufficient. Lenin--in discussing gender relations in the situation of women--makes the issue of political emancipation/democratic rights clearer still when he argues that it is not whether various groups are formally recognized as having rights, but whether they can actually *exercise* those rights and that the precondition for their exercise is economic justice: "democracy does *not* abolish class oppression. It only makes the class struggle more direct, wider, more open and pronounced, and that is what we need . . . The fuller . . . equality . . . , the clearer will the workers . . . see that the cause of their oppression is capitalism not lack of rights" (Lenin, "A Caricature of

Marxism" 73)[7]. What Lenin says of workers in general certainly applies also to lesbian and gay workers.

Until recently the queer left had universalized "coming out" of "the closet" as the precondition for acquiring "political emancipation"/ "democratic rights," turned this concept into a transhistorical category separable from economics and wage labor, and urged all homosexuals to understand their "experience" in terms of "coming out," no matter what other factors (social, cultural, historical, economic . . .) conditioned their lives. As always, the aim of such an idealizing move is to block an understanding of sexual relations as class relations which actually produce sexual (and other) injustices, that is, to separate the analysis of sexual practices "above all . . . from a given stage of the mode of production" (Marx and Engels *The German Ideology* 61). My goal here is to reconceptualize the sexual in historical materialist terms as an inaugural step towards a Red Queer Theory: my argument is that the "the closet" and "coming out" are ideological constructs which change historically depending on changes in social relations and the state of class struggle; that struggle for queer emancipation must be reconnected to questions of the mode of production and class and therefore transformative economic change; that "freedom" must be re-understood not as the freedom to fantasize (desire) but as freedom from need; that because of historical circumstances, same-sex relations have now taken their place in liberal Western democracies not as a legitimate necessity, but as an "alternative lifestyle"--for those who can afford it. Captured within the profit imperative of capitalism, the queer lifestyle is legitimized, on the one hand, as a model form of consumption and deployed, on the other hand, as a form of "difference" used by capitalists to pit one group of workers against other groups so as to prevent their solidarity against capitalist exploitation. To achieve freedom from need (that is, to go beyond "political emancipation") requires the revolutionary overthrow of the capitalist mode of production, whose only imperative is profit and whose result is always the exploitation of the many for the benefit of the few, and the establishment of a socialist economy, whose priority is meeting the needs of all citizens. As I have already said, questions of sexuality, race, gender, ethnicity, . . . must therefore be reconnected systematically to the question of class. Such a rearticulation of Queer Theory as Red Queer Theory requires a sustained critique of the dominant understandings of "coming out" and "the closet" from a classical Marxist perspective that reconnects all of those elements that the queer left works hard to disconnect in order to arrive at a knowledge of the social totality. As Lukács argued, bourgeois social logic is founded upon the reification of the discrete, the isolated, and—to use Deleuze and Guattari's word--the nomadic, a process which he says is the result of the "disintegrating effect" of commodity exchange (Lukács, *History*

85), adding however that "this isolation and fragmentation is only apparent" (91).

It is not just committed Marxists who recognize the unproductive character of contemporary gay/queer politics and question the idea of "coming out" as the "solution" to oppression and exploitation: John Weir, once active as a "radical queer" (Weir 256), has recently declared his intention of "going [back] in" the closet as a repudiation of 1990s queer politics because it is nothing but a sell-out to capitalist consumerism on the part of upper middle class homosexuals for whom "the characteristic homosexual act is compulsive spending" (Weir 253). Weir clearly recognizes the disintegrating effects of the 1990s version of "Gay Liberation": "As a group, self-identified gay men . . . want to be entertained and flattered, not criticized . . . [and] are especially resistant to thinking about issues of class and race, and they steadfastly deny their sexism. The irony of gay liberation," Weir continues, "is that it has made room in the mainstream only for those white men who are already privileged, and disinclined to share their wealth" (Weir 254). "There's no distinction anymore," he concludes, "between conservative Republicans and self-identified homosexuals" (Weir 258) because they both share a sense of class-based entitlement to privilege within the capitalist system. Lacking the knowledge necessary to contribute towards transformative social change, Weir ends up basically in the same unproductive, moralistic ideological position as his opponents: what they see as their "rightful entitlement," he sees as "personal selfishness."

Though Weir himself cannot situate his discourses in a broad and productive theoretical and political horizon, his text is nevertheless symptomatic of the fact that by the late 1990s queer left politics and its ideological support, Queer Theory, had reached a point of historical crisis as a result of the exposure of their own internal contradictions.[8] While it originally represented itself as a staunch and implacable enemy of mainstream bourgeois life, Queer Theory is now recognized as nothing but an ideological maneuver to enable the assimilation of queers to mainstream economic practices, which is to say, the assimilation of those on the sexual margins to the free market.[9] In other words, while at the level of cultural politics, Queer Theory promoted the idea of its "opposition" to bourgeois life in the name of sexual "difference," at the level of economics, it was nothing but a tool for assimilating queers to the new post-national capitalist workforce, the kind of workforce required by capitalism in its current global and transnational phase. Among the symptoms of this crisis are the following historical developments: the recognition of the success of queer assimilation by commentators not only from the far right (Norman Podhoretz) but also from the queer left (Daniel Harris); the expressions of anxiety accompanying queer assimilation--"without [oppression], we're nothing" (Mendelsohn 239); the attacks by Queer Theorists on so-called "Left Conservatives"--a euphemism for the revolutionaries struggling against capitalism ("Left Conservatism"); the worry that that some queer leftists express that Queer Theory has become not only embarrassingly "parochial" but "jingoistic" ("Hot Type" A-21); the sudden and "surprising" reorienting of Queer Theory away from "oppositional" critique towards "reparative reading" (Eve Sedgwick, "Paranoid Reading and Reparative Reading"); the public labeling of the star of Queer Theory, Judith Butler, not only as a "hip defeatist" and "America's Emptiest Feminist" but also as a writer and teacher who encourages "successful middle-class people . . . to focus on cultivating the self rather than thinking in a way that helps the material conditions of others" (Nussbaum 44); and, not least, the new affirmation of the closet.

One of the main objections to the classical Marxist critique evolves around the Marxist analysis of the relation of "need" to "desire." Throughout this essay I call attention to the manner in which various contemporary theorists and writers foreground the concept of "desire" to the exclusion of the concept "need." I furthermore argue against what I call desire social theory and for need social theory. The bourgeois left argues that in making this distinction, I am reinforcing a "binary," drawing therefore too sharp a distinction between need and desire, and creating a "foundational" separation between entities that are not only opposed to each other but are in fact implicated in each other. Instead of making such a distinction, they propose that we should see need and desire in what they opportunistically refer to as a more properly "dialectical" relationship. Needless to add that by "dialectical," they mean one should adopt an eclectic (on the one hand, on the other hand) approach. In other words, to argue for the priority of need is to separate the inseparable and fall back on a pre-Nietzschean notion of "causality" which establishes a hierarchy between need and desire. In this regard, it is important to clarify what is at stake in the bourgeois left's urgent efforts carried out in the name of progressive textualities.

Although opposing binaries is said to be part of an attempt to offer more inclusive ways of thinking, respectful of difference, it is quite clear that, at its core, such a move is not so much epistemological (textual) as it is political. It is not really a question either of "causality" or "binaries," broadly speaking, which is the issue for the bourgeois left: it is what is posited as "cause" and what the contents of the binaries are that is really at stake. If the "cause" is posited in such a way that it naturalizes the interests of the ruling class or the binaries are basically supportive of the law of profit, no objections are ever raised. When, for example, Deleuze and Guattari write that "Desire is not bolstered by needs, but rather the contrary; needs are derived from desire: they are counterproducts within the real that desire produces" (Deleuze and Guattari 27), the politics of this move is to deconstruct Marx, who prioritizes need over desire, for instance, when he situates desire in relation to the social relations of production: "Our desires and pleasures spring from society" (Marx *Wage-Labour* 216).

As in all deconstruction, the relation between desire and need--which is posited as a historical necessity in Marx--is transformed into a contingent relation. To be clear: Deleuze and Guattari start out from the assumption of a "playful" "indeterminate" internal and differential "linkage" between all entities, including "need" and "desire," which leads to the conclusion that no decisive determinate relation between them (or any other entities) can ever be established. On these terms, it is therefore impossible to argue, for instance, that the "desiring" practices of the capitalist class have any effect whatsoever on the fulfillment of the needs of the working class. When the anti- and post-Marxist revisionists or left queer theorists argue that there is a "dialectical" relation between need and desire, their notion of the "dialectical" is identical with the notion of post-al "indeterminacy": in other words, "dialectical" is used to mean "differential" in the Derridean sense--there is no way to argue for a determinate relation between need and desire. Of course, as Marx argues, the relation between need and desire is in fact "dialectical," but here "dialectical" presupposes that "need" and "desire" exist not in a relation of post-al "indeterminacy" but in a historically produced tension resulting from social contradictions. The queer left's slogan about the dialectical relation of need and desire is, in short, an ideological ruse, a move to make any questioning of desire impossible.[10]

Two

When we confront the situation that homosexuality has taken on a greater urgency in Western societies in recent times, we face a fundamental philosophical and political question about the status of questions: What makes a social question appear on the historical horizon as at one stage *a question*, then at another stage as *a significant question*, and then at yet another stage as *an urgent question*? Questions simply do not exist in the "timeless," "a-historical" realm of "good/bad ideas"; indeed what makes a question recognizable as a "good/bad idea" are certain historical and material conditions which enable its very appearance. As Marx observes, "Mankind . . . inevitably sets itself only such tasks as it is able to solve, since closer examination will always show that the problem itself arises only when the material conditions for its solution are already present or at least in the course of formation" (Marx *A Contribution* 263). In other words, the appearance on the discursive horizon of certain questions (homosexuality, abortion, coming out, environmental pollution, . . .) is caused by material transformations at the level of mode of production that affect social life at the level of relations of production. What gives questions "priority" is *not* the "abstract value" of the questions in themselves, but their connection to material conditions. *Material conditions set the priorities*: in societies where hunger is the most urgent question, abortion, pollution, sexualities, . . . will have a different priority.

Queer left social theory holds that "coming out" of the "the closet" is the result of *subjective* changes: these changes in social practices are the effect of an emerging consciousness which, having undergone enlightenment ("liberation") through encounter with "progressive" ideas, finds oppression of all kinds immoral, inhumane and unacceptable. On this view, gay/lesbian/bi/ . . . liberation is therefore the result of acts of the consciousness of autonomous agents developing counter-discourses and mobilizing what de Certeau calls new strategies and tactics to open up the space of gay/queer/bi . . . practices.[11] On this account, the Gay Liberation movement presumably came about because homosexuals decided to "rise up and demand [their] rights" (Blasius and Phelan 277) and this outcome is to be understood therefore as a case of individual gays and lesbians, in Marcus's phrase, "making history" (*Making History: The Struggle for Gay and Lesbian Equal Rights, 1945-1990*). Against both this traditional liberal notion and the more recent notions of Gramscian left activism (addressed below)[12], I argue that changes in the relations between gay/lesbian/queer/bi . . . citizens and heterosexual citizens are neither a matter of emerging consciousness nor of ahistorical agency ("it is quite immaterial what consciousness starts to do on its own" [Marx and Engels *The German Ideology* 45]), but of transformations in the mode of production. Hence, the ways in which human beings engage in their sexual practices is ultimately determined by the mode of production. Whereas the queer left continually distracts attention away from economic determinants and "explains" one superstructural effect (sexual practices) in terms of another superstructural effect (changes of consciousness), Marxist social theory explains superstructural effects (changes of sexual practices, changes of consciousness, . . .) in relation to changes in the base: "What [individuals] are . . . coincides with their production, both with *what* they produce and with *how* they produce (Marx and Engels *The German Ideology* 31-32). My analysis argues that "the ideas of the ruling class are in every epoch the ruling ideas " (Marx and Engels *The German Ideology* 59) and therefore that the mainstream "explanations" of "coming out" of "the closet" (and the shifts those explanations continually undergo) are nothing more than elements of bourgeois ideology-- elements in the ongoing class struggle--which have to be critiqued by rereading them as superstructural developments corresponding to changes in the base. To be sure, such a project has its difficulties: the various aspects of a particular mode of production are ultimately inseparable from each other; the shifts and changes in the internal development of any mode of production cannot in any simple way be placed in a linear order; and superstructural changes are so complex and "messy" that it is difficult to sort them out with precision (Marx *A Contribution* 263).

The major ideological shift discussed in this essay can be briefly highlighted as follows: in the first phase--Coming Out as Gay Liberation (from the 1969 Stonewall uprising through the decade of the 1970s), "the closet" was understood as a forced sanctuary (a place of "hiding") and pressure was placed on homosexuals by liberationists to "come out" and thus "make themselves visible." In the latest (third) phase--The Closet Is Sublime (developed since the 1990s in the wake of Queer Theory), the earlier reading has been "reversed" so that now "the closet" is understood as a space of sublime pleasure—a place of self-embracing, self-enclosing. To pressure someone to "come out" is to repress the pleasures of the closet, which is another way of saying to unleash once again, this time from another side, violence on the queer. While in its earliest phase "the closet" was understood as a more overtly *political* and *economic* matter of the relations between different social groups (heterosexuals and homosexuals) determined by objective historical conditions, in the latter "the closet" is reunderstood as a *textual* matter of the relations between the represented and the process of representation, which is assumed to be autonomous and not the result of objective conditions. At the broadest level, the ideological shift I am examining here is explained by the concept of "post-ality," theorized by Mas'ud Zavarzadeh as "all the practices that, as a totality, obscure the production practices of capitalism . . . by announcing the arrival of a . . . radically different and 'new' present'" (Zavarzadeh, 1) inasmuch as the queer left now argues that we are in a "post-closet" moment. At the sexual level, however, it is the specific "post-al" practices instituted by Queer Theory that announce the "new" and remarkable reading which transvalues "the closet." It is no longer a place of hiding but a place of bliss. In other words, as economic injustice has accelerated world wide and class struggle has grown more intense, the queer left has given its ideology a "new" twist with The Closet Is Sublime--which is the ideology of not "coming out"--so as to push the lesbian, gay, queer masses into a deeper and deeper pleasure-saturated quietism. There is, of course, an interphase in the genealogy of the closet, which I call The Closet as Media Hype.

The struggle for gay freedom in the U. S. had its beginnings in the postwar economic expansion called The Long Boom. The Long Boom (from the end of World War II to roughly the Oil Crisis of 1973[13]) was a time of mass production practices; the dominance of nation-states[14]; U. S. post-war economic hegemony; high and rising worker expectations; and the supposed *embourgeoisement* of the U. S. proletariat. The U. S.'s post-war economic dominance brought its citizens a new level of prosperity and, with the consequent re-ordering of social priorities, such questions as sexual orientation, which up to that time were relatively less important, began to come to the fore. Mass production processes were developed to enable large-scale industrial production and have classically been associated with a male labor force and with the corresponding social recognition and preferential treatment of the male as a family's "breadwinner." Structured in large part by the nation-state system[15] in which immigration flows were highly regulated and the supply and re-supply of workers was an internal, national question,[16] capital divided workers (among other ways) by favoring those who were *reproductive* as well as the *productive*.[17] No doubt, as in other times and places, large numbers of homosexual workers passed for "straight" and the sexually/gender different worker, even though not formally "out," was perhaps sometimes recognized as such through unmarried status or other condition and often channeled (through social pressures and expectations) into certain (often less remunerative) jobs (hair dresser, teacher, musician, artist, . . .). Taking place towards the end of the Long Boom, the Stonewall uprising and the Gay Liberation movement are basically a demand that, like other marginalized groups, those on the sexual margins have the "democratic right" to participate in the mass production processes and the mass forms of exchange which characterized that period and to benefit from the greater income and greater purchasing power (the new system of exchanges) which prevailed in mass production jobs.   In other words, in spite of his/her difference, the gay/lesbian/ . . . worker demanded the right that his/her/ . . . needs--from housing to health insurance--be met and met on the same level being enjoyed by straight citizens.   Again, however, the demand for the "democratic right" of inclusion in mass labor is not--under capitalism--a solution to inequality. Since under capitalism all labor is exploited, the relation between the gay worker and the straight worker is not, at the most crucial level, that of a "sexually" marked "privileged" vs. an "unprivileged" worker: both the straight and gay worker--like the male and female worker, the white worker and worker of color, . . . --are simply assigned different positions in the social division of labor. These positions, which change historically over time, are of course created in capitalism's interest: to simply "switch positions" or change the hierarchy of inclusion/exclusion in wage labor--while it may be locally ameliorative--ultimately provides no effective redress of exploitation itself.

　　　　In any case, while it does indeed play a role, the demand for such a "right" through "activist agitation" is not the *cause* of social change, but instead an *effect* of changes in production practices and in what Marx calls the "working day." Capitalism structures the "working day" in two elements: the period of necessary labor (which provides a subsistence life for workers) and the period of surplus labor (to produce profit for the capitalist); and capital always strives to maximize the latter in order to increase profits. Under mass production, the working day was characterized by such specific features as assembly-line production and a managerial method (Taylorism) which segmented production into its most simple elements so that any worker--even one with little training--could perform the requisite tasks. The result of these practices was the *de-skilling of labor*, which enlarged the pool of workers for the production of profit, increased the number of workers able to compete for the same jobs and simultaneously robbed them of a major ground ("skills") for demanding higher wages. Under these conditions, which also made the workday highly mechanical and monotonous, the arguments for Gay Liberation were basically arguments against the prevailing social division of labor produced by the mode of production, that is, arguments against the increasing alienation of wage labor and the heightened worker competition and growing objectification and commodification created by post-War capitalism. "Coming out" in the Gay Liberation/Long Boom phase involved a recognition of the *structural* interrelation between different levels of exploitation and oppression: at that time Gay Liberation attacked and critiqued not simply heterosexism but "the system" of capitalism that naturalized privilege. Not simply a plea for social and cultural "inclusion," then, the Gay Liberation movement aimed at economic inclusion: at one level, at opening up various modes of employment to all people (regardless of sexual or other differences) but, beyond that, at recognizing and breaking the chain of worker alienation in general. In this phase of "coming out," the sexual margins were able to make overt and clear connections between the subjective, the political and the economic, between the struggle for democratic political rights and the struggle for economic access: "I have a recurring daydream. I imagine a place where gay people can be free. A place where there is no job discrimination, police harassment or prejudice" (Teal 281). In making these connections, the Gay Liberation movement was closer to Marx and Engels's insight that "'Liberation' is an historical and not a mental act, and it is brought about by historical conditions, the level of industry, commerce, agriculture, intercourse . . . " (Marx and Engels *The German Ideology* 38).

The Recession interphase (stretching roughly from the Oil Crisis of 1973 through the Tax Bill of 1993) was marked by significant historical changes: the Long Boom ended; the U. S. was challenged not only by the Oil Cartel but by the other emerging capitalist economies in Europe and Asia; and in the face of 18% interest rates, Carter was defeated in 1980 and the Republicans captured the White House for the next twelve years and put in place national policies hostile to the effective organization of workers to demand their rights (Reagan, for example, demolished the air traffic controller's union). It was a time not of "boom" but of economic uncertainty and downturn: although the twenty-eight-year Long Boom phase saw five recessions in the US economy (1948-49, 1953-54, 1957-58, 1960-61, 1969-70), the significantly shorter, nineteen-year transitional phase saw four recessions (1973-75, 1980, 1981-82, 1990-91) and they were longer-lasting.[18] This transition phase--anticipated in and emblemized by the NASA Apollo moon-shot program (with its high-tech production: automation, mainframe computers, information technologies, technological elites, . . .)--inaugurated the tendencies most fully developed in the (next) Age of Difference when capitalism underwent a number of dramatic shifts: from a more "rigid" to a more "flexible" mode of accumulation, from low tech to high tech, from mass production to batch production, from mass market to niche market, from manufacturing to service work, and away from manual toward knowledge work. With the end of the Long Boom, it is said, "Fewer and fewer people in the West experience work" as the act of transforming "the natural world . . . into tangible goods" (Allen 535) and large segments of the work force are turned into "knowledge workers."

In the Long Boom, mass production involved a "structured" workday: full-time work and the "social wage" (pay with benefits) were regarded as the "norm." As mass production lost its historical effectivity in the increasingly labor-hostile phase of Recession, "structuredness" itself seemed to "seriously hamper" "corporate capital's global mobility" (Tabak 92). In the face of growing economic uncertainty and instability, work practices shifted sharply towards deregulation, informalization, and casualization. Reaganomics--which dominated the last years of the transitional Recession phase--was synonymous with these developments: Reagan's policies helped to curtail the "capacity of state apparatuses to monitor and police 'social' wage arrangements--that is, employment covered by labour codes and legislation regulated by the state" and to "increase the amplitude of 'casualization' of work" (Tabak 105). As a result, "part-time and contract jobs"--that is, "casualized" work (work without such benefits as health care, pensions, . . .)--"became an indispensable part of the world of work in the 1980s" (Tabak 105) and the notion of full-time employment as the work "norm" began to crumble. Capitalists, of course, touted the casualization and informalization of the working day ("flextime" is one example) as a form of worker-sensitive flexibility on the part of corporations, as a "personal convenience" and "benefit" to labor. It was nothing of the kind: the shift towards a more "flexible" working day/mode of production (inaugurated in a time of economic uncertainty and tighter profit-margins) and towards "just-in-time methods" (Allen 552) was a drive to make work more "market-mediated" (Tabak 105), which is to say, to make production processes more sensitive to--more tightly correlated with--quickly shifting market conditions (increasingly rapid fluctuations in supply, demand, finance, prices, sales, consumption, . . .).

In the most recent economic phase, which I call The Age of Difference, capitalism has taken on an increasingly global and transnational form and, as of February 1, 2000, the US had experienced "with 107 months of expansion" the "longest" "economic boom in history," ("Business and Finance" A-1), accompanied by a bullish stock market that has seen the Dow Jones averages rise from around 3300 in early 1993 to over 11,000 in August of 1999 with a yet higher spike on December 31, 1999. However, in sharp contrast to the Long Boom when economic growth raised workers's wages, benefits, confidence, and demands, this most recent economic expansion is marked by worker "insecurity" (Mischel 7). It is important to emphasize that this "insecurity" is not merely a "state of mind" but a marker of the objective material conditions of workers. It is widely recognized that while the share of social wealth held by the owning classes has dramatically expanded, "the typical American family is probably worse off near the end of the 1990s than it was at the end of the 1980s or the end of the 1970s despite an increase in the productive capacity of the overall economy" (Mishel 2), that American workers are "working longer for less" (Mishel 5), that workers are experiencing "greater [job] insecurity" (Mishel 7), that the "acceleration of capital [as opposed to wage] income growth in the 1990s" (the stock market boom) has "overwhelmingly benefited the richest families" (Mishel 3), and that "since the mid-1980s, poverty rates in the United States have failed to respond to economic growth" (Mishel 9).

The Long Boom was, in its structure, more or less a continuation of the "'Fordist accord' reached in the 1930s and 1940s" (Tabak 92). Ideologically the 'Fordist accord' signaled capital's (temporary) acceptance of some of labor's demands. The subsequent shift away from formalized mass production practices and toward the casualization of work, the niche market, and the economics of difference was part of the breaking up of the "Fordist accord," a breakup which was itself linked with the question of gender and the status of worker minorities. In order to increase profits, capital "bypass[ed] the Fordist accord" (Tabak 92) by decreasing the amount of "social wages" paid (getting rid of benefits), by making more work "part-time," by assigning "part-time work to women" (Tabak 93), and by hiring more "non-unionized wage workers, made up mostly of women and 'minorities' of all shades" (Tabak 92). In the shift toward flexible accumulation, the emphasis on service jobs combined with the broader tendencies towards the feminization, minoritization, and casualization of work converged to place workers in a new ideological position. Thus, the shift to "flexible technology finds its counterpart in the formation of flexible workgroups and social innovations such as 'quality circles'" (Allen 550). By the late 1990s, the casualization of the working day had reached so high a level that "in the U. S., fewer than one-third of Americans now have a workweek of standard 9-to-5 days, and that share is shrinking" (Brady 94).

Whereas in the Long Boom the emphasis was on "manual" labor, industrial production, and the manufacture of "tangible goods" that satisfy objectively recognizable human needs, in succeeding phases the emphasis is on "knowledge work" in service jobs more concerned with making things go more "smoothly" in intersubjective terms by responding to "differences." Whereas the former produces an ideology of common interest, the latter produces an ideology of social fragmentation and pluralistic differences. Whereas in the Long Boom, the emphasis of Gay Liberation was on inclusion in the common economic resources of capitalist democracy *in spite of differences,* in the Age of Difference, the emphasis of Queer Theory is on inclusion in global capitalist democratic rights to consumption *tailored to differences.* Whereas in the Long Boom, workers saw themselves as sharing a form of alienation produced by a structure (capitalism), in the Age of Difference, they are encouraged to focus increasingly on how they are divided at the cultural level by their own specific forms of self-alienation ("split subjectivity") which, in bourgeois ideology, are interpreted as specific forms of deeply subjective "difference." The lessons workers are supposed to learn in the Age of Difference is that their cultural "differences" are "theirs" (not structurally created but products of "self-invention") and that these differences are so deeply ingrained that they can never be overcome so as to produce a "commonality" in any zone (least of all, the economic).

In order to naturalize the current conditions of "flexible accumulation," the dominant ideology in the Age of Difference has shifted attention entirely to the cultural level, has canceled any sense of the "common," has utterly fragmented the social, and has posited a "pluralistic" world of utterly incommensurate differences. This fragmentation must be conceived not simply in spatial but also in temporal terms. Thus another significant ideological change brought in by the Age of Difference is the deconstruction of history itself: post-al theory not only declares the "end of history," but such queer left commentators as William Haver theorize the queer subject as the "promiscuous" "sexual nomad" (Haver 142) who inhabits a completely different mode of temporality, a new "contingent historicity" (143) in which "duration is in fact irrelevant" (142). History is celebrated in post-al theory as a sequence of "singular" events. The bourgeois notion that we are today living in a "post-historical" era is basically an ideological ruse to produce what Lukács called a fragmented consciousness that obscures the knowledge of the social totality that will lead to class consciousness. The underlying determinants of this new ideological notion of "history" (the "Constant Now" [Brady 94]) are, as always in bourgeois historicism, tied to technologism. Bill Gates articulates this technologism when he writes that today business is being conducted "@ the speed of thought" (Gates). Commodification has, in other words, reached into all parts of life so that we live now on a "timeless schedule" (Brady 96). Which is to say that the market now mediates everything all the time. So that by the 1990s the awareness of any connection between the working day and such social issues as Gay Liberation was more or less completely severed--leading to what I shall discuss shortly as the third moment of coming out, The Closet Is Sublime.

The present historical moment has thus become the time of the (niche) market: the time of difference, identity, and singularity, a moment when such concepts are celebrated in bourgeois ideology in various forms, but most famously by Derrida in the notion of *différance*. This is as good a place as any to say once again (see Morton, "Queerity and Ludic Sado-Masochism") that *différance* is not simply a textual construct aimed at freeing "difference," that is to say, it is not simply a notion expressing, as Derrida indicates, the "irreducibly polysemic" (Derrida "*différance*" 8) character of all texts/meanings/representations/ . . . ; it is rather a textual alibi for a politico-economic concept aimed at reproducing the "ruling ideas." *Differánce* is just such an alibi: it naturalizes the specific requirements of the forces of production.

Three

The enabling condition of Coming Out as Gay Liberation is the moment of Stonewall (1969) and the decade of the 1970s, which must be understood in relation to post-World War II economic developments and the rise of transnational capitalism. As I have already indicated, this moment's enabling condition is the post-war Long Boom of economic expansion in the West, roughly 1945-73. In this moment, "coming out of the closet" meant coming into an "identify" within a political movement in recognition of the reality of social injustice as a set of material conditions and not an abstract "idea." The people who "came out" in the Stonewall uprising were not middle or upper class persons but, for the most part, "drag queens, dykes, street people, and bar boys" (Adam 75)—persons, in other words, who "couldn't wait," not because of their personal and subjective "excitement" but because they were objectively under more intense (economic) pressures of class and sexuality and therefore had, compared to other lesbians/gays/queers, less to lose by "coming out." They were not simply in the grip of "new ideas" or "witnesses" who learned the purely cognitive lessons of other marginalized groups in the civil rights and feminist movements, but persons who were more intensely subjected to oppression along the axis of sexuality and exploitation along the axis of class. As, for example, the Chicago Gay Liberation manifesto (1970) made clear, the reason for "coming out" was not to express a "lifestyle" but to protest a whole range of objective social, political, and economic conditions (employment, housing, laws, education, medical care, . . . [Jay and Young 346-52]) which limited the lives of the great masses of lesbians and gay men and made them think of themselves as "refugees from Amerika" (Jay and Young 339), where

"Amerika" stood for a complex *structure* of oppression and exploitation. That is to say, for many at this time the "closet" is defined as a set of life-limiting material conditions. In other words, during the Long Boom period of "mass production and mass markets" (Allen 546), "mass" means "standardized" semi-skilled jobs and "standardized" products aimed supposedly at raising the standard of living for all. In fact, the very concept of "the masses" suggests the goal of producing a "good life" for all workers, yet certain groups of workers remained marginalized. The sheer fact of continued exclusion from the widespread Long Boom prosperity, which as is always the case under capitalism was making a small fraction of the citizenry very rich and keeping others in need, gave rise to political resistance. Significant elements of the Gay Liberation movement of the early 1970s were militantly anti-assimilationist: as one historian reports, "Boston's *Fag Rag* attacked assimilationist goals in no uncertain terms: 'We do not want a slice of the pie; the pie is rotten" (Loughery 334). Similarly, the Chicago manifesto (September 1970) gave special emphasis to the connection between sexuality and class when it observed that though "homosexuals have been oppressed in all societies" (Jay and Young 346), under capitalism it is "homosexuals from the proletariat . . . [who] lead a particularly prison-like, straight-jacketed existence . . . [b]ecause of their particular relation to production" (351). By the phrase "homosexuals from the proletariat," the manifesto pointed not to a small or select number but to the vast majority of lesbians and gay men in the U. S. By the phrase "their particular relation to production," the manifesto pointed to the way in which (like women workers and workers of color) gay and lesbian workers (those recognizable as such) were routinely excluded from certain professions and jobs and relegated to "less desirable" (lower-paying) work. As Jay and Young put it, "coming out of the closet" was—in this moment—a demand not for reform but for revolution: "American society had to change from top to bottom in order to end oppression" (Jay and Young xix).

In their ongoing revisionist readings of the moment of Gay Liberation today, collaborationist queer ideologues do everything they can to erase the question of production (work) and focus all attention on consumption (pleasure). The queer left is today trying hard to perpetuate the myth that the so-called sexual liberation movement was an effective political development that has in fact "liberated desire" and produced among vast segments of the U. S. population a historically decisive and increased degree of sexual pleasure and satisfaction. In the wake of this supposed "success" of sexual liberation, all that is needed today is just further enhancement of an already achieved sexual liberation. Exemplary here is the recent "history" of Gay Liberation offered by Michael Bronski, who (reading the situation in the 1960s back through the pleasure-saturated prism of bourgeois queer views of the 1990s) argues that homosexuality should be regarded strictly as a "problem of pleasure" (Bronski 132), that sex in general is to be treated as an autonomous activity (pleasure, he declares, "is an end in itself, as well as a conduit to more pleasure," Bronski 133), and that queers should reject any effort to relate sexual pleasure to what he mockingly refers to as "the more 'important' aspects of life: work, family, and productivity" (Bronski 132). The bankruptcy of such views is demonstrated by the fact that three decades after the "sexual revolution" has supposedly performed its magic, the *Journal of the American Medical Association* reports that in the U. S. of the 1990s, "sexual problems are widespread" (Laumann et al., "Sexual Dysfunction" 544).

Four

If in the moment of Stonewall the closet was a set of life-limiting material conditions, in the Reagan years (the economic period of Recession) it became a space of post-material desire,[19] when coming out moved up the social ladder, a moment extending throughout the decade of the 1980s and into the early 1990s, a time dominated by the fiscally conservative politics of Thatcher/Reagan/Kohl/ . . . , when economic expansion was fueled not so much by production (the economy is relatively weak) as by consumption financed by borrowing (monies injected into the economy by "tax cuts" which eventually make the national debt soar). The simulacral quality of this moment was articulated, for instance, in the 1980 presidential campaign when Ronald Reagan's tax-cutting plan to revive the flagging capitalist economy was labeled as "voodoo economics" and "economics with mirrors" (Harvey 329). The mid-1970s were the beginning of the period in US economic history which commentators associate with the "death" of the "Middle Class," a "truly historic transfer of resources toward the wealthy" (Cassidy 118), "an explosion" of wealth "at the top" (Reich 32): it was, in other words, the beginning of a time when "living standards have fallen or stagnated for the majority of Americans, while a small minority ["the richest five per cent"] have enjoyed a bonanza" (Cassidy 114). The Age of Recession was therefore the moment of "prosperity" as veneer or artifice, its artificiality underscored by the fact that it correlates not with improvement but decline in the material conditions of workers, that is, a decline in the material conditions of the vast majority of citizens. As Reagan's treatment of the air traffic controllers and other union-busting practices demonstrated, this prosperity was achieved more obviously at the workers' cost. In this moment, the concern was not with economic justice but with expressions of taste through fashion and through the idea that subjectivities are constructed not through production but through consumption, not through the social division of labor but rather through the development of various consumer "lifestyles."

The interpretation of homosexuality as a "lifestyle," is of course a class interpretation; the great masses of lesbian and gay workers cannot afford to participate in what Nicola Field has very effectively critiqued as the "lifestyle market" (Field 50-71), cannot in other words afford the level of consumption pictured as the "lesbian/gay lifestyle" in the pages of such glossy magazines such as *Genre, Out, The Advocate,* . . . John Cassidy's plaintive question "Who Killed the Middle Class?" still betrays-- through its use of "who" instead of "what"--the dream that capitalism can be made to work for everyone, while the actual objective conditions Cassidy reports on only confirm Marx and Engels's analysis that under capitalism's necessarily exploitative structure, "instead of rising with the progress of industry, [the modern labourer] sinks deeper and deeper below the conditions of existence of his own class" (Marx and Engels, *Manifesto* 32). When Cassidy reports that this growing inequality frightens even capitalism's titans of finance who fear that we may not "be able to go forward together as a unified society" (Cassidy 113), these are code words pointing to the fear of a future all out class war.[20] Gone now, along with worker optimism, was the exuberance of Gay Liberation, which connected sexuality to class and was oriented towards questions of meeting the needs of masses of people.

In the Recession phase, there appeared on the social horizon a rapidly expanding zone of *culturalist* discourses about the sexual margins where a tremendous "simulated optimism" was produced; this rapid expansion, however, was only possible because the question of "the closet" was appropriated by the media elite and others who had media access. In this moment, the "closet" was turned into a metaphor. Actually throughout this period, it was increasingly difficult for the workers to make their needs a part of the discussion of public policy about any issue because the state monopolized the public sphere by monopolizing the media so as to sustain its agenda of dis-investing in public projects. Maintaining dis-investment as the conservatives' political priority depended in turn on obscuring the obligations of the state to attend to the needs of the working class, including working-class queers and indeed on obscuring—to the extent possible--those needs themselves. Under these conditions, "coming out" of "the closet" became a practice of the privileged whose ideological goal was to demonstrate that under late capitalism there need be no connection between economic exploitation and sexual oppression, that it was indeed possible to "make it" and be lesbian/gay/queer at the same time. In the Recession period, then, the terms "closet" and "coming out" were taken over by complicit queers who set out to "prove" that there need be no necessary "stigma" attached to being queer under capitalism. As Field points out, these queer/gay/lesbian entrepreneurs were actually just selling "a designer lifestyle and an off-the-peg social identity" (Field 1); they were, in other words, simply representing lesbians and gays as a new and "special" group of "consumers." Their worry was that even to hint at a serious social stigma against homosexuals might redirect attention away from sexuality as a set of *cultural* practices and re-relate it once more to material conditions. For them, even to hint at all at production pointed "dangerously" back to the kind of revolution-oriented understanding of the closet that previously prevailed in Gay Liberation. This is the moment of the queer as floating signifier, of "making things perfectly queer" (Alexander Doty).

Symptomatic of this moment of The Closet as Media Hype was Michelangelo Signorile's *Queer in America: Sex, Media, and the Closets of Power* (1993), which—in a parody of revolutionary Gay Liberation— ended with "A Queer Manifesto," which redirected attention away from class difference and even from difference itself by arguing that "It is essential that we put our differences aside, at least for this crucial moment in history . . . and focus not on that which divides us, our genders, races, classes, ages, political ideology—but on the one powerful enemy we all have in common: the closet" (367). Far from being a revolutionary, Signorile, whom *Newsweek* magazine included (along with such other celebrities as Pat Buchanan, William F. Buckley, Jr., William Bennett, Lynne Cheney, Pat Robertson, Dan Quayle, Camille Paglia, Ted Turner, George Will, . . .) in one of its annual rosters (1992) as a member of the cultural elite ("The Newsweek 100" 38), was only interested in "reforming" relations between gays and straights in an effort which only strengthens the class system: his target was not capitalism but "all the closeted people in power today . . . abusing their power, ignoring homophobia, working for institutions that oppress us . . . all in order to preserve their closets" (Signorile 93). Like the rest of the queer left, Signorile assumed that homophobia is not a structure of oppression produced by a class society, but a set of personal prejudices that should be erased all the way up to the top of the social ladder.[21] Signorile's book was heralded by the queer left as "one of the most important books of the twentieth century"[22]; but the book is not important in the sense of containing "important" ideas (it is by no means a work of intellectual significance, though it has considerable interest as ideology) but because it is concerned with privileged people and institutions important to the status quo, that is, with people like Signorile himself.[23] Signorile targeted for outing powerful people ("the most influential people at the very top," xv) in three centers of power: "the media industry, centered in New York," "the political system, centered in Washington," and "the entertainment industry, centered in Hollywood" (xiv-xv). The book is merely another "performance" in the ongoing bourgeois Culture Wars: it "staged" as a media event a "showdown" between what it represents as the "queer community," on the one hand, and closeted media moguls, politicians and entertainers, on the other--that is, between two sectors of the bourgeoisie. What the book occludes is the fact that the condition for resolving this struggle is to leave capitalism's exploitation of workers intact. Signorile was challenging closeted brokers in liberal capitalism's power centers to "come out" and help their fellow queers to combat the "misrepresentation" of homosexuals by such politically conservative persons and groups as Patrick Buchanan, Jessie Helms, Jerry Falwell, the Roman Catholic Church, the Christian Coalition, ... What the book leaves unsaid, of course, is that members of liberal capitalism's power elite are only too eager to help capitalism meet the new imperatives of the multicultural workplace, will gladly fight for such a workplace against bourgeois reactionaries with outmoded ideas,[24] and will therefore support (at least some aspects of) the queer left agenda: implicit in this "agreement," of course, was the idea that the queer left will accept the present economic structure and the exploitative conditions of the workplace which go along with it. By engaging in this battle on these terms, the queer left implicitly encouraged working-class queers to just be glad they had a job, forget about exploitation, and keep the tacit agreement with the power structure that the "war over sexualities" would only be (recognized as) a "culture" war and never a "class" war.[25]

Five

After all the "rage" mustered against the closet just a few years ago when the practice of "outing" was a national queer pastime, it is very telling to observe that the present ideological shift—the current moment of The Closet Is Sublime—is marked precisely by the insistence not to "come out of" but—on the contrary—"to remain in" or "go back in" the closet and that today the closet is being *affirmatively* re-valued by the queer left as the site—in the words of one commentator—of "claustrophiliac ecstasy" (Casarino 203).

By the late 1990s, the Western bourgeoisie had so thoroughly appropriated the question of "other sexualities" as simply a question of desire and lifestyle and so completely erased common needs from the horizon of discussion that the subject of the closet became the subject of pure speculation on desire and the generic vehicle for his/her thought was no longer the "outward-directed" *manifesto* but the "inner-directed" *meditation*. In this ideological phase, which continues into the present, the bourgeois queer is so secure in the assumption that both his needs and his desires will be dependably fulfilled—they are commodities he can purchase because of his privileged economic position created by the surplus labor of others—that neither desire nor need is any longer even in question for him: hence, suddenly, other questions are "affordable." "Forgetting"—as he characteristically does—that time for speculative thought is itself purchased at the expense of someone else's labor, the bourgeois gives himself joyously over to idealist speculation and, spiraling in a contemplative inwardness, imagines that history itself is "under the sway of ideas" (Marx and Engels *The German Ideology* 61), that ideas are "self-generating," or are "'forms of self-determination'" (61). In this moment, we witness Queer Theory's entry into its final stage of "pure" metaphysics, when the pleasure-saturated bourgeois queer—who is now simply unable to imagine a better future—treats even the idea of "coming out" (which like other ideas may conflict with one's desires) with suspicion and poses previously (for the queer) "unthinkable" questions: Why come out at all? Doesn't the closet itself afford pleasures? If you come out, where do you go? Today's queer, in short, accepts--unlike the Gay Liberationist--the alienation of labor and commodification as transhistorical situations rather than as historical conditions that are subject to transformation. This is the moment of Queer Theory's fullest realization of its neo-conservative project. It is no longer either class or even cultural conflict that is seen as the source of social change: for Queer Theory, today is the time for the kind of pure mysticism advocated, through a revival of Bergson, by Deleuze and Guattari.

The queer left's new suspiciousness about "coming out" was signaled in several texts of the 1990s. For instance, there was the dialogue about "coming out" between James Creech and Neill Matheson articulated in Creech's book *Closet Writing/Gay Reading: The Case of Melville's Pierre* (1993) and in Matheson's critical review of Creech's book published in *diacritics,* "Identifying (with) the Queerness of Melville's *Pierre*" (1997). Although the interest of these texts lies elsewhere, they address a number of familiar theoretical issues. On one level, they re-stage the contestation over the meaning of sexual difference: is it to be understood as an identifiable subject position standing in determinate (binary) relation over against other subject positions (a position one takes on in "coming out"--this is the position Creech defends under the term "gay"), or as an unstable and fluid space of indeterminate supplementarity beyond all binaries where no position is finally "identifiable" (this is Matheson's deconstructive position allied with the current notions of the "queer")? According to the former understanding, one's sexual identity becomes an identity one reveals by the deliberate step of "coming out," an identity that forms the basis of a political program; according to the latter, "queer" is that which is "beyond identity," that which refuses identification and positioning, refuses capture within society's codes and conventions. The former leads to a mode of "identity politics" that justifies itself by seeking "grounds" in a determinable "identity," while the latter leads to the ongoing (ethical) deconstruction of "identity politics" and the marking of all identities as unfounded/unfoundable "performativities." On another level, these texts re-stage the equally familiar contestation over whether we should understand desire as a set of social (not natural) practices that are knowable, decidable, and historical (as part of conscious and rational "actions") or as an unknowable and indeterminate entity that produces the play of the signifier and the subversion of all fixed meaning (that renders all human "actions" as "performativities" beyond the control of "consciousness/reason"). For his part, Creech seems to endorse the "historical" mode of "knowing" (he bases his reading practice on his own "history" as a "gay man") and also seems to accept the principle of "constructionism," but he nowhere offers a theory of knowledge, or history, or of social construction and thus ends up leaving all these concepts in a theoretical limbo so that they are therefore--in effect if not in overt intention--as good as "naturalized." Against Creech's claim that deconstructive reading practices are "a-historical," "unpositioned," and reach for a "false objectivity" (beyond personal identification), Matheson proposes that deconstructive reading demonstrates "the impossibility of occupying a neutral, objective position free from forms of projection, identification, interestedness" (Matheson 31). Yet for deconstruction, the "force" that shapes the "forms" of this "interestedness" is desire, something that is by definition unknowable.

By the time of the Creech-Matheson exchange, the questions they re-articulated (determinacy/ indeterminacy, the queer as strictly a category of "desire," identification, identity politics, . . .) had already been debated exhaustively. Furthermore, as a result of recent debates over the meaning of "materialism," new horizons had already been opened and contemporary theory had been placed on new boundaries: by the late 1990s it was no longer credible to pretend to discuss "theory" by simply opposing one form of desire-theory against another, when it has been effectively argued that that all desire-based theory is class-interested and when need-theory (Marxist materialist inquiries) had been strongly rewritten into these contestations. All forms of desire-theory are idealist through and through and serve the bourgeois purpose of occluding and rendering "'impossible" and "unintelligible" historical materialist analyses which struggle to produce–for the proletariat--class consciousness and an inclusive knowledge of the social totality. In the end, the "debate" between Creech and Matheson represents a "family quarrel" among bourgeois critics and represents the typical occlusionary idealist move: as a defender of deconstruction, Matheson is a practitioner of an anti-theory form of theory; as an opponent of deconstruction and defender of a "gay reading" (which, as he explains it, is a purely experienced-based understanding of the social that will always limit the conclusions one can draw to the local and the particular), Creech is a practitioner of a very localized mode of theory that can never allow any claims about the social totality. Creech constructs a narrative by which his own "coming out" as a gay man coincides with his abandonment of deconstructive reading practices. He represents deconstructive reading by reference to Barbara Johnson's essay on Melville's *Billy Budd*—which he identifies as a mode of anti-foundational reading that he rejects as ineffective for gay studies because it tries to be "non-identificatory" and "abstractly objective" and renders all meaning--including that of "gay identity"--indeterminate and undecidable. Instead of deconstructive reading, Creech advocates a "frank" mode of "gay reading" founded on his self-identifying as a gay male reader. Matheson can respond that Queer Theory's (deconstructive) understanding of subjectivity in terms of desire-driven performativity means that, since repressed (fluid and ever-changing) desire is always in the process of being released, every subject is caught up in a state of "coming out," and therefore--as a consequence of this ongoing process--it makes no sense to speak (as Creech wants to do) of a determinate point in one's life of decisive "coming out." By hinting that "coming out" is not really a "big deal" after all, Matheson's deconstruction of Creech's discourses, which renders Creech's position rather "quaint" and "naïve," helps create for the late 1990s a decided and emphatic suspiciousness about the significance of "coming out" as an effective political act.

Since it does not add to the basic philosophical and theoretical issues they address, the exchange between Creech and Matheson is of interest more for its timing, serving as a symptom of larger tensions and contestations in Queer Theory, than for its contribution to Queer Theory. Perhaps the twist Creech adds is that he ("surprisingly"?) turns deconstructive theory into a kind of "closet" from which he also pretends to have "liberated" himself. But in the final analysis, while endorsing "coming out" in a literal social sense, Creech--through the localizing limitations he places on all theory--just turns theory itself into a closet. The upshot of this discussion is the re-emphasis of two different forms of anti-theory theory--and this is taking place at a significant historical turning point, in the wake of a renewed and deepened historical materialist critique of bourgeois queer studies. That is to say, the upshot of this exchange is simply two versions of "diminishment": on the one hand, Creech's gesture of "support" for "coming out" restricts the significance of the move by localizing, experientializing, and naturalizing it; on the other hand, Matheson's deconstruction of Creech's discourses (which, because Creech has not been able to offer a sustained or effective broad critique of deconstruction and post-al theory in general, rather easily renders Creech's position "unsophisticated," "old-fashioned," and "naïve") produces a suspiciousness about the significance of "coming out" by rather quietly and calmly reaffirming the notion that in the late 1990s "coming out" can really no longer be considered a "big deal."

The coming full (and deeply subjectivist) revaluation of the understanding of the closet which I shall shortly elaborate is also hinted at in a 1996 essay on "Coming/Out" by Samuel Delany, who remarked that "it might be better" not to consider "coming out" historically "as a point effect" separating a "*before*" from an "*after*," but as an "attitude," a "disposition," a "mood" (Delany "Coming/Out" 96). And reasons (linked to "economic" issues—meaning predictably those associated with consumption and queer-targeted advertising and not production and class) "to displace" "the closet" from its "totalizing centrality" in Queer Theory have recently been articulated by Eric Clarke (Clarke 59). At any rate, the "debate" between Creech and Matheson is symptomatic of the anxiety of the queer left since the 1990s in the face of the patent fact of the widely recognized "success" of the queer left's assimilation to capitalism.[26] This increasing tension in queer left discourses from the late 1990s onwards shows up in the new tendency to minimize the importance of "coming out" of "the closet," not only on the left but also on the right. The queer left's "anxiety" about assimilation is linked to the straight right's new-found "calmness" about gay/queer assimilation, a calmness illustrated in Saul Bellow's latest novel, *Ravelstein*, a *roman á clef* about his long-time friend and colleague at the University of Chicago, conservative writer Allan Bloom, author of *The Closing of the American Mind*, a book celebrated by the right for its reactionary attack on the left-leaning developments of the 1960s and the subsequent reforms introduced into American higher education. Some commentators have suggested that Bellow's "revelation" not only that Bloom was homosexual but also that he died of AIDS is a "betrayal" of friendship through the disclosure of facts "long kept quiet out of respect for Bloom's privacy" (Tanenhaus A-26). If it can be said to betray anything, what Bellow's novel betrays is that today the question of "coming out" is so routinized and accepted by the mainstream that "coming out"/"outing" has achieved the status of a topos in the Western literary canon (that is to say, in a novel by a Nobel prize winner). In other words, Bellow "outs" Bloom because homosexuality has been effectively assimilated and simply is no longer "a big deal." Of course, the queer left, which by virtue of its ready assimilation is dramatically exposed as suddenly not-so-left anymore, reacts not only with anxiety but also with an extremely hostile rejection of what is to its left—revolutionary Marxism. Thus, for example, Steven Seidman's essay, "Are We All In the Closet? Notes Towards a Sociological and Cultural Turn in Queer Theory" (1998), reports what Seidman calls an empirical change in gay/queer attitudes and interests by which "the closet, coming out, and declaring a public sexual identity are no longer the key narrative figures in terms of which homosexuality is understood" (Seidman 180).[27] True to form, Seidman combines this supposed "revelation" with an emphatic re-expression of the common cliché (presented as a "new" insight) that dismisses Marxism because of its "materialist and class reductionism" (187). This theme is being reiterated again and again, among other places in Eve Sedgwick's essay "Paranoid Reading and Reparative Reading," the introduction to her recent book, *Novel Gazing*. Sedgwick argues passionately that it is now time to abandon the practice of critique and the exposure of overlooked differences and, predictably, the form of critique Sedgwick most strongly denounces is Marxist ideology critique. Producing differential readings, one should keep in mind, is the very practice Eve Sedgwick used with such remarkable success to launch her own career. Yet suddenly, after years of practicing critique herself, Sedgwick is no longer interested in Derridean/Foucauldian/ . . . differential reading, but in "unity"; and her recipe for "unity" is what she calls "reparative reading." One has to ask what historical changes are today driving Sedgwick and other members of the queer left to express a desire for "unity"? The answer is that reparative reading is itself a mode of mainstreaming Queer Theory. In other words, the "unity" achieved by reparative reading is Sedgwick's response to class struggle: reparative reading is aimed at the blurring of social antagonisms and at the affective "healing" of economic wounds.

Six

The rethinking of the closet that most fully exposes the complicity of the bourgeois left with transnational capital today is "The Sublime of the Closet; or, Joseph Conrad's Secret Sharing," by Cesare Casarino. It is a text whose understanding of the world is founded on three major conceptual assumptions of bourgeois theory: (a) the Kantian revival in cultural theory in the 1980s promoted by Lyotard, Courtine, Miller, Norris, Žižek, Hutchings, . . . ; (b) the neo-Marxist theory of history as rewritten by Antonio Negri; and (c) Bataille's notion of a general economy of (addictive) excess. Casarino's essay is of special interest because his "meditations" (Casarino 202) mark the historical moment of the advancing *institutionalization* of the new closet-affirming ideology of The Closet Is Sublime. Aware that he is engaging with a trope that has organized much queer writing for a very long time, one that has in fact passed into wide usage in late twentieth-century popular culture,[28] Casarino nevertheless declares the topic far from exhausted: according to him, the closet's "queer political *puissance* . . . has yet to be fully acknowledged, let alone unleashed" (200). The author no doubt sees his text as such an "unleashing"; but the question remains, what exactly is "unleashed"? What is "unleashed," it turns out, is a conservative resignification of "the closet."

Regarding the sublime which lies behind and informs the current ideological turn of The Closet Is Sublime in general and behind Casarino's essay in particular, we must remember that, according to the received view,[29] Kant is the author of what is perhaps "the greatest single book in philosophy" (Solomon and Higgins 208); "the ultimate champion of the Enlightenment in Germany" (206); and a writer who made

"Reason, the watchword of the Enlightenment, . . . the primary player in [his] supremely rational philosophy" (207). One must immediately add that this modernist evaluation of Kant as one of Western philosophy's major defenders of reason has been abandoned through a re-reading which emphasizes his deployment of the concept of the "sublime." In the first paragraph of the "Analytic of the Sublime" (*The Critique of Judgment*), Kant uses the notion of the sublime to suspend and undermine the capacities of reason by proposing that the pleasures of the sublime do not depend on a "definite concept" (Kant 90), involve "an absence of anything leading to particular objective principles" (92), and are furthermore "singular" (90). Kant ultimately defines the sublime as "that, the mere capacity of thinking which evidences a faculty of mind transcending every standard of sense" (98). Kant thus ties the "understanding" of the sublime not to reason but to feeling, intuition, and sensibility: it belongs, in other words, not to the domain of "pure reason" or "practical reason" but to aesthetic judgment, which is "subjectively and not objectively determined" (98). In recognition of the importance of this reversal, one critic wrote that in the dominant literary and cultural studies, even when the "sublime is not offered as a formal concept, . . . it is nevertheless a guiding theme" (Silverman and Aylesworth xii). Against the dominant view, George Lukács clarifies Kant's role in bourgeois thought by locating Kant as part of a general movement in bourgeois philosophy he calls "the destruction of reason" and puts forth a Marxist critique of the "subjective-idealist weaknesses" of Kant by stressing Kant's "equating" of dialectics with "intuition" (sensibility) (*The Destruction* 139), an equation that lies behind Lyotard's reading of dialectics and informs its post-al rejection. Lukács's critique of Kant needs to be brought up to the present so as to take into account such later developments as the Kantian renaissance in literary and cultural studies which started in the 1980s.

The "Kantian renaissance" and the valorization of the "sublime" form an important element in the post-al project of the marginalization of "reason" exemplified in the work of Jean-François Lyotard, who—one commentator has suggested—has written in "book after book, a new *Critique of Judgment*" (Lyotard and Thébaud 15). Commenting on the centrality of Kant and the category of the sublime in Lyotard's project of marginalizing "reason," Serge Trottein has recently remarked that "for Lyotard . . . [p]ostmodern means sublime" (Trottein 73) The marginalization proceeds by shifting attention almost entirely away from Kant's first two critiques to the third, which is taken to represent a subversive subtext that undermines the first two: that is to say, "knowledges" produced by "pure reason"/"practical reason" are subverted and rendered ultimately "indeterminate" by the operations of "judgment," which is a "savviness" founded *not* on reasons or concepts but--formed by "experience"--on "sensibility/intuition" which finds its most

characteristic and "irrational" moments in the experience of the "sublime."
Like Derrida, Lyotard does not deny the existence of "truth": what he
does deny is that we can rely on what we call "truth" in making
judgments about social life and its problems (*Just Gaming*). In other
words, we can have truth and we can have judgment, but we cannot
have both at the same time: thus, our judgments of social issues are
ungroundable in any determinate reliable knowledge and are therefore
fundamentally contingent and irrational. Lyotard argues that our
judgments—just like our experiences of the "sublime," according to
Kant—"are not regulated by categories" (Lyotard and Thébaud 15), that
in life we must necessarily "decide," but we must decide "without criteria"
(Lyotard and Thébaud 17). We do not need "a discourse that states what
justice is in order to then practice it" (Lyotard and Thébaud 25). In this
perspective, social life is constituted by a series of autonomous--
singular--language games for which there is no common measure: "The
social universe is formed by a plurality of games without any one of them
being able to claim that it can say all the others" (Lyotard and Thébaud
58). What Lyotard concludes from this interpretive maneuver is that it is
"inherent to oppression to import into a language game a question that
comes from another one and to impose it" (Lyotard and Thébaud 53).
Hence it is "oppressive" for workers (who are engaged in their own
autonomous discursive game) to (im)pose their questions about
"exploitation" or "need" or . . . on capitalists (who are engaged in their
own autonomous—desire-driven—discursive game). Lyotard goes on to
argue that "For me, rational politics, in the sense of the concept, is over,
and I think that that is the swerve of this *fin-de-siécle*" (Lyotard and
Thébaud 75). The sublime is, of course, that category which post-al
theorists celebrate as representing the unrepresentable: the supreme
and illimitable disruption of concept and rationality. What Lyotard says is
true of the beautiful contains elements even more true of the sublime:
that the "feeling of the beautiful is a reflexive judgment, singular
(although it claims universality), immediate, and disinterested"
(Lyotard,"The Interest"109). Hence the connection between Lyotard's
interest in the "singular" as opposed to the "universal" and his
theorization of the postmodern as a rejection of "totality" (*The
Postmodern Condition* 82), which is to say a rejection of any possibility
that any common measure can be applied to the various discourses that
circulate in the "public sphere." Lyotard subverts the possibility of having
a knowledge of the social totality by using the concept of the sublime to
displace the understanding of the "public sphere" as the space of shared
concepts and suggesting that what is "common" are "singular" and
"unshare-able" moments. In the end, the idea that each social group is
engaged in an autonomous "game," that what they have in "common" is
"singular" and "unshare-able," implies that there is no coherent
explanation of the operations of the social totality, that there is no

knowable underlying structure connecting the space of the worker to the space of the capitalist and therefore no way to know and explain their relation as a relation of "exploitation." In other words, in the Kantian renaissance inaugurated by post-al theorists, the category of the "sublime" ("intuition"/"sensibility"), which for Kant was operative in the domain of the aesthetic, is transformed by post-al theorists into the operative modality of all judgment in the social sphere. Hence, our understanding of social life is transcoded as a matter of "aesthetics" and our judgments about social life are said to have nothing to do with "need" (economics) and everything to do with "desire" (pleasure). To sum up what I have so far said about the transformation of the sublime from its modernist (Enlightenment) ideological mode to its postmodernist (anti-Enlightenment) ideological mode: for Kant the sublime is that which is so "large" that the mind cannot encompass it ("*Sublime*," he says, "is the name given to what is absolutely great" in the sense of "what is beyond all comparison," Kant 94); for Lyotard the sublime is the name given to the ultimately unknowable Other.

My argument is that to bring about social change, such as a change in sexual politics, requires structural change. Working towards structural change requires a knowledge of the social totality and such a knowledge is not aesthetic (singular) but systematic (total), and systematic knowledge cannot be produced through the exercise of "taste," "intuition," . . . , but only through the exercise of human reason in its praxical encounter with historical problems. Knowledge is the effect of the contradictions between the forces of production and the social relations of production and not a personal effect. The sublime is popular because bringing rational politics to an end allows one to embrace a "politics" that allows for the reform of singular practices (sexual politics) without changing the system (capitalism). Thus the kind of conceptual "structural" explanation of the "closet" offered earlier in the 1960s which connected questions of sexual oppression (desire) to questions of employment, housing, medical care, education, . . . (need) has been "superseded" by today's "sublime politics." Casarino's text is a performance of this sublime politics: how to relegitimate capitalism with a new (left) rhetoric that aims not at freedom from necessity but sensibility for all. How to be "practical" and perform the compatibility of the free market and queer sensibility; how, in short, to show that freeing the queer does not require the overthrow of capitalism. His text provides a lesson in the "new" form of "queer" reading for the late 1990s which is remarkable not only for its sheer comfortableness with and uncritical acceptance of post-al dogmas and clichés (presented in the name of the "new") but also for its reformist and anti-militant, passive, and subjugationist quietism and its embrace of the complacencies of pleasure. Casarino's reading lesson shows--as Weir angrily noted—that, by the 1990s, the distance between Log Cabin Republican queers and bourgeois left queers had in fact disappeared. The "new" notion of the "sublime of the closet" is nothing more than a lesson in queer Republican pragmatism.

The occasion of Casarino's text is a reading of *The Secret Sharer*, Conrad's tale of the complicity between a fugitive (and murderer) pulled to safety from the ocean and the narrator who furtively aids him, a ship's captain with his first commission who—under "odd" circumstances—hides the fugitive in his own personal quarters to keep his presence unknown to others on the ship. It is thus an "anxiety-ridden" story of "fear of discovery" (211-212); and the "sharing" of tight, claustrophobic quarters Casarino celebrates as "claustrophiliac." *The Secret Sharer*, we are told, repeats a pattern characteristic of much of the fiction by Conrad, who is, Casarino believes, the master not merely of the "narrative caesura" but of "*the caesura as narrative,*" one who tells tales that evoke a "state of expectant, atemporal, and placeless suspension" (211). The "quietude" that Casarino finds in Conrad's fiction, in other words, becomes an alibi for legitimizing the quietism of his own essay. In this tale, narrator and fugitive live (close) together for some time as in a "breathless pause" (211). Conrad, however, is not the only— or even the main—practitioner of "the caesura" involved here: the author of "The Sublime of the Closet" repeats the quietism he attributes to Conrad's text in the rhetoric of his own essay, and installs quietism ultimately as the (metaphysical) principle of the closet, which he celebrates as a space of shared isolation and loneliness. Casarino performs quietism and passivity in his essay by using distancing pronouns ("One has always wondered . . . , 202; "One has at times felt . . . , 203; "one cannot but be forced . . . , 203); by situating himself as merely an "onlooker" of his own reading ("we will watch and participate in the unfolding of the spectacle of the sublime of the closet," 201; "Let us spy on these first few moments . . . ," 219); by emphasizing the affective rather than conceptual dimension of his own discourses (he reproduces the "empathetic sharing" which he regards to be the—specifically "same-sex"—core of Conrad's tale from the outset with his extensive "acknowledgments"); by relegating conflicts over explanatory concepts to footnotes so as to leave his main text devoted to the evocation of mood through expanding tropes; and by overtly adopting the "meditative" mode (202), which has become--in the Age of Difference--the required form for writing on difference. What evolves from this discursive matrix is a notion of the closet as the space of "nonrelational pleasures" (203), the "absence of history" (210), the "suspension" of the dialectic (204), the doubling of desire which is a "desire of doubleness" (222), the imposition of anonymity ("everything and everybody remains forever nameless," 223), and the erasure of language (so as to leave only the "sublime expanses of silence," 224). This construction of the "closet" as a non-dialectical space outside history marked by passive subjection leads to the conclusion that ultimately "The sublime of the closet . . . is *not* a coming out" (203). We are not to "come out of the closet" because such an act merely "feeds back into the very problem it was meant to solve" since coming out means "coming-to-visibility as a specifically nameable body" and "a particularly vulnerable target" (204). Besides—and here is the politically telling conclusion—the closet is, after all, the space of unending--sublime--pleasure, of "claustrophiliac ecstasy" (203). Again, the sublime of the closet is "not a coming out but rather an overcoming: a coming pure and simple" (206).

Casarino's notion of the closet represents nothing less than what Marx called the "reactionist" triumph of the pathologizing and infantilizing discourses of psychoanalysis, articulated along the two axes of connections and disjunctions between modernist and post-al theory. Along one axis, this notion of the closet absorbs the modernist idea of "alienation," which results from the "disappointing discovery" that the world is itself a closet. Freud teaches this lesson when, for instance, in *Civilization and Its Discontents*, he first argues that "what decides the purpose of life is simply the programme of the pleasure principle" (Freud 25). He then observes that since requirements of civilized life inescapably place constraints on the search for libidinal gratification, then the very condition of adulthood is permanent frustration (which leads, he says, in many people, to a "strange attitude of hostility to civilization" [38]). Thus psychoanalysis teaches that the entry into social life cannot offer "liberation" or "freedom" because the world is itself a system of unavoidable constraints. In Lacanian terms, the socialized subject— robbed of the symbiotic relation with the body of mother and motivated by unslakeable "desire"—slides interminably along the chain of signifiers, playing with those poor (civilized) "substitutes" which make social life possible but never really "satisfy" and are therefore themselves "constraints." Life is thus a repetition of the primal "trauma" of separation and is therefore one long "sickness." Thus "modernist alienation" is carried over into the notion of the world as "text-house" (to which there is no "outside")—of language, of institutions as structures of closed systems of power/knowledge (Foucault), of ideology (Althusser), . . . All of these little narratives are, of course, variations on Nietzsche's master narrative of the will-to-power (repeated in Casarino's notion of "*puissance*"). Nietzsche, Freud, Lacan, Derrida, Foucault, represent their narratives of the world as analyses of the world as such. However, what they represent as the conditions of the world are in fact the historical conditions of a particular social mode of production--capitalism. Freud's alienation is not inherent in the world, but, as Marx shows in the *Manuscripts of 1844*, is instead the effect of "alienated labor." The alienated world of the modernist and post-modernist narratives is the alienated world of capitalism. To be more specific, against Casarino's reading of Conrad (celebrating the "closet") which reveals (the latest stage of) the queer left's thoroughgoing complicity with capitalist ideology, Lukács again provides an exemplary counter-reading of "modernist alienation" ("paralysis in the face of the unintelligible power of circumstances" under capitalism, Lukács *Realism* 36) in his treatment of Kafka as the bourgeois writer whose "*angst* is the experience *par excellence* of modernism" (36) and who sees the human subject as so enveloped in alienation that there is no vital and growing relation between the self and itself, the self and others, the self and the world: one is either incarcerated in a castle and put on trial, turned into an insect with an imprisoning exoskeleton, or . . . In short, as Lukács argues, "alienation" is not a transhistorical existential state of being: it is the historically produced situation in class societies. Similarly, when Casarino describes the "state of mind" he finds evoked in Conrad's fiction as a "state of expectant, atemporal, and placeless suspension" (211), he is himself in fact evoking for the reading subject the very state of mind required by contemporary production practices. In other words, Casarino (as writer and pedagogue) is placing the reader in the subject position which accepts without question such ideas as cultural and social fragmentation, the dissociation from the historical past, the sense of living in a "timeless time."

Along the (post)modernist axis, the emphasis in "The Sublime of the Closet" is on the pleasure principle in its updated form which represents everything as a repetition of *jouissance*: not only must we confront the fact of modernist alienation (the world itself is a closet—now of course understood in terms of the laws of signification) but also realize that, after all, there is finally so much pleasure in the closet that there is no incentive to leave it anyway. The world is the space of the relational and the historical, which means by definition that it is--under the regime of private property--the space of encounters with the Other, which means endlessly repeated "traumas." To remain in the "closet" is to avoid trauma by embracing the closet as the universal condition of the world. To "come out" is to misrecognize a modernist delusion as emancipation. To entertain any emancipatory gesture is the mark of a complete lack of savviness. We must conclude, according to Casarino, that *jouissance* is finally the source of the "sublime" closet's "queer political *pouissance*" (200), a power that has yet to be fully realized and "unleashed" (200). To justify remaining in the closet, we must, we are told, produce another grand Foucauldian reversal of thinking so as to realize that it is "*jouissance*" in the space of the closet that in fact generates the world, that is the motor of history (not class struggle): the closet becomes in this moment the world's "prime cause." This move, of course, just makes the closet a variant of the post-al proposition that desire is the prime force in the construction of the subject and of the social.

In Gay Liberation, to break out of the closet was to help bring to public awareness some new historically generated and more urgent social questions and to move into the world to claim a place for same-sex relations as social needs and place their discussion and resolution in the public sphere using the powers of rationality. Today's queer left "reveling" in the closet's "sublimity" is a rejection of such public marking and of rationality itself, which is to say a rejection of the very terms of social life. The subject of the "sublime closet"—who, according to Casarino, occupies a post-ideological space free of commodification (227)--can reject the world as site of social struggle in order to save the self from further "trauma" only because—under the present conditions of capitalism--the increasingly comfortable upper middle class queer is so "sure" that he can ultimately rely on "others" who struggle ("produce") for him. In order to aestheticize his life and anesthetize himself and block his awareness of the necessity of "historical relationality" mediated through systems of economic exchange and understood and explained through concepts produced by reason, the queer left subject now devotes his thought and rhetoric to actually obliterating the very notion of the "Other." Whereas Signorile (in his "manifesto") called on queers to "put aside their differences" to fight a common enemy (the closet), for Casarino the closet has become the queer's "best friend." In the sublime closet, something strange happens to the very notion of difference--the battle cry of the queer left: when each person is trapped in her/his own unique Lyotardian singularity, all persons are finally the "same" in their (singular) "difference." "Difference" or textual effect in post-al theory has, from the first, been a decoy for (social) class. It was a concept emphasized at the height of social struggles in the 1960s to divert attention away from class (difference): the "real" difference became not the difference of economic access but the differences of gender, sexuality, race, . . . In Casarino, one sees the final act in this staging of difference. In the wake of the "triumph" of capitalism and the regaining of confidence by the ruling class, difference posited even as textual difference is still seen as a sign of "tension." All differences are therefore erased and the social is rewritten as consensus and sameness. Red Queer Theory, however, refuses to give up difference as the difference of class.

It is not only remarkable that queer studies has arrived at a point of celebrating the pleasures of the closet and rejecting "coming out" as a deluded modernist notion, but also that it here makes an idealizing leap from the notion that homosexuality involves "same-sex" desire (an idea which in no way requires the elision and neglect of differences between lovers, whether two women or two men) to the thorough fetishizing of sameness and erasure of difference. Just as quietism does not in any simple manner "originate" in Conrad's text but is produced by Casarino's reading, Casarino's own text is the site (as he says Conrad's is) of a "paroxysmal escalation of redoubling" (220). By the conclusion of his essay—which endlessly circulates and recirculates the figure of the "double"—Casarino redoubles the closet over and over again so that there is indeed no outside the closet and so that difference is suspended and the world is itself redoubled as the narrative of caesura and the caesura of a narrative. With a somewhat different language, Casarino is fulfilling Sedgwick's prescription of reparative reading (such ideological shifts are not "personal" but historical) by positing the world as a world of passionate consumption in the desire for the Same and producing a "metaphysics of sameness" in the interest of escaping "trauma" by erasing conflict as an excuse for reveling in the melancholy pleasures of the closet, which is desperately threatened by the un-Same. The un-Same is of course the allegory of the "other class" and encountering that other (class antagonism) is for Casarino the "trauma" of life--a concept that Laclau and Žižek have made popular in their anti-communist propaganda which now passes for "theory." Of course, out of a very conventional professional self-interest, Casarino must from time to time suddenly suspend the metaphysics of sameness when he steps back to regard his own text, as he does in various footnotes: it would of course be the end of his career for an academic to suggest that his writing is nothing but a repetition of the Same (a "redoubling"). Casarino therefore self-consciously and in highly defensive footnotes tries to "prove" that his theory of the closet moves discussion beyond the familiar. He follows the dominant ludic logic: he, for example, suggests that his representation of the issues oscillates between "something like a theoretical step backward and a theoretical step forward" (209 n.13]. Yet he nevertheless tries to distinguish his work from that of Judith Butler, on the one hand, because "it does not share her concern for the symbiotic questions of parody and subversion" (205 n.7) and from that of Eve Sedgwick, on the other, because unlike himself she constructs "the closet as a relational structure" (209 n.13). In his actual practices, Casarino is in tune with Butler for many reasons but not least for rendering the "Other" but a parody of—an entity subverted by—the "Same." Similarly, Casarino's reading is a reparative reading and is a redoubling of Sedgwick—practitioner of the associative "a-logic" of the trope and the fetishizer of the "white glasses" (see Morton *The Material Queer* 18-19). Casarino, like Sedgwick and contrary to his formal declarations, does not abandon all sense of human connection but establishes the mode of connection not as understanding—as we saw in relation to Kant--but as empathy enabled by melancholy "fellow-feeling."

Yet Casarino's "same-ing" is not a self-generating idea, but is instead produced by historical and material conditions that can be specified and analyzed. Facing the emerging contradictions of global capitalism, the bourgeois subject simply "does not know" what determines his present advantage and dreams up "ideas" (in this case, the closet) as ultimate cause. When this subject is reminded of the "other," he apprehends it in dreamy and mystifying terms that hides the underlying violence that turns it into the "same"--as Casarino's text demonstrates.[30] It opens with this dedication: "To a nameless traveler on the Djakarta-Yogyakarta Express on a winter night, 1983: it was with you that I first shared the transport of enclosure" (199). The dedication is an allegory of the mastery of the West, of the Westerner taking his pleasure in and through the "East." The epigraph articulates the very exploitative process of globalization by evoking (as the emblem of the interpretation of "sharing" that is to follow) an anonymous encounter in which the Western consumer--in the once more repeated gesture of "same-ing"--does not even bother to name the "other," the producer of "claustrophiliac" pleasure. Of course, behind this pleasure-full fantasied notion of the railroad as an emblem of "romance" lies the relation of rail travel to wage labor and capital: the railroad is part of capitalism's constant revolutionizing of the mode of production driven by the "need of a constantly expanding market" which "chases the bourgeoisie over the whole surface of the globe" (Marx and Engels, *Communist Manifesto* 21). Behind Casarino's anecdotal epigraph of "desire" and "travel" lies the familiar capitalist logic of "same-ing": "The bourgeoisie, by the rapid improvement of all instruments of production, by the immensely facilitated means of communication, draws all, even the most barbarian, nations into civilisation. . . . It compels all nations, on pain of extinction, to adopt the bourgeois mode of production; it compels them to introduce what it calls civilisation into their midst, *i. e.,* to become bourgeois themselves. In one word, it creates a world after its own image" (Marx and Engels, *Communist Manifesto*, 22). Casarino's de-historicized queer representation of "desire" on the "Djakarta-Yogyakarta Express"--which creates the world in his own image--diverts attention away from the long history of Western imperialist ravishment of Indonesia (which continues today ["Indonesia's Downward Spiral"]) and exoticizes it: turns it from a historical place of exploitation into a space of specular bliss.

In the final analysis, Casarino's meditation on the "sublime" closet re-asserts--in typical post-al fashion--the individual not as an agent of history but rather as the subject of de-regulated pleasure. It is nothing more than an attempt to provide a kind of "speculative" respectability for one of the most banal of bourgeois practices, self-care: "I care about myself; my desires are the same as the desires of the world; they constitute the world for me; leave me alone in the closet (the world is one anyway)." At this historical stage of capitalist development, then, the queer left—clinging in desperation to the notion that mental states (and not structures of exploitation) are finally what makes the world the way it is and accepting Žižek's recommendation, "Enjoy Your Symptom!"—suddenly represents the closet as not a closet at all because it is self-chosen, as if self-choosing can be the ultimate level of analysis within a structure of exploitation. This is to say that once again the queer left enacts masochism—Casarino's "claustrophiliac ecstasy" is the pleasure in submission—which because it is self-chosen is represented as *not* masochism at all.[31] From here it is but a short step to fetishizing (identifying through the process of "same-ing" with) the "jack boots" (literal or figurative) which administer masochistic *jouissance*. Those who fetishize and aestheticize rather than historicize pleasure are always already leaving the door open to the "jack boots."[32]   Given the psychoanalytic substructure of Casarino's text, it is worth remembering that in *Civilization and Its Discontents*, a book which helped to launch the understanding of life in terms of de-historicized pleasure, Freud—writing between the World Wars and contemplating war's causes—while mindful of the threat of fascism minimizes it and saves his strongest attacks—as the bourgeois queer left clearly does today—for communism. Freud remarks, for instance, that "the interest of work in common" does not hold "civilized society" together (Freud 69) and shortly thereafter adds— so as to further dismiss critical Marxist categories—that "aggressiveness was not created by property" (71). These anti-Marxist observations build towards a "climax" when he then places "anti-Semitism" side by side with what he calls the Soviet "persecution of the bourgeois" (73) and ponders the following question full of obvious self-interest: "One only wonders, with concern, what the Soviets will do after they have wiped out their bourgeois" (73). Given the pathologizing character of Casarino's re-understanding of the closet which redoubles Antonio Negri's and Slavoj Žižek's aestheticizations of the social, I conclude that the present moment of "the closet is sublime" is undoubtedly "a theoretical step forward" for the bourgeoisie and "a theoretical step backward" for the world's working masses.

Seven

Given the impossibility of altogether ignoring the increasing injustices of class division, it is not surprising that Casarino and others on the queer left are eager to represent themselves as committed to "history," "materialism" and some form of "Marxism"--the kind of "Marxism" outlined, for example, in *Marxism Beyond Marxism* (Makdisi, Casarino, and Karl). There, like many other post-al leftists, Casarino sets aside the materialist theory of history Marx and Engels outlined in *The German Ideology*, developed in the *Grundrisse*, and rigorously theorized in *Capital*. Instead he follows Negri, whose reading of Marx focuses on a revisionist reading of the *Grundrisse,* which has become canonic for post-post-Marxism (as bourgeois theory becomes more institutionalized, more "post"'s have to be added to Marx!). Both in its formal organization as a notebook and an outline of issues and in its development of such concepts as the relation of art to material forces, the book provides an occasion *to trope* Marxist concepts (Makdisi, Casarino, and Karl 8). In their introduction, the editors insist that they are speaking of and for "communism"; however, not only do they dissociate themselves from what they call the "statist communism" (which has always been an idealist ruse in bourgeois social theory) of the former Soviet Union and Eastern European countries, but they also redefine communism--using the Romantic poetry of William Blake as their tutor-texts--in the typically "harmless" post-al manner as any and all forms of "antagonistic relation to various realities and various official modes of community" (2-3). Their Negrian "communism" is finally based on a notion of labor as the direct effect of the "body" (not as the social relations between labor and capital). It is, in other words, a sensualized communism! In their texts, "communism" becomes "a fundamentally transhistorical history of struggle and desire" (3). Under this Blakean communitarianism (represented as communism), even those "resisters" like William Greider who recently wrote a moralistic tract for *The Nation* against (he too quotes Blake) the "'Dark Satanic Mills'" of capitalism as it exists today and for a "reformed" global capitalist economy, would qualify as a "communist" (which simply gets redefined as the belief--in Greider's words--that "we are all in this together now, rich nations and poor alike, all riding on the same runaway train" (Greider 12) that is, the train of global capitalism, which simply needs to be "adjusted" not rejected and replaced. For Casarino, communism is a state of the body--sensual labor--that has nothing to do with class, labor, capital, exploitation, revolution, . . . but is instead the kind of sensual "concern" (cf. sexuality in Butler) that Marx and Engels critique in, among other texts, *The Communist Manifesto*. Casarino's Negrist version of "Marxism"--moving "beyond" Marxism--interprets cultural production as autonomous by relying on a post-al reading of the *Grundrisse*.

As an example of such a reading, we can take the passage at the end of the introduction where Marx (discussing Greek art and Shakespeare) comments as follows: "As regards art, it is known that certain periods of its florescence by no means correspond to the general development of society, or, therefore, to the material basis, the skeleton as it were of its organisation (Marx *Grundrisse* 46). Post-al theorists and critics take this statement about the arts (which they read as standing as a synecdoche for cultural production and the superstructure in general) to mean that Marx here abandons base/superstructure dialectics. The Negrist and other post-al readings, however, are based on a textual forgetfulness. The forgetfulness that does not remember that Marx almost immediately insists that "Greek art and epic poetry are bound up with certain forms of social development"—that the social and the artistic are "inseparably linked" (Marx, *Grundrisse* 47). Bourgeois critics typically dismiss the base/superstructure relation as "oversimplification." But even Terry Eagleton--by no means a classical Marxist--concedes that "Marx is clear that these two aspects of society do not form a *symmetrical* relationship . . . Each element of a society's superstructure . . . has its own internal evolution. . . . yet . . . in the last analysis, art is determined by [the] mode of production (Eagleton 14). The post-al queer left, however, rejects the determination of the superstructure by the base and regards history to be not the history of changing modes of production and modifications within the prevailing mode of production, but a complex network of undecidable "events" in the various "multiform" elements of culture (Foucault, "Nietzsche, Genealogy, History"; but also Teresa L. Ebert, "(Oc)Cult of the Post-al"). For Casarino and the other followers of Negri, history is what Christoph Cox proposes it to be in his reading of post-al theory: "The past is not a sequence of former presents, and the present not their progressive comprehension. Rather, the past is the field of the trace--a nontotalizable, variegated, and shifting field of forces that are either dormant or active. It is a differential field of traces, nonpresences constituted only within a network of differences" (Cox 127). In other words, "history" is "an incessantly destructuring structure that *plays*" (Cox 129). If there is an acknowledgement of some form of determination, it is only a kind of spectral "overdetermination" (Cox 129), the effects of the field of forces that is so complex as to render any knowledge of determination impossible. In other words, Casarino's notion of "history" is a post-al history that accepts the (post)structuralist and (post)modernist de-historicizing of history[33] and proposes, like post-al theory generally, that "things have changed so much" that Marx's mode of analysis must be significantly modified, if not abandoned altogether. Negri proposes that there has been "a new subjective determination" (Negri 82), that is, a mutation in the proletariat that has transformed the worker who is no longer the "mass worker" but the already "socialized worker" who "has an antagonistic character" (84) that is not so much "logically determined" (that is, not a conscious antagonism born of a commitment derived from a rational understanding of the logic of capitalist exploitation) but spontaneously produced (an intuitive result of the worker's experience under capitalism, 87). What Negri proposes as the new class of "socialized workers" (alongside but different from the class of "mass workers") constitutes for him a kind of proletarian "avant-garde" that *spontaneously* leads a resistance to capitalism that a "changed" capitalism has itself induced.

What Negri endorses as the workers' "spontaneity" is actually the trope of the body. When Negri posits this "worker antagonism" as "polyvalent" (Negri 87), he provides the ground for Casarino's appeal to the kind of "spontaneous resistances" of subjects celebrated in Romantic poetry: "the uncanny, multiform, refractory and communist others of and within--and beyond--capital" (Makdisi, Casarino, and Karl 12). In Negri's form of "historical materialism," workers are not part of a class constituted by the mode of production, but instead any persons who feel themselves to be "oppressed." Negri thus foregrounds as the basis of social injustice "oppression" (power relations) and not "exploitation" (the labor relations that form power). Hence, once again, as in Foucault, exploitation as the cause of social injustice is replaced by "oppression." For these neo-, and post- Marxists, the dialectic of history is not driven by class struggle, but by what Laclau and Mouffe and Žižek (following Lacan) formulate as the "antagonisms" sparked by various forms of cultural oppression. In the end, while Casarino and other Negrists still speak about something called "capitalism," unlike Marx who is quite clear and unyielding on the point that capitalism stands or falls as a structure of labor exploitation, they imagine capitalism to be nothing more than an allegorical figure representing the "multiform" modalities of cultural oppression.

Eight

The notion of dialectics as an aleatory "motion" undulating through various marginal and marginalized groups and not as material relations in class struggle informs both Casarino's and Judith Butler's views of Queer Theory. The bankruptcy of anti-materialist and anti-Marxist Queer Theory has become so clear today that even Butler, rather than rejecting Marxism outright, now claims that "queer studies" constitutes "an important return to the Marxist critique of the family" (Butler "Merely Cultural" 276). However, in her opportunistic appropriation of Marxism, she makes sure to dismiss all *sustained* historical materialist understandings of Queer Theory (Morton, "The Class Politics of Queer Theory").[34] What Butler means by "Marxist critique" deserves attention. Her notion of the "material" is, of course, the very one critiqued by Marx and Engels in *The German Ideology*. Her claim to "materialism" rests on the notion that queer persons "get hurt" (bodily) by economic practices, such as (for example) "those instances in which lesbian and gays are rigorously excluded from state-sanctioned notions of the family (which is, according to both tax and property law, an economic unit)" or are "deauthorized by the law to . . . receive the property of dead lovers" (273). So, for Butler, the "material" refers to being literally "hit" by economic forces; thus presumably if Steve Forbes were diagnosed with AIDS tomorrow, he too would fall--to follow Butler's own language--into the "class" of those "suffering" from "the profit-driven organization of health care and pharmaceuticals" which "impose differential burdens on those who live with HIV and AIDS" (273). The fact that Forbes is a private owner of means of production and makes "profit" (that is, exploits surplus labor) does not make any difference in Butler's account of "materialism." The profit maker (bourgeois) and the person whose labor is exploited to produce profit (proletariat) are the same in Butler's "Marxist critique": in effect, therefore, there are no property relations between the two, there are no classes. Like the work of the queer left as a whole, Butler's "materialism" is aimed above all at erasing class and class struggle (while pretending to do the opposite) and at doing so on the model of Foucault, who erases the difference between the powerful and the powerless. What Butler's notion of the "material" aims to produce is what Marx and Engels reject (the "material" as a "sensuous" consciousness of "suffering"--the "affective"); what Butler rejects is what Marx and Engels promote (the "material" as the historically produced conditions of differentials in "suffering"--the suffering of working-class lesbians and gays as opposed to the suffering of Steve Forbes). Butler's "materialism" is a version of that "matterism" which Marx and Engels found and rejected in Feuerbach, who did not "see how the sensuous world [of "suffering"] around him is, not a thing given direct from all eternity, remaining ever the same, but the product of industry and the state of society . . . " and "an historical product" (*The German Ideology* 62). Of course, for Marx and Engels history is the history of class struggle and not a series of aleatory performative moments, as it is for Butler and Queer Theory. On the one hand, then, Butler wants to be seen as endorsing some kind of "Marxism," while, on the other, she attacks and dismisses what she calls a "resurgent [Marxist] orthodoxy" as a "theoretical anachronism" (Butler 268) which damages the Left by rendering questions of other social differences (gender, race, sexuality, . . .) "secondary and derivative" to questions of class.

Butler's embarrassment, which is caused by her evasive politics that is an exemplary case of bourgeois "radical" fence-sitting, has led to such tremendous anxiety in "Merely Cultural" that she ends up constructing retrograde arguments by deploying naturalizations to which she pretends, most of the time, to be opposed. She claims, for instance, that the new social movements (including the gay/lesbian/queer movement) are "resented" by the "resurgent Marxist orthodoxy" because of "the vitality that such movements are enjoying" (268). She fails to historicize and explain the conditions which produce that "vitality" and thus "naturalizes" while claiming to oppose naturalizing. Here "vitality" is a code word for the accommodationist and the acceptable. Butler even goes so far as to deploy the notion of the "popular." In her discussion, however, the "popular" has nothing to do with people (as in working people) but is a trope, as I suggested, for the consensual, the accommodationist, and the collaborationist. Within Butler's frame, in which gender, sexuality, race, are the primary sites of inequality and are therefore the terrain of social struggle, it is hard to see why, for example, EXXON, AT&T, TEXACO, and other transnational corporations are just as busy as Butler is to end sexism, racism, genderism, . . . How does Butler explain her alliance with EXXON? The fact is that by focusing on gender, race, sexuality, . . . these allies (Butler, EXXON, . . .) direct attention away from questions of class and in doing so support the regime of wage-labor and today's intensifying capitalist exploitation.

It is not only the "content" of Butler's text but also its rhetorical framework that deserves attention: before getting down to the "serious" conceptual issues of political economy, the opening section frames the issues by reasserting the reversibility of all positions through the desire-ing lens of performativity and parody. In the climate since the 1990s, as the transfer of economic resources upwards from the masses to the few has accelerated and the economic determinants of social injustice have become increasingly patent to everyone, the ruling class's queer pataphysicians are finding their sublime indifference to questions of class more and more embarrassing and are beginning to comment, although in a hesitant and tentative manner which hints at their great discomfort in entering such unfamiliar (and basically distasteful) territory. Butler's essay is marked by such tentativeness: she targets for discussion a group of "resurgent" (268) orthodox Marxists who "for the moment" (265) she refuses to name and whose specific critiques of her work she refuses to cite on the grounds that she wants to focus on issues not persons. In actuality she refuses to refer to specific writers and texts here so that she, a leading "defender" of "difference," can lump all of "them" together and reduce them and their ideas to caricatures. Like Casarino, in other words, Butler ends up "same-ing" the Other. Instead of engaging directly with the "resurgent" orthodox Marxists, Butler pretends to have a serious discussion of "materialism" by directing her readers's attention to a writer, Nancy Fraser, who agrees with her that classical Marxism is irrelevant (Fraser 287). (Butler's text and Fraser's "response" are so important to the Anglo-American radical left for setting the limits of the "allowable" left discussion of the issues that they were promptly printed in both *Social Text* and *New Left Review*.) While Butler's main effort is to make a gesture towards questions of need (to show that Queer Theorists do not entirely neglect such issues), her framing of her entire text and her opening insistence that all are inevitably implicated in the parodic and in performative emotionalism marginalizes the question of "need": in her prefatory comments, Butler is merely repeating her basic position that desire is the governing force of social practices. Her anxious avoidance of contesting critics demonstrates that the goal of her essay is not at all a serious intellectual engagement with, but the marginalization of the critique-al other (how easy it is to marginalize the already marginalized) and the shoring up of the emotional solidarity of lesbian/gay/queer academia behind desire theory.

Nine

As Butler's text indicates, the queer left has increasingly had to acknowledge that it is engaged not in a "merely cultural" war but in an class war, that it is caught up in class struggle on the side of privilege, and that its main fight is against revolutionary Marxism, not against the political right (the latter fight is part of an inevitable struggle between various bourgeois class fractions, the ongoing battle between the progressive sector of the bourgeoisie and "those portions . . . whose interests have become antagonistic to the progress of industry" [Marx and Engels The *Communist Manifesto* 493]). It is also clear that the Sublime Closet exemplified in Casarino's text does not merely exemplify "general tendencies" (the displacement of politics by ethics and aesthetics) but is in fact constructed out of very precise attacks on the basic premises of that form of theory firmly committed to the resolution of class conflicts, classical Marxism. Thus, like all other instances of "quietism," Casarino's "quietism" is only a cover for violent acts of erasure. In this assault on Marxism, Casarino's closest—if never named—ally is Slavoj Žižek. In the struggles beginning in the 1990s, Žižek's work has proved very helpful to the bourgeois academy and the culture industry in providing an effective mode of ideological mystification. Žižek's usefulness is a result of the fact that, like Butler, he is adept at equivocation: saying and un-saying at the same time, taking a position and vacating it simultaneously. And as with Butler, this evasion is praised as a sign of intellectual "subtlety." For example, although he relies on Lacan, his writings appear--unlike Lacan's--to be "sense-full," and although he deploys the premises of (post)structuralist theory, his writings appear--unlike those of the (post)structuralists--to be geared towards providing "knowledge."

Žižek's work not only links the sublime in Kant and Lyotard to the sublime in Lacanian psychoanalysis but also provides at least part of the theoretical ammunition for Casarino's anti-dialecticism, his celebration of the "non-relational," his "same-ing" of the Other, and—above all--his pathologizing of the subject, . . . Žižek is perhaps most helpful because he makes more vigorous, direct, and overt the generally unremarked anti-Marxist politics of psychoanalysis, for example, by arguing against historical materialist dialectics: "Historicity proper," says Žižek—by implication marking Marxism's notion of historicity as "improper"— "involves a dialectical relationship to some unhistorical kernel that stays the same—not an underlying Essence but as a rock that trips up every attempt to integrate it into the symbolic order. This rock is the Thing *qua* 'the part of the Real that suffers from the signifier' (Lacan)—the real 'suffers' (compare Butler's notion of materiality as suffering) in so far as it is the trauma that cannot be properly articulated in the signifying chain" (*The Metastases* 199). Here Žižek is continuing the psychoanalytic war against Marxism which we have already noted in Freud and find again rearticulated in Lacan, who rejects Marxism's "misguided" tendency to explain the causes of social injustice in terms of "conflict, struggle, even of the exploitation of man by man" rather than in the cause he proposes—the intransigences of "the kernel of the real" which is "unassimilable" to the Symbolic (Lacan 53, 55). Against the Marxist argument that social change is driven by the material collision of the forces and social relations of production in the form of class struggle, Lacan and Žižek argue that it is the conflict between the Real and the Symbolic, between "being" and "meaning"—not between historical classes in their relations of exchange of labor power for wages—that lies at the root of every social conflict and, furthermore, that any effort to resolve these conflicts by providing an explanation of them in the Symbolic (the social) always leads inevitably to a brutal totalitarian outcome (Žižek *The Sublime Object* 5). In other words, the pre-social (the psychic natural) is the grounding, foundationalist, and determining force. What Lacan and Žižek propose, in other words, is a form of determinism which is concealed by the formal indeterminacy of their arguments. This is the bourgeois academy's "preferred" form of determinism; but it is a psychic determinism that is informed by the "thing" of Being. To take up a position as a revolutionary Marxist, Žižek— like Cary Nelson--proposes, is to become "perverse": it is to fall into a "'paranoic' over-identification" with "the reverse of Capitalism's universalism" and thus into "perversion as a socially 'constructive' attitude" (Žižek, "Eastern European Liberalism" 40). By emphasizing the pre-social (subjectivity and desire) and not the social (collectivity and reason), Žižek thus supplies an alibi for quietism, for staying in the closet and never engaging in the world's battles. The sublime for Žižek points to an ethics of "aesthetic awareness" in the sense of accepting things as they are--there is no undoing the "trauma," the cause of conflict--and accepting the fact that the best that one can do concerning social conflicts is not to resolve them but endure them and try to "patch things up afterwards" (*The Sublime Object* 5). We are all, on this view, always "traumatized" and in this sense always "ill" anyway: the distinction between the "needy" proletariat and the "exploitative" capitalist is therefore submerged in the "trauma" of Being as such—Being as a general pathology. In Žižek's trope, enjoyment/pleasure/ *jouissance* "metastasizes" into all social practices like a cancer for which there is certainly no "cure" nor is there any effective "treatment."[35] The effect of the post-al theorization of the sublime is to relocate the emphasis in the understanding of "sublimation": while arguing that civilized subjects will always live in a state of "discontent," Freud emphasized that they could learn to accept and work with the "substitutes" or "symbolic counters."

Such acceptance is what Freud understands as "adulthood." For Lacan and Žižek—and their followers in the queer left--Freud's defense of the bourgeois subject did not go far enough, so that for them the emphasis is placed on the *irredeemable inadequacy of all symbolic substitutes and all theoretical explanations (that is, of reason)*: it is therefore under the impact of this ideological shift that queer commentators like Sedgwick can attack persons (particularly Marxists) who want to bring about transformative social change as "paranoid readers" and can conclude with Casarino that "staying in" the closet is preferable to "coming out" (that the closet is "preferable" to the world), and use this "given" as the excuse for obliterating the Other and redoubling the Same. Since there can be no "resolutions" to social conflicts, it is better to "stay out of them" (remain in the closet). Žižek's theory of the "suffering" Real also provides an alibi for the sublime closet's acceptance of pathology by insisting (I shall shortly provide further discussion of this move) that there is actually no such thing as "health" (individual or social), that is, that all conditions and states of life are inescapably and universally "pathological."[36]

Žižek also provides a theorization for the (pathological) "non-relational" character of the closet on which Casarino is silently relying: psychoanalysis "works," according to Žižek, only if the analysand (and the analyst, by the way, has once been an analysand himself) goes through the experience of "subjective destitution," a "Narcissistic loss, . . . a sublime version of utter humiliation, 'de-subjectivization' . . . " (*The Metastases* 168). In this experience, one gives up "personalism" and finds one's "innermost dignity" is converted into "'a piece of shit'" (168). Žižek argues that this "subjective destitution" is the opposite of self-centeredness or solipsism; it is an acceptance not of the centrality of the self, but instead of the self's "non-existence" (170). Yet "paradoxically" this loss of the "self" is still interpreted as a gain: a gaining of entry into a new kind of community of "selves"–like Casarino's community of the sublime closet—radically different from the community of the "world" (171). Žižek exemplifies this new "kind" of community of "self-less selves" with an Other-erasing and racist "sexual" anecdote: in "the whorehouses of old New Orleans," he tells us, the white couple continues copulation even when the black servant enters to deliver drinks because "his gaze did not count as the gaze of another person" (168). The greatest (sexual) intimacy, he goes on to argue a few lines later, is not after all in sexual intercourse (the self in relation to the Other) but in allowing oneself to be watched while masturbating when one risks looking "ridiculous" (as in Casarino, the self with the self with an onlooker) (169). "Same-ing" in Žižek appears as a social "leveling" that, on the one hand, erases difference by insisting--in a simulation of "democracy"--that we are all finally alike because our situation in life is to be measured in terms of "subjective destitution"; this "same-ing," on the other hand, justifies the outcome here, where the black servant's desire is simply "erased," made the "same" and de-othered, and the partner's desire "suspended," so that instead of "relation" the focus is on the self's "desire." "Same-ing," however, is much more than simply a mode of social "leveling"; it is fundamentally a way of denying that social relations are collective (denying that the black servant's and the white master's needs and desires are connected through the circuitry of class society). Marx explains this connectedness as follows:

> In production, men enter into relation not only with nature. They produce only by co-operating in a certain way and mutually exchanging their activities. In order to produce, they enter into definite connections and relations with one another and only within these social connections and relations does their relation with nature, does production, take place. These social relations into which the producers enter with one another, the conditions under which they exchange their activities and participate in the whole act of production, will naturally vary according to the character of the means of production. . . .
> *Thus* the social relation within which individuals produce, *the social relations of production, change, are transformed, with the change and development of the material means of production, the productive forces. The relations of production in their totality constitute what* are called *the social relations, society*, and, specifically, a society at *a definite stage of historical development.* (Marx, *Wage Labour and Capital* 211-212)

Ten

As they encounter the new contradictions of global capitalism, bourgeois apologists are now focusing not simply on the subject's desire nor on desire's "sublimity" but on desire's "pathological" dimension. Increasingly their alibi is this: the domination of desire is inescapable, it cannot be mastered by reason and therefore has the character of an addiction. The assumption here is that the social—as Bataille claimed—is the site of an ungoverned and ungovernable economy of excess. The bourgeoisie, addicted to--and eager to confuse if it cannot totally obscure the recognition of the injustice of--its privileges has decided to justify those privileges by proposing that addiction is an inevitable condition of subjectivity itself. In other words, while the bourgeoisie insists that the problem of need can be set aside, it argues that desire cannot; hence, we are all addicts--irrationally, inescapably, and uncontrollably "dependent" on our desires. According to post-al theory, all subjects are "sick," not just homosexual subjects. As "ill" people, we are not fully accountable for what we do: hence (class) practices are naturalized as the pathology of Being itself--simply as "who human beings are" and "what they do." We are always "driven" by the force of desire, not by historical class interests. Furthermore, by theorizing desire largely in a psychoanalytic frame, the bourgeoisie explains desires/pathologies/ addictions as mainly dimensions of subjectivities rather than of society itself. Against this personalizing of desire, Marx argues instead that "Our desires and pleasures spring from society; we measure them, therefore, by society and not by the objects which serve for their satisfaction. Because they are of a social nature, they are of a relative nature" (Marx *Wage-Labour* 216). The queer left and desire theorists basically argue that people therefore have a "new level" of "democratic rights": they have a "right" to their dependencies and addictions; they have, in other words, a "right" to focus on what Casarino celebrates in the closet--the pleasures of the self. A small "theory" industry is now growing up which-- following the genealogy traced in the writings of Schelling, Heidegger, Žižek, . . . --argues that *Eigensucht* (self-craving) or "addictive creatureliness" is the very defining characteristic of human being, and indeed of God himself (Clark 19).[37] Thus the immersion in the ideology of the sublime is basically an excuse for the bourgeois subject to focus on the "self" and is buttressed by the alibi of inescapable pathology, which is commonly expressed today in the term "addiction."[38] The recent work of Žižek in fact promotes the supposed theoretical prescience of Friedrich Schelling, who celebrated "addictive longing as human" (Clark 29): Schelling is now regarded as the founding philosopher of "addiction" as the ground of human being. He is, however, like Kant before him and Heidegger and Žižek after him, another contributor to the bourgeois project of the "destruction of reason" explained by Lukács.

If all subjects are irremediably addicted (governed by irrational attachments), then it makes no sense to propose a "rational" agenda for moving the discussion of homosexuality out of the medicalized domain of "sickness": the ruling class's pataphysicians are willing to pay this price because at a time like the present when the logic and effects of exploitation are becoming starkly obvious in the chasm between rich and poor within the US itself, the pathologizing of the social helps to heighten the suspicion of reason by turning all reasons--which are, like humanity in general, "sick"--into untrustworthy and illusory rationalizations and to discount any social theory--such as Marxism--which insists on rational analysis of the laws of motion of capital and exposes its exploitative logic. In their desperation to distract attention away from growing economic injustice, bourgeois ideologues do not simply sow the seeds of distrust of reason but in fact take every opportunity to glorify irrationalism: hence the current fascination with--and often outright celebration of--"addiction" as the subject's necessarily "compulsive" behavior marked by desire. Instances of the bourgeois fascination with addiction appear in cultural interpretations in the work of such post-al and queer left figures as Avital Ronell, Richard Klein, Žižek, and Eve Sedgwick and its impact is congealed in the 1997 special issue of *diacritics* (Redfield) devoted to addiction as a manifestation of engagement with the "sublime of culture."

I will focus here mainly on Sedgwick and Žižek; but I want to begin by pointing briefly to the role of Avital Ronell's *Crack Wars: Literature Addiction Mania* in providing the main outlines of the genealogy of post-al addiction theory in the US academy and in providing the linkage between taking drugs and reading (and enjoying) literature as a synechdoche for making meaning in general, the latter being, according to her, an addiction to intertextuality (understood as the mutual addiction of texts to each other), which is an addiction to what she calls "tropium" (Ronell 29), that is, the unstoppable "play of the signifier." Pathologies are actually social, not individual, and social pathologies are (unproductive) responses to social contradictions; they are a displacement of energies that would be better directed to resolving social contradictions into a zone of "excess," a "displacement" that represents the subject's "giving up on" social contradictions as "unresolvable." It is hardly surprising, then, that contemporary capitalist societies (supposedly the ultimate place of fulfillment of "human possibilities" and "human happiness")--where citizens are taught the ludic lessons that excess is the very fundamental and inescapable condition of human life and that social contradictions are *unresolvable in principle*-- are marked by numerous various social pathologies, including "addiction." The fascination with addiction in the 1990s—the years of new boom and great affluence for the upper middle classes and of growing "excess-ive" social practices—as undecidably both a cause and an effect of social ills is a consequence of attempts to substitute, in the tradition of conservative thinkers from Burke through Hayek to Fish and Rorty, "habits and customs" for class struggle as the dynamics of the social. "Habits and customs" are rewritten by Freud and the poststructuralists as social sites of pleasure. Freud insists that all social practices are motivated by the pleasure principle and Barthes claims that all understandings of the texts of culture are inescapably a performance of the "pleasure of the text." With Nietzsche as her tutor, Ronell teaches that the "history of narcotica . . . is almost the history of culture" and that "*narcotics* articulates a quiver between history and ontology" (Ronell 3). If we understand with Ronell that the ontic is more or less what Lacan theorizes as the Real, that which is in excess of the Symbolic (history), then the "quivering" role of narcotics lies in representing that ambivalent (queer) space--which we all in-habit--between our elemental existence (in the Real) and our historical existence (in the Symbolic). Addiction (pathology), in other words, is the condition of human life that continually disrupts the possibility that we can have a dependable conceptual grasp of our human situatedness ("Drugs resist conceptual arrest," Ronell 51), a condition for which there is no "cure": "To get off drugs, or alcohol (major narcissistic crisis)," Ronell argues, "the addict has to shift dependency to a person, an ideal, or to the procedure itself of the cure," Ronell 25). Narcoanalysis, as Ronell names it, is therefore equivalent to social analysis itself. "Economics" enters Ronell's narcoanalysis in the sense I referred to before, as Bataille's economy of desire that runs "parallel" to the economy that answers to need: that parallel economy is—for Ronell as for other post-al theorists--a "crash economy, an exhorbitant expenditure with no reserve" (Ronell 109).

Eve Sedgwick, too, has inquired into what has become in Queer Theory the "topos" of addiction ("Epidemics of the Will") and has observed that, *pace* Lacan and Žižek, it is not the Real but capitalism that is responsible for the pathologization of subjectivities. Thus, like Butler, Casarino, and the queer left in general, Sedgwick must also make a gesture towards "radical politics" by "critiquing" capitalism. However, the capitalism she targets is not the capitalism critiqued by Marxism. Like the capitalism Derrida targets (he is concerned with financial institutions, with interest and not with surplus value), Sedgwick's is "another" capitalism, where labor and class are not the issue. So, according to her, capitalism has deployed the discourse of pathology in order to posit a zone of "non-pathology" which can only be reached by consumers who assert their "healthy wills" in acts of "free choice" in buying capitalism's supposedly "health-providing" goods (diet foods and supplements) and services (personal trainers). The effect of capitalism which Sedgwick therefore deplores is not the exploitation of the labor of masses of workers by capitalists but rather cultural capitalism: capitalism's production of what she calls "epidemics of the will," the production of supposedly "sick" consumers' demands for supposedly "health-giving" products. In actuality, while the most easily recognized impulse of Sedgwick's essay is its "attack" on capitalist commodification, at a more significant level it is actually an attack on acts of "will." Like Žižek, she is arguing that they are themselves a form of sickness. After the post-al deconstruction of subjectivity, agency, and will, the only kind of "will" the post-al queer left is willing to talk about is what John H. Smith has called a "queered" will, that is, a "undecidable" will "permeated by a radical ambivalence" (John Smith "Queering the Will" 7). Whatever her stated views of capitalism and/or psychoanalysis may be, it is clear that any reservations Sedgwick has--and her complaint is not about the exploitation of workers but about capitalism's "manipulation" of consumers--are the product of affect (her ongoing fascination with feelings is exhibited in the book she recently co-edited, *Shame and Its Sisters: A Silvan Tompkins Reader* [Tompkins]). The best that she can offer for the evidently irresolvable dilemma captured in the harsh binary of addiction vs. health is to replace the term "addiction" with the "softer" and less "judgmental" term "habit." Her title, "Epidemics of the Will," enacts a by now routine and banal Foucauldian reversal that pathologizes (assaults) not those who "go with the flow" (as she does) in an unreasoning and affective-reliant manner but those who exercise their will in the name of a cause, that is, those who are politically militant for a "reason." Unlike others who more openly glorify "addiction," Sedgwick tries to articulate--in the name the "feminist" and queer cultural left --a ("softened" and "sympathetic") understanding of it (that is "one step to the side of" addiction, 138) as "habit" and celebrates "habit" as a "sheltering habitation" for the self (138), a ready justification for *Eigensucht*. David Clark's post-al investigation of Heidegger's "addiction" to Schelling similarly treats "addiction" in significatory terms as a "*figure of understanding*" (Clark 8). Instead of offering a materialist analysis of such social problems as addiction, Sedgwick turns them into problems of representation: so, for her, addiction is not so much a material social problem with a solution as it is troubling allegory of social life which can only be re-read "sympathetically"(reparatively) and shifted into an alternative narrative register. Her suggestion that the self is in need of "protective sheltering" rather than critique is part of the genealogy of Casarino's "sublime closet."

As recent developments--such as the present stage of The Closet Is Sublime--show, there is, as always, an unevenness in the development of the dominant ideology which appears as "differences" in the tactics and strategies deployed by various bourgeois queer factions competing with each other to see who can most effectively serve ruling class interests. Sedgwick's brand of Queer Theory is an eclectic, accommodationist blend of pragmatism, postmodernism, and feminism (with which she here mixes a weak notion of commodification). This focusless, eclectic and evasive "theory" allows her room to maneuver in the interest of always representing herself (in whatever vocabulary she happens to be using at the time) as "sympathetic" to marginalized-- particularly queer--groups. Here again we can see how Casarino's differently inflected romantic (Blakean) and affective discourses converge with Sedgwick's, despite his claims to be "different." As I have hinted, the "difference" is only a question of the unevenness of their relation to dominant ideas. The underlying justification for Sedgwick's eclecticism is that what matters in social life is not politics or economics but affect or "good-heartedness": in her view, the problem of the closet is ultimately what the gay writer Paul Monette called its "stunting of the heart" ("Guest Opinion" 40). Sedgwick's nearly universal appeal to bourgeois readers lies in her eclectic, "flexible" (that is, evasive) approach to all questions: her stress on affect is justified simultaneously by both conventional humanist understandings of subjectivity as unified, coherent, and extra-textual and by post-al understandings of a desire-driven subjectivity as split, incoherent, and textual. In other words, her work becomes a useful site for bourgeois "consensus." The down-side of this eclecticism represented as "breadth" is that her work exposes so obviously the underlying political unity between old and new bourgeois theories and undercuts the claim of the latter to be working in different political and economic interests.

The convergent interest of psychoanalysis and Queer Theory in the project of "sheltering" ("closeting") the (bourgeois) psyche is further developed in one of Žižek's most recent texts, *The Abyss of Freedom*, in which he engages, in passing, the topic of the queer. Repeating Queer Theory's already established tendency, Žižek proposes two forms of homosexual identification in contemporary society: one has a "horrifying aspect," "horrifying" because it calls up a "pre-Oedipal oral-anal introjection, swallowing up the partner," while the other is a "latent homosexual identification as the cohesive force of society" (*The Abyss* 19). Following the familiar argument that sexuality as we know it (as defined in the "masculinist" Symbolic) is basically homosexual (homosocial), he further develops a "sophisticated" and "cosmopolitan" reading of sexuality by following Lacan to propose that the only true heterosexuality is "lesbian sex, the only one in which the otherness of our partner is maintained" (56), while all other sexuality is homosexuality which is itself further divided into "gay sexuality and (straight) heterosexuality" (56). Thus by working within a framework of psychoanalytic reversals already widely used by bourgeois theorists today, the apparently heterosexual Žižek (like the also heterosexual Sedgwick) gives the now requisite impression of "sympathy" with other sexualities. If his attribution of a "horrifying aspect" of homosexual identification at first makes homosexual readers "suspicious," his attribution of a "horrifying aspect" to heterosexual relations mitigates the tension (25). In Žižek's theory of sexual intimacy (whereby we confront not just a Barthesian blissful--and "beautiful"--*jouissance*, but more significantly an "ugly *jouissance*" [21]), the "ultimate problem in intersubjectivity is precisely the extent to which we are ready to accept the other, our (sexual) partner, in the real of his or her existence--do we still love him when she or he defecates, makes unpleasant sounds?" (25). In the last analysis, Žižek's theory of homosexuality is by no means "sympathetic" to homosexuals, since it is merely a "sophisticated" version of the typical bourgeois--transhistorical--understanding; but we need to give it a more sustained and specific class reading.

On the one hand, Žižek postulates a "horrifying homosexuality" (which the bourgeois heterosexual theorist proposes as a form of "ugly jouissance" associated with the oral and the anal), which is a *literal homosexuality*--literal in the sense of pointing to the actual homosexual practices that are (at least formally) "distasteful" to the bourgeois sensibility; on the other hand, he postulates a generalized homosexuality (as a socially necessary homosociality) which is a merely *tropic homosexuality*--in that it is a "cleaned up" version of homosexuality not associated with any ("dirty" or "clean") bodily practices at all. Of course, the bourgeois aversion to dirt is not a materialist consideration (not, say, the recognition that one needs clean tools in order to work productively) but a question of class status (the bourgeois doesn't do--and the petty bourgeois doesn't aspire to do--the kind of work that gets his hands "dirty").

Without bringing to bear on the question of "coming out" a rigorous historical materialist analysis, many queer studies writers (cf. Creech) have already expressed their uneasiness with the move of *troping* sexual practices and detaching them from their supposed literality and "objectivity." Leo Bersani, for instance, has repeatedly complained that much Queer Theory erases the specificity of gay male sexual practices (*Homos* 61). If one turns sexual practices into a trope, one also turns "the closet" into a trope and erases the material conditions that produce "closets" in the first place. For Bersani, however, the only conditions he regards to be "material" are the actual sexual--physical, bodily, sensual--practices of gay men, not the condition of class struggle. When Bersani comments that some of Sedgwick's claims are a bit sweeping (he says "breathtaking," *Homos* 68)--he cites, for instance, her claim that social and cultural interest in homosexuality is universal (*Epistemology* 1)--he gives a hint at the actual role Sedgwick and other queer left ideologues (including Bersani) have all along been playing: they are basically populist demagogues (Bersani commends Sedgwick's "eloquence" [*Homos* x] and is famous for the same expressive quality) saying what (upper) middle class, affluent gays and lesbians want to hear (it will be enough to reform capitalism) rather than pedagogues committed to transformative social change teaching the working class what they need to know (revolutionary class consciousness).

While bourgeois theorists gain power in the culture industry by becoming more and more allusional and tropic, working class lesbians and gay men take up, as a discursive weapon, a new literalism. In their texts, literalism becomes a return to the material reality of late capitalism and although there is no rigorous theory of capitalism developed in their texts, they at least reassert, through the literal, the oppression of wage labor. Thus, such working class writers as Dorothy Allison have, in short, made their lesbian sexual needs and desires--under the impact of class society--quite unambiguously *literal*. Žižek's "sophisticated" metaphorical reading of homosexuality is of course the result of a displacement undergone by the multilingual, multicultural, and cosmopolitan subject who comes to recognize that what is taken as "literal" (that is, "natural") in one social and cultural context is very different from what is taken as "literal" in another social and cultural context and who gives these social differences a tropological reading. The current propagation of that Queer Theory mode of understanding/reading homosexuality known as "queering" is finally nothing more than the queer left's wholesale embrace of the tropological reading which turns a particular socio-sexual need into nothing more than a generalized trope; in other words, it represents the de-materialization of homosexuality which, like all other forms of de-materialization, serves ruling class interests. Once the horizon of understanding difference is established by the literal/metaphorical binary, homosexuals appear to have the following "choice": they must either understand themselves in terms of post-al metaphorics whereby their sexual needs become mere tropes or understand their sexual needs as a "literality." What is of course occluded in this "choice" of a *literal* reading or a post-al *metaphorical* reading--that is, what readers are "sheltered" from--is a historical materialist critique of social practices, which connects the seemingly disconnected (class and sexuality) and produces a knowledge of the social totality and thus marks the historical conditions and limits of hegemonic practices. It is precisely because such a critique provides guidelines for a transformative social change (that the reformist left doesn't want) that it is targeted by post-al theory. The materialist critique concludes that social arrangements are not by definition pathological and unhealthy; that today's "addictions" are not inescapable elements of subjectivity, not psychogenic features of subjects themselves but are shaped by the structure of class relations in capitalist society; that a socially healthy society is one organized around the imperative of meeting all of its members' needs ("needs" that are not transhistorical but change over time); that an "adult" subject is one who accepts the conditionality of life (and sees the notion of "free love" as the idealist illusion it is) and understands his own needs and desires in relation to those of others; and that the subject of the "sublime" closet (for whom the needs of others is irrelevant) is a narrowly self-interested, pathologized, infantile, self-addicted (*eigensüchtig*) subject who constantly proposes illusory (pataphysical) solutions to material social problems.[39]

Whether we are dealing with bourgeois philosophy (Kant, Schelling, Bataille, Butler), psychoanalysis (Freud, Žižek), queer studies (Sedgwick), literary close reading (Casarino), . . . , the same underlying logic is continually re-deployed in all these domains: materialism is not, the bourgeois knowledge industry declares, what Marx says it is (historical conflicts developed through the relations of production/labor) but "something else" (a question of consumption, pleasure, multiple differences, exchange value, indeterminacy, desire, the body, inescapable addiction, . . .). What all these writers are legitimating is this: yes, we are addicted to our privileges, but addictions are constitutive of the subject and therefore not open to change. The closet in its latest transmogrification becomes the emblem of this addiction of the self to the self: narcisopium. The bourgeois culture industry, of course, promotes these apologists for pathologies and addictions as if their writings were all "unique" and "different" and provided something "new"; but in fact the current celebration of the unconscious, addiction, the sublime, . . . is nothing more than a continuation (in a different vocabulary) of earlier bourgeois textual ecstasies--that play-full orgy of signs called pataphysics, an exultation in the absurd, the spontaneous, the bodily, the surreal, the particular, . . . Pataphysics has been--and, as I argue here, remains--an effective discursive tool of the ruling class through which it provides imaginary solutions to social problems, including the problem of marginal sexualities and the question of the "closet."

Pataphysics--the erasure of the possibility of determinate explanations of the social totality, the cancellation of the possibility of a coherent understanding of the "big picture," the fetishization of the particular, the local, and the singular--has recently been returned—as might be predicted during another period of sharpening capitalist crisis—to the foreground of bourgeois thought by Jean Baudrillard in his much cited "millennial" text, "Pataphysics of the Year 2000." That text not only elaborates on the supposed "vanishing or disappearance of history" but also cancels "theory" (reason). In fact, Baudrillard engages in an ironic play with the "physics" (reason) of the social and installs in its place an allusional "pataphysics" of the affective, the uncanny, the enigmatic, the eerie, the spectral. Following that line, Casarino engages pataphysics as the art of the spectral queer. Baudrillard claims that "theory is no longer in the state of 'reflecting' on anything anymore. All it can do is to snatch concepts from their critical zone of reference and transpose them to the point of no return, in the process of which theory itself too, passes into the hyperspace of simulation as it loses all 'objective' validity" (Baudrillard). Yet what Baudrillard announces as the "weakening" of theory is not a *necessary* contemporary social condition but an ideological ploy. Such attacks on reason (troped as "theory") are now routinely cloaked in the rhetoric of radical politics and this supposed radicalism has also been taken over into Queer Theory.

A final exemplary instance. In a new attack on whatever is left of conceptual thinking in the culture industry, Elizabeth Grosz, detecting that Deleuzean spiritualism has been completely absorbed into New Age social practices, has embarked on marketing a new commodity: Bergsonian theosophy. Like all "post" authors, who simultaneously reject politics and call themselves political, she wraps up her anti-conceptualism as a form of radical politics. This is supposed to give her more credibility and enhance her ability to more effectively defend capitalism. In a recent lecture ("Deleuze, Bergson, and Uncharted Futures"), for example, Grosz boldly repeated Cary Nelson's sentiment: "theory doesn't feed people." This is supposed to place her emphatically on the side of "the people," but in the same lecture she does her best to discourage people from thinking and instead encourages them to embrace an amorphous spirituality that makes it impossible to come to any conclusion in life. Postponing decisions (such as, for example, the decision that the present economic system has to be completely transformed) is her goal. For her deciding ("predicting") is itself an act of violence; but she doesn't seem to regard her own aggressive advocacy of ignorance in the name of spiritualistic anti-conceptuality to be itself a violence against people. In the wake of the absorption of Deleuze and Guattari's writings, Bergson's have now become the next source for developing a "fresher looking" form of false consciousness. A false consciousness that reassures people to endure their alienated and fragmentary life and inhibits any attempt to supersede that life as a misguided rationalism. Using mystical meditation to obliterate the political while at the same time calling herself "political" (on this cynical use of the "political," see Ebert, "Beyond 'Enlightened False Consciousness' and For a Red Theory"), Grosz rejects Marxist theory and the politics of "mass movements" guided by theory because she believes that the mind is neither a thinking machine nor a conscious entity (neither matter nor spirit) but an "excessive" material body that delays and disrupts the connection between stimulus and action and diverts the subject's planned actions and transforms them into something unpredictable. Mass movements--she declares--are at an end because no one can "predict" any outcome. Since we cannot know when, why, how things happen or what the future will bring, all that is left is the contemplation of Time—in Bergson's terms, duration. To stay in the closet is therefore to live in a "time" of one's own. Grosz explicitly rejects Marxism on the grounds that stock brokers now read Marx: for Grosz, it is irrelevant to ask why they read Marx or what understanding of his ideas they put forward after reading him. If stockbrokers's reading of Marx discredits Marx, what are we to conclude from the fact that a great number of readers of Nietzsche, Deleuze, Berson, Heidegger, . . . are Nazis, neo-Nazis, and post-fascists? For reactionaries like Grosz, the project of revolution is over and the unfolding of Time is the only serious issue left to contemplate. On the view Grosz puts forward, it is not just homosexuals but all subjects who are in "the closet" today, waiting there for Time to shape history--by itself.

The closet, in the dominant Queer Theory, has become the trope for self-caressing withdrawal from the scene of social struggle: through such concepts as "reparative reading," "the sublime," "claustrophiliac ecstasy," "(self)addiction," . . . , post-al Queer Theory has legitimated the notion of the closet as the site of jouissance and (melancholic) self-reflexivity of the post-socialist nomadic subject. However, the closet is in fact a response to production practices; it is an annex of the system of wage-labor--a place in which inequalities of exchange of labor power for wages are justified by pathologizing resistant sexualities. To affirm the closet by the alibi of "freedom" is to affirm wage labor. What is needed now is not more addictional theories and theories of addiction--not the habituation of queers to the closet--but a Red Queer Theory to open the closet and cut the addictive connections by new reconnectings: reconnectings that put an end to the commodification of human labor by setting people free from necessity. It is only through freedom from necessity that the time of the closet will come to an end.

Notes

[1]For example, Graham-Gibson describes "her" project to mitigate the harshness of capitalism as "theorizing capitalism without representing dominance as a natural and inevitable feature of its being" (5); Nelson urges workers to "unionize" (180); and Delaney promotes the idea that "given the mode of capitalism under which we live, life is at its most rewarding, productive, and pleasant when large numbers of people understand, appreciate, and seek out interclass contact and communication conducted in a mode of good will" (111).

[2]Cary Nelson is, of course, not the only person with entrenched institutional power masquerading as a "leftist" who, using the language of opposition, normalizes capitalism. In the wake of the "fall of communism," left capitalism has in fact become a boom industry. The special issue of *South Atlantic Quarterly* on "Psycho-Marxism: Marxism and Psychoanalysis Late in the Twentieth Century" (Spring 1998), for instance, similarly deploys a left rhetoric as a disguise for the most reactionary theories and views aimed at marginalizing classical Marxism and its revolutionary practices. See the exemplary essay: "Queering the Unconscious." For a sustained critique of Cary Nelson's collaborationist practices, see Mas'ud Zavarzadeh, "Cary Nelson's Homophobia and the Defense of Capitalism."

[3]To be sure, the phrase "coming out" had a history stretching back long before Gay Liberation: earlier however, in the 1930s, say, "coming out" meant to make oneself known to other homosexuals, that is to say, to other persons in "the life" but not "to the world—family, neighbors, colleagues" (Loughery 70).

[4]Still the most recent mainstream "history" of the gay rights movement relies from beginning to end on the trope of the visible/invisible—see Clendinen and Nagourney pp.11 and 573.

[5]United as the queer left is a range of writers with numerous superficial differences; included in its membership are not only humanists (John Boswell, Lauren Berlant, Michael Warner, . . .) but eclectic literary figures and cultural commentators (Edmund White, Tony

Kushner, Eve Sedgwick, . . .), not only Freudians (Teresa de Lauretis, Leo Bersani, . . .) but Foucauldians (David Halperin, Simon Watney, . . .), not only post-structuralists (Lee Edelman, Judith Butler, Elizabeth Grosz, D. A. Miller, . . .) but social scientists (Steven Seidman, Ken Plummer, Barry Adam, . . .), not only conservative apologists (Andrew Sullivan, Camille Paglia, Bruce Bawer, . . .) but neo- and post-marxians and democratic socialists (John d'Emilio, Dennis Altman, Gayle Rubin, Gary Kinsman, David Fernbach, Jeffrey Weeks, Scott Tucker, Samuel Delaney, Kevin Floyd, . . .).

[6]For a recent, sustained discussion of the case for "gay rights," see Nava and Dawidoff.

[7]For a fuller view of Lenin's concern for issues of gender, see Lenin, *The Emancipation of Women.*

[8]For a sustained discussion of Queer Theory's crisis, see Morton, "Queer Theory as Pathos."

[9] Of course, the queer left has also "queered" "ideology," so that they could "quit worrying" about it (quit taking it seriously). See O'Neill.

[10]For an extended instance of the queer left's (reformist) articulation of "dialectics," see Floyd. Predictably, Floyd's appropriation of a Marxist vocabulary depends on emptying it of its explanatory and revolutionary power by, for instance, erasing the determinative relation of base and superstructure ("we should reject Lukács's economistic assumption that . . . " (Floyd 184).

[11]While the historical pressures produced by growing global economic inequality have recently pushed an increasingly embarrassed queer left to gesture towards materialist explanations, those "explanations" are always eclectically and "safely" combined with a thoroughgoing idealism. An example is the recently published text by Dennis Altman who remarks that "it is capitalism, not moral argument, that has rendered homophobia old-fashioned and unacceptable" (in other words, the mode of production has produced social effects) but then goes on to conclude that the problem with Queer Theory is that it "removes the concrete actors [autonomous agents] whose hard work is what made . . . queer theory itself--possible at all" (Altman "From Gay Power" 29). Like others on the queer left, Altman is proposing that capitalism has made homophobia "acceptable," which is a way of saying that homosexuals in some sense "owe" their "freedoms" today to capitalism. What the queer left obscures by this claim is that capitalism creates homosexuality as a particular consumerist lifestyle that only a few can afford and furthermore that, by raising the level of food production, capitalism has not only made it possible to feed all of the world's hungry but also, because it is geared only to profit, blocked that from happening.

---

[12]The Gramscian activists who are discussed in a sustained manner below are, in the words of Charles Anderson, among those "opportunists" who "vulgarize" "aspects of the Marxist model . . . to serve their own political purposes" (Anderson 4). A particular branch of this opportunism has produced what is today called "cultural materialism" tracing its roots to the work of Raymond Williams. As articulated by Scott Wilson, the basic opportunistic assumption of the "culturalist left" is that "the international socialist movement must be abandoned because it implies a universalist and totalizing idea of socialism that ignores specific cultural differences" (Wilson 24). For an exemplary instance of the opportunistic appropriation of Gramsci (through Williams) as it relates to gay studies as a branch of cultural materialism, see Sinfield, *Cultural Politics--Queer Reading* (21-27). As Sinfield makes clear, the key theoretical grounding of so-called cultural materialism is specifically the rejection of the classical Marxist idea of the determination of the superstructure by the base (25). He also makes the reformist (rather than revolutionary) goal of cultural materialism clear when he notes that the target of such activism is not capitalist exploitation but "the cultural degradation . . . associated with capitalism" (24). A much more sustained articulation of the grounds of "cultural materialism"--along with a critique of Sinfield's appropriation of Gramsci as a form of "romanticism"--is found in Scott Wilson, *Cultural Materialism* (see especially 254-257). In an effort to "move beyond" this "romanticism," to "maintain [cultural materialist] theory . . . but [take] it elsewhere," Wilson himself tries to give cultural materialism a more "economic" flavor by drawing on Bataille's pataphysical notion of "general economy." For more celebration of Bataille, see "Georges Bataille."

[13]Regarding the end point of this phase, David Harvey remarks: "It was not until the sharp recession of 1973 shattered that framework [mass production practices] that a process of rapid . . . transition in the regime of accumulation began" (Harvey 140). Regarding its beginning, the significance of World War II has often been noted by commentators on the sexual margins. What is passed off today as "materialist" analysis of the development of the gay/lesbian/ . . . communities in the post-war US society always seeks a multiplicity of causes (if not outright "determinants") outside economics. For example, it is by now a cliché of gay historiography that the war effort itself--the drawing of gay men and lesbians out of small town and rural US and concentrating them into the armed services--had a great impact "on the future of gay life in America" (Kaiser 27). On this narrative, it is "one of the great ironies of gay history" that "the United State Army" was "a secret, powerful, and unwitting engine of gay liberation in America" (27-28). This massive concentration --started during wartime but continued in peacetime--of gays and

lesbians in major US cities such as New York, San Francisco, Boston, Baltimore, . . . was a major underlying impetus for the post-war development for the growth of highly visible "gay communities" (for what Charles Kaiser calls the "Gay Metropolis"). Although the mention of a "causal" condition (war) for the rise of the gay liberation movement looks like a materialist analysis, it turns out to be simply one chapter in the usual idealist narrative of self-determination: "No other group has ever transformed its status more rapidly and more dramatically than lesbians and gay men" (Kaiser vii). Determined as always to read gay liberation as a triumph of gay 'self-invention," bourgeois historians put aside the fact that there had to be underlying infrastructural conditions--structural economic changes driving and enabling urbanization--that made such a concentration possible. While metropolitan--as against rural or small-town--life has supposedly "obvious" advantages to the sexual minorities (opportunities to find like-minded partners), the dominant narrative turns this condition into an "urban romance" and suppresses economic conditions and the life of gay men and lesbians as workers under capitalism. Such interpretations take World War II itself for granted, when in fact we should never lose sight of the political economy of the War. For the bourgeois historian, of course, World War II as a struggle of individuals doing their "duty" in a mythic moral struggle between, on the one hand, the forces of "evil" (the Axis powers--Germany, Italy, and Japan), and on the other the forces of "good" (the Allied powers--mainly England and the US, with the Soviet Union's role heavily downplayed for ideological reasons). In actuality World War II was battle of various imperialist powers over how the spoils of capitalist exploitation were to be distributed. In broad terms, it was a battle between two forms of capitalism: overt fascist capitalism (the Axis countries) vs. liberal democratic capitalism (the Allied countries), in other words, two ways of managing the processes of exploitation.

[14]While it had to some degree a large compass earlier and also later, "US corporate capital" had 'limited reach during the 1930s and 1940s" and "state-mediated flows loomed large throughout the 1950s" (Tabak 90) and in the later decade discussed here.

[15]"State-mediated flows loomed large" (Tabak 90) and there was a "gradual expansion of state structures during the 1950s and 1960s" (Tabak 103).

[16]In discussing the tendencies of economic change, I draw on the work of several writers, among them, Faruk Tabak. While I find much of Tabak's articulation of broad economic tendencies of help, the reader should be aware that Tabak's work is flawed, in my view, in its reliance on the "world systems" theory elaborated by Immanuel Wallerstein and others. By emphasizing the importance of what it calls

"the 'opaque terrain' of employment" (Tabak 89) and production activities outside capitalist wage labor, world-systems theory distracts attention away from capitalist exploitation and blocks the development of revolutionary class consciousness.

[17] While the urgent interest gays and lesbians have recently shown to become parents and raise children is typically given a subjective interpretation (the demand for the "right" to the affective rewards of family life), under capitalism it is also a bid for inclusion in the much-valued category of productive AND reproductive labor. By taking their place as (in some sense) reproductive workers, show that their sexuality also can transcend the level of personal pleasure and emotional reward and fulfill their social responsibilities of sustaining the existing system and enhancing capitalist profits by reproducing workers.

[18] Edward Renshaw observes: "The average duration of the last four recessions is higher for each of our indicators than the average duration for the first five recessions since 1947" (Renshaw).

[19] For a discussion of the "post-material economy," see Heartfield.

[20] As I have already noted elsewhere, this "lack of unity" in the gay/lesbian/queer community is evident from time to time with the resurgence of class consciousness (see especially Morton "The Class Politics" 472).

[21] How the media has recently tried to demonstrate the "success" of this "up-scaling" is evident in reported comments made after the death of Princess Diana, a celebrity representing a most archaic mode of social and economic—feudal—class oppression. A member of Britain's Terrence Higgins Trust for AIDS advocacy remarked—approvingly—that Diana "had an ease with the gay men she met" (Elliott 37). Like the question of "celebrity" itself, the death of Diana is not treated as a starting point for a critique of capitalism as such but only of capitalism in a supposedly "unnecessary" mode of "excess" emblematized not by Diana herself but by the "stalkerazzi," as if "excess"—profit—were not the core mechanism of capitalism as a mode of production, an "excess" that in fact drives the "stalkerazzi."

[22] Larry Kramer's book-jacket comment was reprinted and seconded by *The Advocate*, whose editors said that "even given that man's [Kramer's] propensity for hyperbole, gays and lesbians as well as the publishing industry seem to agree: *Queer in America: Sex, the Media, and the Closets of Power* is a landmark book indeed" ("Cover Story," 33).

[23] Kramer has in fact become so rich by "coming out of the closet" that he recently offered Yale University one million dollars to underwrite a Gay Studies Department. The queer left, proving that its interests are

purely "cultural" and have nothing to do with economic justice, celebrates Kramer's wealth achieved by his complicity with capitalism and interprets Yale's refusal of Kramer's money as "proof" that queer studies is "dangerous" to the status quo! (See Goldstein.)

[24]Marx and Engels explain the relation between such people as Kramer and Signorile, on the one hand, and Buchanan, Helms, and Falwell, on the other, when they argue that "The bourgeoisie finds itself involved in a constant battle . . . [even] with those portions of the bourgeoisie itself, whose interests have become antagonistic to the progress of industry" (Marx and Engels, *Manifesto* 493). They of course explain these intra-class bourgeois battles as one of the results of the fact that "The bourgeoisie cannot exist without constantly revolutionsing the instruments of production, and thereby the relations of production, and with them the whole relations of society. . . . Constant revolutionising of production, uninterrupted disturbance of all social conditions, everlasting uncertainty and agitation distinguish the bourgeois epoch from all earlier ones" (21).

[25]By emphasizing sexual emancipation as a matter of a war with the religious right, the queer left is typically (just like the religious right itself) obscuring the significance of economic injustice. Even Jeffrey Weeks, by no means a Marxist, hints at the historical bankruptcy of the outmoded ideology of religious right and by implication at the bankruptcy of thought on the queer left which overlooks this fact. Weeks points to the irreversibility of secularization in Western cultures: "Yet it seems that despite all the huffing and puffing, the anguished debates and the like, the process of secularisation has gone too far to reverse fundamentally . . . The fevered efforts of religious traditionalists to turn back the tide testifies, I would argue, as much to the success of secularisation as to the power of religion" (Weeks 7). A similar observation about the historical change represented by the "success" of the gay/lesbian/queer movement in joining with (not fighting) the present class system, comes from the neo-conservative right: in a recent essay "How the Gay Rights Movement" won, Norman Podhoretz has conceded that the gay rights movement has succeeded in overcoming resistance to its inclusion in mainstream bourgeois politics (Podhoretz). The major "misrepresentation" produced by the religious right that the queer left works hard to "correct" today is *not* that homosexuality is either "sin" or "sickness," but the kind of claim that Pat Robertson has made that the queer left is a dangerously subversive enemy of capitalism, nothing but an "elite cadre" that merely represents "one of the principal instruments of Marxism" in the US today (Herman 182-83). What this actually means is that there is now a more and more overt competition between the

queer left and the religious right over which groups can be more helpful to capitalism in its current phase.

[26]For a sustained discussion, see Morton, "Queer Theory as Pathos."

[27] See also Seidman, Meeks, and Traschen, another text which marks what it calls "the declining significance of the closet" (27).

[28]The closet, for example, is the governing trope of the late 1990s Hollywood farce, *In and Out*, starring well-known "straight" actors, Kevin Kline and Tom Selleck, as gay men.

[29]Restated once again very recently in a new "history of philosophy" by US academic philosophers (Solomon and Higgins) published by a prestigious university press, Oxford.

[30]On the idea that this way of "understanding" the East that hides tremendous violence is a widespread ideological pattern, see Morton, "Global (Sexual) Politics."

[31]For further analysis, see Morton, "Queerity and Ludic Sado-Masochism."

[32]On the current forms of today's pervasive and growing fascism in the US, see Zavarzadeh, "Making Fascism Fashionable."

[33]Although there appears to be no reference to Negri in Scott Bravmann's recent book, *Queer Fictions of the Past: History, Culture and Difference*, it is informed by the same (queer) left understanding of history. Like Negri and Casarino, Bravmann regards himself to be writing against bourgeois historiography (31), but his notion of the "bourgeois" excludes--typically for the queer left--any rigorous analysis of class and is limited to the heteronormativity of the bourgeois bedroom (see Bravmann).

[34]For another response to Morton, "The Class Politics of Queer Theory," see also Champagne, "A Comment," and Morton, "Donald Morton Responds.")

[33]The idea that all subjects are inescapably "sick" has led to a backlash against a supposedly "politically correct" "healthism." The idea of campaigning against "healthism" (in defense of individual desires/pleasures) is not new to lesbian/gay/queer writing: in the early 1980s, one anthology on the "sex wars" (the fight over sado-masochism) published a "satiric" newspaper report (parodically post-datelined: "Berkeley, July 4, 1984") according to which "a lesbian-feminist smokers' liberation group, Smolda" held a protest against "'heatlhist propaganda which falsely attacks the revolutionary nature of a feminist approach to smoking'" (Tiklicorect 164). In the mid-1990s, pathology has been most fully celebrated in the books of the post-al cultural critic, Richard Klein: *Cigarettes Are Sublime* and *Eat Fat*. By rejecting any ground of social "health," Žižek (like Lyotard, if on somewhat different theoretical grounds)

strongly reinforces contemporary cynicism about the possibilities of revolutionary change and social justice.

[36] The use of the alibi of universal pathology theorized by Žižek and other post-al theorists to undermine the notion of (rational and concept-based) social solidarity has in fact proved so appealing to the culture industry that *Newsweek* now asks the question--and answers it in the affirmative--"Is Everybody Crazy?" The *Newsweek* reporter, pointing out that "ever since Freud, the number of psychiatric illnesses has soared," argues that "mental health" is now considered "a continuum": "At one extreme might be a Ted Kaczinsky, the Unabomber suspect described by his brother's lawyers as obsessive-compulsive, out of touch with reality, delusional, antisocial and paranoid. At the other end of the spectrum lie what are usually considered normal, even wonderful human differences" (Begley 52). In other words, all citizens are now said to have--at a minimum--what might be called "Mental Illness Lite" (Begley 52).

[37] See, for instance, not only Žižek, but also Redfield.

[38] Evidence of the growing academic interest in and "acceptance" of the theory of the subject as "addict" is seen, for instance, in the conference on "Addiction and Culture" sponsored by the Humanities Center of the Claremont Graduate School in the spring of 1996 ("Call for Papers"). Among the subcategories cited for possible discussion is "Consumption and Desire." Another instance, this time of student interest, is a "Call for Submissions"--for a student show titled "Indulgences"-- "in any medium that in some way meaningfully engage the issues of substance abuse and other forms of escapist behavior. The show seeks to call attention to such behaviors by bringing them out into a public forum for discussion and personal revelation." The call for submissions indicates that the show is not simply for "artists who are dealing with these personal issues, but also an opportunity for others to consider their own behavior. In effect, this will call attention to widespread hedonistic, escapist tendencies that are often silenced in our society due to their simultaneous acceptance and prohibition." As an "intriguing" attention-catcher, the flyer poses the (pharmakonic) question: "What's Your Poison?"

[39] Yet, of course, post-al theorists and queer left critics argue the opposite: that the "sublime" subject is not so much infantile as the infinitely generous giver in Bataille's "general economy," the subject of "expenditure" par excellence, one who "shares" (in Casarino's terms) without limit. I would like to examine this claim in greater detail by pointing out that, before Casarino, there was an already established line of post-al ideology which makes this "generosity" a particular property of a de-historicized "homosexual" subject. For example, long before

Casarino, Hélène Cixous and Catherine Clément disconnected gender from class, and set the by definition "generous" homosexual subject starkly over against the supposedly "stingy" masculine, unitary, centralized heterosexual subject who brutally excludes the Other: they thereby provided the queer left—before the development of the "queer"-- with a theorization for the widespread myth that posits the "homosexual" as a person of special "sensitivity" and "sensibility" (a version of that romanticism we have already seen in Casarino) as the exemplary "inventive" subject. According to them,

> There have always been those uncertain, poetic persons who have not let themselves be reduced to dummies programmed by pitiless repression of the homosexual element. Men or women: beings who are complex, mobile, open. Accepting the other sex as a component makes them much richer, more various, stronger, and—to the extent that they're mobile—very fragile. It is only in this condition that we invent. . . . That doesn't mean that you have to be homosexual to create. But it does mean that there is no invention possible, whether it be philosophical or poetic, without there being in the inventing subject an abundance of the other, of variety: separate-people, thought-/people, whole populations issuing from the unconscious, and in each suddenly animated desert, the springing up of selves one didn't know—our women, our jackals, our Arabs, our aliases, our frights. . . . This is what is inscribed in Jean Genet's name . . . (Cixous and Clément 83-84)

The homosexual has, we are told, a "superabundance" of Otherness, out of which she creates through invention and "shares": hence, Casarino's "generous," if implicit, invitation that the reader "enter the sublime closet" with him and partake of its libidinal "plenitude." In other words, Cixous and Clément, implicitly giving a new twist to Kant, proposed that homosexuals are by definition persons with a "sensibility" in tune with the "sublime." Following this theoretical line, which once again turns homosexuality into an allegory of a generalized subjectivity and fails to recognize it as a material and social need, Casarino's subject of the "sublime" closet is therefore represented not as a self-centered infant but an exemplary *philanthropist*, a "lover of men" if not exactly in his particular case of "mankind." The title of "true philanthropist" is, therefore, being claimed today by those celebrating their bi-, tri-, omni-sexuality-- their limitless capacity for pleasure--as a superior form of sexual "plenitude," even a form of "generosity."

Works Cited

Adam, Barry. *The Rise of a Gay and Lesbian Movement.* Social Movements Past and Present. Boston: Twayne, 1987.

Allen, John. "Post-Industrialism/Post-Fordism." In Hall et al., 534-563.

Altman, Dennis. "From Gay Power to Gay Mardi Gras." *Harvard Gay and Lesbian Review* Summer 1999: 27-29.

Anderson, Charles H. *The Political Economy of Social Class.* Engelwood Cliffs, NJ: Prentice-Hall, 1974.

Baudrillard, Jean. "Pataphysics of the Year 2000." http://www2.sva.edu/readings/pataphysics.html.

Begley, Sharon. "Is Everybody Crazy?" *Newsweek* Jan. 26, 1998: 50-55.

Bellow, Saul. *Ravelstein.* New York: Viking, 2000.

Bersani, Leo. *Homos.* Cambridge, London: Harvard UP, 1995.

Blasius, Mark, and Shane Phelan, eds. *We Are Everywhere: A Historical Sourcebook of Gay and Lesbian Politics.* New York: Routledge, 1997.

Bloom, Allan. *The Closing of the American Mind.* New York: Touchstone, 1988.

Brady, Diane. "The Clocks Ahead Will Have Our Own Faces." *Business Week* Aug. 23-30, 1999: 94, 96.

Bravmann, Scott. *Queer Fictions of the Past: History, Culture, and Difference.* Cambridge, England: Cambridge UP, 1997.

Bronski, Michael. "Sex in the '60s, Sex in the '90s: The Problems of Pleasure." *Steam* 2.2 (summer 1994): 132-134.

"Business and Finance." *The Wall Street Journal* February 1, 2000: A-1.

Butler, Judith. "Merely Cultural." *Social Text* 52/53 (Fall/Winter 1997): 265-276. Also in *New Left Review* 227 (Jan./Feb. 1998): 33-44.

"Call for Papers: 'Addiction and Culture.' " *Minnesota Review* 41/42 (1995): [360].

"Call for Submissions." Flyer circulated on the Syracuse University campus, Syracuse, New York, calling for submissions for a show called "Indulgences," Fall, 1997.

Casarino, Cesare. "The Sublime of the Closet; or, Joseph Conrad's Secret Sharing." *boundary 2* 24:2 (1997) 199-243.

Cassidy, John. "Who Killed the Middle Class?" *New Yorker* Oct. 16, 1995: 113-124.

Champagne, John. "A Comment on 'The Class Politics of Queer Theory." *College English* 59 (1997): 350-51.

Cixous, Hélène, and Catherine Clément. *The Newly Born Woman*. Trans. Betsy Wing. Theory and History of Literature, vol. 24. Minneapolis: U of Minnesota P, 1986.

Clark, David L. "Heidegger's Craving: Being-on-Schelling." *diacritics* 27.3 (Fall 1997): 8-33.

Clarke, Eric O. *Virtuous Vice: Homoeroticism and the Public Sphere*. Durham and London: Duke UP, 2000.

Clendinen, Dudley, and Adam Nagourney. *Out for Good: The Struggle to Build a Gay Civil Rights Movement in America*. New York: Simon and Schuster, 1999.

Courtine, Jean-François, et al. *Of the Sublime: Presence in Question*. Trans. Jeffrey S. Librett. Albany: State U of New York P, 1993.

"Cover Story: Queer In America." *The Advocate* April 20, 1993: 33-38.

Cox, Christoph. "The (End of the) End of History." In Herron, et al., *The Ends of Theory*, pp.120-34.

Creech, James. *Closet Writing/Gay Reading: The Case of Melville's Pierre*. Chicago & London: U of Chicago P, 1993.

Davis, Robert Con, and Ronald Schliefer, eds. *Rhetoric and Form: Deconstruction at Yale*. Norman: University of Oklahoma P, 1985.

Delaney, Samuel R. "Coming/Out." In Delany, *Shorter Views* 67-97.

——. *Shorter Views: Queer Thoughts & the Politics of the Paraliterary*. Hanover and London: Wesleyan UP, 1999.

——. *Times Square Red, Times Square Blue*. New York and London: New York UP, 1999.

Deleuze, Gilles, and Félix Guattari. *Anti-Oedipus: Capitalism and Schizophrenia*. Trans. By Robert Hurley, Mark Seem, and Helen R. Lane. New York: Viking, 1977.

Derrida, Jacques. "différance." In his *Margins of Philosophy*, pp.3-27.

——. *Margins of Philosophy*. Trans. A. Bass. Chicago: U of Chicago P, 1982.

Doty, Alexander. *Making Things Perfectly Queer: Interpreting Mass Culture*. Minneapolis, London: U of Minnesota P, 1993.

Eagleton, Terry. *Marxism and Literary Criticism*. Berkeley: U of California P, 1976.

Ebert, Teresa L. "Beyond 'Enlightened False Consciousness' and For a Red Theory." (forthcoming)

——. "(Oc)Cult of the Post-al." *Rethinking Marxism* 9.3 (1996/97): 103-118.

Elliott, Michael. "Diana's Britain." *Newsweek* Sept. 15, 1997: 37.

Field, Nicola. *Over the Rainbow: Money, Class and Homophobia*. London: Pluto P, 1995.

Floyd, Kevin. "Making History: Marxism, Queer Theory, and Contradictions in the Future of American Studies." *Cultural Critique* 40 (Fall 1998): 167-201.

Foucault, Michel. *Language, Counter-Memory, Practice: Selected Essays and Interviews.* Ed. D. F. Bouchard. Trans. D. F. Bouchard and S. Simon. Ithaca: Cornell UP, 1977.

————. "Nietzsche, Genealogy, History." In his *Language, Counter-Memory, Practice.* pp.139-164.

Fraser, Nancy. "Heterosexism, Misrecognition, and Capitalism: A Response to Judith Butler." *Social Text* 52/53 (Fall/Winter 1997): 279-289. Also in *New Left Review* 228 (Mar./Apr. 1998): 140-149.

Freud, Sigmund. *Civilization and Its Discontents.* Trans. James Strachey. New York, London: W. W. Norton, 1961.

Gates, Bill. *Business @ the Speed of Thought: Using a Digital Nervous System.* New York: Warner Books, 1999.

"Georges Bataille: An Occasion for Misunderstanding." Ed. Nelly Furman Special issue of *diacritics* 26.2 (Summer 1996).

Goldstein, Richard. "It's Here! It's Queer! It's Too Hot for Yale!" *Village Voice* 6 August 1997: 58-59.

Graham-Gibson, J. K. *The End of Captitalism (As We Knew It): A Feminist Critique of Political Economy.* New York: Blackwell, 1996.

Greider, William. "Saving the Global Economy." *The Nation* Nov. 15, 1997: 11-12, 15-16.

Grosz, Elizabeth. "Deleuze, Bergson, and Uncharted Futures." Lecture given at a conference on "Becoming Woman" held at the State University of New York at Albany on February 11, 2000.

Hall, Stuart, et al. *Modernity: An Introduction to Modern Societies.* Cambridge, MA and Oxford, ENG: Blackwell, 1996.

Harris, Daniel. *The Rise and Fall of Gay Culture.* New York: Hyperion, 1997.

Harvey, David. *The Condition of Postmodernity.* Oxford: Basic Blackwell, 1989.

Harvey, Robert, ed. *Afterwords: Essays in Memory of Jean-François Lyotard.* Occasional Papers of the Humanities Institute at StonyBrook, no.1. [Stony Brook: Humanities Institute, 2000]

Harwood, Victoria, et al., eds. *Pleasure Principles: Politics, Sexuality and Ethics.* London: Lawrence & Wishart, 1993.

Haver, William. *The Body of This Death: Historicity and Sociality in the Time of AIDS.* Stanford, CA: Stanford UP, 1996.

Heartfield, James. *Need and Desire in the Post-Material Economy.* [Sheffield, England]: Sheffield Hallam U, 1998.

Herman, Didi. *The Antigay Agenda: Orthodox Vision and the Christian*

Right. Chicago and London: U of Chicago P, 1997.

Herron, Jerry, et al., eds. *The Ends of Theory.* Detroit: Wayne State University P, 1996.

Hodges, Andrew, and David Hutter. *With Downcast Gays: Aspects of Homosexual Self-Oppression.* 2d ed. London: Pink Triangle P, 1979. (Available on the Web: URL: http://www.outgay.co. uk/ wdg2.html)

Hopkins, Terence K., Immanuel Wallerstein, et al. *The Age of Transition: Trajectory of the World-System,* London and New Jersey: Zed Books, 1996.

"Hot Type." *Chronicle of Higher Education* Jan. 21, 2000: A-21.

Hutchings, Kimberly. *Kant, Critique and Politics.* London and New York: Routledge, 1996.

"Indonesia's Downward Spiral." *New York Times* Jan. 11, 1998: 18.

Jay, Karla, and Allen Young, eds. *Out of the Closets: Voices of Gay Liberation.* 20th anniversary issue. New York: New York UP, 1992.

Kaiser, Charles. *The Gay Metropolis, 1919-1996.* Boston: Houghton Mifflin, 1997.

Kant, Immanuel. *Kant's Critique of Judgment.* Trans. James Creed Meredith. Oxford: Clarendon P, 1911.

Kinsman, Gary. *The Regulation of Desire: Homo and Hetero Sexualities.* New rev. ed. Montreal, New York, London: Black Rose Books, 1996.

Klein, Richard. *Cigarettes Are Sublime.* Durham: Duke UP, 1995.

————. *Eat Fat.* New York: Pantheon, 1996.

Lacan, Jacques. *The Four Fundamental Concepts of Psychoanalysis.* New York: Norton, 1981.

Laumann, Edward O., Anthony Paik, Raymond C. Rose. "Sexual Dysfunction in the United States." *Journal of the American Medical Association.* 281 (Feb. 10, 1999): 537-544.

"Left Conservatism I and II." *Theory and Event* 2.2 and 2.3. Online journal:http://www.muse.jhu.edu/journal/theory&_event/toc/archive .html/#2.2 and 2.3.

Lenin, V. I. "A Caricature of Marxism and Imperialist Economism." In V. I. Lenin, *Collected Works* 23: 28-76. Moscow: Progress, 1964.

————. *On the Emancipation of Women.* 4th rev. ed. Moscow: Progress, 1974.

Linden, Robin Ruth, et al. *Against Sadomasochism: A Radical Feminist Analysis.* San Francisco: Frog in the Well, 1982.

Loughery, John. *The Other Side of Silence. Men's Lives and Gay Identities: A Twentieth-Century History.* New York: Holt, 1998.

Lowenthal, Michael, ed. *Gay Men at the Millenium: Sex, Spirit, Community*. New York: Jeremy P. Tarcher/Putnam, 1997.

Lukács, Georg. *The Destruction of Reason*. Trans. P. Palmer. Atlantic Highlands, NJ: Humanities P, 1981.

———— *History and Class Consciousness: Studies in Marxist Dialectics*. Trans. R. Livingstone. Cambridge, MA: MIT P, 1971.

————. *Realism in Our Time: Literature and the Class Struggle*. Trans. J. and N. Mander. World Perspectives vol. 33. New York: Harper and Row, 1964.

Lyotard, Jean-François. " The Interest of the Sublime." In Courtine et al., pp.109-132.

————. *The Postmodern Condition: A Report on Knowledge*. Theory and History of Literature, vol.10. Minneapolis: U of Minnesota P, 1985.

————, and Jean-Loup Thébaud. *Just Gaming*. Trans. Wlad Godzich. Theory and History of Literature, vol. 20. Minneapolis: U of Minnesota P, 1985.

Makdisi, Saree, Cesare Casarino, and Rebecca E. Karl, eds. *Marxism Beyond Marxism*. New York, London: Routledge, 1996

Marcus, Eric. *Making History: The Struggle for Gay and Lesbian Equal Rights: 1945-1990. An Oral History*. New York: HarperCollins, 1992.

Marx, Karl. *A Contribution to the Critique of Political Economy*. In K. Marx and F. Engels, *Collected Works* 29: 257-562. New York: International, 1987.

————. *Grundrisse [Economic Manuscripts of 1857-58]*. In K. Marx and F. Engels, *Collected Works* 28. New York: International, 1975.

————. "On the Jewish Question." In K. Marx and F. Engels, *CollectedWorks* 3: 146-174. New York: International, 1975.

————. *Wage-Labour and Capital & Value, Price and Profit*. In K. Marx and F. Engels, *Collected Works* 9:197-228. New York: International, 1977.

————, and Frederick Engels. *The German Ideology*. In Marx andEngels, *Collected Works* 5: 19-539. New York: International, 1976.

————. *Manifesto of the Communist Party*. In Marx and Engels, *Collected Works* 6: 477- 519. New York: International, 1976.

Matheson, Neill. "Identifying (with) the Queerness of Melville's *Pierre*." *diacritics* 27.4 (Winter 1997): 30-45.

Mendelsohn, David. "Decline and Fall: How Gay Culture Lost Its Edge." In Lowenthal 236-251.

Miller, J. Hillis. "The Search for Grounds in Literary Study." In Davis and Schliefer, eds., *Rhetoric and Form*, pp. 19-36.

Mishel, Lawrence, Jared Bernstein, and John Scmitt. *The State of Working America, 1998-99.* Ithaca and London, Economic Policy Institute, Cornell UP, 1999.

Monette, Paul. "Guest Opinion." *Playboy* May 1993: 40.

Morton, Donald. "The Class Politics of Queer Theory." *College English* 58 (1996): 471-82.

———. "Donald Morton Responds." *College English* (March, 1997): 95-97.

———. "Global (Sexual) Politics, Class Struggle, and the Queer Left." *Critical inQueeries* 3.1 (May 1997): 1-30.

———. *The Material Queer: A LesBiGay Cultural Studies Reader.* Boulder, CO: HarperCollins/Westview P, 1996.

———. "Queer Theory as Pathos." *Critical InQueeries* 2.1 (June 1998): 94-127.

———. "Queerity and Ludic Sado-Masochism: Compulsory Consumption and the Emerging Post-al Queer." *Transformation* 1. Washington, DC: Maisonneuve P, 1995.

Nava, Michael, and Robert Dawidoff. *Created Equal: Why Gay Rights Matter to America.* New York: St. Martin's P, 1994.

Negri, Antonio. *The Politics of Subversion: A Manifesto for the Twenty-First Century.* Trans. James Newell. Cambridge: Polity P, 1989.

Nelson, Cary. *Manifesto of a Tenured Radical.* New York and London: New York UP, 1997.

———, and Stephen Watt. *Academic Keywords: A Devil's Dictionary of Higher Education.* New York and London: Routledge, 1999.

"The Newsweek 100." *Newsweek* Oct. 5, 1992: 36-39.

Norris, Christopher. "Against Postmodernism: Derrida, Kant and Nuclear Politics." *Paragraph* 9 (1987): 1-30.

Nussbaum, Martha. "The Professor of Parody." *The New Republic* Feb.22, 1999: 37-45.

O'Neill, Edward R. "Making Ideology Perfectly Queer, Or, How I stopped Worrying and Learned to Love Ideology." *Strategies: A Journal of Theory, Culture & Politics* 9/10 (1996): 94-121.

Podhoretz, Norman. "How the Gay Rights Movement Won." *Commentary* (November 1996): 32-41.

"Psycho-Marxism: Marxism and Psychoanalysis Late in the TwentiethCentury." Special issue of *South Atlantic Quarterly.* Ed. Robert Miklitsch. 97.2 (Spring 1998).

Redfield, Marc, ed. *Addictions.* Special issue of *diacritics.* 27.3 (Fall1997)

Reich, Robert B. "When Naptime Is Over." *New York Times Magazine* Jan. 25, 1998: 32-34.

Renshaw, Edward. "The IS-LM Framework: The Duration of Economic Recessions and the Fed's Recessionary Reaction Function." (http://www.albany.edu/~renshaw/leagin/ess07.html)

Ronell, Avital. *Crack Wars: Literature Addiction Mania*. Lincoln and London: U of Nebraska P, 1992.

Sedgwick, Eve. "Epidemics of the Will." In Sedgwick, *Tendencies* 130-142.

————. *Epistemology of the Closet*. Berkeley: U of California P, 1990.

————. *Novel Gazing: Queer Readings in Fiction*. Durham and London: Duke UP, 1997.

————. "Paranoid Reading and Reparative Reading" You're So Paranoid, You Probably Think This Introduction Is about You." In Sedgwick, *Novel Gazing* 1-37.

————. *Tendencies*. Series Q. Durham and London: Duke UP, 1993.

Seidman, Steven. "Are We All in the Closet? Notes Towards a Sociological and Cultural Turn in Queer Theory." *Journal of European Cultural Studies* 1.2 (May 1998): 177-198.

————, Chet Meeks, and Francie Traschen. "Beyond the Closet? The Changing Social Meaning of Homosexuality in the United States." *Sexualities* 2.1 (Feb. 1999): 9-34.

Signorile, Michelangelo. *Queer in America: Sex, the Media, and the Closets of Power*. New York: Random House, 1993.

Silverman, Hugh J., and Gary E. Aylesworth, eds. *The Textual Sublime: Deconstruction and Its Differences*. Albany, NY: State University of New York P, 1990.

Sinfield, Alan. *Cultural Politics--Queer Reading*. Philadelphia: U of Pennsylvania P, 1994.

Solomon, Robert C., and Kathleen M. Higgins. *A Short History of Philosophy*. New York: Oxford UP, 1996.

Smith, Dinitia. "'Queer Theory' Is Entering the Literary Mainstream." *New York Times* Jan. 17, 1998: B9, B11.

Smith, John H. "Queering the Will." *Symploke* 3.1 (1995): 7-28.

Tabak, Faruk. "The World Labour Force." In Hopkins, et al., pp.

Tanenhaus, Sam. "Bellow, Bloom, and Betrayal." *Wall Street Journal* 2 Feb. 2000: A-26.

Teal, Donn. *The Gay Militants: How Gay Liberation Began in America, 1969-1971*. New York: St. Martins' P, 1995 [1971].

Tiklicorect, Paula. "Smokers Protest Healthism." In Linden, et al., eds. *Against Sadomasochism*. 164-65.

Tomkins, Silvan. *Shame and Its Sisters: A Silvan Tompkins Reader*. Ed. Eve Kosofsky Sedgwick and Adam Frank. Durham: Duke UP, 1995.

Trottein, Serge. "The Beauty of the Postmodern Sublime." In Harvey, Robert 73-84.

Warner, Michael. *The Trouble with Normal: Sex, Politics and the Ethics of Queer Life.* New York: Free P, 1999.

Weeks, Jeffrey. "An Unfinished Revolution: Sexuality in the 20th Century." In Harwood, et al. 1-19.

Weir, John. "Going In." In Lowenthal 252-259.

Wilson, Scott. *Cultural Materialism: Theory and Practice.* Oxford: Blackwell, 1995.

Zavarzadeh, Mas'ud. "Cary Nelson's Homophobia and the Defense of Capitalism." (forthcoming)"

———. Making Fascism Fashionable." *Political Affairs* March/April 1997: 35-37.

———. "Post-ality: The (Dis)Simulations of Cybercapitalism. Book One." In Zavarzadeh et al., *Post-ality: Marxism and Postmodernism.* 1-75.

———, et al., *Post-ality: Marxism and Postmodernism. Transformation 1.* Washington, DC: Maisonneuve P, 1995.

Zizek, Slavoj. "Eastern European Liberalism and its Borderlines." *Oxford Literary Review* 14 (1992): 25-44.

———. *Enjoy Your Symptom! Jacques Lacan in Hollywood and Out.* New York: Routledge, 1992.

———. *The Indivisible Remainder: An Essay on Schelling and Related Matters.* London: Verso, 1996.

———. *The Metastases of Enjoyment: Six Essays on Woman and Causality.* London, New York: Verso, 1994.

———. *The Plague of Fantasies.* London, New York: Verso, 1997.

———. *The Sublime Object of Ideology.* London, New York: Verso, 1989.

Zizek, Slavoj/F. W. J. von Schelling. *The Abyss of Freedom/Ages of the World.* Ann Arbor: U of Michigan P, 1997.

Dana L. Cloud

Queer Theory and "Family Values":

Capitalism's Utopias of Self-Invention

Since the 1992 Presidential Campaign, the phrase "family values" has been a centerpiece of mainstream American political life. In 1992, then-Vice-President Dan Quayle launched a wave of family values hype in the aftermath of the 1992 Los Angeles uprising. Quayle blamed the unrest on the personal failures of Black families rather than acknowledging the extent of class antagonism, poverty, and police violence against minorities in Los Angeles. In addition, Quayle attacked situation comedy character Murphy Brown for having a fictional baby out of wedlock, thus invoking conservative gender and anti-welfare politics. The mass media and both mainstream political parties have channeled this ongoing moral panic about the family through and beyond the 1996 Presidential election.[1] The links among the discourse of family values, the general privatization of social responsibility in capitalist society, and anti-gay policy were clearly established with the signing into law of both the Defense of (Heterosexual) Marriage Act and the Personal Responsibility and Work Opportunity Reconciliation (Welfare Repeal) Act by President Clinton in 1996.

While the Christian right has fueled the moral panic surrounding family values and gay and lesbian rights since the 1950s (Herman), it is important to understand that the current rage over "family values" is connected historically and instrumentally to the capitalist system. Conservative familialism scapegoats and vilifies "unconventional" families—such as those of gays and lesbians as well as of single parents—whose arrangements challenge the modern nuclear family ideal necessary to the reproduction of labor under capitalism. In addition, conservative familialism encourages people to see their intimate, domestic relations as both the source of their most difficult problems and the site of those problems' resolution—even if there are external, social, structural causes of personal crisis.

This article goes beyond the critique of the conservative policies that emerge from and depend upon conservative familialism, to examine familialism's deeper logic of dislocating political attention onto the intimate sphere. I argue that queer theory, in spite of its manifest opposition to normalizing familial discourses, replicates this logic. What queer theory, as a variant of the post-al retreat from class politics, shares in common with mainstream discourses on "family values" is an explicit effort to atomize and privatize the experience of social, economic, and political phenomena—i.e., oppression of gays and lesbians and exploitation of labor in a system that depends on the ideal—as much as the reality—of the nuclear family. Further, queer theory, like family values rhetoric, discredits collective political responses to social problems in favor of ludic textualist strategies. It poses utopian experiments in intimate fulfillment— akin to the 1950s suburban family ideal—in lieu of a collective, political struggle.

This argument may seem counter-intuitive given that queer theorists have come out against the politics of normality behind the gay and lesbian movement's demand for the right of same-sex couples to marry (see Weston; Sullivan). Against the political exclusion represented in modern-day family values crusades, gays and lesbians have attempted to dignify their families of choice by defining them as "normal," "the family next door" (Weston; Sullivan). As a gay family newsletter summarized its purpose, "When our families are isolated, homophobia has its best chance of doing what it does best: eating away at the self-esteem of the members of lesbian and gay families and hurting the cohesion of our families as a whole. . . . At best, society ignores families not formed by heterosexual married couples. At worst, we are routinely and actively discriminated against" (Deaner 1, 6).

For socialists, this approach is defensible but inadequate to end lesbian and gay oppression. The struggle for socialism would ultimately abolish the bourgeois nuclear family as a normative ideal, since the ideology of domesticity justifies the privatization of social responsibility and legitimates women's oppression in a sphere of privatized reproduction. Under capitalism, the privatization of services associated with reproduction—housework, laundry, child care and rearing, food preparation, emotional support, and so on—is profitable to capitalists who do not have to bear any of the costs for these services. Under socialism, the labor now performed in the domestic sphere would become visible as collective, social labor. This total transformation of society is necessary to win real sexual freedom and freedom from exploitation and oppression of all kinds.

However, to the extent that many gays and lesbians are ordinary working people, the right to marry is, materially, part of a fight for health care and other real benefits that can make daily life in capitalism a little easier. And, as Eric Clarke notes, in capitalist society, citizenship is closely tied to property-ownership, which is in turn tied to familial inheritance systems. Thus, Clarke writes, "it is difficult to imagine queers becoming fully enfranchised other than through conformity to this rather traditional notion of marriage" (22). Clarke also encourages readers to understand "the ambivalence of wanting what one has been denied— marriage rights, military service, Hollywood films, corporate advertising— at the same time that what has been denied often proves to be less than what one may want" (65). In so far as defending gay and lesbian "families" can be a form of resistance to gay bashing and homophobia, it should be defended. However, in my view, we must recognize that the assimilationist approach upholds the idea of "the family" even as it attempts to redefine who counts as a family.

The most prominent advocate of gay familialism is the gay former editor of *The New Republic* Andrew Sullivan. He defends "legal homosexual marriage" (172) as "the centerpiece of this new politics" (178). "As a classic public institution, it should be available to any two citizens" (179). Sullivan rejects collective approaches to gay and lesbian liberation, along with worker- and workplace-centered strategies, in favor of privatized marriage and privacy for gays and lesbians. Clearly, Sullivan's aim is to play down any potentially radical challenges to "normal" conduct in capitalist society. This approach, while challenging some aspects of the capitalist family as an ideological norm, preserves the ideal of the family as a "classic public institution," as privileged site of self-development, self-definition, and affiliation. In other words, a relentless focus on "the family" prioritizes the narrow task of protecting or enriching one's private life over a broader program of political struggle.

The emergence in the 1990s of queer theory has produced a critique of strategies that assume equal rights in liberal capitalist society as their end goal. For example, queer theorists Lauren Berlant and Michael Warner write, "The national lesbian and gay organizations have decided to float with the current, arguing that lesbians and gays should be seen just as the people next door, well within a mainstream whose highest aspirations are marriage, military patriotism, and protected domesticity" ("What Does" 345). More recently, Warner (*Trouble*) has argued that when gay men and lesbians defend their sexuality and family lives as "normal," they reify a normalizing and oppressive set of discourses and practices and marginalize alternative sexual identities and practices such as non-monogamy. On the face of it, queer theory has nothing but scorn for the politics of gay familialism.

However, queer theory shares with familialism an emphasis on intimacy as the locus of emancipatory practice. Capitalism constantly translates social problems into problems of personal life, exhorting its subjects toward self-scrutiny, self-development, and self-blame (Cloud, *Consolation*). Queer theory potentially represents another version of a pro-capitalist deflection of political attention and analysis onto private life. It, like "family values" talk, encourages gays and lesbians to substitute private self-invention for political struggle and social change. Of course, "private" life *is* political in capitalist society, since under capitalism, "privacy" names those realms that are obscured from political view and absolved of collective responsibility and public control. Marxist approaches to the family observe how the family and the economy—arenas designated by liberal capitalism as "private" and therefore outside the purview of political life—are material sites of class power connected fundamentally to the requirements of capitalist society. The family is in this light a political institution whose oppressive relations and economic functions are obscured by liberalism—an ideology of individual rights and respect for privacy and private property, no matter what exploitation and abuses of power might occur in the "privacy" of the family and the workplace. Likewise, sexuality under capitalism is invested with political significance, as practices threatening the sanctity of the nuclear family are criminalized and medicalized. As spheres of "privacy" in capitalism, the family and the economy are thereby protected from critique and transformation, although they are sites of oppression and exploitation. Even so, they are not equally proper sites for political organizing and resistance to capitalism. While the economic level is fundamental to the shape of society and therefore can be the site of direct transformative agency, the realm of intimacy does not play this kind of determining role.

For this reason, I find problematic the tendency of feminism and queer theory to hail a "personal politics" that displaces struggle from collective challenges to structural oppression and exploitation to the realm of intimacy. This essay will demonstrate that queer theory has rejected all conceptual explanations (denigrated as "totalizing") for gay and lesbian oppression in favor of a micropolitics of intimate life. This rejection generates mystifying formulations such as "erotic politics" and "enactment of performativity of identities" as pseudo-political strategies. These micro-strategies, based on intimate experimentation, textual play, and lifestyle variation, replicate one feature of "family values" rhetoric: Like conservatives who scapegoat gays and lesbians (along with minorities, women, and the poor) for breaking with the traditional family, queer theorists dislocate responses to oppression away from the realm of economic and political struggle into the arena of intimate life.

My argument proceeds as follows: First, I lay out a Marxist analysis of the origins of gay oppression in capitalism's invention and vigorous defense of the modern nuclear family ideal. Second, I describe how despite an acknowledgment of the historical roots of gay oppression in capitalism, queer theory rejects anti-capitalist struggle in favor of privatizing and atomizing strategies that parallel feminism's rejection of class politics and collective struggle. Third, I contextualize the invention of queer theory as a component of the post-al left's retreat from politics—particularly, *materialist* class politics—in general. Finally, I pose a Marxist politics based on renewed attention to class struggle as the only way to win gay and lesbian liberation. Central to this project is the Marxist challenge to the capitalist family.

The Family and "Familialism" Under Capitalism

Despite the periodic construction in American political discourse of a mythic ideal family (figured as universal and permanent), the actual forms and experience of family life have varied enormously across cultures and time, shifting with the material requirements of a given society. It is widely acknowledged among family historians, Marxist theorists, and even queer theorists that the "traditional" nuclear family form celebrated by conservative familialists developed under capitalism, and, more specifically, under industrial capitalism. Stephanie Coontz (*Social History, Way We Never Were*) documents the evolution of the American family from native American communalism, through colonial craft households, to the industrial nuclear family, which peaked as an ideological norm during the post-war economic boom of the 1950s. Historians have long agreed that the family is not a natural, universal, or permanent institution; rather, kinship organizations change form and function over time and across cultures (Poster, *Critical Theory*). For example, modern norms of family intimacy and maternal devotion to children were unfamiliar to pre-modern families, in which unwanted children were routinely and unceremoniously exposed to the elements, in which the tasks of nursing and raising babies were often farmed out to wet nurses, and in which conjugal intimacy and emotional support were conspicuously absent (Aries; Laslett; Shorter). The modern family was a product of changes in early capitalism which over time separated work from the household, reinforced an oppressively gendered division of labor, and placed an increasing domestic burden on the family as a private unit. As industrialization severed wage labor from the home, it placed increasing burdens for the reproduction and upkeep of workers on women and isolated the tasks of reproduction and homemaking from the broader economic and political sphere.

Even as the ideology of the nuclear family took hold, however, the forces of industrialized wage labor threatened to tear the working class family apart. Long hours, low wages, and inadequate housing have meant that workers have rarely identified with the bourgeois family ideal. For this reason, Barrett and McIntosh make a useful distinction between the actual, unstable and varying experience of diverse families at different moments in history, and "the family" as an ideological construct that has been, in contrast, remarkably consistent and stable for more than a century. Stressing the popularity and normative force of this construct, Barrett and McIntosh write,

> The family remains a vigorous agency of class placement and an efficient mechanism for the creation and transmission of gender inequality. . . This institution is the focal point of a set of ideologies that resonate throughout society. The imagery of idealized family life permeates the fabric of social existence and provides a highly significant, dominant and unifying, complex of social meaning. (29)

The historical variability of the family goes against the ideological common sense of the right suggesting that the nuclear family is a universal, unchanging institution and the bedrock of human existence. In contrast to conservative familialism, materialist histories and theories of changes in the shapes and functions of families develop an understanding of how those changes are produced out of the needs and imperatives of their material, economic contexts.

In this light, materialist theories of the family must theorize not only "the family," but also "familialism," or the production of discourses encouraging a conventional nuclear family ideal. What motivates the periodic moral panic in American history over the alleged decline of the nuclear family? Although familialism has been a recurrent theme of the American political imagination since the mid-1800s, scholars have noted two significant periods in the United States at which familialist discourses have emerged in response to social and political crisis. The 1840s through the turn of the century were marked by a surge of family moralism in response to feminist, anti-racist, and labor movements (Coontz, *History*; Cott). A great deal of the nineteenth-century familialist discourse constructs the middle-class family as a utopian sanctuary (kept by women) of affection removed from the clash of public life.

Nikolas Rose argues that there has been an intensification of the themes of familialist discourses in the 20th century since World War II, notably in the "new" disciplines of child development, family sociology, and social work. These fields developed discourses and regimens training families in their proper conduct—and surveying and blaming them when their personal lives fell short of the ideal. The ideology of the family thus "solves" the actual economic contradictions of capitalism for the capitalists, as familialism can explain and justify exploitation, crisis, and suffering in private terms that absolve the industrial capitalism of blame.

Barbara Dafoe Whitehead, founder of the conservative think-tank Institute for American values, states this theory of crisis and blame quite clearly:

> The principal source of family decline over the past three decades has been cultural. It has to do with the ascendancy of a set of values that have been destructive of commitment, obligation, responsibility and sacrifice. (quoted in Raspberry A27)

In reducing economic and political problems to matters of family responsibility, familialism serves as ideological linchpin of the New Right. Familialism simultaneously justifies the erosion of welfare spending, and backlash against women's and gay and lesbian liberation movements.

Abbott and Wallace explain the logic of family moralism for the New Right faced with the recurring crises of modern capitalism. According to this logic,

> There is a clear mutual reinforcement of social and economic ideologies in the moral New Right; economic and moral decline are not just happening at the same time—the latter is causing the former. To stem the economic decline of capitalist countries it is essential to remoralize them. (7)

The tactic of "remoralizing" social problems such as economic crisis, unemployment, racism, and so forth distracts attention from their structural roots. An alleged "breakdown in family life" becomes the scapegoat for capitalism. In this way "family values" is aligned with the preservation of capitalism and the denial of collective, social responsibility for the egalitarian distribution of resources and material well-being of workers.[2]

This analysis supports what Marxists since Engels' *On the Origins of the Family, Private Property, and the State* have held to be the utility of the family for capitalism. Engels argued that changes in the mode of production, or in the way society produces and distributes the necessities of life, affect the form taken of relations between men and women in the family (Cliff 224). Relying on the research of anthropologist Lewis Morgan, Engels showed that the transition (beginning about eight thousand years ago and lasting for several millennia) from primitive society to modern civilization was foremost a shift from classless, communal societies without states to the first class societies. These first class societies created elaborate social divisions of labor and state apparatuses designed to protect the private accumulation of surplus wealth by ruling classes.

Engels links the emergence of women's oppression to this development. The monogamous, male-headed family rose with the state in class society as a way of controlling women's fertility in order to determine the inheritance of private property. Evelyn Reed comments, "As Engels demonstrates, class exploitation and sexual oppression of women were born together to serve the interests of the private-property system. And they work together for the same ends to the present day" (15). The materialist history of women's oppression understands the family and the subjugation of women to be historically specific phenomena, rather than universal features of social reality.

Furthermore, only since industrial capitalism's severing of production from the household has women's role tended toward isolation in the home. Women's labor in the home becomes essential to capitalist society, as this labor, unpaid and privatized under capitalism, reproduces the work force itself.[3] As Paul Smith writes, "The specific oppression of women in capitalist social formations [is] as the main bearers of the domestic work burden and as occupying an inferior position in social production, aspects which are mutually reinforcing" (207). Capitalism produced and requires the separation of household labor from relations of production and commodity exchange so that it will not have to pay for the services performed in the domestic sphere.

These services include reproducing the work force (which includes providing for family members' nutrition, health, and hygiene), socializing and educating children, and making a haven away from the brutal and unforgiving world of wage labor. In addition, an ideology of domesticity that exalts motherhood and condemns women who work outside the home makes available a devalued sector of wage labor. Discrimination against women, justified by the ideology of domesticity, like racism and anti-immigrant sentiment, lowers wages for all working people by holding in reserve a labor force whose presence is used by capitalists to undercut prevailing wages. In the first volume of *Capital*, Marx notes how an "industrial reserve army" comprising the unemployed or partially employed generally as well as women allows capitalists to "buy with the same capital a greater mass of labour-power, as he progressively replaces skilled labourers by less skilled, mature labour-power by immature, male by female, that of adults by young persons or children" (788). The ideology of domesticity not only burdens women with the tasks of reproduction and nurturance, but also justifies wage differentials in the productive economy, according to which women can be paid less than men. In this way, capitalists can hire more labor-power for the same wages, thus increasing their profits.

The idealized family as ideological norm thus justifies the exploitation of workers, the privatization of social responsibility, and the oppression of women. More than reinforcing heterosexual privilege, the debate over "family values" is fundamentally a contestation over labor and social responsibility. The invention and vigorous ideological defense of the nuclear family supports capitalist social relations. The family serves reproductive and ideological functions even though the only time that the nuclear family ideal was attainable for large sections of the (white) U.S. population was during the decades of the post-World-War-Two economic boom. Before and since then, the ideal has exerted normative force in the lives of those—namely the working class—who cannot "measure up." As Nicola Field explains, the bourgeois nuclear family has been a realistic ideal only for its namesake, the bourgeoisie—who has access to in-home child care, domestic support staff, and the leisure from work to devote to family life.

For workers, the pressures of life under capitalism threaten the stability of the family even as the rhetoric of "family values" attempts to reconsolidate it. As Field puts it, "The working class simply does not have the resources to live up to the family values that are rammed down its throat and so it presents a constant threat to the rule of capitalist order" (21). In other words, familialist discourses in capitalist society blame working class people for poverty, racism, and sexism—problems that capitalism itself produces.

Marx and Engels, in their indictment of the bourgeois family in *The Communist Manifesto*, wrote,

> In its completely developed form this family exists only among the bourgeoisie. But this state of things finds its complement in the practical absence of the family among the proletarians . . . the bourgeois clap-trap about the family and education, about the hallowed co-relation of parent and child, becomes all the more disgusting, the more, by the action of Modern Industry, all ties among the proletarians are torn asunder and their children transformed into simple articles of commerce and instruments of labor. (50)

Even as capitalism "tears asunder" the family ties of the working class, its "clap-trap," periodically revived in a rhetoric of "family values," exerts normative force in justifying exploitation. This analysis explains why, for example, times of economic crisis, social unrest, and heightened class or social movement struggle are accompanied by moral panic about the "decline" of the family. The system matches its disruptive influence with an explanation for poverty that absolves the system of blame.

Marxism, Feminism, and the Family

Feminists have taken issue with this history and theory of the family and of women's oppression, putting forward instead a range of theories of patriarchy. "Patriarchy" as it elaborated by radical feminists (see MacKinnon) is an ahistorical construct suggesting that sex, not class is the basic division in society and that the oppression of women as a sex-class by all men, who are said to control women's labor and sexuality, is a universal feature of human society (Hartmann 15). A central flaw in this theory is that "patriarchy" is not a universal feature of human history and there is no evidence to suggest that men have any inherent interest in dominating women.

In addition, the theory of patriarchy fails to understand that not all men have control over women's labor. Indeed, most men have no control over their own working conditions. Men as a category are not "united" across class in their "shared relationship of dominance over their women." Likewise, women are not unified as a "sex-class," but are divided along class lines (and by racial differences that are also deployed in the service of capitalism) and therefore cannot be (and have never been) unified in any struggle against men. It is corporate boards and CEO's of factories and corporations (the owners and their deputies), mostly men but some women (whose presence in the seats of power is difficult to explain on a patriarchy model), who control the conditions of labor of most men and women in capitalist society and who perpetuate an ideology of women's domestic role and inferiority in other roles in order to diminish women's *and* men's wages.

Marxist-feminists have attempted to refine the concept of patriarchy so as to acknowledge capitalism as a force in women's lives. For example, Fraad, Resnick, and Wolff, writing in a series called "New Directions/Rethinking Marxism," argue that the household constitutes a quasi-feudal economy, alongside but separate from capitalist economic relations, in which women are a class exploited by men. These authors use the language of Marxist economic analysis, arguing that "surplus value" produced by women in the home, in the form of housework above and beyond what it would take to sustain only themselves, is appropriated and accumulated by men. The housewife is "a direct laborer inside the household. . . . The results are use-values consumed by household members: prepared meals, cleaned rooms and clothes, mended furniture, and so on. . . . Her husband appropriates her surplus labor in the form of the household use-values that she produces for him" (6).

Despite the application here of Marxist terminology, these authors elaborate a feminist theory of patriarchy that assumes that women are unified as a class, universally exploited by men; and that the household economy is entirely separate from broader capitalist relations. It turns out that "rethinking Marxism" means rejecting its analysis outright. As Engels and Marxists since his writing have pointed out, women's oppression and isolation in the domestic sphere are not universal phenomena, but are closely linked to the rise of capitalism. Michele Barrett, recognizing these limits of traditional patriarchy theory, has offered an updated, historicized critique of Marxism's account of women's oppression. While conceding the material basis of women's oppression in class society, she argues that patriarchy is less a matter of any universal domination of all women by all men than of the relative autonomy of the *ideology* of gender oppression from its capitalist foundations. In other words, she argues for reconceiving familial and domestic ideologies as they have been elaborated under capitalism as themselves *material*, to be fought as if they had a life of their own. Barrett writes,

> The oppression of women under capitalism is grounded in a set of relations between several elements. Of these perhaps the most crucial are the economic organization of households and its accompanying familial ideology, the division of labour and relations of production. . . . yet the continuance and the entrenched nature of this oppression cannot be understood without a consideration of the cultural processes in which men and women are represented differently—created and recreated as gendered human subjects. Nor can it be understood without an analysis of sexuality and gender identity. (*Women's Oppression* 41-41)

In this passage, Barrett acknowledges the significance of economic organization of society, yet shifts her attention to discourses, "the cultural processes in which men and women are represented differently." In her more recent book, *Politics of Truth,* Barrett retreats even further from materialist analysis, claiming that a purely discursive politics requires "going beyond" a materialism that stresses the role ideologies play in justifying exploitative economic relations of household and production. The move that Barrett makes to redefine ideologies, "cultural processes," and representations as themselves the material basis of exploitation and oppression is common to theorizing in the post-al left. It detaches the subjective experience of oppression and the formation of sexual and gendered identities encouraged by ideologies from any conceptual explanation of origin and motive for that oppression. Barrett's work is part of a more general feminist "retheorization of materialism" (Ebert, "Critiques" 114; see also Stabile, "Feminism" and "Postmodernism") in which discursive determinism—outright idealism—is substituted for a materialist analysis of women's oppression.

The strategies of resistance generated by a theory of sexual oppression as ideologically rather than materially based are textualist, ludic strategies that also characterize queer theory. Feminists like Barrett have revamped the theory of patriarchy in order to suggest that although women cannot share common material interests as a sex-class, they can identify as a unified oppressed group by virtue of their experience of *discourses*. This idealist sleight-of-hand evacuates the political project of women's liberation by eliding class differences among women and forgetting the class struggle. Queer theory and feminism share this textualism which allows sexual-textual identities to become the terrain of struggle. The theory of ideological autonomy of sexual oppression lays the ground for the anti-materialist retreat from class on the part of post-al theorists generally, including queer theory.

Like feminism, queer theory posits an autonomous sexual oppression as a matter of discourse, failing to explain its material basis in the relations of production in capitalist society. Then sex itself becomes the battleground for gay and lesbian liberation, and movement politics fail to address the roots of gay oppression in the nuclear family. For example, Dennis Altman encourages gay and lesbian activists to defend public sex as "the new front line for gay politics" (75). Altman has no way of understanding how to achieve a "freer view of sexuality" (84) other than publicizing his and others' intimate lives.

The Capitalist Family and Gay and Lesbian Oppression

In contrast, a materialist analysis of the development of the family and accompanying familialist ideologies explains why the specific persecution of homosexuals as a category dates only from the period of industrialization. Whereas the oppression of women clearly predates capitalism, the label "homosexual" was first used in only 1869 (Carlin, 64). Carlin describes how the appearance of this and other words to describe specifically homosexual attraction and practice at this time "shows that a new attitude was developing towards men and women who were now seen as having a condition, or a certain type of personality" (65). This is not to say that same-sex love and relationships did not exist prior to the 1800s, nor to say that there were no sanctions against homosexual practices before then. Carlin notes that what was new to the late 19th century was the idea of homosexual *identity*, a label constructed and imposed on gay men and lesbians rather than a natural essence.

Carlin's historical survey of gay and lesbian sexuality, identity, and oppression from antiquity to the present concludes that while same-sex love has been present throughout recorded history, specific social condemnation of it and punishment have not. Most societies other than Western, Christian ones have made a place for homosexuality, but only in ways that do not threaten established institutions and class relations. In ancient Greece and Rome, for example, sexual relations between older men and pubescent boys were encouraged, as long as rules of propriety and status were not violated.

One commonly hears the argument that the oppression of homosexuals arose with Christianity rather than with modern capitalism. And indeed, early Christian texts, arising in the Roman transition from slavery to serfdom, forbade all non-procreative sex. The Christian doctrine stressed the need for production of children as laborers and offered spiritual solace while the Roman Empire crumbled (Carlin 76-77). However, the proscriptions against non-procreative sex did not specifically target or name homosexuals.

Likewise, the period from thirteenth century forward witnessed a massive backlash against sexual permissiveness of any kind, alongside the persecution of Jews and heretics, culminating in the witch hunts during the next several centuries. Again, however, in the late medieval and early modern periods, legislation against and Christian condemnation of "sodomy" included a wide range of non-procreative practices, from homosexual acts between men or between women to bestiality and heterosexual anal intercourse (Carlin 81). The point to be made here is that the issue before the industrial era was non-procreative sex in general, not a specific persecution of homosexuals as an identifiable category. Changes in political and economic life—including the beginnings of separation from work from home—during the Renaissance created new attitudes of freedom toward sexuality, although the end of the eighteenth century saw increasing controversy over sodomy and inklings of a new consciousness about same-sex relations.

In sum, ideological definition of the family and of appropriate sexual behavior are historically variable with other, material, factors. While major political, social and economic crises have always shaped family life and generated new and varied sets of prescriptions and prohibitions, Carlin shows that it was not until industrial capitalism and its need for the nuclear family that homosexuality, as a discrete identity category, became medicalized—as a disease to be "cured"—and criminalized—as an immoral act to be policed—in its own right.

Carlin writes, "The question of same-sex relations has to be seen as linked to the history of the family. . . . The coming of industrial capitalist society brought a whole complex of changes—the separation of home from work, the polarization of gender roles for women and men in these 'separate spheres', and a new stress on individuality and personal life—which opened up a new era in attitudes to sexuality" (65). This "new stress" on individuality and personal life has invested sexuality and the elaboration of a self with paramount significance. Capitalist society produces selves that are preoccupied with their own self-invention. Its goal is to create and sustain the illusion of the subject as a private individual, unconnected to class and labor, and free to choose commodities and pleasures without regard to place within the mode of production. Thus, Carlin adds,

> The position of the family in modern capitalist society, detached from production and redefined as the separate sphere of personal life, has given sexuality a new context and new meanings compared with all previous societies. This means that both gay consciousness and gay oppression as we know them are specific to modern capitalist society. (107)

The family is one site of the politics of intimacy; but queer theory, in hailing the "new meanings" of sexuality "detached from production," is replicating the turn to intimacy as a substitute for collective identification and political engagement.

It is no mere coincidence that the late 19th century marked not only the invention of the homosexual, but also the first eruption of bourgeois lamentation over the threats to the nuclear family. The production of a politics of intimacy on both sites served capitalist society by insisting on self-scrutiny, self-development and self-fulfillment. Waves of moral panic over the family occurred in the context of feminist challenges to the 19th-century ideology of True Womanhood and, importantly, in response to labor unrest during Reconstruction and industrialization. What these simultaneous phenomena tell us is that the oppression of gays and lesbians and the emergence of social hostility to homosexual intimacy and relationships are the products of capitalism's attempts to contain economic and political unrest. Survival of the family as a unit of reproduction and responsibility was crucial during a time of tremendous industrial change and exploitation of workers on an unprecedented scale. At the same time, the production of a homosexual self offered capitalism yet another site upon which to privatize social experience.

Queer theorists have, oddly, confirmed this historical analysis, bolstered by Foucault's history of sexuality, which marks homosexual identity and oppression as products of the industrial era. In the first volume of his history, Foucault notes, "The appearance in nineteenth-century psychiatry, jurisprudence, and literature of a whole series of discourses on the species and subspecies of homosexuality" (101). John D'Emilio also locates the emergence of gay identity and gay oppression with the changes in the family occurring with industrialization. The freeing of the household from the requirements of production and from necessary procreation created space for the construction of gay subjectivity. But because capitalism needs the family to perform services that the state, in its role as defender of corporate profits, is unwilling to support, the emergence of gay identity is accompanied by pro-family, anti-gay politics and discourses. Similarly, Jeffrey Weeks insists that homosexual identity and the persecution of homosexuals are historical products of capitalist society, whose impoverished family ideals must be challenged. Weeks confirms Carlin's historical narrative, noting once again that "The word 'homosexuality' itself was not invented until 1869 (by the Hungarian Benkert von Kertbeny) and did not enter English usage until the 1880s and 1890s. . . The widespread adoption of neologisms such as 'homosexuality' and 'inversion' during this period marks a crucial turning point in attitudes toward homosexuality" and "the emergence of a whole new set of assumptions" (16-17). Thus Weeks dates the medicalization and criminalization of homosexuality, as well as the invention of "homosexual" as an identity category, at the middle of the nineteenth century.

The central implication of this history, for Weeks as for Marxists, is that sexual categories are not universal, but rather are historical products. Moreover, Weeks acknowledges that the sexual category of homosexuals is closely linked to the history of the family in capitalism. Weeks writes, "We live in a culture which is suffused with familial values, and where the language of alternatives is feeble and etiolated" (134).

One might expect, given the close attention to the material history of gay identity and oppression as determined by capitalist social relations, that such analyses would generate political programs rooted in class struggle and a critique of the nuclear family. That is, if the oppression of gays and lesbians is an effect of capitalism's need for the family as a justification for the exploitation of the working class, then only a socialist challenge to capitalism and its family ideals will suffice as a transformative project. As Bolshevik Alexandra Kollontai put it in the context of the Russian Revolution of 1917,

The conservatively inclined part of mankind argue that we should return to the happy times of the past, we should re-establish the old foundations of the family and strengthen the well-tried norms of sexual morality. The champions of bourgeois individualism say that we ought to destroy all the hypocritical restrictions of the obsolete code of sexual behavior. . . . Socialists, on the other hand, assure us that sexual problems will only be settled when the basic reorganization of the social and economic structure of society has been tackled. (237)

While Kollontai urged immediate attention on the part of Bolsheviks to the problems of sexual oppression, she rejected the individualistic, utopian lifestyle experiments of those who thought practicing free love would make the revolution. Her warnings bear directly on a critique of queer theory, which identifies the historical production of gay oppression in capitalism as the problem, but offers only lifestyle experimentation as a solution. Queer theorists are present-day "champions of bourgeois individualism" opposed to the "obsolete code of sexual behavior" as the way forward for gay and lesbian rights, as if throwing off the history of the family is as easy as taking off old clothes.

Weeks' formulation is instructive in this regard. On the one hand, Weeks acknowledges that "a widespread anxiety about the family . . . concerns the contradictory demands made upon the family in a period of rapid social change," involving the increasing economic burden on families and women (142). He goes on to critique the family as "a material and ideological prop of capitalism" and as a site of "gender stereotyping and sexual exploitation" (144).

Up to this point, Weeks elaborates a materialist analysis of the family and its ideological counterpart, familialism. The logical next step would be to suggest class struggle, against capitalism, against rigid sexual and moral codes, and on behalf of services that would socialize the family burden—such as unemployment pay, health care services, free child care, and so forth. Instead, Weeks, like many other queer theorists, produces a program radically disconnected from his analysis. In his chapter "Pretended Family Relationships" (134-156), he explores "the strength of other loyalties that strain against family ties." These alternative loyalties, found in some mystical "subterranean social order" (152), include friendships, subcultural communities of lesbians and gay men, neighborhoods, "network families" (153) of loose groupings bonded together for mutual support, groups of people with AIDS, and other "moral communities" (154).

Weeks' disjuncture, between a materialist understanding of the roots of gay and lesbian oppression and an idealist set of solutions completely severed from an understanding of how oppression works in conjunction with class exploitation, is symptomatic of ludic radicalism more generally. The ludic character of Weeks' recommendations is revealed in his chapter title, "*Pretended* Family Relationships." While gay and lesbian oppression is produced in the material context of capitalism, Weeks suggests that we can "pretend" that the material conditions of oppression have evaporated without a struggle, as if in imaginary play. The "pretend families" that he encourages gay and lesbians to adopt have nothing to do with possessing shared material interest but rather are formed on the basis of psychological need and identification as well as emotional attachment. Capitalists, too, exhort workers to aspire to imaginary families in which they can pretend to be happy, secure, and free. Like Weeks, proponents of conservative "family values" want workers to dislocate political responses to felt exploitation and oppression onto personal life.

As Weeks himself points out, the way in which his "pretend" communities as sites of gay and lesbian self-elaboration are to be understood is "still unavoidably familial" (154). Buy why does Weeks "unavoidably" reproduce the politics of intimacy that he ostensibly rejects when it comes to conservative familialism? Ironically, Weeks sets out a materialist historical analysis, yet omits, despite his analysis of capitalist society, *class* as a source of collective identity, solidarity, and transformative agency. He claims that the goal ahead is not class struggle, but "the attempt to forge a moral language" based on "pluralistic values" (155). In the space of a single chapter, then, Weeks condemns the right-wing proponents of the moral language of family values as capitalist ideologues, then offers only a second moral language, one that is firmly entrenched in an ideology of liberal individualism and tolerance (rather than in a structural critique of the family in capitalism). In this way, Weeks replicates the privatizing moralism of "family values" ideology, foreclosing on the possibility of class struggle that his initial materialist analysis invites. Queer theory becomes, like "family values" rhetoric, a remoralizing discourse.

The omission of class as a category characterizes both queer theory and feminist theory. As I will elaborate below, both reject liberal assimilationist models and universalizing or separatist constructions of identity. In the crisis of identity and action posed by postmodernist retreats from explanatory, collective politics, however, neither looks to the working class as an agent of history, collapsing instead into a mode of identity deconstruction and political inertia. The result is an anti-politics of intimate life that is "unavoidably familial," mirroring conservative family values talk.

Identity, Difference, and Discourse:
The Twin Trajectories of Feminism and Queer Theory

The New Left of the 1960s rejected models for struggle rooted in the working class in favor of political strategies based on the expression of moral outrage and on the experiences of members of groups oppressed on the basis of "identity." As products of the 1960s and 1970s, then, gay/lesbian/queer and feminist theorizing exhibit parallel progressions: from initial liberal, equal-rights/assimilationist stances, through cultural separation and identity politics, to a poststructuralist suspicion of identity and of collective political agency themselves. As a third alternative to the accomodationist liberal stance of equal rights on the one hand and a problematic universalizing of "women" and "gays" on the other, poststructuralism seems to be the only way forward. In reality, however, the move to poststructuralism marks a move to the right among feminist and gay and lesbian intellectuals.

Alongside the rhetoric of family values, poststructuralist discourse theories favor increasing displacement of economic questions in favor of discursive and ideological explanations for the various oppressions feminists, gays, and lesbians took on. Ironically, capitalism requires this displacement and itself constantly translates economic demands and struggles into the terms of lifestyle and identity. This is why, for example, Dan Quayle was at pains to explain away the Los Angeles rebellion of 1992 not as a matter of economic exploitation, poverty, and legitimate anger over racism, but as a matter of family failure and individual moral shortcoming. Quayle offered only a right-wing ideological explanation for the uprising. Similarly, feminism and queer theory often work to obscure the material interests and conditions grounding oppression, explaining oppression only as sets of discourses and identities.

The claim to represent universal womanhood was shattered by experiences in the feminist movement in which women clashed over issues of class, race, and sexuality (see Moraga and Anzaldúa). Carol Stabile writes, "The concept of women as a uniform group proved an inadequate foundation for feminists . . . for although it cannot be denied that most women experience the effects of a profoundly misogynist system they do so in various ways and to varying degrees. . . . By substituting 'women' for 'working class,' feminism tends to deny that not all women share an interest in liberation, much less a common ground for political action" ("Postmodernism" 138). In materialist theory, that common ground for political action comes from the solidarity—across race, gender, and sexuality—of the working class. By working class, I mean the group of men and women of all races and sexual orientations whose labour produces the wealth of society—and the profits for a leisure class who owns the means of production. The working class, united by a common material relationship to the way in which the necessities of life are distributed, shares a material interest in overthrowing capitalism, whereas groups organized around identity often fail to challenge the terms of the profit system, including the normative nuclear family.

I do not mean to say that class consciousness is automatic, nor to argue that race, gender, and sexuality are not significant axes of oppression. There is a tendency for racial and sexual oppression to be co-extensive with class exploitation, alongside a tendency of racism and sexism to be experienced as autonomous from economic relationships. But while a person's *subjectivity* or identity is not a simple matter of class determination, oppression and exploitation *are* directly connected to one's economic status in the relations of production. Marxists believe that there is more to liberation that the invention of alternative subjectivities; an end to poverty, hunger, exploitation, and physical abuse are more central, and require a notion of class interests and class struggle.

What filled the void after the shattering of the dream of universal womanhood, however, was not class politics but identity politics. Broadly speaking, identity politics refers to the notion that people can only fight against their own oppression, which is rooted in specific identities whether they are conceived as socially constructed "locations" or as racial or sexual essences. The latter view, that identities are essential, unchanging facts of life out of which coherent, though isolated, political enclaves might spring, characterizes 1970s and 1980s anti-racist responses to the universalizing tendencies in feminisms. The Combahee River (Black feminist) Collective wrote,

> This focusing on our own oppression is embodied in the concept of identity politics. We believe that the most profound and potentially the most radical politics come directly out of our own identity, as opposed to working to end somebody else's oppression. (212)

As Iris Marion Young points out, identity politics assumes that identity factors such as race, sexuality, and gender (but not class) are fixed, essential determinants of identity. Furthermore, identity politics regards self-definition, "focusing on our own oppression," as an end in itself. Ellen Willis makes a crucial point about the limits of identity politics:

"Though self-definition is the necessary starting point for any liberation movement, it can take us only so far" (xv). This observation is key to a critique of queer theory and family values, both of which center their projects on self-definition and personal development. Such politics cannot transcend the self and therefore cannot pose a collective challenge to capitalism.

The logic of identity politics is, ironically, one of fragmentation and disintegration based upon the assertion of singular identities. About the predominance of identity politics in feminist and gay liberation movements, Sharon Smith comments, "The dominance of identity politics is a guarantee against building a lasting movement" (17). And if women's, gay, and lesbian oppressions are products of the capitalist system and its need for the family, only a "lasting movement" that is public and collective in nature will challenge its hold.

Identity politics fragments movements by disallowing solidarity across "identities" of race, gender, and sexuality; it does not provide a theory linking struggles together. On this model, men cannot fight for women's liberation, white people cannot fight racism, and heterosexuals cannot march next to gays and lesbians against hate crimes. The key to identity politics is the idea that one can somehow explain oppression simply by referring to one's own *experience* of it. In identity politics, there is no attempt to *explain* the origins of and strategies against racism and sexism, as these phenomena are theorized as psychological, experiential events rather than as ideological systems with a basis in material reality.

In practice, identity politics leads to suspicion and distrust among activists. But Willis writes that the problem is not only one of allowing ourselves to be divided and conquered, "but our understanding of what it means to be a principled radical" (xvi). "While the moralists indulge in the American left's long-standing habit of substituting righteousness for thought, the pluralists, in their fear that universal claims or 'totalizing' theories of any sort are inherently repressive, replicate the aversion to 'ideology' that has always made liberals incapable of understanding the social system as a whole" (xvi). Importantly, Willis notes that moralism is no substitute for politics, a point to which I will return in connection to queer theory. Practitioners of identity politics substitute experience for analysis, and self-obsession for action. For example, Steven Seidman considers gay cultural politics to constitute a new, postmodern social movement "whose aim is less 'the end of domination' or 'human liberation' than the creation of social spaces that encourage the proliferation of pleasures, desires, voices, interests, modes of individuation and democratization" ("Identity and Politics" 106; see also "Queer Theory/Sociology").Yet Seidman hails this model, arguing that "communities organized around affirmative gay/lesbian identities yet exhibiting heightened conflicts around those very identities should be the starting point of contemporary gay theory and politics" (129). He admits that this stance is increasingly disconnected from politics on a liberationist model that might advance political understanding and a program for common action and indeed, "the end of domination."

Family values discourse, likewise, aims at rendering the social system as a whole unintelligible by focusing attention on the experience of the family. Familialist ideologues "substitute righteousness for thought," much in the same way that queer theorists self-righteously proclaim the end of collective struggle in favor of developing a richly textured intimate life. For feminists and queer theorists, "sex" stands in for "the family" in this formulation, but the effect is the same: the diversion of our attention and energy, the atomization of our efforts, the evacuation of theoretical, conceptual explanations for social reality.

The poststructuralist move to substitute a notion of plural, discursively articulated, and flexible "differences" for the term "identity," rejected as essentialist, does not overcome the idealist, fragmenting logic of identity politics. While essentialist notions offer the solidarity of shared identity, poststructuralist interrogations of identity generates the politics of difference. Social theorist Jorge Larrain argues in a recent article that identity politics and a poststructuralist "politics of difference" each deploys the identity/difference binary so as to displace the category of class. Poststructuralist versions of identity politics—formulated now as a "politics of difference"—refuse to answer the question of material interest, preferring instead to make identity itself the site of interrogation. Taken to an extreme, this theory poses deconstruction of gender identities in texts as the only possible (a)political act, rejecting any kind of collective, instrumental action toward change.

For example, Judith Butler, who claims to be absolutely opposed to essentialist identity politics, represents this new kind of politics of identity—in which a faith in essential identities is replaced by a critique of subjectivity. In *Bodies That Matter*, Butler insists on the performativity of identity, the existence prior to the "I" who speaks of a set of a discourses "which precedes and enables the 'I' and forms *in language* the constraining trajectory of its will" (225, emphasis added). Therefore any action is by definition the citation of the discourses that precede both the person who acts and the act itself. Subjects on this view are not understood as constrained by or produced within material, economic contexts, but are rather the products of discourses.

On the one hand, Butler is laying out a theory, resonant with Althusserian structuralism and Foucaultian post-structuralism, of the end of human agency, a world in which discourses enact their will *through* the subjects who utter them. On the other hand, Butler insists that a theory of performed, citational subjectivity conceptually restores the possibility of agency to poststructuralist thought. There is an odd utopianism to Butler's project, especially her faith in performativity:

> Performative acts are forms of authoritative speech: most performatives, for instance, are statements that, in the uttering, also perform a certain action and exercise a binding power. . . .
> If the power of discourse to produce that which it names is linked with the question of performativity, then the performative is one domain in which power acts *as* discourse. (*Bodies* 225)

Still there are no discernible agents of history here. "Discourse" in this passage has the power to produce what *it*—not the performer of the utterance—names. Yet, Butler seems to be suggesting that language produces what it names, that to perform queer identity or gender transformation through cross dressing is to actually produce sexual freedom: "the critical potential of 'drag' centrally concerns a critique of a prevailing truth-regime of 'sex'" (233). Only if one conceives of power relations as being constituted by *discourses*, rather than by the material conditions of capitalist society, does it make sense to pose a politics of battling "prevailing truth-regimes." Butler presumes that one can rename oneself and in the naming, and renaming, become free. So, "the increasing theatricalization of political rage in response to the killing inattention of public policy-makers on the issue of AIDS is allegorized in the recontextualization of 'queer' from its place within a homophobic strategy of abjection and annihilation to an insistence and public severing of that interpellation from the effect of shame" (233). Butler reveals queer theory's project as one of recontextualizing words like "queer" without addressing the foundations of heterosexism in the capitalist ideology of the family. In addition, the utopian, textualist spaces of a performative politics are intimate, private spaces. Butler offers not struggle against gay and lesbian oppression but a theater of the self in which intimacy is staged and words are detached from their material referents. The theory of performativity locates agency in the "consciousness" (or parodic awareness of the discursively performed character of one's subject positions) of individuals and not in posing a collective challenge to capitalism.

Further, queer theory backs up political engagement to the moment of self-invention. Warner endorses the "self-shattering impulse" in queer sexuality (Jagose 3). Likewise, Butler's earlier account in *Gender Trouble* of the shifting multiplicity of sexual identity (on the part of drag queens, transsexuals, and so forth) hails parodic performance as a political act. She explicitly redefines politics: "The deconstruction of identity is not the deconstruction of politics; rather, it establishes as political the very terms through which identity is articulated" (*Gender* 148). In other words, cross-dressing or otherwise deconstructing gender categories in the performance of everyday life is the only thinkable transformative action. The goal, Butler writes, is the "denaturalization of gender as such" (*Gender* 149). Thus, her suspicion of foundationalism leads to a politics of identity deconstruction.

Collective structural politics gives way to a world view in which "strategic raids" on the gendered meaning system displace the project of transformative change. Barbara Biesecker, following deCerteau, hails a feminist rhetorical practice that shuns outdated notions of unity in favor of *techne*, defined as

> a kind of 'getting through' or ad hoc 'making do' by a subject whose resources are necessarily located in and circumscribed by the field within which she operates . . . a bringing-about in the doing-of on the part of an agent *that does not necessarily take herself to be anything like a subject of historical or . . . cultural change.* (155, emphasis added)

"*Techne*," then, refers to the relentless and endless process of self-invention in which one becomes mired forever in the struggle over the terms of one's identity. Like Butler, Biesecker heralds the end of political agency and social transformation and celebrates the necessity of "making do" with capitalism as it is. Because the "subject's" resources (which are defined here as discursive) are determined prior to the individual's utterance or action, the "subject" cannot be an agent of change, cannot analyze society, strategize transformative projects, or act in solidarity with others. This defeatism about the project of changing society results from the post-al rejection of the notion that oppression and exploitation are materially real outside of discourses or that we can know, explain, and act on our social conditions. In the absence of concepts or explanations, the only recourse for the "subject," embedded in discourses not of her own making, is to play with the texts of her identity. The vision of post-al feminist theory is a bleak one, mired in theories of helplessness and defeat disguised as new theories of invention and creativity.

The anti-politics of *techne* describe and valorize identity play (performative subversion of the gender code, playful misreading of popular texts) as a primary strategy. For this reason, Teresa Ebert (*Ludic Feminism*; "Critiques") critiques recent poststructuralist feminisms as "ludic" feminism that abandons the project of transformative social change. Ebert recalls a telling passage from Marx's critique of the idealist "young Hegelians": "They are only fighting against *phrases*" (Marx and

Engels, *German Ideology* 149). The passage continues, "They forget, however, that to these phrases they themselves are only opposing other phrases, and that they are in no way combating the real existing world when they are merely combating the phrases of this world" (149). For Ebert, "what is at stake in this displacement of the economic by discourse is the elision of issues of exploitation and the substitution of a discursive identity politics for the struggle for full social and economic emancipation" ("Critiques," 146).

Queer theory, like poststructuralist feminism, tells the story of the emergence of a new politics, heavily informed by poststructuralist assumptions, as the corrective to both assimilationist and universalizing strategies and as a progressive development in the struggle for gay and lesbian liberation. Thus, Lisa Duggan comments, "I want to take up the position of 'queer' largely in order to criticize the liberal and nationalist strategies in gay politics and to advocate the constructionist turn in lesbian and gay theories and practice" (11). This brief statement summarizes the narrative of feminist and queer theory, from liberal through separatist to discourse-oriented ("constructionist") politics. Class struggle is not a stop on the identity-politics theory train. Similarly, T. Anthony Slagle heralds queer politics as a move away from essentialist identity politics to more open-ended, theatrical strategies in a "politics of difference." And Michael Warner introduces the edited collection *Fear of a Queer Planet* with the words,

> The preference for "queer" represents, among other things, an aggressive impulse of generalization; it rejects a minoritizing logic of toleration or simple political interest-representation in favor of a more thorough resistance to regimes of the normal . . . 'Queer' therefore also suggests the difficulty in defining the population whose interests are at stake in queer theory. (xxvi)

Like Biesecker, Warner has trouble identifying the agents of social transformation. And like Butler, Warner heralds a politics of discourse, suggesting that claiming the word "queer" entails "resistance to regimes of the normal." Queer theory offers ultimately conservative, utopian, fragmenting, and privatizing strategies on behalf of an unidentifiable collective in a political vacuum. At the same time, it ignores the questions of need, class interests, and the necessity of a transformative political project.

Queer Theory's Theatrics of Intimacy

In its idealism, its privatism and its utopian moralism, queer theory becomes a mirror image of family values discourse. As a consequence of translating political resistance into interrogations of identity, queer theory exalts the performative and the theatrical. If sexual identities are little more than textual works in progress, it follows that constructing elaborate gender-bending performances would come to substitute for collective political activity. As Butler explains, if there is no performer prior the performance, "gender is a kind of imitation for which there is no original" ("Imitation," 21). Working from this assumption, Warner suggests that queer activists make politics out of "tempered rage and carnivalesque display" (*Fear* xxvi). Warner's language reveals an accomodationist stance; playful performance allows only for the expression of "tempered," stylized anger in a ludic frame. Similarly, Slagle heralds Queer Nation's revisions in the concept of politics. They have "changed the meaning of activism," he writes, from public demonstration to the construction and display of an outrageous self-image. All of these queer theorists replace politics with performances staged in a theatrics of relentless self-invention. The purpose of such performances is only to shock bourgeois voyeurs, not to challenge the structures of wage labor and family mandates that generate gay and lesbian oppression under capitalism.

"Theatricalization" is so implicitly foundational to post-al dogma that it is taken as a self-evident good. Thus Andrew Parker can indict Marx and Marxists of being "anti-theatrical" without ever considering Marx's reasons for rejecting theatricality as a substitute for politics. Parker writes, "Marxism's constitutive dependence on the category of production derives in part from an antitheatricalism, an aversion to certain forms of parody that prevents sexuality from attaining the political significance that class has long monopolized" (19). It is, of course, true that Marxism does not attribute to sexuality the centrality of class nor to the theater the centrality of the workplace, but this is not due to some determining predisposition against the performing arts, as Parker implies. Rather, Marxism rejects performative gender politics because sexuality does not constitute the basic division in capitalist society—class does. And it is because sexuality—as a discursive identity construct—is not the theoretical analog of class that Marxism suspects theatrical metaphors in political contexts.

Performance metaphors are fundamentally idealist, suggesting that play with ideas, texts, and characters—as if they are autonomous from relations of production—can replace challenges to the capitalist system. Teresa de Lauretis writes that the project of queer theory is "to articulate the terms in which lesbian and gay sexualities may be understood and imaged as forms of resistance to cultural homogenization, counteracting dominant discourses with other constructions of the subject in culture" (iii), and to "recast the terms of discourses. . . and to rethink the sexual" (xvi). It is unclear how recasting the terms of discourse can end gay and lesbian oppression, since such oppression is not merely a product of "cultural homogenization." Marx and Engels were quite clear in *German Ideology* about such ludic politics in their critique of the Young Hegelians, where they comment, "It is quite immaterial what consciousness starts to do on its own" (159). By this Marx and Engels meant that idealist efforts to transform consciousness without challenging the material conditions of consciousness, the consequences of such efforts would be, quite literally, "immaterial."

Michael Warner epitomizes the idealism of consciousness trying to act on itself, redefining politics as "a fantasized space where all embodied identities could be visibly represented as parallel forms of identity" (*Fear* xix). The theatrical spaces of queer resistance showcase the sheer fantasy of consciousness attempting to act on itself. Warner's description of a purely textual, virtual rebellion captures what Francis Mulhern describes as the post-materialist dissolution of politics into culture: "It leaves no room for politics beyond cultural practice . . . There is no space, and in fact no need, for struggle if all popular culture, abstracted from the historical realities of inequality and domination, is already active and critical, if television and shopping are already theaters of subversion" (40). In a recent interview, Warner offers "queer world making" as an alternative to what he regards as a conservative program of normalizing gay and lesbian life. The strategy he suggests is explicitly theatrical and utopian. He states, "There is something transformative about those moments of mutual display, like Stonewall, that are not merely corporatized and regimented." In addition, he argues that public sex cultures make possible "the imagination of an alternative world. . . . There is something fundamental about the spatial imagination in convincing people that it would be possible to remake the dominant culture: what if every place were like this?" (Jagose 4-6).

While I, too, yearn for a remaking of the dominant culture in which gays and lesbians are not policed, medicalized and otherwise normalized, a Marxist analysis rejects the utopian emphasis on imagination and display rather than systematic revolutionary organizing that can target the material base of gay and lesbian oppression. Moreover, queer theory's theatricalism does not break with a capitalist commitment to private accumulation and self-elaboration.

Thus it may be illuminating to point out that familialist ideologues also rely on the theatrics of intimacy. The 1959 "Kitchen Debates," in which then-Vice-President Richard Nixon theatrically displayed the domestic accouterments of the American family to Russian Premier Nikita Kruschev during the American Exhibition in Moscow, are one example of staged familialism and the celebration of capitalist self-invention. The theatrics of domestic superiority suggest a similarity between queer theory's politics of intimate display and "family values": Both offer an ideological defense of privacy against a collectivist, transformative politics. Historian Elaine Tyler May writes,

> For Nixon, American superiority rested on the ideal of the suburban home, complete with modern appliances and distinct gender roles for family members. He proclaimed that the 'model' home with a male breadwinner and a full-time female homemaker, adorned with a wide array of consumer goods, represented the essence of American freedom. (16-17)

Nixon's own remarks about the essence of American freedom are instructive: "To us, diversity, the right to choose, . . . is the most important thing" (quoted in May, 17). As in queer theory's defense of self-expression and sexual freedom, intimate choices define the cold-war domestic utopia. Queer theory, like cold-war conservatism, celebrates the "right to choose" in the spaces of domesticity and consumption. Both queer theory and the suburban family ideal are idealist moral visions that translate political struggles into theatrical displays of pleasures and choices.

The cold-war family was, as May explains, an expression of both optimism and middle-class affluence on the one hand and cold-war anxieties over the possibility of nuclear war on the other. Undoubtedly, the vision of a prosperous suburban family living the dream of security and harmony amid new appliances in the kitchen and tricycles on the sidewalk depended upon the relative economic stability of the period between 1945 and 1973. David Harvey argues that despite the tensions of racism and the eruptions of social movements during the 1950s and 1960s, "material living standards rose for the mass of the population in the advanced capitalist countries," enabling the spread of the "benefits" of mass production and consumption to some layers of the working class, even as new assembly-line techniques also regimented and disciplined workers (140). Harvey argues that post-war Fordism—assembly-line mass production on an unprecedented scale—alongside the geopolitical hegemony of the United States "meant a whole new aesthetic and a whole new way of life" (135). This new way of life was expressed through the proliferation of consumer choices and the celebration of consumption. The family was the site of mass consumption and the expression of the dream of eternal American prosperity.

The recession of 1973 marked an end to that dream. To maintain profitability, capitalists introduced a new regime of what Harvey calls "flexible accumulation," marked by increased internationalization of capital, innovations in production, flexibility with labor and resources, and rapid growth in the service sector. In recent decades, under the banner of flexible accumulation, employers have taken advantage of weak unions to push for overtime, replacement of unionized with non-union workers, speedups, wage and benefits reductions, and irregular work hours. Gone are the eight-hour day and the family wage, replaced by workers holding multiple part time jobs, or working split shifts, or working from home (Harvey 149-150).

Workers have paid for the shift to flexible accumulation with lower wages, reductions in benefits, and longer work hours. In this context, conservative familialists offer a vision of the cold-war family as a utopian corrective. It is as if the rehabilitation of intimate life could restore the material conditions that generated the 1950s nuclear family ideal. The intimate utopias offered by queer theorists are functionally similar to this familialism, except that queer theory offers not the stable family of Fordism, but rather invents a new, flexible consumer to match the regime of flexible accumulation. Harvey explains that in late capitalism, the mass consumption society based on the family is replaced with a yuppie culture stressing individualized consumption and spectacles of increasing individuation (179). In an un-critique-al mode, Anthony Giddens takes the dynamic transformation of capitalism described by Harvey as a sign of the actual disorganization and democratization of capitalism itself. He celebrates the formation of new subjects who can replace political engagement with lifestyle elaboration and therapy. He writes that in "late modernity," "The self is seen as a reflexive project, for which the individual is responsible. . . We are, not what we are, but what we make of ourselves" (75).

Giddens' faith in the "self-made" man echoes the Horatio-Alger ideology of liberal capitalism that justifies class-based exploitation, alongside racial and gender oppression, by promoting individual opportunity and responsibility. Giddens' mistake is to assume that the invention of flexible selves in discourse corresponds to an actual loosening of capitalism's grip on our lives or to an egalitarian economic restructuring of society. In reality, the ideology of flexible selfhood and individual lifestyle choice is a cover for the ongoing relations of exploitation in capitalist society. The resonance between Giddens' giddiness over the infinite malleability of the self and Butler's notion of performativity should be self-evident. Giddens and queer theorists are caught in a loop of imaginary self-invention as a substitute for collective political activity geared toward the real transformation of society.

In post-al queer theory as in the politics of family nostalgia, the utopian fantasies of consumption attempt to both deny and justify the continuing reality of a society divided by inequalities of class. Both utopian visions assume the affluence and leisure necessary to the obsessive elaboration of an intimate life as the conditions of freedom— within, not in opposition to, capitalism.

Harvey notes the tendency of "flexible" capitalism to produce spectacles in which the self is incessantly and elaborately reinvented through the interplay of commodities and discourses. Thus the performative dimensions of queer theory are closely tied to its textualism, or the centering of an entire transformative project on the close readings of literary and other cultural texts. Eve Sedgwick defends this textualist project in her book *Epistemology of the Closet*. In this work she performs readings of literary works from the late 19th and early 20th centuries to describe the tense co-existence of essentialist, separatist ("minoritizing") depiction of male homosexuality on the one hand, alongside theories that posit a flexible, contingent sexuality. While her readings are convincing as descriptions of the texts under consideration, it is not at all clear how such quasi-deconstructive literary readings achieve any practical political end. Likewise, Diana Fuss writes, "Many of the current efforts in lesbian and gay theory, which this volume seeks to showcase, have begun the difficult but urgent *textual* work necessary to call into question the stability and ineradicability of the hetero/homo hierarchy" (3). Given the emphasis on the textual autonomy rather than on the material roots of gay oppression, it is no wonder that in the same paragraph Fuss asks, "But how, exactly, do we bring the hetero/homo opposition to the point of collapse?" (3).

From a materialist perspective, the attempt to fight phrases, to bring linguistic constructions and categories to "the point of collapse"— without at the same time addressing the material bases of such constructions (capitalist class relations)—entails a reactionary politics. "Family values" talk offers a similar idealist response to capitalist exploitation and the difficulties working class people have in supporting themselves and their families. The Republican National Convention in 1992 featured "family values night," during which speaker after speaker attempted to "fight back" feminist and working-class challenges to the Right with a discourse of utopian intimacy. Marilyn Quayle acknowledged this motive explicitly in her speech to the Convention:

I came of age in a time of turbulent social change. Some of it was good, such as civil rights, much of it was questionable. But remember, not everyone joined the counterculture, not everyone demonstrated, dropped out, took drugs, joined in the sexual revolution or dodged the draft. Not everyone concluded that American society was so bad that it had to be radically remade by social revolution. Not everyone believed that the family was so oppressive that women could only thrive apart from it.

Quayle offers the utopian family as a "solution" to political strife and radical challenges to the social order. Significantly, she states, "Not everyone concluded that American society was so bad that it had to be radically remade by social revolution." Idealist, utopian, and domestic salves for the ills of capitalist society are posed here as an alternative to the radical remaking of society (see also Cloud, "Rhetoric of Family Values"). Likewise, queer theory has concluded that capitalist society is not so bad as to require revolution. Rather than radical projects, rooted in historical analysis and an understanding of the importance of collective struggle, queer theory offers a domesticated vision that appears to critique the oppressiveness of the bourgeois nuclear family but instead replicates its logic of intimacy and self development.

Queer theory, like the rhetoric of family values, offers what Fredric Jameson calls a "fantasy bribe" to the public in the form of utopian, textual identity play. But this bribe covers the ideological conservatism of a discourse that celebrates the complete collapse of collective struggle in favor of intimate experimentation and self-absorption. Familialist ideologies similarly articulate the yearnings of ordinary people for a better life but turn those desires inward on themselves. Likewise, queer theory's prescriptions for intimate self-expression and development are ultimately conservative in their effects in the academy and for gays and lesbians who are seeking political direction.

In looking to the places of consumer pleasure, queer theory offers a politics that very often hails the commodification of sexuality and identity. Put bluntly, its politics are pro-capitalist and therefore cannot challenge gay and lesbian oppression at its source. About lesbian chic, Danae Clark writes, "Once stripped of its political underpinnings, lesbianism can be represented as a style of consumption linked to sexual preference. Lesbianism, in other words, is treated as merely a sexual style that can be chosen—or not chosen—just as one chooses a particular mode of fashion for self-expression" (197). Similarly, Eric

Clarke explains that this sort of commodified "visibility politics" offers nothing like real democratic representation in a political sphere (58).

In a contradictory way, capitalism requires both the privatized family, to which gays and lesbians could pose a threat, and the flexible consumers of queer self-invention. Both the post-war family and queer self-invention are sites of flexible and ever-increasing consumption masquerading as political fulfillment. As Eagleton puts it, "Difference, 'hybridity,' heterogeneity, restless mobility are native to the capitalist mode of production, and thus by no means inherently radical phenomena" ("Where Do" 64). This is not to say, however, that attacks on gays and lesbians in the media, by the police, the military, in the law, and by gay-bashers are on the wane or that gays and lesbians are not oppressed. Despite the liberalization of domestic partnership laws in some states and communities, we are witnessing the intensification of anti-gay sentiment in conjunction with the emphasis on "family values" as a response to social crisis. It is just that when the legitimate anger of gays and lesbians is channeled by queer theory in consumerist directions, it serves rather than challenges the capitalist relations that produce homophobia in the first place.

Donald Morton ("Ludic Sado-Masochism") notes the growing mainstream acceptance of sado-masochistic sexuality in films such as *Exit to Eden*. He argues that such representations should not be embraced as political victories for groups who engage in non-normative sexual practices. I would also urge caution, not out of sexual prudery or an aversion to private role-playing, but rather out of the recognition that to count such representations as emancipatory political acts does not challenge capitalism's hegemony. Far from it: To celebrate flexible new subjects who create themselves through consumption in a proliferation of spectacularized sexual practices like sado-masochism is to become complicit with capitalism's strategies of recuperation and containment. Such practices serve as fantastic compensations and imaginary neutralizations of actual power relations in society. Those who would celebrate sado-masochism *as political* (rather than strictly personal or private) activity elide questions of real, material power in society—as if one can overcome the exploitation and oppression suffered in capitalist society by choosing who's on top and who's on bottom.

"Erotic Politics" and the Public Sphere

At the crux of queer theory's anti-concept, anti-materialist stance is the conflation of public and private implied in phrases such as "erotic politics" and "revolution of desire." Like "family values," the queer theory lexicon distracts us from the institutions, structures, and public relations of power and toward the experience of private life as both cause and solution of gay oppression. Like sexologists and regulators of sexual desire across the last century, queer theorists put gay and lesbian liberation in terms of private, moral, sexual behavior. For this reason it is strange and even Orwellian that queer theorists have taken up the language of public sphere theory to describe their project. For example, Lauren Berlant and Elizabeth Freeman's celebratory essay "Queer Nationality" describes the way in which Queer Nation adopts and subverts symbols of American nationalism such as flags, pledges of allegiance, and prayer in "the production of a queer counterpublic out of traditional national icons, the ritual places of typical public pleasure (parades, malls, bars, and bodies), and the collective identities of consumers in the mode of mass culture" (215).

Similarly, *Warner* suggests that queer theory's program is "to mess up the desexualized spaces of the academy, exude some rut, reimagine the publics from and for which academic intellectuals write, dress, and perform. . . . 'Queer' gets its edge by defining itself against the normal" (*Fear* xxvi). There is a clearly audible moralistic tone to such statements: the idea of queer theory is to regulate the deregulation of desire, exhorting theorists to "exude some rut" as a strategy. Such programs demonstrate how queer theory is the flip side of sexology and familialism, obsessed with the performance of sexual acts and interpersonal connections. Warner also spins out the other anti-political thread of queer theory: its emphasis on textual manipulation by academics who do not *act* to make history but rather "write, dress, and perform," its construction of an apolitical fantasy in which social relations are simply "reimagined." Warner admits that this project is one of "universalizing utopianism" (*Fear* xxvi).

Despite the clearly privatizing force of this argument, Warner (and Berlant and Warner, "What Does" and "Sex in Public") invoke public sphere theorists Hannah Arendt and Jurgen Habermas (see Warner, *Fear* xxvi) in support of their project, which they see as somehow building publics or counter-publics. Seen from a Marxist perspective, Habermas' project is liberal and utopian in orientation (like that of queer theory). Yet he makes it clear in his writing that what he is arguing *against* is the increasing interpenetration of personal and political life and the displacement of critical debate by the kind of consumerist spectacle hailed by Berlant, Freeman, and Warner.

Habermas' argument is that after the bourgeois public sphere reached its peak of vitality in the 1800s, the pressures of special-interest politics and privatized consumer capitalism began to take their toll on public life. In a society in which engaged public dialogue has been exchanged for mass culture media hype and commodity marketing, the ability to frame social issues as problems of structure and collectivity is weakened. The result is the "refeudalization" of the public sphere, in which a participatory public is exchanged for the spectacular display of autocratic power.

In contrast to a privatized social realm, Habermas poses the ideal of the public good achieved through rational debate. Habermas has faced criticism for narrating the fate of the public sphere in contemporary capitalist society as a story of degeneration from the Enlightenment ideal, which as Michael Schudson warns us, was already imbued with the imperatives and marked by the exclusions of capitalist social relations. Furthermore, Habermas' vision of democratic public life presupposes a measure of economic equality and the diminishing of the power of the market, conditions that can only be met in the present by way of a politics of struggle against capitalism. In this struggle, the political cannot be rendered ever more pure and separate from economic relations of capitalist exploitation, but rather must be geared toward transforming those economic relations. Ultimately, Habermas defends a utopian liberalism that presumes that one can (and capitalists will, voluntarily) set aside economic interests during political deliberation. He laments the emergence of class struggle and the labor movement as symptom of the public's decline into interest politics rather than of its democratic expansion. By privileging *dialogue*—in some imagined space of harmony and common interest—over *dialectics*—the process of social transformation through class struggle, his argument begs the question of whether one can achieve a democratic public life in a capitalist society divided by class in which the interests of the few control the institutional spaces, media outlets, and terms of discussion. In other words, socialist economic relations are a prerequisite of a democratic political life, which cannot be "talked" into being.

Even so we can use Habermas' deep critique of the collapse in capitalist society of social experience into private life. Despite the inability of Habermasian liberalism to comprehend class antagonism as public, there is something to its valorization of *publicness* and its refusal to call the personal ruminations and self-ishness of people in private, "politics." Eric Clarke attempts to bring class politics to queer theory through Habermas, arguing that neither the politics of normality nor the politics of queer visibility can escape the distorting influence of the market on modern publics, that tolerance and visibility are not enough. Even liberal theories of the public sphere enable us to challenge the dubious claim that queer theory's carnivalesque sexual spectacles constitute "publics" (as they are much more about "privates").

Berlandt and Warner invoke Nancy Fraser's amendment to Habermas, her notion of *counterpublics*, as a way of coding sexual display and self-invention as transformative or emancipatory political activity. Fraser argues that rather than idealizing the gender-exclusive and fundamentally inegalitarian Enlightenment public sphere, we should attend to the multiple, culturally specific, oppositional publics that allow participants "to speak in one's own voice, and thereby simultaneously to construct and express one's cultural identity through idiom and style" (126). Oddly, however, the emphasis here on "idiom and style" echoes Habermas' description not of democratic publicness but of a feudal publicity "wedded to personal attributes such as insignia (badges and arms), dress (clothing and coiffure), demeanor (form of greeting and poise) and rhetoric (form of address and formal discourse in general)" (Habermas 8).[4] Donald Morton argues that "like other bourgeois modes of understanding, what ludic theory, including queer theory, aims at finally is the collapse of the nonpersonal or public space into the personal and private space. Thus queer theory in all its variants works to displace gender as a category in an analytical, concept-based materialism" in favor of allegedly disruptive freedoms and pleasures" ("Politics," 141).

"Family values" is another bourgeois mode of understanding that "aims at finally . . . the collapse of non-personal or public space into the personal or private space." Only a commitment to textualist utopias allows Berlant and Warner to claim about their project, "This work aspires to create publics, publics that can afford sex and intimacy in sustained, unchastening ways" ("What Does" 343). Tellingly, Berlant and Warner put their vision in consumerist terms: Their sexualized "public" is one "that can afford sex and intimacy" as a lifestyle choice. Their language quite resembles Nixon's conservative defense of the family as the place of consumer choice. More recently, Berlant and Warner have extended this argument in an article appearing in a special issue of *Critical Inquiry* on intimacy. They write, paradoxically, "There is nothing more public than privacy," arguing that pornographic theaters, strip joints, and other "queer zones" are public, political spaces ("Sex in Public" 547). What makes their article interesting for my purposes is that they explicitly critique the conservative rhetoric of family values as utopian, acknowledging that familialism displaces structural critique and privatizes social experience (549). At the same time, however, they replicate the displacement and the privatization of familialism in their celebration of a sexualized queer world (551).

This declaration that privates are public is a neat trick of doublespeak. Berlant and Warner appear to disavow "the utopian wish behind normal intimate life" ("Sex in Public" 567). However, while they indict bourgeois heteronormative sexualized spaces as "intimate utopias," they definitionally exclude by fiat queer sexualized spaces from that category. They do not consider the possibility that the politicization of intimacy—heteronormative or queer—is a strategy rooted in bourgeois society. Berlant and Warner's resort to the language of the public sphere—right alongside the language of affluence and consumption—suggests the limits of both queer theory—which makes a politics of public sex—and of liberal models of the public sphere that can be read in support of a purely sexual-textual anti-politics. As Field puts it, "It is inconceivable that any kind of oppression can be got rid of simply by wishing or 'imagining' it away" (54). Models for ways of talking—or of having sex—will not address the roots of gay and lesbian oppression in the family under capitalism. One must defend a public of another sort: space for critique of and education about capitalist society and the history of struggle against the exploitation and oppressions it produces, *and* a commitment to collective action against the capitalist system itself.

Queer theory, on the other hand, is constituted within the general post-al rejection of materialism and class politics. As a number of materialist scholars have argued (see Anderson, *Considerations*, *Origins*; Callinicos; Cloud, "Socialism"; Eagleton, *Ideology*, *Illusions*, and "Where Do"; Ebert, *Ludic Feminism;* Norris; Wood, *Retreat* and *Democracy*; Wood and Foster, "Marxism," *In Defense*; Zavarzadeh; Zavarzadeh, Ebert, and Morton), postmodernist, poststructuralist and post-Marxist theories are idealist/textualist and relativist in their implications. As Zavarzadeh argues, these are theories that come from an elite class perspective, produced in order to justify a set of textualized and commodified desires and pleasures. They ignore questions of human need and material interest in favor of textual play. They leave critique—and the possibility of real social transformation—behind in their flight from any explanatory theories of oppression and exploitation. As Donald Morton notes in an exchange with Dennis Altman, postmodern, poststructuralist analyses "end up endorsing the idea that all 'global' phenomena are so complex that no determinate or coherent explanation of them can be offered" ("Global [Sexual] Politics" 3). In such discourse "complexity" and "subtlety" become euphemisms for an unwillingness or inability to offer political explanations of the world. Post-al theorists claim the political credentials of the left, arguing all the while that collective struggle is dead or irrelevant. Queer theory exhibits the symptom of this defeat in its retreat into micro-strategies of intimacy that, ironically, echo the strategic micro-focus of capitalism on the family. Turned inward on ourselves, we pose little threat to the system that requires the oppression of gays and lesbians.

Capitalism's Intimate Utopias

Like the "universalizing utopianism" of queer theory, "family values" exhibits a utopian dimension in the construction of a fantasy of a better life. In the contemporary moral panic over the family, scapegoating of gays, lesbians, women on welfare, and "deadbeat" Black men is counterpoised to the image of an idyllic 1950s family, secure in the embrace of maternal love. This utopianism gestures toward a mythic place where the conflict and hardship of the American Dream in disarray can be imagined away. As a 1992 *Newsweek* article put it, "There is a yearning for the security associated with the good old days." When shown a photograph of an ideal family having a barbecue, "one woman said, 'I know the "Ozzie and Harriet" stuff is impossible, but I miss the *familyness* of it'" (Klein 22).

The simultaneous acknowledgment of both the impossibility and desire for "familyness" marks a contradiction in "family values" rhetoric. It claims to want to strengthen families—and gestures toward a time when *some* families thrived—while telling poor families that they are on their own, sink or swim. The utopian dimension of "family values" rhetoric humanizes and rationalizes the ongoing erosion of federal material support for struggling families. The fantasy keeps us from focusing on the present. And like the queer theory utopia, it is also a fantasy closely bound up with ideals of self-expression through consumption, of making a textured intimate life out of the fabric of consumer capitalism.

This analogy should serve as a warning about the proliferating fantasies of queer theory, in which gay oppression and the struggles of the working class family for survival can be somehow "imagined away" through textual play, consumer spectacle, and the performative construction of citational identities. The 1950s ideal family is a similar ideological dream of endless consumption and self-fulfillment. Engels, in his critique of the utopian socialists of the 19th century, wrote,

> The solution of the social problems, the Utopians attempted to evolve out of the human brain. Society presented nothing but wrongs; to remove these was the task of reason. It was necessary, then, to discover a new and more perfect system of social order and to impose this upon society from without by propaganda, and wherever it was possible, by the example of model experiments. These new social systems were foredoomed as Utopian; the more completely they were

worked out in detail, the more they could not avoid drifting off into pure phantasies. (121)

The fantasy lives of queer theorists, rapidly becoming a hegemonic articulation of pro-gay politics in the academy (see Morton, "Politics of Queer Theory"), serve as a diversion from the practical political struggle required to win not only gay and lesbian liberation but an end to a class reality belied by the utopian family image.

However, a gay and lesbian challenge to "family values" could point the way toward a strategy of liberation linked to the struggle for socialism. What is achieved under the banner of family values by the right goes well beyond the vilification of homosexuality: After two decades of falling wages and a massive upward redistribution of the world's wealth, politicians—and queer theorists—offer only dreams of private fulfillment as compensation. Attacks on welfare and other social programs, the scapegoating of Black men in the wake of the 1992 Los Angeles uprising, the blaming of poverty, racism, and crime all on the failures of families suggest that to target the family is to challenge the capitalist system that requires it. Because the rhetoric of "family values" represents a broad offensive against the working class on the part of the right, a willingness to contest familialism on behalf of gays and lesbians can be generalized as a fight against capitalism itself.

Clearly, the liberal-assimilationism represented by Andrew Sullivan is an inadequate formulation of this challenge. The moderate demand to legitimate gay families on the same privatized terms as the normative nuclear family is not enough. Queer theory says that it wants to get beyond a pro-family stance. Yet instead of recognizing the links through "the family" among struggles against homophobia and those against poverty and racism, queer theory also operates on the same terms as "family values" talk. By arguing for a response on the terrain of intimacy and consumerism, queer theory fails to challenge the roots—in capitalism's needs for the heteronormative nuclear family—of homophobia and sexual oppression. A program conceived merely as a "revolution of desire" can only sustain a capitalist system that denies basic means of survival to the poor amid fantasies of private freedom, fulfilling intimacy, and spectacular plenty.

Notes

[1] As this revised essay goes to press, the 2000 Democratic National Convention is under way in Los Angeles. On August 14, President

Clinton, in his speech to the convention, closed a summary of his administration's meager family-oriented initiatives with the words, "This is what it means to value families." In ending welfare and beefing up the police state during his two terms in office, Clinton linked "family values" ideologically with "personal responsibility," indicating the conservative effects of privatized responses to social crisis.

[2] This function of family values ideology is evident in the context of discourses about AIDS. For example, Cindy Patton shows how Africans with AIDS are stigmatized by international health officials on the basis of their lack of "family values": "The African family's purported problem is its similar inability to construct itself properly as a small, well-disciplined unit . . . the pamphlets posit the family as the idealized site for support, care, and education" (134). As Patton explains, this rhetoric justifies underfunding education, community organizing, and blood-banking as material solutions to the AIDS crisis. Similarly, Simon Watney demonstrates a link between familialism and AIDS in Britain: Official discourses construct AIDS as a spectacular threat to family life, thus upholding familial norms and justifying political repression against gay men in particular. Even these queer theorists must acknowledge that the discourse about homosexuality is linked to the preservation of the capitalist family.

[3] There is some debate over the role performed by housework in or alongside capitalist social relations (see Berk; Boydston; Fraad, Resnick, and Wolff; Wang), with some Marxist- and socialist-feminists claiming on the one hand that housework is itself directly productive of value in the capitalist economy, by virtue of its reproduction of laborers. On the other hand, some feminist analyses argue for a conception of the capitalist family as an entirely separate patriarchal economy in which women are a caste or class exploited by men (Fraad, Resnick, and Wolff). Neither of these positions—one collapsing housework into the capitalist economy, the other positing the domestic sphere as the site of a separate, patriarchal oppression—explains the complex relation of housework and women's oppression to the capitalist mode of production. Paul Smith argues against feminist theories that suggest that Marxism ignores or marginalizes housework and domesticity as analytical concepts. To the contrary, Smith argues, "It is not Marx's theory of value which marginalizes domestic labour, but the capitalist mode of production" that has pushed the necessary labor of social reproduction into a domestic realm marginal to the capitalist economy (215). In other words, Smith is arguing that under capitalism, the work performed by women (most of the time) in the home never enters into the circulation of the economy. It is socially necessary but not productive labor. "The reproduction of labor

power takes place outside the capitalist mode of production, although of course in a manner determined by it" (214).
[4] More recently, in *Justice Interruptus*, Fraser recognizes the necessity of a materialist project, which she calls a "politics of redistribution," alongside a textualist project of cultural deconstruction. The concept of the counterpublic can be appropriated to describe materially transformative social movement projects such as the labor movement. However, as the concept is appropriated in queer theory, it describes a spectacular, personalistic, and staged publicity that is fundamentally at odds with Habermas' project.

Works Cited

Abbott, Peter. and C. Wallace. *The Family and the New Right*. London: Pluto P, 1992.

Abelove, Henry, Michele Aina Barale, and David Halperin, eds. *The Lesbian and Gay Studies Reader*. NY: Routledge, 1993.

Altman, Dennis. "Sex: The New Front Line for Gay Politics." *Socialist Review* 12 (5, 1982): 75-84.

Anderson, Perry. *Considerations on Western Marxism*. London, Verso, 1976).

_____. *The Origins of Postmodernity*. London: Verso, 1998.

Aries, Peter. *Centuries of Childhood: A Social History of Family Life* (trans. Robert Baldick). New York: Vintage, 1962.

Barrett, Michele and Mary McIntosh. *The Anti-Social Family*. London: Verso, 1982.

Barrett, Michele. *The Politics of Truth: From Marx to Foucault*. Stanford: Stanford UP, 1991.

_____. *Women's Oppression Today: Problems in Marxist-Feminist Analysis*. London: Verso, 1980.

Berk, Sarah Fenstermaker. *Women and Household Labor*. London: Sage, 1980.

Berlant, Lauren. "Intimacy: A Special Issue." *Critical Inquiry* 24 (1998): 281-288.

Berlant, Lauren and Elizabeth Freeman. "Queer Nationality." In Warner, 193-229.

Berlant, Lauren and Michael Warner. "Sex in Public." *Critical Inquiry* 24 (1998): 547-560.

_____. "What Does Queer Theory Teach Us About *X*?" *PMLA* 110 (1995): 343-349.

Biesecker, Barbara. "Coming to Terms with Recent Attempts to Write Women Into the History of Rhetoric." *Philosophy and Rhetoric* 25 (1992): 140-161.

Boydston, Jeanne. *Home and Word: Housework, Wages, and the Ideology of Labor in the Early Republic.* New York: Oxford UP, 1990.

Butler, Judith. *Bodies that Matter.* NY: Routledge, 1993.

_____. *Gender Trouble: Feminism and the Subversion of Identity.* NY: Routledge, 1990.

_____. "Imitation and Gender Insubordination." In Fuss, 13-31.

Callinicos, Alex. *Against Postmodernism: A Marxist Critique.* NY: St. Martin's P,

Carlin, Nora. "The Roots of Gay Oppression." *International Socialism* 42 (Spring 1989): 63-113.

Clark, Danae. "Commodity Lesbianism." In Abelove, et al., 186-201.

Clarke, Eric O. *Virtuous Vice: Homoeroticism and the Public Sphere.* Durham: Duke University Press, 2000.

Cliff, Tony. *Class Struggle and Women's Liberation.* London: Bookmarks, 1984.

Cloud, Dana L. *Consolation and Control in American Culture and Politics: Rhetorics of Therapy.* Thousand Oaks: Sage, 1998.

_____. "The Rhetoric of Family Values: Scapegoating, Utopia, and the Privatization of Social Responsibility." *Western Journal of Communication* 62 (1998): 387-419

_____. "Socialism of the Mind: The New Age of Post-Marxism." In Herbert Simons and Michael Billig, eds. *After Postmodernism: Reconstructing Ideology Critique.* London: Sage, 1994. 222-251.

Combahee River Collective. "A Black Feminist Statement." In Cherrie Moraga and Gloria Anzaldúa, eds., *This Bridge Called My Back: Writings by Radical Women of Color.* New York: Kitchen Table/Woman of Color P, 1983. 210-218.

Coontz, Stephanie. *The Social Origins of Private Life.* London: Verso, 1988.

_____. *The Way We Never Were: American Families and the Nostalgia Trap.* New York: HarperCollins, 1992.

Cott, Nancy. *The Bonds of Womanhood.* New Haven: Yale UP, 1977.

D'Emilio, John. "Capitalism and Gay Identity." *Making Trouble: Essays on Gay History, Politics, and the University.* New York: Routledge, 1992. 3-16.

Deaner, Cheryl. "We're Looking Good." *The Family Next Door* 2 (6, June-July 1995): 1, 6.

deLauretis, Teresa. "Queer Theory: Lesbian and Gay Sexualities." *differences* 3.2   (1991): iii-xviii.

Duggan, Lisa. "Making It Perfectly Queer." *Socialist Review* 22 (Jan.-March, 1992): 11-31.

Eagleton, Terry. *Ideology: An Introduction*. London: Verso, 1991.

_____. *The Illusions of Postmodernism*. London: Blackwell, 1996.

_____. "Where Do Postmodernists Come From?" *Monthly Review* 47 (3, 1995): 59-70.

Ebert, Teresa. "(Untimely) Critiques for a Red Feminism." *Transformation 1* (Spring 1995): 113-149.

_____. *Ludic Feminism and After*. Ann Arbor: U of Michigan P, 1995.

Engels, Friedrich. *On the Origins of the Family, Private Property, and the State*. New York: Pathfinder, 1972.

_____. "Socialism: Utopian and Scientific." *Selected Works* vol. 2. Moscow: Foreign Languages Publishing House, 1962 (1883). 92-155.

Field, Nicola. *Over the Rainbow: Money, Class, and Homophobia*. London: Pluto P, 1995.

Foucault, Michel. *The History of Sexuality* vol. 1. Trans. Robert Hurley. New York: Random House, 1980.

Fraad, Harriet, Stephen Resnick, and Richard Wolff. *Bringing It All Back Home.*   London: Pluto P, 1994.

Fraser, Nancy. "Rethinking the Public Sphere." In Craig Calhoun, ed. *Habermas and the Public Sphere*. Cambridge, Mass.: MIT P. 109-142.

Fuss, Diana, ed. *Inside/Out: Lesbian Theories, Gay Theories*. New York: Routledge, 1991.

Giddens, Anthony. *Modernity and Self-Identity*. Stanford: Stanford University Press, 1991.

Habermas, Jurgen. *The Structural Transformation of the Public Sphere* (trans. Thomas Burger and Frederick Lawrence). Cambridge, MA: MIT Press, 1988.

Hartmann, Heidi. "The Unhappy Marriage of Marxism and Feminism: Towards a More Progressive Union." In Lydia Sargent, ed., *Women and Revolution*. Boston: South End Press, 1981. 1-42.

Harvey, David. *The Condition of Postmodernity*. Cambridge: Basil Blackwell, 1989.

Hennessy, Rosemary. "Queer Theory, Left Politics." *Rethinking Marxism* 7 (3, 1994): 85-111.

Herman, Didi. *The Antigay Agenda: Orthodox Vision and the Christian Right*. Chicago: University of Chicago, 1997.

Herman, Ellen. *Romance of American Psychology.* Berkeley: University of California Press, 1994.

Hocquenghem, Guy. *Homosexual Desire* (trans. Daniella Dangoor, pref. Jeffrey Weeks). London: Allison and Busby, 1978.

Jagose, Annamarie. "Queer World Making" [interview with Michael Warner]. *Genders* 31 (2000): online version http://www.genders.org/g31/g31_jagose.html.

Jameson, Fredric. "Reification and Utopia in Mass Culture." *Social Text* 1 (1980): 130-148.

Klein, J. Whose values? *Newsweek* (June 8, 1992): 19-22.

Kollontai, Alexandra. "Sexual Relations and the Class Struggle." From *Selected Writings of Alexandra Kollontai* (trans. Alix Holt). Westport, CN: Lawrence Hill, 1977. 237-249.

Larrain, Jorge. "Identity, the Other, and Postmodernism." *Transformation* 1 (1995): 271-289.

Laslett, Peter. *Household and Family in Past Time.* Cambridge, UK: Cambridge UP, 1972.

MacKinnon, Catherine. *Toward a Feminist Theory of the State.* Cambridge: Harvard UP, 1989.

Marx, Karl. *Capital,* vol. 1. Trans. Ben Fowkes. New York: Vintage, 1977.

Marx, Karl and Friedrich Engels. "Manifesto of the Communist Party." *Selected Works* vol. 1. Moscow: Foreign Languages Publishing House, 1962. 34-65.

_____. "The German Ideology, Part I." In Robert Tucker, ed., *The Marx-Engels Reader.* New York: Norton, 1978 (1846). 146-200.

May, Elaine Tyler. *Homeward Bound: American Families in the Cold War Era.* New York: Basic Books, 1988.

Morton, Donald. "Birth of the Cyberqueer." *PMLA* 110 (3, May 1995): 369-381.

_____. "Global (Sexual) Politics, Class Struggle, and the Queer Left." *Critical InQueeries* 1 (3, 1997): 1-30.

_____. "Queerity and Ludic Sado-Masochism: Compulsory Consumption and the Emerging Post-al Queer." *Transformation* 1 (Spring 1995): 189-215.

_____. "The Politics of Queer Theory in the (Post)Modern Moment." *Genders* 17 (Fall 1993): 121-150.

Mulhern, Francis. "The Politics of Cultural Studies." *Monthly Review* 47 (3, 1995): 31-40.

Norris, Christopher. *What's Wrong With Postmodernism?* New York: Harvester, 1990.

Parker, Andrew. "Unthinking Sex: Marx, Engels, and the Scene of Writing." In Warner, 19-41.

Patton, Cindy. "From Nation to Family: Containing African AIDS." In Abelove et al. 127-138.

Poster, Mark. *The Family and the Mode of Information. Critical Theory and Poststructuralism.* Ithaca: Cornell UP, 1989. 143-169.

Quayle, Daniel. Remarks to the Commonwealth Club of California, May 19, 1992. Text obtained from Lexis/Nexis database.

Quayle, Marilyn. Remarks to the Republican National Convention, 1992. Text obtained from Lexis/Nexis database.

Raspberry, William. "Back to the Family." *Washington Post* (July 24, 1992): A27.

Reed, Evelyn. "Introduction." To Friedrich Engels, *On the Origins of the Family,   Private Property, and the State.* New York: Pathfinder, 1972. 7-22.

Reeves, Jimmie and Richard Campbell. "Family Matters." *Cracked Coverage.* Durham: Duke UP, 1994. 184-309

Rose, Nicolas. *Governing the Soul.* London: Routledge, 1990.

Schudson, Michael. "Was There Ever a Public Sphere?" In Craig Calhoun, ed. *Habermas and the Public Sphere.* Cambridge, Mass.: MIT P. 143-163.

Sedgwick, Eve Kosofky. *Epistemology of the Closet.* Berkeley: U California P, 1990.

Seidman, Steven. "Identity and Politics in a 'Postmodern' Gay Culture: Some Historical and Conceptual Notes." In Warner, 105-142.

_____. "Queer Theory/Sociology: A Dialogue." *Sociological Theory* 12 (1994) 166-177.

Shorter, Edwin. *The Making of the Modern Family.* New York: Basic Books, 1975.

Slagle, R. Anthony. "In Defense of Queer Nation: From Identity Politics to Politics of Difference." *Western Journal of Communication* 59 (2, Spring 1995): 85-102.

Smith, Paul. "Domestic Labour and Marx's Theory of Value." In Annette Kuhn and AnnMarie Wolpe, Eds., *Feminism and Materialism: Women and Modes of Production.* London: Routledge and Kegan Paul, 1978. 198-219.

Smith, Sharon. "Mistaken Identity: Or, Can Identity Politics Liberate the Oppressed?"
International Socialism 62 (Spring 1994): 3-50.

Stabile, Carol. "Feminism and the Ends of Postmodernism." In Rosemary Hennessy and Chrys Ingraham, Eds., *Materialist Feminism: A Reader in Class, Difference, and Women's Lives (*New York: Routledge, 1997): 395-408.

_____. "Postmodernism, Feminism, and Marx: Notes from the Abyss." In Ellen Meiksins Wood and John Bellamy Foster, eds., *In Defense of History* (New York: Monthly Review P, 1997): 135-149.

Sullivan, Andrew. *Virtually Normal.* New York: Knopf, 1995.

Wang, Huei-ju. "Women's 'Oppression' and Property Relations: From Sati and Bride-Burning to Late Capitalist 'Domestic Labor' Theories," in this volume.

Warner, Michael. *Fear of a Queer Planet.* Minneapolis: U Minnesota P, 1993.

_____. *The Trouble With Normal:Sex, Politics, and the Ethics of Queer Life.* New York: Free Press, 1999.

Watney, Simon. "The Spectacle of AIDS." In Abelove, 202-211.

Weeks, Jeffrey. *Against Nature.* London: Rivers Oram Press, 1991.

Weston, Kath. *Families We Choose.* NY: Columbia UP, 1991.

Willis, Ellen. *No More Nice Girls.* Hanover and London: Wesleyan University Press, 1992.

Wilson, Colin. *Socialists and Gay Liberation.* London: Socialist Worker's Party, 1995.

Wood, Ellen Meiksins and John Bellamy Foster, eds. *In Defense of History: Marxism and the Postmodern Agenda.* New York: Monthly Review Press, 1997.

Wood, Ellen Meiksins and John Bellamy Foster. "Marxism and the Postmodern Agenda." *Monthly Review* 47 (3, 1995): special issue.

Wood, Ellen Meiksins. *The Retreat From Class.* London: Verso, 1986.

_____. "What is the 'Postmodern' Agenda?" *Monthly Review* 47 (3, 1995): 1-12.

Young, Iris Marion. "Gender as Seriality: Thinking About Women as a Social Collective." *Signs: Journal of Women in Culture and Society* 19 (1994): 713-738.

Zavarzadeh, Mas'ud. "Post-Ality: The (Dis)Simulations of Cyber-capitalism." *Transformation* 1 (Spring 1995): 1-75.

Zavarzadeh, Mas'ud, Teresa Ebert, and Donald Morton, eds. *Post-Ality: Marxism and Postmodernism. Transformation* 1 (1995).

Bob Nowlan

Post-Marxist Queer Theory

and "The Politics of AIDS"

> "The class struggle is sharpening. For now, the combatants on the other side of the trenches—the ruling class—are much more acutely aware of this than most of us are. But that is likely to change. And sooner rather than later."

> --Shelley Ettinger, "Afterword," *The Roots of Lesbian and Gay Oppression: A Marxist View*[1]

One

That progress toward ending the global AIDS epidemic has been very slow has everything to do with "politics."[2] Although there appears to be wide agreement on this premise, this essay opposes the dominant understanding of "politics"–specifically "the politics of AIDS"--circulated by queer left critics within the United States and Western Europe, especially the United Kingdom, in the years that have passed since "AIDS" was first "discovered." My aim here is to contribute to the development of a Marxist theory of "the politics of AIDS" first by situating the issues within the current ideological climate and then by critiquing the work of Cindy Patton and Simon Watney, whose writings are symptomatic of the dominant mode of queer left investigation of AIDS issues. Unlike the understanding of politics promoted by the queer left, my Marxist understanding foregrounds the question of need[3] and the question of class and therefore examines the discourses of culture and the significations of cultural texts as ideology in the classical Marxist sense of representations of the opposing material interests of different classes. When bourgeois theorists deploy the concept of ideology, they treat it as a cross-class effect of all discourses/representations/ textualities: on their view, ideology is a language effect and thus all uses of language are ideological in the sense that they produce not "truths" but merely textual "truth-effects." The result of such an understanding of ideology is to render all knowledges--as mere "knowledge-effects"-- equally unreliable. By contrast, I take ideology to be representations of class interests--general social materialities: representations, in other words, of the material logic of organization of society as a whole. Ideology critique is therefore the investigation of texts in relation to how they naturalize the economic interests of the ruling class and how they are positioned in class struggle.

In today's world of sharply increasing class disparities that are being accelerated by capitalism in its current globalizing form, it is more urgent than ever to oppose the bourgeois understanding of "the politics of AIDS," which relies on a purely discursive and theoretically eclectic understanding of the social inspired by Foucault (whose strong grip on bourgeois queer theory is signaled by the fact that he has lately been "sainted" by the queer left [Halperin, *Saint Foucault*]) that disconnects and localizes such issues as race, gender, class, sexual orientation, public health, ... on the grounds that each of these discursive zones requires its own specific and separate theorization, and on the ludic "politics" of "free play" theorized by Derrida, who argues, for instance, in his canonic essay "différance," that in considering all issues, philosophical, political, social, medical, sexual, . . . , "we must conceive of a play in which whoever loses wins, and in which one loses and wins on every turn" (20)--theoretical moves which only mystify and thereby sustain social inequality. By contrast, my approach rejects that linguistic idealism--consistently masked by post-al theorists as "inscriptive materialism" (see Warminski's "Introduction" to de Man's *Aesthetic Ideology*)--that underpins today's discussions of queer left politics (including the "politics of AIDS") and that has informed and dominated the queer left's discussion of all social issues from the early writings of that queer theorist before the letter Roland Barthes, for whom "everything is left to the power of the discourse" (*Sade* 136-137), to the equally influential recent (queer) writings of Judith Butler, where it reappears under the categories of "performativity" and "citationality."[4] The underlying idealist assumption of ludic queer theory—as of linguistic post-al theory in general--is that social issues are most fundamentally conditioned and shaped by the illusory, misleading, and unreliable conceptual categories constructed in the operations of language. Against this view, I follow here the argument of Marx and Engels in *The German Ideology* that "Language *is* practical, real consciousness" (Marx and Engels *Collected Works*, 5:44), by which they mean that language is itself both product and enabler of the social intercourse needed to carry out the requirements of production. It is in this broad Marxist context that Voloshinov regards the "sign" to be not simply a formal entity but "an arena of the class struggle" (Voloshinov 23). I am therefore arguing that it is not language but the mode of production which ultimately shapes and conditions the social and our understandings of it. At the broadest level, my aim here is to transform the queer left's notion of "the politics of AIDS" into an investigation of "the political economy of AIDS," that is, to situate questions which the dominant queer left critics treat in an experientialist, localized, pragmatic, reformist, and textuo-idealist fashion in the larger historical, structural, and material context of orthodox Marxist political economy that sees the base (mode of production) as ultimately determinative of the superstructure (the social institutions such as law, the family, philosophy, religion, love, friendship, public health, . . .).

The Marxist proposition that "The ideas of the ruling class are in every epoch the ruling ideas" (Marx and Engels, *Collected Works,* 5:59) applies to the contemporary discussions of AIDS: the "politics of AIDS" as formulated by the queer left is--in spite of claims to the contrary--fully complicit with ruling class (capitalist) interests, since its basic goal is to displace the revolutionary Marxist understanding of AIDS ("political economy") which works towards meeting the health care (and other) needs of all citizens (and therefore situates AIDS in relation to such other issues as breast cancer, sickle-cell anemia, environmental pollution, . . .) and to install in its place a merely reformist "politics of AIDS" which treats AIDS as a "separate" health issue of "special populations" and which is designed only to improve the health care for those (queer and other) citizens of the bourgeois and petit-bourgeois classes. In their inquiries into the "politics of AIDS," queer theorists such as Patton and Watney follow uncritique-ally the assumptions of post-structuralist and post-modernist theory in order to create the impression that orthodox Marxist social (including health care) analysis is—in the words of one leading bourgeois theorist, Judith Butler--"anachronistic" (Butler "Merely" 268). As Butler's recent attacks on Marxism ("Merely Cultural" and her remarks at the Left Conservatism Conference held in January, 1998, at the University of California, Santa Cruz ([http://www.jhu.edu/journals/theory_&_event/ v002/2.3q_ and _a. html]) clearly show, the contestation over questions of need (in relation to desire) have grown increasingly sharp in recent times, as global social inequities have accelerated. Her attack on what she calls "economism" indicates that under current sharpening conditions of class struggle, bourgeois theory has reached a new stage in which it is not enough to be "post-Marxist": the queer left has to declare itself--clearly, undeniably, and decidably--"anti-Marxist." Before getting to the specifics of the anti-Marxist "politics of AIDS" in the work of Patton and Watney, it is necessary to indicate at the outset how the queer left's program of post- (that is, anti-) Marxist social theory has been developed out of the writings of such post-al theorists as Derrida and Foucault.

Deconstruction's influence on the queer left's "politics of AIDS" can be seen mainly in the absorption of the Derridean (*Dissemination, The Gift of Time, Glas, The Ear of the Other*)--and to a lesser extent de Manian (*Allegories of Reading, Resistance to Theory, Aesthetic Ideology*)--notion of the indeterminacy/undecidability of all conceptual meaning which underlies the very (re)understanding of the "gay" as the "queer." Queer left praxis focuses not on seeking to create and conform to a new (sexual) identity but rather on refusing to accept and conform to any stable (sexual) identity whatsoever: thus Lee Edelman proposes that queers should "reinvent the politics of sexuality by insisting on the fluidity of differences without the need to affirm the difference of a cordoned-off 'politics' or 'activism'" (Edelman 31), and refuse to work within the bounds dictated by any conceptual categories which define "political activism" like any other category by "setting limits" to it. Instead, Edelman urges queers to embrace a "passive agency, an agency that acknowledges its inescapable participation in the production of social effects while acknowledging its inability to control the effects in whose production it thereby figures"--an agency whose foremost commitment is toward steadily striving to keep open space for "the unexpected," for "a zone of possibilities in which the embodiment of the subject might be experienced otherwise" (30-31). As Edelman himself is well aware, this queer left understanding of sexual difference simply reflects "a certain bourgeois aspiration to be always au courant" in its conception of "queer" "as the endlessly mutating token of nonassimilation (and hence as the utopian badge of a would-be 'authentic' position of resistance)" and in the end produces nothing but a version of identity politics as "postmodern commodity fetishism" (31). Given the fact that the queer left's notion of a completely fluid and unstable sexual difference/identity/desire has been effectively assimilated to capitalism today as a reinforcement of its interpellation of the subject as endlessly consuming subject (in Daniel Harris's terms, the homosexual as "strategic shopper" [Harris, 78]), the political bankruptcy of Edelman's "token" notion of "queer resistance" is starkly evident. It is significant to note that while Edelman advocates a passive agency for the queer left, his own institutional practices are quite aggressive. For example, according to the *Chronicle of Higher Education* (July 3, 1998), Edelman has actually insisted that, as a condition for accepting a new position in the Department of English at the State University of New York at Stony Brook, the University will have to give a position to his partner also. Far from being an instance of "passive resistance," this move of Edelman's is instead an instance of active (if not coercive) insistence.

By following post-al theory's privileging of the notion of the ultimate undecidability/indeterminacy of all social meanings, queer left politics--as an instance of deconstructive performativity and micropolitical discursive "resistance"--sees all "norms" as its enemy, not just the heterosexual norm but even the "norm" of social justice--and is therefore devoted to the subversion of all normative understandings. Its "politics" rests on the post-al assumption that oppression comes from the "regulatory" operations of clear concepts themselves: as Barbara Johnson has put it, "Nothing could be more comforting to the established order than the requirement that everything be assigned a clear meaning or stand" (Johnson, 30-31); and, in the words of Judith Butler, identity categories [represented through stable concepts] tend to be instruments or regulatory regimes, whether as the normalizing categories of oppressive structures or as the rallying points for a liberatory contestation of that very oppression" (Butler "Imitation" 13-14). What, on this view, most needs to be resisted are all concepts/discourses, since they are based on normative binaries which always operate by producing inclusions/exclusions (regulation) that are by definition "oppressive."

What post-al—including queer left--politics occludes is the fact that while binaries and norms ("regulatory regimes") can indeed be "deconstructed" in signifying practices as a rhetorical act, they cannot simply be "dispensed with" or "erased" because they are not mere linguistic or semiotic products but material practices produced historically by the laws of necessity, that is to say, by the material requirements of the mode of production and not by the "playfulness" of language. Under any given mode of production, relations of production are "regulated" by historically produced material requirements. Every society will therefore have its "norms" and "regulations" that are the inevitable material requirements of its mode of production. Given the material necessity of "norms" and "regulations," it follows then that far from being a politically "neutral" exposure of how signifying practices are always "oppressive," the post-al promotion of undecidability/indeterminacy (the deconstruction of "norms" and "regulations," the attack on "clear meaning") is actually an idealist rhetorical maneuver, an ideological maneuver of ruling class philosophers and critics aimed at obscuring the material determinants of social practices and at convincing citizens that all forms of knowledge are ultimately unreliable, especially that form of knowledge of the social totality that explains social injustice in the determinate, material terms of class struggle. Instead of calling, as Marxism does, for a determinate social and economic justice through revolutionary means, post-al politics (including queer left politics) substitutes "cultural justice," which is an indeterminate—fluid--"justice" that shifts constantly—and cannot therefore be clearly conceptualized as the basis of political praxis-- according to the constantly shifting differences of various cultural identities/differences/desires (Andrew Ross, *Real Love: The Pursuit of Cultural Justice*).

If Foucault has long been, in David Halperin's words, "a compelling model for an entire generation of scholars, critics, and activists" (Halperin 7), that is basically because he decisively shifts attention from the exploitation of labor to diverse forms of power and oppression; announces—like Derrida and all other post-al ideologues-- the end of the real possibility of systematic and structural analysis of the social and the end of any system-structural social change to overcome exploitation; and diverts the focus of critical and oppositional praxis from the global to the local, from "structure" to "event." In other words,

Foucault rejects in different terms all theories that claim to explain the system-wide and structural causes of injustice in the social totality. In the place of a structure and a system, Foucault introduces a multiplicity of simultaneously operating discursive formations of social regulation which he terms "technologies." He names, as the "four major types": "(1) technologies of production, which permit us to produce, transform, or manipulate things; (2) technologies of sign systems, which permit us to use signs, meanings, symbols, or signification; (3) technologies of power, which determine the conduct of individuals and submit them to certain ends or domination, an objectivizing of the subject; (4) technologies of the self, which permit individuals to effect by their own means, or with the help of others, a certain number of operations on their own bodies and souls, thoughts, conduct, and way of being, so as to transform themselves in order to attain a certain state of happiness, purity, wisdom, perfection, or immortality" (*Ethics* 224-225). Although Foucault remarks that "these four types of technologies hardly ever function separately" (225), there is clearly no necessary determinate relation between them (such as a determinate relation between production and the other "technologies"). When he adds that "each" technology is "a matrix of practical reason" (225), he furthermore reinforces the assumption that there is no inclusive theory that comprehends all these social practices. In Foucauldian theory, politics can only be a micropolitics of resistance that can no longer be lasting system-wide transformation or even substantial reformation but only temporary disruption and destabilization, since the latter is all that is "realistically"--pragmatically--possible. His emphasis on the Kantian category of "practical reason" (as opposed to "pure reason") is meant to situate the politics of these "technologies" within the domain of an experience-oriented "everyday" praxis. On this model, which shifts attention away from the social as a determinate system and structure shaped by material questions of need to the question of the specificity of the subject's "desire," politics is subsumed within ethics, in particular an ethics of self-assertion and self-actualization through self-invention and self-stylization. Although Foucault cautioned against the notion that "ethics is synonymous with the care of the self" (*Ethics* 285), such a conclusion can plausibly be drawn from his work and indeed has been drawn by neo-Foucauldian queer left writers who base their understanding of sexuality on it. For example, in *Gay and Lesbian Politics: Sexuality and the Emergence of a New Ethic*, Mark Blasius equates "ethics" with "care of the self" and repeatedly reasserts the Foucauldian formula ("sexual behavior is . . . a practice through which one constructs oneself [45]; "lesbians and gay men invent themselves" [183]; "lesbians and gay men virtually invent a way of life" [192]; "it is a practical creation of the self" [203]). This "new" Foucauldian ethics is an ethics of witness to and testimony for the strivings (for self-assertion and self-actualization through self-invention and self-stylization) of the distressed, the displaced, the dispossessed, and the downtrodden "other"; and an ethics of somatic, even visceral identification for the subject understood as a direct participant within an activist practice of especially immediate and physical "resistance" (*Discipline and Punish*) with whatever social groups are--at the given local place and in the given immediate time where the happens to be--the most thoroughly dominated and subjected by "power" (*History of Sexuality, vol.1*). Foucault's conception of power is of power which is both always everywhere and nowhere at the same time, a power which is unconditioned and undetermined, which, as a mysterious trans-substantial, trans-immanentist force, is beyond explanation and resistant to transformation *(History of Sexuality, vol.1)*. Foucauldians tend to assert that it is an illusion to believe that substantial social progress can be achieved, at least at this historical moment within modern society, through revolutionary social transformation. The aim of "resistance" on the part of the dominated/subjected subject is instead "survival." And yet this quite obviously limits "resistance" to finding the best way to cope, and as far as possible flourish, within existing social arrangements. Thus, even Foucault's own "activist" involvement in street battles with police does not testify to a greater radical authenticity as opposed to others who did not similarly "put their bodies on the line" as frequently as Foucault did (contrary to the claims of Foucauldian critics of Marxism such as Patton and Watney). Rather, it confirms how committed Foucault was toward contributing to the localizing reformist bourgeois project of preserving the status quo (with a human face). Moreover, Foucault's political activism is exemplary of the politics as ethics (and aesthetics) his theory advocates--directed toward limited, ad hoc, piecemeal, and localist reforms, but even more than this, toward a politics of mere "resistance." Foucauldian politics ultimately refuses to confront, challenge, and work to change *economic* structures, processes, and relations, and is therefore not concerned with bringing about substantial transformation at a fundamental, system-structural level. Foucault's own commitment to "indeterminacy" (a notion more commonly associated with Derrida and de Man) is clear when he remarks that "genealogy" is concerned not with "the anticipatory power of meaning" but only with "the hazardous play of dominations" ("Nietzsche, Genealogy, History" 148). For the question of AIDS, it is urgent to point out that Foucault extends his Nietzschean skepticism specifically to the discourses of science and medicine.

This skepticism is evident in the use Foucault makes (in his essay, "Life: Experience and Science") of the idea of "error" he draws from the work on science and scientific knowledges of Georges Canguilhem. As Foucault points out, Canguilhem develops (in *The Normal and the Pathological*) the notion that "life has led to a human being that is never completely in the right place, that is destined to 'err' and to be 'wrong'" (*Aesthetics* 470). In other words, life is defined as that which is "capable of error" (476), which is a way of saying what post-al queer theory has come to say: that the pathological (as *error*) is always already inscribed in the "true," the "right," the "normative." Just as Derrida proposes the notion that textuality is governed by the "alea," Foucault follows Canguilhem in proposing that "error is the permanent contingency [alea] around which the history of life and the development of human beings is coiled" (477). (I leave aside the almost biological "fatalism" that is mystified here as self-reflexivity.) On this view, which Foucault himself adopts, not only is knowledge in general always inscribed with "error," but in particular medical knowledges are NOT to be regarded as adequate and reliable accounts of objective conditions but as discursive formations that are always already marked with "error." As Foucault observes in his essay "On the Archaeology of the Sciences," "What must be characterized as clinical medicine is the coexistence of [a set of] dispersed and heterogeneous statements; it is the system that governs their distribution, the support they give to each other . . . .The rule of formation of these statements in their heterogeneity, in the very impossibility of their integration into a single syntactic chain, is what I shall term enunciative divergence. . . And I shall say that clinical medicine is characterized, as an individualized discursive set, by the divergence or the law of dispersion which governs the diversity of its statements" (*Aesthetics* 315). In other words, what governs the production of medical knowledges are NOT historical and objective conditions, but the rules internal to discourses themselves which are always marked by "error." Thus, for Foucault, . . . language is NOT— as Marx and Engels argue in *The German Ideology*—formed out of social necessity and shaped by and capable of approximating the objective historical conditions of production (including medical conditions); on the contrary, language is about language and cannot therefore give us reliable knowledges of objective conditions. Furthermore, when Foucault declares that, in the study of discursive formations, "the distinction between scientific and nonscientific is not pertinent: [that discursive formations] are epistemologically neutral" (Aesthetics 325), he is basically arguing that discourses and the knowledges they articulate cannot be prioritized or ranked in terms of their "truthfulness" or their connection with objective conditions. If all discourses are equally "true"--which is to say, of course, that they are equally "false," equally full of "error"—then of course the proletariat's claim that it is exploited under capitalism is no more "true" than the bourgeoisie's denial of its exploitative practices. In his essay, Foucault makes it quite clear that he values Canguilhem's work because it is a critique of epistemological claims, the claims to objectivity, of scientific knowledges. If, as Foucault remarks, we can recognize two incompatible and incommensurate kinds of theory/philosophy, "a philosophy of experience, of meaning, of the subject, and a philosophy of knowledge, of rationality, of the concept" (*Aesthetics* 466), then Canguilhem and Foucault himself are practitioners of the former and not the latter. Such a valuing of a philosophy of experience as separable from a philosophy of the concept has the political effect so desirable to bourgeois ideologues of placing experience beyond the reach of concept-based ideology critique.

Such notions as shifting justice and the undecidability of all knowledges--which Foucault's work supports--certainly raises a number of critical questions for public health: What, for example, does the "queering" of all knowledges including the knowledges of science--the rendering of the knowledges of medical science "uncertain" and "unreliable"—mean for "the politics of AIDS"? To those suffering from so serious an illness, what possible benefit can derive from the queer left's declaration of the impossibility of a reliable and certain (medical) knowledge? Is the effect of such a declaration the "freeing" of desire from the illusory chains of reason (as post-al theorists claim), or is it merely an ideological maneuver to lower the working masses's expectations of the health care system, a move quite convenient to capitalists who do not wish to be taxed to support public health? This rejection of the idea of reliable knowledges, the rejection of any determinate theory of the social, and the consequent rejection of the analysis of economic structures and class struggle as socially determinate is precisely what makes the queer left's politics in general--and its "politics of AIDS" in particular--not merely post- but anti-Marxist.

Two

In the late 1990's, AIDS remains--in most affected parts of the world--a pandemic of massive and tragic proportions, yet in the economically advanced capitalist democracies, it is undergoing a historical change through medical advances producing drug-cocktail therapies that are transforming--for those who can afford it--what was only a short time ago an inevitably fatal syndrome into something more like a manageable "'chronic' disease" (Gagnon and Nardi 3). While bourgeois commentators (who cannot ignore these remarkable transformations) are sometimes satisfied to speak vaguely of "changing times" in relation to "HIV/AIDS" (Levine, et al.), these historic changes must be examined and accounted for in determinate and specific— politico-economic--terms. Thus like organ transplants and other scientific advances, the new AIDS treatments—developed under capitalist exploitation--are prolonging life for a very small fraction of the world's relatively wealthy citizens while remaining entirely out of reach of most people suffering from the disease. In the wake of new medical treatments, the conservative gay writer Andrew Sullivan was emboldened in November, 1996, to declare the "end" of the AIDS epidemic (Sullivan "When Plague Ends") and *Newsweek* magazine followed up a few weeks later with an article on "The End of AIDS?" (Leland). However, the "end of AIDS" Sullivan envisioned (whether actual or not) was an "end of AIDS" only for those in the owning class whose privileges Sullivan has always worked to defend. In other words, while under current economic, social, political, medical, . . . conditions, some are experiencing remarkable progress in the treatment of the disease, countless others are experiencing deprivation and death. In the gay/lesbian/queer . . . global community, this progress in AIDS treatment is being largely enjoyed by those in what bourgeois sociologists call like to call "the middle class" who can afford the new drugs, a situation resulting largely from the widely recognized and much heralded *queer assimilation to capitalism.*

No investigation of the political economy of AIDS in the 1990s can afford to overlook the fact that queer assimilation to capitalism in the US, which is showing the way for other core countries, has reached a stage of unquestionable "success": Richard Mohr, for example, has recently declared that "America is at a turning point on gay issues and is undergoing an important structural change that bodes well for the long haul" (Mohr 332) and Daniel Harris writes that this change is the result of "the accelerating pace of . . . assimilation into mainstream society" (Harris 4). Charles Kaiser's articulation of this "success" has been even bolder. In his recent study of the "gay metropolis" (which is literally New York City, but figuratively "every place on every continent where gay people have found the courage and dignity to be free" [Kaiser xii]), Kaiser claims to be telling "the story of an amazing victory over adversity: how America's most despised minority overcame religious prejudice, medical malpractice, political persecution and one of the worst scourges of the twentieth century to stake its rightful claim to the American dream—all in barely more than half a century" (vi). Yet both the anxiety and guilt which accompany this "success" are also readily evident today, for instance, in the uneasy triumphalism of the *Village Voice's* 1998 'queer" issue (its annual commemoration of Stonewall): while the cover declares that "it's a gay world. straight people just live in it" ("The Queer Issue" 1), the lead article inside acknowledges that successful assimilation means the assimilation into capitalism of the queer "middle class" (Goldstein 49) and expresses a fear of the "banalizing impact of mainstreaming— . . . that it means the end of gay culture" (Goldstein 44). The queer left's enthusiastic embrace of capitalism is amply documented in *The Rise and Fall of Gay Culture* by Harris, who—rejecting a Marxist interpretation that is seriously critical of capitalism--insists that "the commercialization of gay culture was not an act of rape, of colonialist expansionism, of an unprincipled oppressor preying upon the defenseless minority that groveled at its feet," and that on the contrary "the selling of gay culture was . . . a profitable intersection of interests . . . that homosexuals have fought long and hard to bring about" (Harris 6). Thus, according to its own spokespersons, what was once pitched as "gay liberation" has been taken over in the 1990s by a queer mainstream composed of energetic and compliant marketeers. In order to encourage and reinforce the process of assimilation and smooth its path to "success," the bourgeois queer left has been busy in the past few years trying to use its "economic muscle" through "strategic acts of shopping" to effect reformist "change" (Harris 78), which is to say that the queer left has--knowingly--been in full complicity with "the economic exploitation of homosexuals" (Harris 83). The reformist practice of "strategic shopping" (instead of the revolutionary practice of class struggle) is, of course, a well-established dogma in contemporary left circles (for example, Yudice and Fiske). These practices have their root in de Certeau's thesis of "tactics" and strategies" in *The Practice of Everyday Life*. Their newly achieved "success" (assimilation) has made queer ideologues even more acutely attentive to ruling class interests and sensitive (from the ruling class perspective) about the ever-widening global economic disparity between the owning class and the working class and of the ever-widening class inequality of access to medical treatment for all illnesses, including treatments for AIDS. In the wake of queer assimilation and the queer left's abandonment of any residue of interest in struggling against capitalism, the queer left's understanding of "the politics of AIDS" has reached a new phase in the US today: as Gagnon and Nardi put it, the late 1990s is the period of "transition between the era of AIDS and the era of post-AIDS" (Gagnon and Nardi 13), a time when HIV/AIDS no longer has "first place in the panoply of gay issues" (13). This is the case because the goals the queer left set for AIDS intervention (the reformist goal of increasing the access of middle class gay men and other middle class minorities to specific treatments and specific resources of the bourgeois health care system, NOT radically changing that class-based health care system itself to provide equal access to all) have more or less been reached. As Harris points out, the assimilation of queers to capitalism (and the smooth connection of middle class queers to the corporate health care system) is a project that has found "an unlikely ally in the epidemic" (Harris 236) because the epidemic has been the occasion for corporate America to demonstrate—through advertising and much publicized philanthropy--its "compassion" and "good samaritanship" (236). In this era of "strengthened bonds between the gay community and the business world" (236), the queer left has simply accepted the fact that "the politics of AIDS" is ultimately just the politics of "the market." For the queer left, what passes as "politics" is nothing but an internal competition between consumers (now including openly queer consumers) to get corporations to produce products to meet "queer desires" and a competition between different branches of entrepreneurs in the pro-capitalist queer community. In this competition, queer marketeers, who are successfully commodifying the "gay lifestyle" for sale on the market to those who can afford it, are competing with drug marketeers, who are likewise selling health care to those who can afford it. Both groups, in other words, are competing against each other for the consumer dollar and both groups are competing for relative advantage in a class-based exploitative system which is structured on the sole imperative of producing profit and fights desperately against the mere mention (much less the institution) of an alternative economic system—socialism—which, moving beyond class society, is structured on the "other" imperative of fulfilling the needs of all citizens. That the queer left's approach to AIDS has indeed been a politics that leaves the economic status quo intact is clear from Mark Blasius's Foucauldian analysis of "the politics of AIDS." As Blasius remarks, "A 'politics of AIDS' problematizes the exercise of power by people who would tell us how to live through their knowledge . . . of risk factors for contracting the disease, through their medical knowledge of how to preserve the lives of those who have the disease, and through their knowledge of how to 'cope' with the cultural manifestations of the disease" (Blasius 165). The Foucauldian approach to AIDS has therefore been an attempt to intervene in "these 'pastoral' forms of power" which "operate through techniques of subjection" (165). Blasius makes it clear that these negotiations over power start from and remain within--in the manner recommended by de Certeau--the established "specific power relations in 'everyday life'" (165). In other words, these negotiations are strictly reformist since they take place within the established economic status quo.

It has to be emphasized that the situation at the end of the 1990s is highly contradictory: it is precisely during this period of queer assimilation that all workers (straight/lesbian/gay . . .) have simultaneously grown increasingly aware of global capitalism's exploitative practices and have seen their health care privatized under the management of HMOs and accountants concerned only with profit. Under these conditions, it has become much more likely that members of the working class—whatever their sexuality/ethnicity/race/gender . . . -- will lose faith in the possibilities of capitalist reformism, recognize more clearly the consequences of the fact that "the class struggle is sharpening," and take up an active role against ruling class interests. To offset this possibility, the queer left has not simply "passively"—to use Edelman's word--accepted its assimilation to capitalism but has in fact launched a vigorous pro-reformist and anti-revolutionary—pro-capitalist and anti-Marxist—campaign, expanding throughout the decade, aimed at convincing workers to be loyal to capitalism no matter what the cost and at frightening them away from the revolutionary movement.[5]

Three

The discussion of AIDS (like that of all social questions) has to be situated in the contemporary ideological climate: it must therefore be emphasized that what the queer left has long been promoting as a "subtle," "sophisticated," and "undecidable" "post-Marxist" social theory has turned more and more sharply, obviously, and decidably into one that is virulently "anti-Marxist" and pro-capitalist. In the wake of Stonewall, when questions of need were more prominently foregrounded, many gays and lesbians embraced revolutionary Marxist explanations of social injustice and analyzed questions of sexuality in terms of such categories as production, class, labor, exploitation, . . . However, since the beginning of the 1990s—marked by the arrival of "queer theory," by the successful "assimilation" of middle-class queers to capitalism, by the near wholesale rejection of questions of need and the saturation of all social institutions and practices with questions of desire (inspired by dominant ideology provided by post-al theory)--there has been a growing queer left attack on revolutionary Marxism, under various code-words, for instance, "Bolshevism" for Ellis Hanson and "orthodoxy" for Judith Butler.[6]

An exemplary instance of this anti-Marxist gay theory is Simon Edge's recent book, *With Friends Like These: Marxism and Gay Politics*. Edge tries to place his readers in an "autonomous" space beyond conventional notions of left and right, emphatically rejects revolution in favor of reform, and endorses treating sexuality—like all other social practices and issues--on a subjectivist and experiential basis. Because it makes the special claim of being based on an "insider's knowledge" of Marxism (the author declares himself a "former Trotskyist--now happily out and proud as a separatist," 3), Edge's book seems to acquire greater politico-intellectual authority than most other denunciations of revolutionary theory. Like other recent queer apologists for capitalism, Edge—following the lead of such virulently anti-Bolshevik writers as Simon Karlinsky[7], many of whose reactionary views he specifically cites-- makes a sharp attack on revolutionary orthodoxy, arguing specifically that the idea "that the socialist tradition, with the Bolshevik Revolution at its apogee, has an exemplary record on gay issues" is a "bare-faced lie which should be exposed once and for all" (4). What most gay/lesbian/queer . . . readers of Edge's diatribe may likely not recognize is the subterfuge by which Edge makes his "argument." Because the bourgeois academy and the allied culture industry has been so successful in excluding revolutionary Marxist knowledges from general circulation, most readers will not "know" when he is speaking "authoritatively" about Marxism from "inside," and when he is just spouting the most banal, commonsensical "complaints." To convince his audience of his authenticity and the authority of his "thinking," Edge starts out by insisting that he still takes Marxism seriously, that the Marxist theory of homosexuality "is a good one," and that it "provides a more convincing explanation of lesbian and gay oppression than the alternative theories" (8). He then immediately and without any theoretical argument at all abandons Marxist theory and accounts for his disillusion with Marxism not on theoretical grounds but on the grounds of "personal experience." Rejecting not just Marxist theory but theory per se, Edge recommends that readers follow (albeit at a very commonsensical and non-philosophical level) the "projects before principles" approach to politics made famous today by Richard Rorty.[8] Like Rorty, Edge approaches social questions through empirical experiment and experiential pragmatism: forget about theory and objective explanations of social injustice, he recommends, and instead "Do X and see how you feel." As a model, Edge offers his readers the template of his own life narrative: he "came out in 1988 around the same time [he] joined the S[ocialist] W[orders] P[arty]" (11), was warned away from the gay scene by his Trotskyist mentors (12), then went on the "scene" and found it "profoundly liberating . . . and left the SWP shortly afterwards" (12). Thus subjectivism (how a particular person "feels" after engaging in particular social practices) completely displaces any objective analysis of the social totality. Far from being a historical materialist or "Marxist insider's" account, Edge's purely idealist text supports an autonomous lesbian/gay movement making headway through "capitalist consumerism"[9]; argues that under capitalism successful reforms have--pragmatically--been achieved that have improved the lot of most homosexuals; assumes that historical change and homophobia are not politico-economic and structural but the results of voluntarist actions and prejudicial "attitudes." Without ever explaining his non-Marxist understanding of the relation of sexuality to class, Edge attacks revolutionary Marxism as basically a heterosexist plot and appeals to lesbians and gays to embrace assimilation to capitalism. His argument rests on the underlying classist assumption that what's good for the lesbian/gay/queer . . . bourgeoisie is good for the lesbian/gay/queer . . . proletariat. Edge's basic strategy is the one the bourgeoisie has always used: he tries to frighten lesbian and gay readers by putting forward as exemplary of Marxist views a distorted notion of Marxist sexual theory according to which homosexuality is a "diseased" form of sexuality produced by class societies, a form which will therefore disappear after the revolution. Again, such a version of "Marxism"—promoted by a writer with the supposed "authority" of a one-time "insider"--overlooks the most basic elements of the historical materialist view: the fact that historical materialism regards all modes of sexuality to be affected (though not "caused") by the mode of production (whatever that mode might be) and forgets especially Marx's forceful rejection of the notion that historical materialism is a form of utopian thinking that can "predict" the future. Edge's text provides a clear signal of the pro-capitalist queer "left's" growing desperation: at a time when the contradictions of liberal capitalist democracy and the limits of capitalist "reformism" have become increasingly clear and when more and more working class lesbians and gays may find Marxist explanations more compelling than ever, Edge tries to warn them away from historical materialism with the fiction that revolutionary Marxists are not interested in "finding the best strategy to overcome gay oppression . . . [but only in] winning lesbian and gay recruits to a wider struggle against capitalism" (46). Thus, the ideological function of Edge's text is to defend the status quo and the interests of the ruling class by dividing workers from each other along the lines of sexual difference.

Edge also endorses "strategic shopping" by arguing that capitalism has proved "'it can as easily deliver gay liberation as Gucci loafers'" (14) and argues that gays and lesbians should therefore continue the "consumerist" approach to "liberation" because they don't really know yet—experientially--how far capitalism will go to accommodate their interests and they therefore need to test capitalism's limits further. However, any one-time Marxist "insider" should already know that contradictions of the liberal capitalist state dictate that it can only go so far in eradicating homophobia, just as it can only go so far to eradicate sexism and racism. While it is very much in the interests of capital to accommodate to the facts that today's workplace is indeed a "multicultural workplace" and that workers with sometimes vastly different understandings of social and cultural values and issues must be able to work effectively together, it is also in the interests of capital to emphasize social and cultural differences as a source of suspicion and division between elements of the workforce so that the members of each group will see their interests as basically opposed to the interests of the other groups rather than seeing that indeed the interests of all workers worldwide are basically opposed to the interests of the ruling class. Under capitalism, homophobia is therefore, on the one hand, a threat to the requirements of cooperation in the workplace which capitalists must minimize for the sake of productivity and, on the other hand, a useful tool for dividing and controlling workers. Edge asks his readers to believe in a version of capitalist "trickle-down" theory; while he recognizes that it is middle-class gays who are the ones benefited most under capitalism (not everyone can buy Gucci loafers), he argues that the "bartenders, shop assistants, office workers and rent boys . . . are just as much a part of the gay scene as the accountants and fashion designers" (22). Of course, that working class gays and lesbians in some way take part in the same "scene" as bourgeois gays and lesbians--that there is an overlap of "physical presence"--hardly erases their class differences.

That members of the working class as well as multi-millionaire Hollywood celebrities are both "present" at a Los Angeles Lakers basketball game does not erase the class differences between them. Here, posing as an authority on Marxism, Edge repeats the banal, intellectually and theoretically empty notion of a social "unity" based on physical "co-presence" that Lenin once critiqued as the "elementary ignorance" which assumes that "'the social form of labour' 'amounts' to 'working under one roof'!" (Marx, Engels, Lenin 347).

Edge's reasonable sounding practical approach to social questions is nothing more than a cover for the queer left's complicity with capitalist exploitation. Edge concludes his book by recommending that the same pragmatism and experientialism should be applied to AIDS, where it will—he proposes--bring about a more "honest political response" to the disease (52). (As I shall shortly indicate in my discussion of the work of Patton and Watney, the queer left's approach to AIDS has already accepted this kind of pragmatism and experientialism, which assumes a theoretical separatism—that desire is separate from need and requires a theory not determinately related to need—because queer/gay/lesbian/. . . persons *experience* these dimensions of their lives as "separate.") What Edge's version of "honesty" means--as his book makes clear --is to completely set aside any consideration of the political economy of AIDS in historical materialist terms and to simply take the pragmatic position which says "we are doing the best that we can under the present conditions" and NOT working in any effective way to bring about fundamental change in the "present conditions." Taking the "experiential" and "pragmatic" response to AIDS will leave things as they are: instead of health care—like food, clothing, shelter, education, ... –being acknowledged as needs that the politico-economic system should dependably fulfill *for all*, it is seen simply as a commodity one can have *only* if one has the ability to pay.[10]

Four

Little effort need be spent on establishing that the dominant queer academy's writers on "the politics of AIDS" have wholeheartedly accepted the post-al theoretical framework for their investigations. Such exemplary texts as Simon Watney's first book, *Policing Desire: Pornography, AIDS and the Media* not only foregrounds "desire" (as opposed to "need") as its privileged category but also adopts the Foucauldian notion of "power" (not exploitation) as the central political category (*Policing* 16) and collapses questions of politics into the "matter" of signification. In fact, he opens the book with the announcement that "this . . . will be a book about representation, written from the belief that we can only ultimately conceive of ourselves and one another in relation to the circulation of available images in any given society" (*Policing* 8). In another canonic text of AIDS literature, *Sex and Germs* Cindy Patton explicitly declares that "the post-structuralist philosophers offered the most useful tools for understanding the sex wars and the AIDS sex panic" (*Sex* 108) and, from Patton's subsequent description of these "tools," it seems that Foucault has provided by far the "most useful."

This is "old news": what is much more politically significant is the fact that Patton and Watney have found it urgently necessary to couple their post-al analyses of the AIDS global epidemic with a broad and ongoing attack on historical materialism. In other words, in taking up questions of public health, they find it absolutely necessary to attack the only theory that threatens the capitalist system of exploitation which gives a material advantage in medical treatment to the queer (as well as straight) upper middle class. Instead of an analysis that relates the injustices of AIDS health care to the structural inequalities under capitalism, they recommend instead the "hopeful" *utopian* pathway of subjectivism, experientialism, and pragmatic ameliorative reform of medical care. They are, in other words, engaged--in a more and more overt manner--in the class struggle *on the side of the bourgeoisie.*

In their various texts, Patton and Watney manage to repeat a whole series of by now routine and very tired anti-Marxist--especially anti-Bolshevik--clichés. Watney's first book, *Policing Desire*, written in the mid-1980s, is full of exuberant confidence that "the politics of AIDS" could be effectively reduced to a Foucauldian "politics of representation," and Watney therefore has little to say about Marxism. However, by the publication a decade later of *Practices of Freedom* (1994), when economic injustices are increasingly glaring and representationalism is patently suspect and bankrupt, Watney alters his approach. He tries to place his representationalist politics in a "historical context" by suddenly "remembering" his own personal "history." So like Edge, collapsing "history" into "personal history," Watney situates himself as a one-time pro-Marxist "insider" (as a member of the British Gay Left Collective of the 1970s) who, having thought through the political issues long before the AIDS epidemic, had rejected Marx and Lenin in favor of Freud, Gramsci, and Foucault (*Practices* xi). While Watney (like Edge, who says he firmly believes in the validity of the Marxist theory of sexuality) nominally insists that it is necessary to provide a class analysis of British society (he formally acknowledges the "centrality of class in British society," *Practices* 132), it is "impossible" (according to him) to "understand or intervene in the political struggles around AIDS in class terms alone" (*Practices* 132), as if that is what Marxism tries to do: in actuality, the Marxist approach—instead of disconnecting sexuality from race or sexuality from gender or sexuality from class (as Foucault teaches his followers to do) rigorously relates and connects questions of desire to questions of need, relates and connects the issue of class to other issues of race, gender, sexuality, . . . In other words, Marxism argues that the capitalist mode of production shapes the social relations of production and shapes the consciousness (including the sexual/race/gender . . . consciousness) of those living under capitalism and that any social analysis which fails to explain the shaping effects of the mode of production on all social practices is inadequate to the task of accounting for social injustice. It is because Marxists are uncompromising on this insistence on the necessity of an analysis of the interconnectedness of these issues that Watney accuses them of following the path of "puritanical separatism" (*Practices* 152). It is in fact the followers of post-al theory like Watney who are setting up a "separatism" at the theoretical level by which they insist–like Foucault with his doctrine of "emergence" ("Nietzsche, Genealogy, History," 148ff.)—that each social problem (race, class, gender, . . .) belongs to an autonomous realm of its own and therefore requires its own autonomous (separate) theory. This is separatism with a vengeance. Like Edge, Watney asks his readers to agree with his rejection of Marxism simply on the basis of a narrative of his own personal "experience" as a one-time "insider" (who got "out") and by *ad hominem* attacks on Marxists as merely "self-righteous" people (*Practices* 132), and not by providing rigorous critiques of Marxist theory. Like the writers already discussed, Watney rejects any form of system-structural analysis of the social totality. In fact he is opposed to any notion of what he calls a "unified homophobia," any analysis based on a "functionalism which glimpses either a unified purposive state or coherent collectivity of 'heterosexuality' at work behind social and psychic attitudes towards AIDS" (*Practices* 13). In other words, in typical post-al fashion, Watney, who has accepted the post-al notions of desire, irrationality, indeterminacy, incoherence, specificity, anti-foundationalism, de-structuring, . . . , rejects out of hand Marxist social theory which relies on such concepts as "functionalist" "need" (material priorities), "unity" (the social totality), "coherence" (rationality), "purposiveness" (determinateness), or "collectivity" (worker solidarity).

Like Edge, Watney--who argues that in the AIDS debates what is ultimately at stake are "fundamental questions about the meaning of democracy in modern British society" (*Practices* 153)--urges queers to work "pragmatically" within the status quo. Watney is explicit in delineating the ultimately "pragmatic" trajectory of his AIDS activist praxis: "all along my aim has been to contribute what I could to the design and implementation of rational, humane and demonstrably effective social *policies* [my emphasis] in relation to AIDS" (*Practices* xviii). By focusing his aim on "policies," Watney is of course accepting that changes within the structures provided by existing social institutions and enterprises will prove sufficient, and that there will not be any need to transform these institutions and enterprises to realize his goal. Watney believes that his aim can be achieved by supporting the greatest possible local autonomy for the varied particular "communities" which must confront HIV and AIDS in their own unique ways. Insofar as it is necessary to work beyond one's own local and particular community, it is necessary to "lobby and organise on behalf of changes in the law and greater Parliamentary political representation" (*Practices* 44). This is, Watney conceives, the short-term goal of British AIDS activism as it organizes and operates on a national scale; "in the longer term," the objective must be to reform the system of British national government so that it would proceed on the basis of a written Constitution, with a Bill of Rights, as is the case in the United States (*Practices* 45). Watney here implies, in a position very much akin to that of the American Civil Liberties Union, that this kind of foundational document (leaving aside, for the moment the epistemological incoherence involved in the demand for a founding text by an anti-foundationalist queer writer) is necessary because it can provide effective protection for "minority communities" in a "democratic society." Of course, this kind of position abstracts politics from economics, accepts the bourgeois demarcation of "private" versus "public" as if this were simply as innocent and neutral as it is conventionally ideologically represented to be, and conflates formal with substantial democracy. The fact that Watney considers anything beyond constitutional reform to be impractical and unnecessary is further underlined when he praises the late Princess Diana at the end of his essay "Short-Term Companions: AIDS and 'Popular Entertainment'" for her ability "to fully understand the significance of re-narrating AIDS as a national issue" (*Practices* 220). As Watney elaborates, "after all, who could be better placed to extend popular notions of national identity than the most glamorous and popular embodiment of British nationalism" (*Practices* 220). As this remark indicates, Watney is interested in "extending" "popular notions of national identity" so that these will include people living with AIDS, and, in particular gay people living with AIDS. The nation need not be in any way fundamentally--that is *systemically* or *structurally*--transformed so as to overcome and abolish anachronistic institutions like the monarchy, the peerage, and the aristocracy, together with the bourgeois expropriation of surplus value from surplus labor (evidently the constitutional reforms Watney favors will be compatible with maintaining Britain as a constitutional monarchy); it only needs to be somewhat more generously inclusive in its prevailing ideological manifestations, and it will be enough if its feudal and bourgeois elites offer a "kinder and gentler"--and more "glamorous and popular"--face to the oppressed and exploited masses of the larger British population.

Like Edge, who "switched" from a Trotskyite to a gay bar-scene "collectivity" because the experience of this move made him "feel better,"

Watney uses the notion of "collectivity" in a manner designed to mystify and confuse his queer readers while appealing to their feelings of "moral outrage" to make them "feel better." He marshals queer outrage by arguing that "Aids [sic] has been used quite cynically to shore up the fabric of the ideology of patriotic heterosexuality," and to defend "the family," the "sacred and largely imaginary locus of neo-conservatism" from external and internal opponents which threaten to bring about its "imminent collapse" (*Policing Desire* 15-16). According to Watney, it is "this dream-like fantasy of a nation which only exists as individuals in closed family units, supervised by government," that neo-conservatism "both draws on and wishes to impose with the full force of law," and it is in this respect that AIDS has been used to represent a crisis not only in "family values," but also, and directly following from this "decadent" "assault" on the family, a crisis as well in consent to state power and government authority. Watney contends that representations of "the AIDS crisis" have been used by neo-conservative forces as a key part of a much larger effort to rally individuals to re-identity with the nation: and, in particular, to re-identify with a highly conservative and exclusive image of what national identity can and should involve. This is an identity that tends to delegitimate identity within collectivities other than the nation and the family. Watney charges that neo-conservative use of AIDS has been part of an even larger ideological assault "on all social values rooted in collectivities which are incompatible with . . . individualist absolutism"("Taking Liberties 24), and, furthermore, that it is "very clear that the collective response to AIDS by so many lesbians and gay men is deeply threatening to the ruthless individualism of much contemporary conservative culture, which lacks any vision of community beyond the impoverished ideals of 'family' and 'nation'" (*Policing Desire* xii).

Watney claims that conservatives are engaged in an ideological maneuver to resecure traditional notions of collectivity (traditional notions of selfhood, family, nation, . . .): by marshalling their "moral outrage" in defense of such notions, they simply "make themselves feel better." Yet Watney is only producing the same ideological maneuver in reverse: he is writing not to educate his readers about the laws of necessity that determine and shape the social totality but basically to make himself and his queer left readers "feel better" by defending the new notions of collectivity compatible with capitalism in its latest stage (contemporary notions of self, family, nation, . . .) that are threatening the old ones. No more than the conservatives against whom they are fighting do queer left writers like Watney or Patton provide a rigorous materialist explanation of how social change comes about, and in this particular case, how it is that new notions of collectivity are now superseding old notions. As Marx observes, "At a certain stage of development, the material productive forces of society come into conflict with the existing relations of production . . . Then begins an era of social revolution. The changes in the economic foundation lead sooner or later to the transformation of the whole immense superstructure. In studying such transformations it is always necessary to distinguish between the material transformation of the economic conditions of production . . . and the . . . ideological forms in which men become conscious of this conflict and fight it out" (Marx *A Contribution* 21). In its latest stage, capitalism has created a new social formation of which the newly assimilated queer subject is one part. Because Watney's queer leftism is, in the last analysis, only a cultural leftism, the "collectivity" it completely ignores is the one produced by global capitalism: the systematic collectivization of workers of the world whose labor is exploited to produce profit for the ruling class.

In her discussion of the "politics of AIDS," Patton repeats the same anti-Marxist, "separatist" theoretical moves we have seen in Edge and Watney: in *Sex and Germs* she claims that Marxism conceives of sexuality in an economistically reductive fashion that cannot acknowledge sexuality "as a separate form of oppression" (*Sex* 103), cannot appreciate "the profound and anarchistic possibilities of liberating sexual identity from gender, class, race" (*Sex* 153), and is thereby unable to account for the "autonomy" of "sexualities" as discourses and practices (*Sex* 109), of "the body as the site of human subjectivity" (*Sex* 106), and the extent to which language and discourse in fact "create subjectivity" (*Sex* 108). In all these comments, Patton is simply repeating (like a mantra) the most familiar clichés of (bourgeois) post-al theory: she puts these ideas forward as seemingly uncontestable (as needing no theoretical argument), as if it is self-evidently necessary for the sexual margins to accept the currently dominant dogma about the "autonomy of sexuality" from race, class, gender, . . .

Patton makes a sweeping indictment of Marxism by arguing that its "inability to value sexual expression inverts marxist/socialist analysis of sexuality" and that this shows up in the ways that Marxist socialists 1. tend to view "the proliferation of sexual practice within the gay male community . . . as excess, rather than decrying the *lack* of free sexual expression within the heterosexual nuclear family (worker or not)"; 2. rarely place sexuality "on a par" with "'material' needs, even though sexual practice and identity are profoundly interconnected with material relations"; and 3. tend to "duck the topic" of sexuality "despite ample excellent historical work by feminists and lesbian/gay historians that [shows] throughout industrial history 'workers' have sought out and structured a sexual world" (*Sex* 154). Here Patton follows the usual activist pattern of celebrating a particular resistant social group's efforts to "make its own history" without explaining that this history-making is always conditioned and shaped by the historical circumstances created by productive practices. Furthermore, she attributes to Marxists the notion that sexuality is not "on a par" with material needs. In fact, Marxists *do* recognize sexual needs among others, but they know what

Patton ignores: that there are always priorities among needs (food, shelter, clothing, . . .) and that it is not people but objective historical conditions which ultimately set those priorities for society.

Given this supposed failure of Marxism, Patton sees it as "no great surprise" that the Marxist socialist left "did not leap up for duty in the AIDS crisis, even though the people with AIDS included activist leftists, racial minorities, working-class people, women, prostitutes, and drug users" (*Sex* 154). Patton is basically repeating the (false) claim that Marxism has no theory of sexuality and therefore cannot respond to questions about sexual practices or even to illnesses associated in any way with sexuality. Marxists certainly *do* care about AIDS as a disease and about the plight of AIDS patients, but they insist that AIDS be understood not in isolation but in relation to other health issues such as breast cancer, sickle-cell anemia, environmental pollution, . . . that is to say, within the context of public health for all. She forgets that her own notion of the "autonomy" of social differences would lead exactly to the kind of "disinterest" she falsely attributes to Marxists: under her notion of "autonomous desire" and its consequently "separatist" politics, different social groups would have a difficult time explaining to themselves why they should ever be interested in the problems of other groups (except for forming ad hoc, occasional, and temporary coalitionist alliances in emergency circumstances). The queer left insists on treating the AIDS epidemic--like everything else--as an "autonomous" issue, in the manner of mainstream "issues politics." Marxism does have a theory of sexuality, but it is obviously one that Patton, Watney and the other members of the queer left *do not like* because it relates all social (including sexual) practices to the shaping effects of the social division of labor and the mode of production in a class society and starts from the assumption that social issues are (I repeat) NOT prioritized by the free choices of individuals (particular people are therefore not to blame) but by the material requirements of the mode of production.

Patton devotes a great deal of rhetorical energy to breaking up worker solidarity, specifically by encouraging gays and lesbians to think of themselves as inevitably "at odds" with (separate from) heterosexuals: Marxism, she claims, consigns gays and lesbians "to the list of people who must be tolerated despite some peculiar difference" (*Sex* 153). Like Edge, Patton dismisses "the marxist/socialist tradition" for "having no good answer" as to "how to strategize for sexual liberation" (*Sex* 153). Like Edge, she charges Marxists with "erotophobia," with viewing "the proliferation of sexual practice within the gay male community . . . as an excess, rather than decrying the *lack* of free sexual expression within the heterosexual nuclear family (worker or not)" (*Sex* 154). Taking need into account, Marxists must indeed make a distinction between social problems created by excess and social problems created by lack. Unable to recognize this theoretical distinction, Patton, like other desire-theorists, assumes that "the proliferation of sexual practice" is a sign of increasing "freedom" and in itself produces more "freedom" and that it is the "heterosexual nuclear family" as such ("worker or not") that is unfree (here she treats the "family" specifically as a trans-class concept). She completely "neglects" to articulate the Marxist view by which sexuality, like any other issue, should be treated as a scientific question and theorized as a social issue of equality. She fails to explain how "more sex" of any kind will overcome the massive world-wide deprivation produced by an economic system that fails to satisfy workers's basic needs. It is indeed "excessive" to assume that "more sex" and "more sexual pleasure"—of any kind for any one--is the answer either to hunger, poverty, homelessness, the inequalities of the health care system, . . . or to homophobia itself. Like the rest of the queer left, Patton defines homophobia in an entirely subjectivist fashion (in her words, as "the fear of homosexuals or homosexuality," *Sex* 153), that is to say, as a "bad attitude" or "state of mind" of individuals, when in fact homophobia is a structural relation of inequality produced in the social relations of production under the capitalist mode of production. Patton argues that where gay/queer "liberation" is concerned the differences break down between "the left" and "the right"--both being supposedly dominated by non-promiscuous heterosexuals who have all too "blindly" and all too "docilely" submitted themselves to the acceptance of the social regulation of sexuality. As before on the question of "excess," Patton neglects here other theoretical distinctions. The right attacks homosexuals (in order to separate gay from straight workers) by wielding "promiscuity" as a moral category in defense of bourgeois marriage which is to say basically in defense of the orderly transfer of private property under capitalist inheritance laws. The Marxist left fights for free sexual expression and therefore is in solidarity with homosexuals who struggle for equality in meeting their material needs (food, clothing, health care, education, employment, housing, . . .). At the same time, however, it sees the queer left's demand for utterly unregulated sexual behavior (its defense of what it calls "promiscuity") as a demand that ignores the material constraints need inevitably places on desire and, as such, as a commodification of sexuality, that is, as nothing but a fulfillment of the capitalist free market's demand that citizens be encouraged to understood themselves as consumers with insatiable appetites for more commodities.

Patton foregrounds the experiential as the basis of knowledge, a move (as we saw) fully licensed by post-al theory (following the work of Canguilhem, Foucault, . . .). Because of its devastating effects upon the physical body, it is not surprising that much critical analysis of the politics of AIDS has been centered upon opposing ways of discursively representing the physical body of those who have been infected with HIV and those who are struggling to live with, while suffering and dying from,

AIDS--as well as the physical body of those who are suspected as either definitively responsible or peculiarly at risk for contracting (and spreading) HIV. This has led AIDS activists to focus upon the relationship between knowledge and experience, and in particular, toward suspicion about and hostility against all knowledges that do not either directly emanate out of or directly respond to the exigencies of the everyday experience of those who are, in one way or another, immediately "living with AIDS." For instance, in *Inventing AIDS*, Patton attempts to balance the "esoteric" knowledges derived from science with the "exoteric" knowledges supposedly derived from different kinds of "thought communities" and their different "thought styles," and in particular with knowledges supposedly derived from "lived experience," in a model not based upon "translation" from realm to realm but rather upon "co-evolution or negotiation" between realms (*Inventing* 72-74). Similarly, in *Sex and Germs*, Patton argues that conceptual models which abstract and generalize from particular instances of sexual practice "must not substitute for speaking about the real feelings and activities of an individual" (*Sex* 111). Likewise, in *Last Served? Gendering the HIV Pandemic*, Patton critiques AIDS relief workers for failing to respect the "local, often informal networks where much crucial folk knowledge about sexuality and social norms circulate"; it is necessary to "translate" "government/non-government ways of doing" into "women's ways of knowing" in order adequately to reach women, and these latter ways of knowing are, it seems, the results of women's experience of acting and relating as women in society (*Last* 79). While it is undoubtedly important to understand diverse experiences, and especially how they have been socially constructed, it remains questionable from what philosophical and political framework one becomes "truly open-minded" in "listening" to and "learning" from those whom one seeks to serve, as Watney likewise advocates (*Practices* 173). Although this may seem like critical self-reflexivity, it in fact can quite readily turn out to be the opposite, by accepting the liberal humanist positions that no one can, or should, "speak for the other"; that everyone's level and kind of knowledge, derived from their own individual lived experience, is "equally worthwhile"; that individual experience *is* ultimately uniquely individual; and that everyone should, furthermore, both "have the right to their own opinion" and "respect each others' right to their own opinions." Unfortunately, the "commonsense" of "lived experience" is ideologically determined as much if not far more than is "science": "experience" is neither auto-intelligible nor an immediate source of knowledge about itself. To experience an event is simply to have lived through it. What an experience is *understood to mean* depends upon what *frames of intelligibility* are brought to bear to make sense of the experience, and different frames of intelligibility will lead to different interpretations and evaluations of what this "same" experience was all about. The meaning of experience is in fact a crucial site of *ideological conflict and struggle*, as different ways of making sense of a single experience will lead to different ways of making use of this experience in support of different ends and interests. To think that experience itself produces the consciousness which makes sense of itself is to suffer an empiricist illusion which is in fact worse than an illusion: it is to accept the still predominant--liberal humanist--ideological understanding of "the individual" as independent of the shaping influences of social forces, as an autonomously self-determining agent of her own destiny who simply thinks and feels as she, this sovereign and transcendent subject, wills and/or chooses. Within bourgeois society, only the bourgeoisie maintains the material prerequisites to even approach such a position. Whenever others accept the illusion that they are as free as the bourgeoisie, they of course are gravely mistaken--and what's worse, are unable to inquire critically into the interests at stake in the production of both their seeming "freedom" and their real "unfreedom" because they do not even recognize this gap between appearance and reality.

Five

Following Foucault (who follows Canguilhem), both Watney and Patton believe "the politics of AIDS" must include a critique of science and scientific knowledges: the question is what are the effects of the kind of skeptical Foucauldian critiques they make. The mere promotion of skepticism toward and distrust of science leads ultimately to a naive and dangerous embrace of anti-intellectual populism and even irrationalist mysticism. Watney believes it is "progressive" to urge his readers to reject the "generally supine faith in medicine" to which most contemporary British citizens, he contends, still subscribe with little question or qualification (*Practices* 194). The irrationalism can be seen, however, when Patton argues, for instance, that AIDS activists have put their efforts into "studying the wrong information" throughout most of the first decade of organized community response to AIDS, in "trying to beat the odds by acquiring expertise in epidemiology instead of using and adapting their existing knowledge of their own socio-sexual milieu" (*Fatal* 102). Although Patton contends she wants to challenge "the basis of the cultural acceptance of science's claims, not the results of its work" (*Inventing* 55), it is not surprising, given the pragmatic logic of this contention, that it proves difficult for her in practice to differentiate sharply between the two. For instance, Patton suggests that the cultural privilege granted science over "para-science" is without foundation because "the language used in science and para-science rests on the same metaphors of self/other, origin/return that structure the myths and stereotypes which make visible institutional patterns of stigmatization and discrimination" (*Inventing* 5). In other words, Patton's post-al reading of science and para-science once again foregrounds language, signification, representation, . . . as the source of the "problems" with scientific thought in general and AIDS science in particular. In actuality, the problem is instead how science is conducted, as part of what, and for what, within what kind of system of social relations and according to what kinds of political imperatives. It is the *ideological* reification of science conducted under the ultimately effective control and according to the interests and needs of capital that is the problem, not the inherent tendency of "science logic" to "reify itself" so as to support its "own" agenda of "policing society" (*Inventing* 99).

In a recent book, *Fatal Advice: How Safe-Sex Education Went Wrong,* again Patton tries to evade any coherent, causal, structural explanation of social issues by displacing the determinist Marxist concept of the "state" with Foucault's "pluralist" notion of "governmentalities." In spite of the fact that to some people, Althusser ("in the last instance") went too far in distancing the economic from the social and the cultural, Patton specifically rejects Althusser because his ideas of the explanatory force of ideology and his theory of the state apparatuses are still too devoted to giving a rigorous theoretical explanation of the social totality. Patton contends that "coming to think of ourselves is a much more fragile process" [than comprehended in Althusser's notion of subjectivity] (*Fatal* 9). Here, under cover provided by the term "fragile," Patton--like other desire-theorists--tries to render subjectivity as too mysterious and unknowable to be grasped by rational understanding. So Foucault's concept of "governmentalities"--referring to various incommensurate modes of relating bodies, space and administration--is far more helpful in making sense of the ways in which AIDS has functioned politically to resecure American national identity in the 1980s and the 1990s than Althusser's concepts of ideology and the state, the Repressive State Apparatus, and the Ideological State Apparatuses. In an effort to give her rejection of Marxism legitimacy, she suggests in her "Conclusion: From Visibility to Insurrection: a Manifesto" that she herself had earlier subscribed to an emancipationist model for AIDS activism that was still too Marxist.

It is important to examine more fully what is at stake in Patton's rejection of Althusser, whose name she is using basically as a convenient metonym for a theoretically rigorous and serious Marxist understanding of ideology. When Patton says that even her earlier own AIDS activism still seemed to share too much of a Marxist residue, she means she was not yet sufficiently "pragmatic" in her approach to social issues. Following Foucault's lead in shifting from a historical analysis that foregrounds structure to one that foregrounds "events," Patton declares that "Practices are an interaction that occurs on the practical level. They refer to actual events or moments: making a film is a practice, having sex is a practice" (*Sex* 109). What she is rejecting in particular in her own and other queer left practices is any "residue" of the Marxist notion of the determinate connection between ideology and social practices or the Marxist notion that beneficial social change can be encouraged through a rigorous political praxis based on a rigorous theoretical grasp of the issues. She observes that "in marxian theory 'praxis' is the embodiment of theory in the real world" (*Sex* 109-110) and that even some forms of "orthodox feminism" have—mistakenly--followed the Marxist notion that "practices" are "directly related to ideology" (*Sex* 110). For this rigorous notion of the determinate relation between class-based understanding of ideology and a connection of ideology and theory to praxis, she substitutes (following Foucault) the idea that "each practice must be carefully analyzed relative to many discourses" (*Sex* 110).

It is of course this discursive/ideological/theoretical/praxical . . . "eclecticism" (by which different social issues of class, sexuality, gender, . . . are systematically disconnected from each other, rendering impossible a coherent grasp of their connections) that orthodox Marxism rigorously and emphatically rejects as a form of bourgeois mystification and therefore as a compromise with the status quo. Today's growing and virulent hostility to Marxism—more specifically, Bolshevism--is a result of the bourgeois (including queer) left's awareness that Bolshevism completely and uncompromisingly rejects theoretical eclecticism, experientialism and pragmatism. Drawing on Marx and Engels's defense of principled (rigorously theorized) praxis, Lenin most trenchantly and uncompromisingly re-articulated revolutionary Marxism's objections to eclecticism as the characteristic mode of reading/writing/thinking of bourgeois ideologues. In *What Is To Be Done?* Lenin speaks of "the general European phenomenon" (which may be recast today as the global bourgeois phenomenon) by which the demand for "freedom of criticism does not imply substitution of one theory for another" but instead "implies eclecticism and lack of principle" (*What Is To Be Done?* 91). Theoretical eclecticism opens the door precisely to a "pragmatic" social practice, that draws at one moment on one set--and at the next moment on another contradictory set--of theoretical principles.

Patton argues that there is a more or less permanent theoretical stalemate between Marxists and the queer left: "Lesbians and gay men within the left and leftists within the lesbian and gay movement have developed various analyses suggestive of a coherent theory, but neither the left nor the lesbian/gay liberation movement has made a substantial theoretical impact on the other" (*Sex* 153). However, what Patton represents as a stalemate is actually a mark of the class contestation over the interests represented by Marxism, on the one hand, and queer theory, on the other. This presumption that neither side has a "theory" that can comprehend the "theory" of the other side, that, in other words, there is a permanent impasse between the queer left with its desire-theory, on the one hand, and Marxists with their need-theory, on the other, is nothing but a repetition of an ideological--pragmatist—reading. Patton's statement with regard to questions of homosexuality is nothing but a repetition--at the level of sexuality--of Richard Rorty's general claim (*Contingency, Irony, Solidarity*) that there is no way to "hold self-creation and justice, private perfection and human solidarity, in a single vision," that "there is no way to bring self-creation together with justice at the level of theory" (*Contingency* xiv). To develop her "politics of AIDS," Patton, therefore, repeats the alibi bourgeois philosophy has always offered for adopting the position of pragmatism. Such a pragmatist "solution" is a thinly disguised defense of the status quo and an aggressive attempt to legislate it.

All Marxists—but especially queer Marxists--have to directly confront Patton's charge that the "failure" of the gay and lesbian attempt "to form a coalition with the left" (*Sex* 152) is to be laid at the feet of "the straight left" (*Sex* 152). In her discussion of these issues, she sometimes appears to be speaking generally about "marxists/socialists" (including orthodox Marxists) and at other times to be talking about "new left theories" (*Sex* 152) which of course are different because the New Left is explicitly marked as "new" by its acceptance of the autonomy of various political groups. For the latter, it makes sense to refer to "the straight left," but for classical Marxism the term is problematic if it is used to mark a social difference (sexuality) that serves as the basic political priority: workers' solidarity is premised not on their denying their other cultural identities, but on their theorizing the relation of those cultural identities to their class position. Patton promotes the idea that the "cultural oppression of lesbians and gay men has not been understood by the left" and that Marxism has found "lesbian and gay liberation cultural critique and agit prop incomprehensible" (*Sex* 153). On the contrary, Marxists (straight, queer, . . .) find the queer left's form of separatist cultural critique all too comprehensible as an evasion of economic and class issues, as an evasion of theorizing the constraints need places on desire, as a compromise with capitalism. Among the questions that neither Patton nor Watney can answer are these: Since it can be argued that their mode of post-al social theory reduces everything to "desire," why is their reduction of social "matters" to "desire" any better than Marxism's reduction of social "matters" to "need" (assuming for the moment that their charge of Marxist "reductionism" is accurate)? Bourgeois ideologues write as if "reduction" were not the necessary condition for producing conceptual explanations of social phenomena. They furthermore not only write as if Marxists are guilty of "reductionism" while they themselves are not, but also pretend that Marxists perform their reductions "in secret" and thus their "reductionism" provides an occasion for a sensational political "exposé." In actuality, Marxists very publicly advocate for the explanatory power their "reductions" can achieve: as, for example, when Lenin observes that "The theory of the class struggle . . . represents a tremendous acquisition for social science for the very reason that it lays down the methods by which the individual can be *reduced* to the social with the utmost precision and definiteness" (emphasis added, Marx, Engels, Lenin 368). Moreover, since the political and social theory promoted by bourgeois ideologues is itself "separatist" (while they claim that Marxist social theory is "separatist"), why is their mode of "separatism" better—apparently self-evidently better--than Marxism's mode of "separatism"? While theoretically Marxism does insist on relating and connecting practices in the social totality, it can be affirmed that although it doesn't *create* separations (no theory creates anything; being itself a material practice, theory *is created* by the historical conditions that are in turn determined by the mode of production), Marxism does recognize the "separation" (in the sense of "antagonism") between the classes—bourgeoisie and proletariat— created by the capitalist mode of production. As Marx and Engels write, "Within the antagonism as a whole, the private property owner represents the conservative side and the proletariat the destructive side. From the former comes action for preserving the antagonism; from the latter, action for destroying it."[11] Watney and Patton reject out of hand what Marxism acknowledges as "separation" because that "separation" (class antagonism) points to the enormous gap between the class interests of the ruling class on whose behalf they write and theorize and the vast majority of the world's citizen-workers (gay, straight, . . .) whose interests are—in spite of their protestations to the contrary-- completely beyond the queer left's concern. Furthermore, as Marxism argues, the overcoming of the separation (the superseding of the "antagonism" which is part of a "dialectical historical relation") will mean the end of class struggle, the end of class society, and thus the end of the class privileges which Patton and Watney enjoy and wish to see continue. (Marx and Engels again: "Then [with the victory of the proletariat] both the proletariat itself and its conditioning antagonist— private property—disappear."[12])

What Patton and Watney are rejecting in rejecting Marxism is— broadly speaking—theory understood as a form of knowledge that explains the objective conditions of the social totality as it is shaped by the mode of production, which is of course at the present moment the global capitalist mode of production. In commenting on the question of knowledge of the objective and the necessity of concepts, Engels argues that although concepts do not "coincide" with objective reality, they serve as abstract "asymptotic approximations" to it which are absolutely necessary for social practices: "But although a concept has the essential nature of a concept and cannot therefore *prima facie* directly coincide with reality, from which it must first be abstracted, it is still something more than a fiction, unless you are going to declare all the results of thought fictions because reality has to go a long way round before it corresponds to them, and even then only corresponds to them with asymptotic approximation" (Selsam and Martel, p.179).   If all knowledges, as post-al theorists claim, are unreliable in the sense that none of them can be said to correspond to the objective conditions in the world, then there is no basis on which to work effectively for a transformative politics of AIDS or anything else. If there is no reliable objective knowledge—no knowledge that is effectively "founded" in objective conditions, then the claim that there is such a thing as class struggle or that we have in fact entered an era of global capitalist exploitation are simply narrative representations whose "truth" is as illusory as that of any other narrative representation (for example, the pro-capitalist narrative representation by which "what's good for General Motors is good for America"). In the ultimate analysis, what Watney and Patton are primarily rejecting is the commitment to a rigorous revolutionary theory. They very well know that, as Lenin long ago clearly stated in a patent rejection of pragmatism and the kind of compromise on principles that bourgeois ideologues, "Without a revolutionary theory there can be no revolutionary movement. This idea cannot be insisted upon too strongly at a time when the fashionable preaching of opportunism is combined with absorption in the narrowest forms of practical activity" (*What Is To Be Done?* 110).

Six

        That the queer left's "politics of AIDS" is focused exactly on an "absorption with the narrowest forms of practical activity" and is basically hostile to rigorous theory which it desperately wants to "by-pass" is exemplified in the way Patton, in *Fatal Advice,* simply intensifies the localism by calling for a supposedly "new" stage of queer left politics as an "ob-scene" politics. According to Patton, who continues to follow the Nietzschean model of the "politics of suspicion," it is necessary to recognize today the extent to which the ACT UP and Queer Nation models of "shock-politics" "subversionism" have been effectively accommodated and contained within a new "national pedagogy" which is working to renegotiate and resecure the category of national citizenship and yet to do so in ways that are subtler and more complex than was the case with initial responses to AIDS. In other words, the earlier stage of "the politics of AIDS" as a politics of discursive/ significatory/ representational subversion, has lost its effectivity and the queer left must now adopt new subversive practices. This new national pedagogy teaches citizens that it is right to be "sympathetic" to those particularly at risk for contraction of HIV and eventually the development of AIDS. At the same time, however, the normative--straight, white--citizen is addressed "as naturally and literally HIV-free" and therefore as in little need to practice safe sex. Safe sex is for the racial and sexual other, for whom the citizen may well, and indeed even "should," sympathize, but *from whom* one must nonetheless distinguish one's self. Gays who are willing to "heterosexualize" themselves--to conform to heterosexual standards for social-sexual identity and practice--are "allowed" into the province of national citizenship, and so are upstanding, "white-acting," middle class blacks and other people of color, although both of these groups are still marked as of ultimately lesser value within this space of partial inclusion, and must attest to this valuation by relating to the dominant in shame-facedly self-apologizing ways. According to Patton, this readjustment of the category of national citizenship, and of the proper mode of conduct of "the citizen" versus "the other" functions to divide minority racial and sexual communities between those who are now acceptable as second-class citizens, and those who will remain defined and targeted as "deviant" and/or "primitive" non-citizens, thereby in turn conquering the prospective threat of resistance and opposition arising from these now divided minority communities.

Given this development, Patton argues, in relation to the future course of queer politics (her answer to "What Is To Be Done?"), that the new dissident educators and activists need to do more than produce shocking cartoons and confrontational slogans. They must develop better means of mobilizing the practical logics of erotic survival that already exist in communities, learning how and when these evolve in relation to the range of texts that intrude into or circulate beyond their borders. Reimagined sexualities--sexualities imagined beyond the nation--must become embedded in everyday life, not set apart as exceptional or extraordinary (*Fatal* 139).

Patton, in short, is here once again primarily concerned for "queer survival," for survival of the queer as a markedly different and, especially dissident, subculture in relation to the dominant "heteronormative" culture. It is important to find ways to resist being absorbed, coopted, contained, and reduced, and it is for this reason that she proposes it is time to move beyond a politics focused on "visibility" toward a politics "that implodes vision into space" (*Fatal* 140). In order to do this, queer politics must become an "ob-scene politics," a politics which works from the space of "the abjected, the meaningless, the thing that does not try to recover meaning but tries to secure the space *prior to the visibility*, prior to information" (*Fatal* 141). As such, this is queer politics as usual: the queer politics of deconstructing all knowledges and stable identities. According to Patton, "ob-scenity is a kind of palpable presence that is not so much invisible as it is detectable only on a different, potentially more disturbing, more *radical* level as a more deeply embodied volume"; "ob-scenity as politics" means "placing our bodies in an insurrectional posture prior to staging, *being there before*," between--and beyond--intelligibility in terms of questions of visibility and invisibility (*Fatal* 141).   In working to "complicate and confound heterosexuality," the aim is "to create more space for sexual alliances" (*Fatal* 154) among ob-scene subjects that are open to exploring diversely innovative varieties of sexual practice, according to the free-floating dictates of their "desiring bodies" (*Fatal* 148); as Patton sees it, "our bodies *already know*" (*Fatal* 169).   What Patton here presents as something new and fresh is just a recycling of Barthes' very old claim that "The pleasure of the text is that moment when my body pursues its own ideas--for my body does not have the same ideas I do" (*The Pleasure* 17). It would, however, be a mistake to equate the "body's ideas" with conceptual thinking, since post-structuralists and post-Marxists like Paul Smith who go along with post-al theory explain the body as the "enigmatic body" as "what cannot be accounted for by our legitimized systems of representation or our rationalized procedures of interpretation" (Schefer x). As Smith makes clear, this notion of the "enigmatic body" that resists rational understanding but is nevertheless the main "force" or "locus" of social praxis has as its ultimate goal the cancellation of determinism: it takes us back to Merleau-Ponty's "body theory" in *The Phenomenology of Perception* which asserts: "Nothing determines me from outside, not because nothing acts on me, but on the contrary because I am from the start outside myself and open to the world" (Schefer xiv). This "openness to the world" of the human body, which makes it a constantly changing, indeterminate and therefore "enigmatic" space is the space celebrated, for example, by the queer theorist, Elspeth Probyn (*Outside Belongings*) who like Schefer and Smith focuses on the body as a site that "opens onto" the "other": "At the edge of ourselves we mutate; we become other" (Probyn 34). Probyn, who like other post-al theorists practices what she proudly calls a "sociology of the skin" (Probyn 5),   understands the body not as the determinate and determined site of labor, class, . . . but as the site of desire-spawned "singularities . . . that overpower any generalization" (Probyn 21).   As is typical of desire-theorists, Probyn is exceedingly hostile to Marxism which foregrounds questions of need: she, for example, attacks Marxist analyses of sexuality because (she says) they "threaten to fuel an already dichotomous and divisive situation within cultural theory" and because of "their relentless negativity" (Probyn 139). In her drive for a supposed "openness" and "inclusiveness," Probyn attacks any form of critique that operates by negation (as if "negation" were the subjective "choice" of Marxists rather than a historical necessity): directing her anger at Marxists, Probyn conveniently neglects to provide a rigorous account of the manner by which capitalism--in its exclusivist drive for profit (which her writings support)--consistently manages to "negate" the needs of the working class. Patton's call for an "ob-scene politics" is just the recycling of the by now rather tired post-al notion of the "enigmatic body" (not the mode of production) as the motor of social change.

Despite Patton's claims to the contrary, this "ob-scene" politics is nothing but an on-going program for shocking the sensibilities of the bourgeoisie. And despite her claims for the novelty and innovativeness of this program, it is fully in line with logical tendencies of bourgeois queer theory and practice from the beginning of its emergence nearly a decade ago. Whether focusing on the politics of AIDS or on some other issue, it ultimately seeks only to find a way to preserve a space to remain as queerly different as possible within contemporary late capitalism without striving to change anything whatsoever fundamental about the larger society within which it seeks to carve out a space for "dissidence." Such a politics is just another version of liberal reformism: its goals are merely to get governmental and non-governmental agencies to respond more quickly and fairly (in a very local, class-determined sense) to the most immediately and urgently practical of needs of historically marginalized communities--principally, of course, lesbigay/queer communities--while at the same time striving as far as possible to direct and control this response in a way that will enhance and increase the space for a supposedly "autonomous self-determination" within and by these same communities. All this means ultimately is that the dominant queer theory accepts political struggle within bourgeois society as a form of "managed competition" among diverse oppressed and exploited groups which are in effect set up to fight against each other for means of amelioration made available through the (re)distribution of the "public wealth" that is left over after capitalist profits and superprofits have been satisfied.

When it is good for business (that is, when it helps bring up the rate of profit), capital is always able to make partial and limited concessions to the interests and needs of at least the most powerful of the oppressed and exploited in return for their support of its continued right to maintain and reproduce its control over the production and distribution of socially produced wealth. Moreover, capital grants concessions in ways which work to divide and conquer the opposition, by supporting and even increasing relative--class—disparities. If the global class divisions among homosexual men and women as well as among people with AIDS can be maintained and even extended--thereby at the same time maintaining and extending as well the stability not only of capitalist political and ideological hegemony but also of capitalist profits and superprofits--then there is no reason to doubt that capitalist states will continue to institute piecemeal reforms that respond to the needs of those suffering from homophobic discrimination, prejudice, and violent abuse, and the needs of those living with and dying from AIDS as well as struggling against and suffering from AIDS-phobic discrimination, prejudice, and violent abuse. Yet it will do this in highly uneven ways which in fact always work to benefit some gays and lesbians and some people with AIDS at the direct expense of others. At the same time, the extremely limited resources available for such public dispensation, and the highly disparate allocation of these resources across the various nations of the "developed" and the "developing" "worlds" means that--especially in the midst of the currently continuing global recession (and, in much of the "developing" "world" this is in fact a continuing and even worsening state of actual economic *depression*) and a huge global "debt crisis" and pervasive fiscal "austerity"--whatever amelioration is made available will be woefully insufficient to address the enormity of these social problems.

The queer left's notion that the prevailing situation in health care is simply "a sad but inevitable reality" which "has to be accepted" is nothing less than a pragmatic acceptance of the regime of wage-labor-capital. It is this relation of labor and the social relations of property that it produces, that need to be addressed. What is needed is not an "obscene" politics, but rather a revolutionary praxis that can transform the existing health care system that commodifies the human body and turns its illnesses into profit.

Notes

[1]Ettinger, p. 95.

[2]For a more extended discussion of many of the issues addressed in this text, see my forthcoming book, *Queer Theory and the Politics of Radical Social Change: a Marxist Critique.*

[3]On the question of need vs. desire, see, for example, Heartfield.

[4]Butler, *Gender Trouble* and *Bodies That Matter.*

[5]At best, the queer left can tolerate descriptions of the life experiences of working class lesbians and gays in the US (as, for instance, in Susan Raffo's collection called *Queerly Classed*), or voyeuristic accounts of the sex lives of citizens of the former Soviet Union and the Eastern socialist countries (as, for instance, in David Tuller's *Cracks in the Iron Closet: Travels in Gay and Lesbian Russia*) or --in the zone of analytic writing--the theoretically confused, eclectic, and non-rigorous social democratic writings of artists and critics like Tony Kushner, Scott Tucker, and Dennis Altman (see representative texts in Works Cited). It sometimes shows a more sustained interest in post- and neo-Marxist social analyses such as that found in *The Regulation of Desire: Homo and Hetero Sexualities* (now in a second, revised edition) by Gary Kinsman, who--like the queer left in general--accepts the

necessity of some kind of class inquiry. The queer left finds "marxism" tolerable on one profoundly reactionary condition (which Kinsman, by the way, fulfills): that "historical materialist" (Kinsman 23) analysis be detached from the tradition of "political economy" (23) and purged of so-called "economic determinism" (23), that is, purged of exactly what is most threatening to the status quo--its rigorous connecting of the cultural to the economic.

[6]See Butler, "Merely Cultural," and Hanson, "The World's Oldest Living Bolshevik." Since others have already critiqued the texts of Hanson and Butler, I direct the interested reader, for the former, to Zavarzadeh and, for the latter, to the essays by Cloud and Morton in this volume.

[7]See, for instance, Karlinsky's "Russia's Gay Literature and Culture: The Impact of the October Revolution" and his more recent essay in Hekma.

[8]See, instance, Rorty's "First Projects, then Principles" and his diatribes against Marxism-Leninism in his *Achieving Our Country: Leftist Thought in Twentieth-Century America.*

[9]This same pro-queer-consumerist position is endorsed by Alan Sinfield, who in his recent *Gay and After* remarks: "My view is in certain circumstances we have some economic leverage, and we should use it" (Sinfield 164).

[10]The effect of the acceptance of commodification in recent discussions of AIDS is seen in *Policing Public Sex: Queer Politics and the Future of AIDS Activism* (edited by Dangerous Bedfellows), where the "critique" of capitalism is only a complaint about those instances when capital, as a result of changes in the mode of production, displaces one kind of commercialism in the interests of another kind—as in the case of the "renewal" of 42nd street in New York City and the displacement of its famous sex businesses (see the text by Serlin). This "complaint" lies at the core of the new book by Samuel Delany, *Times Square Red, Times Square Blue.*

[11]The original reads: "Innerhalb des Gegensatzes ist der Privateigentümer also die *konservative*, der Proletarier die *destruktive* Partei. Von jenem geht die Aktion des Erhaltens des Gegensatzes, von diesem die Aktion seiner Vernichtung aus." (Marx and Engels, *Die heilige Familie*, p.37. The translation is mine.

[12]The original reads: "Alsdann ist ebensowohl das Proletariat wie sein bedingender Gegensatz, das Privateigentum, verschwunden." *Die heilige Familie*, p.38. The translation is mine.

Works Cited

Altman, Dennis. *Homosexual Oppression and Liberation.* New York: New York UP, 1993.

------. "Rupture or Continuity? The Internationalization of Gay Identity." *Socia Text* 48 (Fall 1996): 77-94.

Barthes, Roland. *Sade, Fourier, Loyola.* Trans. R. Miller. New York: Hill and Wang, 1976.

------. *The Pleasure of the Text.* Trans. R. Miller. New York: Hill and Wang, 1975.

Blasius, Mark. *Gay and Lesbian Politics : Sexuality and the Emergence of a New Ethic.* Philadelphia: Temple Up, 1995.

Butler, Judith. *Bodies That Matter: On the Discursive Limits of Sex.* New York: Routledge, 1993.

------. *Gender Trouble: Feminism and the Subversion of Identity.* New York: Routledge, 1990.

------. "Imitation and Gender Insubordination." In Fuss, 13-31.

------. "Merely Cultural." *Social Text* 52/53 (Fall/Winter 1997): 265-276.

------. Response to the Audience. Left Conservatism Conference. University of California, Santa Cruz. January 31, 1998. (http: //www.jhu.edu/journals/theory_&_event/v002/2.3q_and_a.html)

Dangerous Bedfellows. *Policing Public Sex: Queer Politics and the Future of AIDS Activism.* Boston: South End P, 1996.

de Certeau, Michel. *The Practice of Everyday Life.* Trans. S. F. Rendall. Berkeley, U of California P, 1998.

de Man, Paul. *Aesthetic Ideology.* Ed. and Introd. Andrzej Warminski. Minneapolis: U of Minnesota P, 1996.

------. *Allegories of Reading.* New Haven: Yale UP, 1986.

------. *The Resistance to Theory.* Minneapolis: U of Minnesota P, 1986.

Delaney, Samuel R. *Times Square Red, Times Square Blue.* New York: New York UP, 1999.

Derrida, Jacques. "différance." In *Margins of Philosophy*, 1-28.

------. *Dissemination.* Trans. B. Johnson. Chicago: U of Chicago P, 1983.

------. *The Ear of the Other: Otobiography, Transference, Translation.* Ed. C. McDonald. Trans. P. Kamuf. Lincoln: U of Nebraska P, 1988.

------. *Given Time: I. Counterfeit Money.* Trans. P. Kamuf. Chicago: U of Chicago P, 1994.

------. *Glas.* Trans. J. P. Leavey. Lincoln: U of Nebraska P, 1990.

------. *Margins of Philosophy*. Trans. A. Bass. Chicago: U of Chicago P, 1982.

Edelman, Lee. "The Mirror and the Tank: 'AIDS', Subjectivity, and the Rhetoric of Activism." In Murphy, 9-38.

Edge, Simon. *With Friends Like These: Marxism and Gay Politics*. London: Cassell, 1995.

Ettinger, Shelley. "Afterword: The Struggle Continues." In McCubbin *The Roots* pp.87-96.

Fiske, John. *Understanding Popular Culture*. Boston: Unwin Hyman, 1989.

Foucault, Michel. *Aesthetics, Method, and Epistemology*. Ed. James D. Faubion. *Essential Works of Foucault, 195401984*. Ed. P. Rabinow. Trans. R. Hurley and others. Vol. 2. New York: New P, 1994.

------. *Discipline and Punish*. Trans. A. Sheridan. New York: Vintage, 1995.

------. *Ethics, Subjectivity and Truth*. Ed. P. Rabinow. *Essential Works of Foucault, 1954-1984*. Ed. Paul Rabinow. Trans. R. Hurley and others. Vol. 1. New York: New P, 1997.

------. *The History of Sexuality, Volume I: an Introduction*. Trans. Robert Hurley. New York: Pantheon, 1978.

------. "Nietzsche, Genealogy, History." *Language, Counter-Memory, Practice: Selected Essays and Interviews*. Ed. Donald F. Bouchard. Trans. Donald F. Bouchard and Sherry Simon. Ithaca, NY: Cornell UP, 1977, 139-164.

Fuss, Diana, ed. *Inside/Out: Lesbian Theories/Gay Theories*. New York and London: Routledge, 1991.

Gagnon, John H., and Peter M. Nardi. "Introduction." In *In Changing Times: Gay Men and Lesbians Encounter HIV/AIDS*. Ed. Martin P. Levine, Peter M. Nardi, and John H. Gagnon. Chicago and London: U of Chicago P, 1997.

Gay Left Collective. "Why Marxism?" In *Pink Triangles: Radical Perspectives on Gay Liberation*. Ed. Pam Mitchell. Boston: Alyson, 1980.

Goldstein, Richard. "Queering the Culture." *The Village Voice*. June 30, 1998: 39, 44, 49, 52.

Halperin, David M. *Saint Foucault: Towards a Gay Hagiography*. New York, Oxford: Oxford UP, 1995.

Hanson, Ellis. "The World's Oldest Living Bolshevik." *Lesbian and Gay Studies Newsletter* 24.3 (Fall 1997): 18-19.

Harris, Daniel. *The Rise and Fall of Gay Culture*. New York: Hyperion, 1997.

Heartfield, James. *Need and Desire in the Post-Material Economy*.

Sheffield, ENG: Sheffield Hallam University, 1998.

Hekma, Gert, Harry Oosterhuis, and James Steakley, eds. *Gay Men and the Sexual History of the Political Left.* New York, London: Haworth P, 1995.

Johnson, Barbara. "Is Writerliness Conservative?" In Johnson, *A World of Difference*, 25-31.

------. *A World of Difference.* Baltimore and London: Johns Hopkins UP, 1987.

Kaiser, Charles. *The Gay Metropolis, 1940-1996.* Boston, New York: Houghton Mifflin, 1997.

Karlinsky, Simon. "Russia's Gay Literature and Culture: The Impact of the October Revolution." In *Hidden From History: Reclaiming the Gay & Lesbian Past.* Ed. Martin Duberman, Martha Vicinus, and George Chauncey, Jr. New York: Meridian, 1990. pp. 347-364.

Kinsman, Gary. *The Regulation of Desire: Homo and Hetero Sexualities.* 2d rev ed. Montreal, Quebec; Cheektowaga, NY: Black Rose Books, 1996.

Kushner, Tony. "A Socialism of the Skin." In *Taking Liberties: Gay Men's Essays on Politics, Culture & Sex.* Ed. Michael Bronski. New York: Richard Kassack, 1996.

Leland, John. "The End of AIDS?" *Newsweek,* Dec.2, 1996: 64-69.

Lenin, V. I. *What Is To Be Done?* In his *Collected Works.* Vol. 4 (The Iskra Period, 1900-1902), Bk. 2. Trans. J. Fineberg. Ed. A. Trachtenberg. New York: International, 1929.

Levine, Martin P., Peter M. Nardi, and John H. Gagnon, eds. *In Changing Times: Gay Men and Lesbians Encounter HIV/AIDS.* Chicago and London: U of Chicago P, 1997.

McCubbin, Bob. *The Roots of Lesbian & Gay Oppression: A Marxist View.* 3d ed. (originally titled *The Gay Question*) New York: WW Publishers, 1993.

Marx, Karl. *A Contribution to the Critique of Political Economy.* Ed. M. Dobb. New York: International, 1970.

Marx, Karl, and Frederick Engels. *The German Ideology.* In *Collected Works*, Vol.5 (Marx and Engels 1845-1847), New York: International, 1976, pp.19-608.

------. *Die heilige Familie.* In Marx and Engels, *Werke*, Bd. 2: 3-223.

------. *Werke.* Bd. 2. Berlin: Dietz Verlag, 1962.

Marx, K., F. Engels, and V. Lenin. *On Historical Materialism: a Collection.* Moscow: Progress Publishers, 1972.

Mohr, Richard D. "A Gay and Straight Agenda." In *Same Sex: Debating the Ethics, Science, and Culture of Homosexuality.* Ed. John Corvino. Lanham: Rowman & Littlefield, 1997.

Nowlan, Bob. *Queer Theory and the Politics of Radical Social Change: a Marxist Critique*. Urbana, IL: U of Illinois P, forthcoming.

Patton, Cindy. *Fatal Advice: How Safe-Sex Education Went Wrong*. Durham, NC: Duke University Press, 1996.

------. *Last Served: Gendering the HIV Pandemic*. London: Taylor and Francis, 1994.

------. *Inventing AIDS*. New York: Routledge, Chapman, and Hall, 1990.

------, and Janis Kelly. *Making It: a Woman's Guide to Sex in the Age of AIDS*. Ithaca, NY: Firebrand Books, 1987.

------. *Sex and Germs: the Politics of AIDS*. Boston: South End Press, 1985.

Probyn, Elspeth. *Outside Belongings*. New York and London: Routledge, 1996.

"The Queer Issue." *The Village Voice*. June 30, 1998.

Raffo, Susan, ed. *Queerly Classed: Gay Men & Lesbians Write about Class*. Boston: South End P, 1997.

Rorty, Richard. *Achieving Our Country: Leftist Thought in Twentieth-Century America*. Cambridge, MA: Harvard UP, 1998.

------. *Contingency, Irony, and Solidarity*. Cambridge: Cambridge UP, 1989.

------. "First Projects, then Principles." *The Nation* December 22, 1997: 18-21.

Ross, Andrew. *Real Love: The Pursuit of Cultural Justice*. New York: New York UP, 1998.

Schefer, Jean Louis. *The Enigmatic Body: Essays on the Arts*. Ed. and trans. Paul Smith. Cambridge: Cambridge UP, 1995.

Selsam, Howard, and Harry Martel, eds. *Reader in Marxist Philosophy: From the Writings of Marx, Engels, and Lenin*. New York: International, 1963.

Sinfield, Alan. *Gay and After*. London: Serpent's Tail, 1998.

Sullivan, Andrew. "When Plague Ends: Notes on the Twilight of an Epidemic." *New York Times Magazine*, Nov. 10, 1996: 52-62.

Tucker, Scott. *The Queer Question: Essays on Desire and Democracy*. Boston: South End P, 1997.

Tuller, David. *Cracks in the Iron Closet: Travels in Gay & Lesbian Russia*. Boston, London: Faber & Faber, 1996.

Voloshinov, V. N. *Marxism and the Philosophy of Language*. Trans. L. Matejka and I. R. Titunik. Cambridge, MA: Harvard UP, 1986.

Warminski, Andrzej. "Introduction." In de Man, *Aesthetic Ideology* 1-33.

Watney, Simon. *Policing Desire: Pornography, AIDS, and the Media*. Minneapolis: U of Minnesota P, 1987.

------. *Practices of Freedom: Selected Writings on HIV/AIDS*. Durham, NC: Duke University Press, 1994.

------. "Taking Liberties: an Introduction." *Taking Liberties: AIDS and Cultural Politics*. Erica Carter and Simon Watney, eds. London: Serpent's Tail and ICA, 1989: 11-58.

Yudice, George. "Civil Society, Consumption, and Governmentality in an Age of Global Restructuring: An Introduction." *Social Text* 45 (Winter 1995): 1-25.

Zavarzadeh, Mas'ud. "The Spectre That Haunts Desire: Red Baiting As Queer Funstering." *Lesbian and Gay Studies Newsletter* 23.1-2 (Spring/Summer 1998): 3-4.

------. "The Spectre That Haunts Desire-2: Anti-Communism in Contemporary Queer Theory, or How the Queer Market Is Reacting to Donald Morton's Red-ing of Queerity." *Critical inQueeries* 2.1 (June 1998): 147-152.

Jennifer M. Cotter

Sexual Harassment as/and (Self) Invention:

Class, Sexuality, Pedagogy and (Creative) Writing

For the **Revolutionary Marxist Collective** at Syracuse University
—Solidarity, Critique.

One

The contemporary knowledge industry has put into motion a massive machinery of diversion which appeals to the logic of supplementarity in order to conceal material exploitation by deconstructing the difference between "exploiter" and "exploited." This logic has been enabled by post-al theorists such as Ernesto Laclau and Chantal Mouffe who claim that: "'Society' is not a valid object of discourse. There is no single underlying principle fixing—and hence constituting—the whole field of differences" (*Hegemony* 111). In short, according to this logic there is no objective ground upon which to stand in order to determine the historical validity of one kind of knowledge or political practice over another (as I will demonstrate below, such theorists do argue that there is a material reality however, they understand this "material reality" ahistorically, as an inert matter of the body or the originating "trauma"). Further, since all reality is theorized as a differential "text" subject to the laws of "excess," arguing for the possibility of historical knowledge of objective reality is itself understood as a reification that blocks the "subversive" play of difference in meaning. On these terms, "inasmuch as the field of 'society in general' has disappeared as a valid framework of political analysis, there has also disappeared the possibility of establishing a general theory of politics on the basis of . . . categories which fix in a permanent manner the meaning of certain contents as differences which can be located within a relational complex" (*Hegemony* 180).

In such a political climate the social, rather than being an arena of decisive and conclusive political contestation, is understood as a continuum (with no origin and no end) of multiple alternative and playful possibilities. Far from producing a "radical" trend in left practices, this political climate has made it virtually impossible to conclude and decide on a plan of collective action—other than the "plan" to remain politically undecided, self-reflexive and "open." As a result, the collective intervention into and social transformation of the material conditions of exploitation and oppression has been given up in favor of the more "spontaneous," "overdeterminate," and more "playful" political practice of producing "subversive pleasures" within existing social arrangements. Since post-al politics forecloses the possibility of producing historical knowledges of the objective structures of global capitalism, its explanation of the "autonomy" of social struggles (which denies that it is a theory of autonomy) is largely articulated at the level of the *effects* of these structures in the identities produced from them. In short, the presupposed "autonomy" of social struggles gets articulated as "competing," yet "intersecting" and *self-inventing* differences so that, as post-al feminist and queer theorist Judith Butler claims: "to prescribe an exclusive identification for a multiply constituted subject, as every subject is, is to enforce a reduction and a paralysis . . . at the expense of race or sexuality or class or geopolitical positioning/ displacement" (116). However, if we cannot account for the structures that give rise to the seemingly disconnected issues of class, gender, race, sexuality, . . . and can only understand these structures in terms of their identity effects, and further, if no priority can be established for social transformation, then we can only understand the operations of social oppression on the most particular, local level: a "case-by-case" basis.

Meanwhile capital is *systematically* exploiting the majority of people on the planet; it is *systematically* (re)producing and making use of social differences such as race, gender, and sexuality to assist in masking and maintaining this exploitation. Capital is *systematically* producing flexible subjects who will think in terms of fulfilling individual desires, who will adjust to the changes capital has made in the name of fulfilling these desires; flexible subjects who, because of their historically and materially produced (thus changeable!) incapacity to think and act in systemic and collective terms, will be more easily, among other things, inculcated into labor forces that help capital re-privatize historical and material gains made by workers in previous moments of struggle. These strategies of subjectivity are useful for the ruling class but not workers. As Donald Morton has argued, they are crucial in producing a new mode of "high risk" capitalist entrepreneurs whose ruthless and reckless practices know no limits to making profit off of others (Morton 211-213). This "high risk" is further reproduced among the petit-bourgeoisie who, working as managers in the interests of a "high risk" capitalist class, will use excessive and violent practices to maintain, control, divide and subordinate workers. In other words, the strategies of self-invention, promoted in the ludic queer theory of Butler and others as the "cutting edge" of radical politics, is part of a much larger strategy of subjectivity in capitalism: the entrepreneur as self-inventing subject.

By naturalizing the undecidability of meaning, post-al theories of invention erase the knowledges necessary for the direct intervention into material conditions by means of revolutionary praxis. For these theories, the only way to produce change is through a pedagogy of pleasure which promotes the subject's spontaneous "creativity" to invent a "new wor(l)d order." In doing so, these pedagogical strategies present a world in which the liberation of interpretation and the liberation of desire are ends in themselves—as if producing "subversive pleasures" through a "redescription" or "remetaphorization" of exploitation and oppression were tantamount to the revolutionary social transformation of material relations under capitalism. Consequently, a Red pedagogy of critique and collective needs that aims to produce systemic knowledges to enable more effective intervention into and transformation of capitalist social relations of production, is represented as a "dogmatic" practice which blocks the subject's "subversive" performance of desire by insisting on collective principles and a fixed axis of action. Emancipation (collective freedom from exploitation in a society based on producing for need, not profit) is itself under erasure by a pedagogy of pleasure. This is owing to the fact that a pedagogy of pleasure aims to displace collective needs with the "subversive reversibility" of "autonomous" desire—claiming that any determination of collective needs is *always already* based on desire. This brings the "new" and "progressive" post-al feminist and queer theories of desire, which retheorize desire as what Jane Gallop calls a "defiant perversion of any norm," surprisingly close to such neo-conservative strategies as those of dominant "creative writing" pedagogies in which "creativity" has now been redefined as "letting it all hang out." This is because these seemingly "disparate" practices within the pedagogy of pleasure are actually strategies of "anything goes" capitalism which promote the progressive, "creative" subject as the entrepreneur of desire who knows no limit to making profit out of personal pleasure, and unleashes this desire on others in order to maintain the regime of profit.

In short, this post-al diversion away from explaining the systematicity of exploitation and oppression is a legitimation of the current backlash by capital against all marginalized groups, waged in order to increase its rate of profit in a time of economic crisis. The effectiveness of this backlash is in capital's "divide and conquer" tactic of individualizing various social struggles, representing them as autonomous from each other. If instances of social oppression can only be understood on a "case by case" basis—on the terms of local strategies, not collective principles—then the "resolution" of such problems can only be determined by what is most pragmatically "effective." However, without a systemic analysis of social oppression, "what is most effective" is really a cover for what is most "convenient" for those who are already relatively privileged within existing social arrangements. Such a logic leads to a form of petit-bourgeois reformism in which what puts the least pressure on "the center" is "what works."

This form of petit-bourgeois pragmatism—to act on what is convenient—is legitimated in the post-al academy through a pedagogy of pleasure which promotes desire as a trans-social and natural "given." It does so through a whole range of pedagogical practices aimed at producing self-serving subjects who will uncritically accept and maintain existing social arrangements in the name of the pursuit of the ethics of the "care of the self" (as Foucault calls it). As part of this ensemble of pedagogical practices, seemingly "different" and "opposed" theories help legitimate desire as an autonomous social practice.

In this text I will investigate the ways in which some of the dominant political and pedagogical theories, such as "Creative Writing" theories and ludic postmodern feminist and queer theories, renaturalize desire through the notion of "invention"—a technology of subjectivity that promotes a "trans-social" subject who acts on her "own" dehistoricized desire in the name of "intuition" or "discursive repetition." Through a historical materialist analysis of gender, class, sexuality, invention, creativity, performance and desire, I will demonstrate how the ensemble of discourses in the pedagogy of pleasure promote the entrepreneurial subject of capitalism and serve to mystify exploitation and oppression—including violence against women—in order to maintain the regime of profit. In order to do this I will undertake a "reading" of a concrete instance of sexual harassment, its conditions of possibility, and the consequences that are engendered from it. Specifically, I will focus on my own formal grievance against a Syracuse University Creative Writing faculty member for sexual harassment. But first, it is necessary to point out that I bring this incident and corresponding events up NOT to write an article in the spirit of "intimate criticism" or "confessional feminism": reformist social practices in which the purpose of "criticism" is to privilege the experiences of the victims of social oppression by reading these experiences through the "tropes" of race, gender, sexuality, and class. Such a practice is reformist because it reduces social oppression to its effects in experience, and refrains from investigating the objective conditions of existence which produce these various forms of social oppression and make them available to "experience." In doing so "intimate criticism" dematerializes various forms of social oppression (consequently re-understanding them as tropes of self-writing). This ends up acknowledging the existence of these forms of oppression without providing the means to critique and intervene in their material causes.

If it is to be fully understood, the problem of sexual harassment cannot be reduced to my "personal" experience of it, nor can it be reduced to experience itself. Sexual harassment is a *social* issue that is part of a much broader *system* of economic exploitation and its corresponding forms of social and political oppression. Sexual harassment is a manifestation of a larger conflict and struggle between the ruling class and workers access to, ownership of and control over material resources: the means of production and the products of collective labor. It therefore cannot be understood adequately on the "personalizing" terms of individual experience. Instead it must be read symptomatically, as an articulation of the social relations of production. With this in mind, I bring this issue up to produce knowledges of sexual harassment on the materialist grounds of a Marxist *public* critique: a revolutionary social practice in which the purpose of critique is to uncover the relations of production (based on the exploitation of labor) which produce and maintain various forms of social oppression (such as sexual harassment), through an intervention into the dominant discourses and practices that legitimate these relations. The purpose of uncovering these relations is to produce revolutionary knowledge that can enable the collective transformation of them in order to produce a new society free from exploitation and oppression.

Two

On Friday, March 31, 1995, I was sexually harassed by Professor Stephen Dobyns a well known creative writer and Syracuse University faculty member. Although I did not know Professor Dobyns very well and had little contact with him, he evidently knew who I was and was familiar with my political commitment to revolutionary Marxism and the global emancipation of women. Approaching me at a gathering held by a creative writing student in celebration of his fiction reading earlier in the evening, Dobyns immediately initiated a series of aggressive and hostile remarks and actions: First, Dobyns addressed me by saying "Hello Pol Pot" and I brushed off the comment by saying that I was not connected with that regime. Second, he proceeded by putting his arm around the man next to him, gesturing toward me and leering at me while telling this man "I'm looking at her breasts right now." When I was angered and walked away Professor Dobyns called after me "You stupid Stalinist bitch!" I refused to be intimidated by his remarks and did not accept them in silence by saying, "You are a tired old man, aren't you?" To this Dobyns responded by throwing a drink in my face.* Following this incident I learned from several other graduate students that this kind of sexual intimidation was evidently a pattern on the part of Professor Dobyns (which was documented by the time my case reached

---

*Dobyns, of course, has disputed my entire account of the incident. For example, in his testimony, he insists that what he said was "Don't look at her breasts" instead of "I'm looking at her breasts." However, in either case, the University found the remark suggestive and a form of sexual harassment.

a formal University hearing and included three reported acts of physical assault and multiple instances of verbal sexual harassment against other students and faculty).

On Monday, April 3, 1995 I filed a formal grievance letter to the Affirmative Action Officer at Syracuse University against Professor Dobyns for sexual harassment of a visual, verbal, and physical nature. Along with sending this letter to the Affirmative Action Officer, I sent it to various deans and all of the faculty and graduate students in several different departments in the College of Arts and Sciences, the College of Visual and Performing Arts, the Law School, the School of Education and the School of Social Work at Syracuse University. In addition, I faxed this letter to various local and national newspapers, television stations, and radio programs as well as journals in the Humanities. These actions were to emphasize the fact that sexual harassment is a public and social issue, not a private and personal matter. Three days after submitting my grievance with the Affirmative Action Officer, Syracuse University suspended Professor Dobyns with pay from his teaching and advising duties for the rest of the semester (the end of which was approximately three weeks away). I also wrote and distributed, with the help of the Revolutionary Marxist Collective at Syracuse University, an "Open Letter to the Syracuse University Community on Institutionally-Shielded Sexual Harassment" which began to address the conditions within the Department of English at Syracuse University, its Creative Writing Program and the University itself, which helped perpetuate this broader social problem. Among other things this text included a critique of the theory of "creativity" and the pedagogies founded upon it. It argued that in the post-al academy, "creativity" is turned into a mode of entrepreneurship, in which it is redefined as "the freedom to do whatever one wants." Moreover, such a mode of "creativity" is used to discourage any principled commitment to progressive political and social theory and practice and further, to legitimate reactionary social practices.

In response to my formal grievance and open letter, the subsequent series of texts that I wrote and co-wrote, texts circulated by the Revolutionary Marxist Collective at Syracuse University, and those texts circulated by a small core of Creative Writing students and faculty who refused to defend Professor Dobyns' sexist practices, a series of reversals took place in order to whitewash the issue of sexual harassment and exempt Dobyns from any responsibility. Besides a group of staff workers that I will discuss below, the Revolutionary Marxist Collective was the only organization at Syracuse University to *publicly* come forward and give uncompromising support to my formal grievance harassing me or any other student (which he denied) but for his long term problem with alcohol and depression. Deploying familiar strategies to "reinvent" himself, Dobyns managed to take the reader through his depression, denial, hopelessness, recognition, "and the struggle to abolish sexist violence. Feminists and the faculty and students in "Women's Studies" remained utterly silent throughout my struggles. Two days after the circulation of my grievance letter, Professor Dobyns circulated his own text: an "apology" *not* for sexually miraculous" recovery, and newfound hopefulness (all of which has occurred between Friday, March 31, 1995 and Wednesday April 5, 1995 when he first circulated this text—less than a week!).

In this text Dobyns admits: "On Friday night, March 31, I . . . threw a drink into Jennifer Cotter's face" (Dobyns, *The Syracuse Herald-Journal* 4/6/95: A-16). For this he claims to be "profoundly sorry" and states that his actions were unjustifiable, yet exempts himself from responsibility by claiming that "if I had been sober I would have realized that." In short, Dobyns individualizes his actions as a simple "fluke" of his alcoholism, in no way connected to his institutional status as a professor and a celebrity writer. In fact, his apology which describes how he was caught in a cyclical relation between suicidal "depression" and "drinking" is really an elaborate rewriting of the significance of his institutional authority and a mystification of his pattern of intimidation toward his female students. On the one hand, Dobyns denies that his sexually harassing and abusive practices have anything to do with the production of a hostile work environment for his graduate students (both the women who were the targets of his abuse and the men who did not want to participate in cultivating such an environment). Dobyns is careful to point out that his practices which occurred "while drinking" never got in the way of his academic and scholarly duties: "I met my classes, I had conferences, I wrote, even though I was hung over." What Dobyns erases in this revisionist self-writing is that he cannot casually step outside of his position of institutional authority and that sexually harassing students outside of the classroom immediately sets up sexual hierarchies inside the classroom and limits the extent to which his "community" of writers actually includes and takes seriously the intellectual contributions of women.

While Dobyns claims that his institutional position bears no weight upon his abusive practices toward his female students, on the other hand, it has everything to do with his alcoholism and the personal depression he feels outside of the classroom. For Dobyns, his "wish to die" was part of a response to the fact that he had no one to discuss his depression and drinking with because his social status had alienated him from others. To this end he states: "I had nobody with whom to discuss this. I was, after all, the director of a program, a well published writer and it seemed that every day another person would tell me how fortunate I was." In short, according to Dobyns, his institutional authority does not extend into spaces outside of the classroom and in his personal life as long as it is a question of those in a position of relative institutional subordination. Yet it clearly has a bearing on his own life and "personal" practices outside the classroom when it is a question of his own interests. This opportunistic "blurring" of institutional lines is precisely what enables Dobyns to mystify his position of relative institutional power and authority, and minimize the sexist violence he perpetrated against myself and others.

While he could, (to use one of Dobyns' terms) "control" himself enough to fulfill the obligations of his professional career, apparently he could not prevent himself from sexually harassing me: "The result of this behavior was my insult to Jennifer Cotter . . . I do not know her, I have hardly ever spoken to her, she was simply the pretext. I was unhappy, I was drunk and she was there." Despite the fact that his harassing remarks (e.g.., "Hello Pol Pot," and "You stupid Stalinist bitch!") indicate that he was obviously conscious and coherent enough to recognize who I was and single me out and ridicule me on the basis of my gender ("bitch") *and* my political ideas (what he calls "Stalinist"), his depression and drinking according to his "logic" exempt him from having to account for using myself and other women as objects upon which to unleash sexist violence. In short, the logic of Dobyns' "apology" claims that I and others were not the victims of his sexually harassing practices rather, he was the "victim" of depression, of his institutional power ("Director of Creative Writing"), of unsympathetic ears, of his own celebrity status, of loneliness and, most prominently, of alcohol. Yet, the logic that legitimates violence against women for "just being there" is not a product of alcoholism (an individual's singularity), it is (as I will discuss below) the product of a much wider systemic backlash against feminism and as a result a backlash against women. Dobyns' own personalizing narrative of alcoholism, however, was not enough to exempt him from responsibility. Others had to come to the rescue of a social and academic order that had produced and legitimated sexual aggression and harassment against women. As I have already suggested: Dobyns' practices were not idiosyncratic or singular and the system that had sustained them had to be defended. In an interview with *The Syracuse Post-Standard*, English Professor John W. Crowley added another level to this chain of defense by reversals. He argued that American male writers have historically been the "victims" of alcoholism and "addiction" (McKeever, "Alcohol Woes" C-4).

This set of reversals was evidently quite effective for Dobyns as, in response to a formal hearing in which the University "concluded that Dobyns sexually harassed [me] on the night in question and, furthermore, that he had engaged in a pattern of behavior that created a hostile environment for some of his students and colleagues" (Morrow, *Syracuse Record* 7/24/95), the University gave Dobyns merely a two year suspension, only *one* semester of which was without pay. In addition, in what the University called a "harsh" punishment, Professor Dobyns was "required" to provide proof to the University of continued treatment for alcoholism, engage in 170 to 200 hours of community service in the Syracuse area with "organizations that seek to meet the special needs of women," and pay me $600 compensation for wages lost from missing work. To call a semester of suspension without pay, community service, and compensation of the victim "harsh" is, of course, another legitimation of the systemic aggression and harassment against women. Dobyns has openly admitted that he has "no economic reason for teaching"—and thus this lack of a semester of pay is of no consequence to him (Buckley 10). What this "punishment" really represents for Dobyns is a year and a half of paid vacation time for sexually harassing his students. The "severity" of such a punishment is even more ludicrous in light of the fact that the preceding year Syracuse University actually fired two professors for sexually harassing their students. In other words, because of Dobyns' commodifiable textwares, and because he has celebrity status and marketability for Syracuse University, he is considered to be "above" the "standards" and "principles" set forth by Syracuse University in its sexual harassment policy in which it claims that: "sexual harassment corrodes the values most central to the mission of the University. Avoiding its occurrence is of the highest priority" (*Faculty Manual* 37). Far from maintaining a principled commitment to ending sexual harassment as Syracuse University claims, in actuality it demonstrates an unprincipled approach to sexual harassment; it approaches sexual harassment on a case-by-case basis, which enables the University to do whatever is most *convenient* for its marketability. Furthermore, the community service that Dobyns must perform in actuality represents the University's refusal to make its expressed "commitment" to ending sexual harassment a fundamental part of a university education. This is manifested in its "individualizing" of the problem of sexual harassment (locating it within the behavior of just one person), and pushing this problem off onto a smaller organization with considerably less resources, who is as a result to be burdened with the responsibility of "educating" him. To date, Dobyns refuses to fulfill any of these obligations and has not returned to teaching at Syracuse University. In effect, Syracuse University has wasted one and one-half years of tuition dollars to reward a professor who basically refuses to fulfill even the most minimal of democratic standards.

The most aggressive reversal (the assumptions of which I will discuss at length) was led by Tobias Wolff, Mary Karr, Brooks Haxton and others (highly privileged members of the Faculty who had benefited year after year from the lavish attention and financial support of the University's administration), who attempted to shore up the politico-pedagogical bankruptcy of the Syracuse University Creative Writing Program. They argued that the S.U. Creative Writing Program was the "victim" of a "totalitarian" Marxist attempt to rid Syracuse University of

Creative Writing and, by implication, to rid the world of "creativity," "individuality," and "artistic freedom of expression." Underpinning this logic is a set of assumptions that the Syracuse University Creative Writing Program shares with the dominant form of creative writing pedagogy in the United States which depoliticize art and place the "free expression" of the "individual" as the most urgent task over and above freedom from exploitation.

Three

This view of "creativity" is manifested in Dobyns' poem "Allegorical Matters" (*The American Poetry Review* 24.2 [March-April 1995]: 3). At the core of this allegory is a rehearsal of the abstraction of "artistic expression" from its social, historical, political, and economic conditions, and an ideological legitimation of violence against women under the guise of defending "artistic freedom." On one level "Allegorical Matters" appears to recognize the total collapse and historical bankruptcy of the heterosexual male subject as the standard of "normalcy." Yet on another level this "appearance" of recognizing multiple sexualities is a ruse for this "norm," as the "recognition" is underwritten by a privileging and naturalizing of a heterosexist and sexist desire. This contradiction is manifested in the poem from the beginning when the narrator invites the reader to participate in a "heterosexual male fantasy" in which the reader is to imagine himself as a man sitting on a park bench approached by a "universally" beautiful woman who removes her halter top, reveals her breasts (which the narrator instructs us to compare to "ripe fruit"), and presses them against his face. The narrator subsequently instructs the reader: "Eagerly,/ you embrace her but then you learn the horror because while her front is young and vital,/ her back is rotting flesh that breaks away/ in your fingers with the smell of decay" ("Allegorical" 3). In other words, the narrator invites the reader to partake in this fantasy only to discover the "horror" of the feminine (its "rotten backside"), which naturalizes "hatred" for women. The poem is, in other words, a representational reversion of the misogynist imaginary: it provides an ideological alibi for violence against women by presenting women as a source of decay, destruction, death and "horror" (and thus a cause for "hatred"). Well aware of historical challenges to narratives of masculinity and heterosexuality and of public contestation over the social conventions and cultural codes of gender, the poem sets out from the onset to mock public critique and an open investigation into the social uses toward which these narratives are put. While the narrator is rehearsing this fantasy in the beginning of the poem, he interjects parenthetical qualifiers in order to ironically qualify the emerging feminist codes (which the subtext of the poem regards as "political correctness"):

"Let's say you are a man (some of you are)/ and susceptible to the charms of women/ (some of you must be) . . . A beautiful woman approaches. (Clearly,/ we each have his or her own idea of beauty/ but let's say she is beautiful to all.) . . . (Let's say you are an admirer of bare breasts)" ("Allegorical" 3). Through the construction of the narrator who ironically qualifies this fantasy at every turn, Dobyns marks an "awareness" of challenges to traditional notions of masculinity and heterosexuality in order to parody and mock them.

In short, this "awareness" is quite trite and superficial as this poem actively works to restore—through making fun of feminist critique—a time when "men were men and women were women." That is, a time presumed to be without challenges to the naturalization of gender and sexuality. In its parody of feminist codes in order to "subvert" them, the text also manifests a *mourning* for the coherency of the heterosexual male subject: "Some of you are [men] . . . and *must be* [susceptible to the charms of women]" ("Allegorical" 3; emphasis added). At the same time the narrator appears to call attention to the "multiple" and "particular" (by the very fact that he must "qualify"), he assumes the "naturalness" of "heterosexual male" desire, by using the qualifiers to eliminate the desires of "others," in order to enable the narrative to proceed coherently: "let's say you are a man . . . let's say she is beautiful to all . . . let's say you are an admirer of bare breasts" ("Allegorical" 3). While Dobyns "formally" allows for multi-normalities, those who respond to a particular desire are *men*—and the standard for "masculinity" (for a "real man") in this text is he who has the same sexist and heterosexist "desire" as the narrator. As a result, the "invitation" initiated at the beginning of the poem is not an ideologically "innocent" invitation rather, it is a call for *men* to *identify* with a heterosexist desire (one that assumes "heterosexual male" desire as natural, universal, and obvious) and the disappointment of leaving it "unsatisfied."

This point is reinforced by what the female figure with the "rotten backside" represents. Rather than calling into question this heterosexist fantasy as a reactionary fantasy that objectifies and fetishizes the female body in order to reinscribe women as the sexual playground (i.e., "in the park"!) for the natural(ized) desires of "real men," this poem in actuality advances a sexist attack on women for not living up to the expectations of such a fantasy. In short, "Allegorical Matters" is a song of mourning and melancholia (as Freud would call it) lamenting the loss of the object of desire. The "half-rotten" woman does not fully satisfy the desire of "real men." The woman is deceitful: while her "front"—the visible surface—is appealing, this *hides* something unpleasant, incomplete and corrosive. For Dobyns this fantasy is "bankrupt" not because it is sexist but because it cannot be fulfilled: women create "the *illusion* of an eternal present" ("Allegorical" 3; emphasis added). This is because women, on the poem's terms, are corrosive, rotten, and deceitful and therefore never live up to their promises; in short, they are "immoral." Such a construction of "femininity" is precisely one of the ideological alibis that legitimates violence against women. The "hidden immorality," the "ruse" of "woman" gives license to men to treat them as (dis)simulations, as lies toward which abuse is justified. Such a construction "reverses," in the cultural imaginary, the systematic violence against women under capitalism by making so called "real men" (those whose desires correspond to this fantasy) the "real victims" of the "hoax" called "woman." Harassment, violence, and abuse toward women are simply "what they deserve" for "victimizing" men through being "liars" and "cheats."

The sexual politics of this poem are concealed and legitimated by what Dobyns later introduces in the poem as "the ruthless necessities of art"—a space "free" from political and social contestation in which the artist does not have to account for his "aesthetic" practices on social and historical terms. In other words, this is a space of "free invention" in which the artist-as-individual, not a collectivity of people, invents the norm. The legitimation of such a space becomes apparent in the poem when the narrative is interrupted by a "meta-narrative" in which the "author" (who initially is the narrator who invites the reader to partake in this fantasy and is now the subject of the narrative) must confront the readings that "a trio of experts" (Dobyns' term for theoreticians) have produced of his story. As Dobyns presents them, these theorists—whose assumptions are grounded in psychoanalytic, deconstructionist, and feminist theories—represent the "suppression" of the artist's "everyday desire." In order to understand social norms of collectivity and critique as an "outside" force that *suppresses* artistic freedom of expression, Dobyns necessarily presupposes the existence of a transcendent human consciousness and innate desire. In the face of these "expert" readings and the "weight of their disapproval" the author "censors" himself and refrains from the "spontaneity" of his desires: "He scratches under his arm and suppresses a belch," he thinks twice about stepping on an ant in front of the experts, "he would like to be elsewhere, perhaps home/ with a book or taking a walk" ("Allegorical" 3). In short, Dobyns offers a narrative of petit-bourgeois escapism ("elsewhere") from the pressure of social and political critique (at "home" instead) and toward the care of the "soul" ("with a book") and the "self" ("taking a walk"). Through this narrative of "escape" these rather banal examples of "desire" are really a promotion of desire as a transhistorical and "natural" human "instinct"—as the product of a trans-social subject. Consequently, beneath this mourning for the lost object of desire is another lamentation; a lamentation for the *unrestrained* exercise of desire—where desire, as such, is understood as autonomous from and fundamentally opposed to social relations. In the dominant creative writing pedagogy "unrestrained desire" is represented as "natural" insofar as it is understood to be "repressed" by social forces not produced through the social relations of production.

Dobyns promotes such a notion of the subject by positing that the artist is ruled by "intuition." In fact, the creative writing industry as a whole legitimates the naturalization of desire through this invention of "intuition." "Intuition" is that characteristic which exempts the artist from accounting for his social practices on historical terms. Dobyns states that "material comes to the creative artist through intuition; he or she rarely chooses it consciously. And when the material comes, the creative artist is not allowed to reject some part of it because it is horrible or disgusting; the writer cannot refuse it by imposing upon it an everyday subjectivity"—that is, the norm of a collectivity ("Voices" 22). It is upon these grounds that Dobyns and others who advance the dominant creative writing pedagogy, legitimate social oppression and exploitation. By representing themselves as the "rebels" for "truth" against the "authoritarianism" of "political correctness" (i.e. "everyday subjectivity") they redefine "creativity" as the freedom to "let it all hang out": the freedom for the reckless exercise of one's hatreds, prejudices, and appetites. Yet, what is twisted as "political correctness" and subjected to endless jokes by right-wing polemicists as well as state jokesters is of course nothing more than a limited liberal awareness of the "other": the other's social being, her life and practices, her equality and freedom. This is, in fact, the limit of liberal politics, which are based on bourgeois individualism: the same freedom that Dobyns allows himself as a creative writer, he denies the "other" by the ruse of "political correctness." For Dobyns, respect for the other's social existence is "political correctness"; the satisfaction of one's own desires is "freedom." The intuitive subject has insight to such "freedom" because he only acts on "internal" impulses and desires, not collective social principles. Yet in understanding these "impulses" as natural, the desire to sexually harass, to gay bash, to rape, to accumulate and profit off of the labor of others all become ahistorical, unchangeable, and uncontrollable desires.

By abstracting desire and "artistic expression" from the social relations in which this desire and its expressions are actually produced, Dobyns and the creative writing industry end up supporting a reactionary Right Wing desire to "save" the supremacy of the white, middle-class, heterosexual male. Using the guise of "neutrality," Dobyns argues that "free art" is opposed to "partisan art"—or partisanship in general—which "instead of posing questions, gives answers" ("Voices" 22). According to Dobyns, "partisan art" such as "anti-war poems . . . radical feminist, black, gay, and Marxist poems . . . speaks to those already convinced of its truth or bullies those who aren't" ("Voices" 22). In other words, Dobyns proceeds with the assumption that we can only "intuit" reality (we cannot produce historical knowledge of objective social conditions) and therefore we must occupy an "undecidable" stance in relation to social contradictions. Any other stance would be "too dogmatic." Of course, this fetishizing of the question and undecidability is the bedrock of all post-al pedagogies, which aim to problematize the "politics of truth" rather than explain the social and economic interests behind particular "truths" (or what Marx calls the "economics of untruth"). In post-al pedagogies, one cannot posit an "outside" to a particular "truth" in order to determine its historical and material validity, as to posit an outside is simply to extend the discursive "inside." Historical knowledge cannot be produced and therefore a determinate position cannot be taken. Following this logic, in his anti-intellectual mode Dobyns does not realize that he upholds norms identical to those whom he rejects: he is just as much an advocate of the "undecidable" and the "supplementary" as any deconstructionist such as de Man, Laclau and Mouffe, Derrida, Butler, Lyotard, ... Fetishizing the question and avoiding answers by calling them totalitarian ("bullying") is, moreover, a petit-bourgeois managerial strategy of containment. It silences the decisive, purposeful, and principled commitment to social change by putting in its place pragmatics, indecision, and opportunism. As a result, "unrestrained" expression is expression that does not have to account for the advances of oppositional struggles and their social theories: of feminism, of anti-racism, of gay liberation, of anti-imperialism, or of Marxism. Far from remaining neutral, Dobyns not only laments but revives the supremacy of the "white," "middle class," "heterosexual," "male" subject as the measure of neutrality. What Dobyns pretends to "give" in the form of liberal "sensitivity" to and "tolerance" of discursive differences ("we all have our own opinion"), he takes back with a vengeance by making dominant modes of intelligibility the standard of neutrality. In doing so he renaturalizes socially produced differences and renders the violence inflicted against people that gets legitimated through the production of these "differences" as aleatory—as a "fluke."

However, sexual harassment and other forms of social violence can by no means be understood as "flukes." Sexual harassment is a tool of the ruling class and is best understood on the terms of exploitation. It is part of the vast machinery of ruling class practices designed to ideologically legitimate class based society and conceal over and maintain its process of exploitation: the process in which the working class is compelled to work part of the working day to reproduce its own means of subsistence and the rest of the day to produce surplus-value for the capitalist. Sexual harassment is a concentration of practices that help to legitimate capitalism by reinforcing, exacerbating, and intensifying gender differences so that they can be used as tools of exploitation. In its ideological legitimation of exploitation, capitalism produces and reproduces social and historical differences such as "gender" and "race" in order to use them as instruments of exploitation, divide the working class to prevent it from effectively fighting this exploitation, and produce specialized markets for consumption.

Sexual harassment contributes to the justification of the economic exploitation of women and helps to maintain a politically divided labor force that is, as a result, prevented from collectively fighting the entire system of exploitation and oppression. It is symptomatic of much broader strategies of violence against women in the international division of labor, used to "cheapen" labor-power and keep women more vulnerable and less resistant to the global logic of capitalist exploitation. As Maria Mies has argued, "violence against women and extracting women's labour through coercive labour relations are . . . part and parcel of capitalism" (171). Violence against women is not, as bourgeois feminists of "patriarchy" assume, a product of the "uncontrollable" and "innate" desires of men unleashed on women (the exercise of internal "power"); it is a tool for the private appropriation of socially produced wealth. Moreover, what is crucial to understand here (and this is where my understanding of the material basis of sexual harassment is in contestation with Mies' as well), is that sexual harassment is enabled by *private ownership* (not the other way around) in which a small fraction of people, the ruling class, own the means of production and the products of that production, and the vast majority of people own only their own labor-power to sell in order to survive. It is in class based systems, where one group monopolizes socially produced wealth at the expense of the vast majority (who are denied economic access) and, therefore, has command over the labor of others, that the domination of women and the exploitation of women's labor is materially supported and reproduced.

The history of violence against women and the isolation and exclusion of women from social production (by restricting women to social reproduction) produced in earlier stages of capitalism has set up enabling conditions for an extremely cheap labor force that can be easily manipulated depending on what will make the most profit for the capitalist. Now, in a time of economic crisis, and a subsequent increase in ruthless and reckless global inter-capitalist competition, more women are being proletarianized on a global scale than ever before. The crisis of capitalism that is the effect of the fall of the rate of profit, requires capital to push down the cost of labor to increase or at least maintain the rate of profit, and those workers (often women) whose *historical* conditions of life have made them more economically vulnerable (and thus more easily exploited) are drawn into wage-labor to help capital stave off crisis.

On the one hand, these shifts in the mode of production, which require the increased cooperation of male and female workers, have opened up the possibility for women, who were previously relatively isolated from each other, to develop collective practices with each other and male workers to resist, intervene in, and transform the conditions of their exploitation. Yet, to suppress the development of collective revolutionary praxis, capitalist relations of production require an increase in managerial strategies that will maintain gender distinctions in order to (re)produce a labor force that will be more easily exploitable by capital. As part of these strategies there has developed a significant backlash against advances made by women all over the globe, which includes both covert ideological violence through the "repetition," and "recitation" of gender norms in the media and educational systems, and the development and maintenance of practices of overt physical violence against women.

In suppressing the material, historical and political dimensions of art through the invention of an apolitical "force" such as "desire" or "intuition," the creative writing industry helps legitimate the backlash against those struggling against systematic exploitation and oppression. Under the guise of neutrality, creative writing pedagogy "invents" a trans-social subject that actually serves to legitimate the production of *antisocial* subjects who, in the face of the pressure of principled political practices, retreat from world-historical events into the more "comfortable" and "familiar" domain of the body and personal pleasure (e.g., "he would like to be elsewhere, perhaps home/ with a book or taking a walk"). This is ultimately a class narrative for the privileged liberation of the bourgeois subject of desire in which freedom of expression is the freedom to act on whim; the freedom to do whatever one wants, including the freedom to unleash this desire on women and others.

Under the pressure of increasing social and economic contradictions, more recently creative writing pedagogy has had to "acknowledge" the politics in creative writing but does so by presenting a vacuous notion of politics itself. Erasing politics as class struggle, that is, the struggle for social transformation, Dobyns argues that "all literature is political whether the writer is responding to a sunset or expressing indignation over the world's many injustices. It is political because not only does it make us aware of the world, *it helps us live within the world.* But a distinction can be made between the political and the partisan" ("Voices" 22; emphasis added). This innocuous notion of politics, which substitutes politics as revolutionary social transformation (which determines social priorities and guarantees economic access for all) with politics as strategies of adjustment to the status quo, is really an ideological alibi that helps conceal exploitation by presenting the "world" as a neutral zone without class antagonisms and social oppression in which it is possible to take a political position without being partisan. It further conceals and maintains social alienation, what Marx explains as the process in which workers confront the products of their own labor as a force alien to them (*Capital, Vol. 1* 990). Deploying modes of creative writing pedagogy which argue for politics as "freedom of expression" while occluding the material conditions necessary for equal access to such "expression" (that is, freedom from exploitation), Dobyns presents politics as the struggle to adjust to the existing "world." These ruling class strategies present the "world" as an ahistorical, natural given—an empirically fixed entity—not a product of social labor which can be collectively transformed. This is most strongly manifested in the poem when the "author" provides his explanation to the "experts" for his fantasy: ". . . don't we become blind to the world around us?/ Isn't what we see as progress just a delusion?/ Isn't our country death and what it touches death?" ("Allegorical" 3). Presenting the artist as the "subtle" reader who gives us new insight into the operations of the world, Dobyns in actuality rejects the knowledges that can explain this social alienation (which the poem accepts as "given").

This appeal to "contemporary theory" while still preserving capitalist relations of production is symptomatic of a much larger trend within creative writing and the literary and cultural industry as a whole to update its exchange value in the academic marketplace. Post-al theory, under the pressure of increasing economic and social contradictions in the international division of labor, claims to produce a "liberating" social theory for marginalized social groups. In doing so it criticizes Western thought as inescapably "political" and "ideological" and basically the biased product of the white, middle class, heterosexual male, who represents himself as the "normative subject" of all thought. Dobyns and others advancing "creative writing" pedagogies are having to respond to the same material contradictions and account theoretically for their "politics." But this "politicization" ends up being more of a marketing strategy and an evasion of the actual causes of social injustice. This strategy is deployed in *Colors of a Different Horse: Rethinking Creative Writing Theory and Pedagogy*, which attempts to relegitimate realism by appealing to the (post)structuralist injunction against binaries in order to break down boundaries between "creative writing" and "theory." In its introduction one of the editors argues that in the debate between "theory" and "creative writing" "a potentially more productive approach to take is to redefine arguments across boundaries as dialogues with the self" (Ostrom xvii). Such an approach is meant to "help" the creative writing instructor "open up" to theory by "questioning" her own resistance to it through re-understanding the "theorist" as a person with flaws like herself and "theory" as just one of a series of texts to play with in the workshop. By playing with and parodying theory in her classroom she can "defang theory . . . and help us remember the extent to which our enterprise is mutual" (xviii-xix). Theory in this context is not understood as the historical concepts and analytical practices which make possible a materialist critique that can demystify the social structures that give rise to exploitation, oppression, and alienation. Theory is emptied of its explanatory content and instead becomes a means to justify ones own legitimacy in the marketplace without interrogating the structure of exploitation upon which this legitimacy and class privilege is founded. Theory becomes simply another "text" for "self exploration" and "self expression."

Yet it is precisely this rejection of social theory as explanatory critique that prevents people from understanding the conditions under which they live. If people do not have access to the historical concepts and analytical practices necessary to understand the social arrangements of which they are a part, they will see these not as historical conditions that can be changed through collective praxis, but as fixed, unchangeable, and natural givens in which they are "trapped." Instead of understanding their conditions of life as social and taking collective action to change their world, they treat this oppression (manifesting itself as personal unhappiness and unfulfilled desires) as a personal tragedy. Their goals become not changing the world and the conditions themselves, but the suspension of their own unhappiness. Under these conditions people seek violent "remedies" such as the abuse of children, gay bashing, violence against women, rape, sexual harassment, etc. *"Freedom of expression" without freedom from exploitation is the ruse of the "Liberal" state*: it is a means of crisis management to "help" people "survive" within relations of exploitation without collectively transforming them. Yet to encourage "survival" without social transformation (adjusting to existing social relations) is to teach people to adjust to their own exploitation. By "neutralizing" politics and theory, and concealing its own *partisan* position in protecting existing social arrangements, the dominant form of creative writing pedagogy exempts itself from having to explain exactly what the "problem" is with the *specific* political and theoretical positions it opposes. Consequently, it reveals that far from being concerned with preserving "freedom of expression" the dominant mode of creative writing that Dobyns represents actually contributes to *policing* social theoretical knowledges and radical political praxis in the name of a "nonpartisan" creativity of "free expression."

Under the guise of protecting "freedom" and advancing a progressive position this notion of "creativity" ("to do whatever one wants") legitimates the most reactionary, aggressive, retrograde and brutal sexist practices. Further, by elevating this to a disciplinary and artistic level as the "authentic" mark of creativity, Dobyns and his allies in the culture industry, are blocking other students and faculty from mobilizing their creative practices and art in the service of fighting reactionary social relations. In short in the name of "freedom" this produces an absolute pressure on students and faculty not to act (as evidenced by the fact that the twelve witnesses who knew of Dobyns' sexually harassing practices all along, felt completely unable to do anything about it until the issue was made public). While Dobyns (and others) reject my Marxist notion of socially progressive knowledge, which he called "Stalinist" (the trope in bourgeois discourse for totalitarian), the use of "creativity" and "free expression" as an alibi for sexual harassment marks a backlash against the struggle for social emancipation of all other concerned students and faculty. A telling example of this is the subsequent harassment and intimidation that former Director of Creative Writing Michael Martone received when he refused to remain complicit and silently protect sexual harassment by speaking out against the hostile work environment created by the past silence in the Syracuse University Creative Writing Program, and openly calling for Dobyns' resignation on the basis of his past practices. As a response the "old guard" (led by Tobias Wolff and including Mary Karr, and Brooks Haxton), the most effective collaborators for institutionally shielding sexual harassment at the Program level, attempted to have Michael Martone officially removed from his position as Director. While they did not succeed with an official mandate by the Department of English, for all intents and purposes, they did effectively succeed in marginalizing and alienating both Martone and Assistant Professor Melanie Rae Thon—the only two Creative Writing faculty members who took a public stand against Dobyns' sexual harassment practices—so that both felt compelled to leave the Program. As an article in a student newspaper, *The Summer Orange*, reports: "Martone said he left because he feared retribution by his colleagues . . . He said if he had remained at SU, it would not have been a good working environment" (Mehta, "Three Years" 10). In short, the "old guard" advancing "freedom of expression," far from fostering an "open environment," had created an environment that forced out the faculty members in the Creative Writing Program who immediately stood up against Dobyns and *dissented* from the whitewashing of his sexually harassing practices.

The defense of "freedom of expression" without freedom from exploitation and oppression is really a bankrupt notion of "freedom" which serves as an alibi for sexual harassment by promoting the creative subject as the entrepreneur of desire. The argument for the unregulated exercise of personal pleasure promotes a culture of consumption in which it is understood to be "creative" to consume, and any mode of consumption—including sexual consumption in which "art" routinely uses violence against women as part of its exchange value—is understood to be an expression of artistic creativity and the mark of "true liberation." Yet what such a politics occludes is the regime of profit and wage labor that undergirds the *production* of the commodities that are consumed. The redefinition of "creativity" is not the only strategy used to occlude production and displace it with consumption. The "creativity" of "Creative Writing" is not a freestanding practice rather, it is a more pronounced articulation of mainstream notions of pedagogy which aim to produce subjects who will invent newer and newer modes of consumption. The pedagogical practice that endorses "creativity" as "intuition" or "unrestrained expression" is part of a much larger strategy of the *pedagogy of pleasure* in the bourgeois knowledge and culture industry aimed at legitimating compulsory consumption and subordinating more layers of social life to the dictates of commodity production and exchange.

Four

The pedagogy of pleasure, as might be expected from any historically constructed set of practices, is also deployed in the dominant discourses and practices in contemporary studies of gender and sexuality. Like the "creative writing" regime of truth, these post-al knowledges are also founded upon the "autonomy" of the desire of a subject free from economic determination. Post-al feminism and queer theory to a large extent have been part of a much broader diversion from politics as the revolutionary struggle to transform the social relations of production and toward a notion of politics as the production of pleasure within existing social relations. Advanced by such theorists as Rubin, Meese, Probyn, and Grosz this can be seen in the turn of feminism, aided by the emergence of ludic queer theory, from focusing on gender to focusing on sexuality and "desire" as autonomous practices separate from gender and class—which is to say, free from the constraints of patriarchy and capitalism. Articulating "sexuality" as the new "supplement" on the discursive horizon that "subverts" and "disrupts" the "center" (of "gender" and "class"), ludic theories of desire understand freedom of sexuality to be tantamount to the deregulation of all collective principles. For this new wave of ludic theories of desire, desire is "always already" a disruptive force that "perverts" any attempt at the production of knowledge and collective solidarity in the struggle for a society that produces for need. Producing for need is impossible according to ludic theories of desire, which understand desire as prior to need. Any collective attempt to prioritize basic needs is understood as an attempt to generalize the desires of some as needs for all. For ludic theories, needs are always already only effects of subjective desires and it is desire that produces need. Yet, it is only from the standpoint of the ruling class—those who have their basic needs met—that desire undergirds collective needs. Opposing *all* collective norms is a marker of class privilege in its erasure of a collective society in which "the free development of each is the condition for the free development of all." If desire is to be equated with the disruption of *all* norms, then collective struggle for social emancipation (which requires a commitment to collective principles) is represented as an unnecessary or impossible means for social change.

On the terms of post-al theories of desire, the historical and material basis of sexual harassment is impossible to determine because such a determination requires principles of analysis and the production of coherent knowledges of the larger system of oppression and exploitation of women. At the same time, these theories claim to be "more historical" and "more material" for denying the possibility of reliable knowledge of objective reality. Yet, for post-al politics, the "historical" is really understood as the process of signification while the "material" is defined in terms of what Red Feminist Teresa Ebert, in her book *Ludic Feminism and After*, calls "matterism": an idealist construction of materialism that equates material reality with "inert objects," and the experiences, sensations, and pleasures of the body. One particularly prominent example of the post-al feminist erasure of the historical and material basis of sexual harassment can be found in the writings of Jane Gallop. In the wake of accusations against her for sexual harassment of two of her female students, Gallop has been at the forefront of extending retro-feminist and post-feminist attacks on the opposition to sexual harassment and violence against women. Gallop's whitewashing of violence against women is often presented in a "high theoretical" mode that purports to overcome epistemological inadequacies undergirding existing sexual harassment policies and identitarian forms of feminism. However, as I will demonstrate, this veneer of "high theory" and epistemological "sophistication" is actually a ruse for a return to the "self-evidency" of "experience," the desires of the ruling class, and the transparency of consent. It is a ruse that effectively erases the unequal power structures in the workplace for women (and workers generally)—structures that are themselves enabled by social relations of production in capitalism in which a few who own the means of production are able to appropriate the surplus-labor of others and command over their labor. In order to produce the material conditions necessary for all workers—including all women—to be emancipated from exploitation, violence, harassment, and oppression, it is imperative to abolish the system of private ownership that allows for a few to command over the labor of others.

In her essay "The Teacher's Breasts," Gallop on one level presents herself as a "sophisticated" and "nuanced" reader/writer who is "aware" of the historical basis of gender and sexuality and "rigorous" in acknowledging it. She argues against the identity politics (what she calls "maternal" or "good girl pedagogy") prevalent in the traditional Women's Studies classroom on the grounds that it fixes gendered meaning by assuming a "mother/daughter" relationship as the foundation for teacher student relations. This identity politics advances a simple reversal of gender relations by valorizing women's experience and "feminine" attributes (such as "nurturance," "caring," "community," etc.) without investigating the "historicity" of such experiences and attributes. In doing so, traditional feminist teaching, Gallop says, ends up promoting a notion of gender that is "idealized, decontextualized, and removed from history" (*Pedagogy* 87). It is this "idealized" understanding of gender, Gallop claims in *Feminist Accused of Sexual Harassment*, that is behind current policies against sexual harassment which go beyond the "traditional" case of *quid pro quo* harassment (barter of sexual favors, etc. for job security, grades, etc.) involving a man in a higher position of institutional power who harasses a woman in a lower position of institutional power. For Gallop, those policies that problematize same-sex harassment, the harassment of workers by institutionally powerful men *and* women, and the limits to consent in consensual relations between faculty and students, are part of a "protectionist" effort that makes "sex" and multiple forms of sexuality criminal. Moreover, she contends that recent policies are anti-feminist because they discriminate against "powerful women" and construct women as "victims" incapable of making their own "choices."

They do so, according to Gallop, because they confuse "gender discrimination" with "sex." For Gallop "sexual harassment is criminal not because it is sex but because it is discrimination" (*Feminist Accused* 10). By "discrimination" Gallop means overtly targeting a particular social group. If sexual harassment does not target women only or isolate any particular group, according to Gallop it is not "harassment," it is merely sexual. Thus, when a professor advances a post-al pedagogy of desire and "sexualizes" the workplace consistently for all students, she is not discriminating and thus should not be accused of harassment. On these terms, extending the scope of anti-harassment policy beyond *quid pro quo* discrimination against women by men is to enforce a "bloated general application" which criminalizes sex: "when it is possible to conceive of sexual harassment without discrimination, then sexual harassment becomes a crime of sexuality rather than of discrimination" (*Feminist Accused* 10). Consequently, Gallop claims that it is necessary to restrict anti-sexual harassment policy to gender only, so that it does not encompass sexuality. Yet, what Gallop effectively erases in this retheorization are the unequal power relations between a tenured professor and her students and, moreover, the creation of a "hostile work environment" in which the desires of the institutionally powerful have free reign at the expense of the material and intellectual needs of the majority. Discrimination is not merely the effect of isolating a particular group, it arises as a result of material inequality in class societies in which the needs of many are subordinated to the desires of a privileged few.

By restricting a theorization of sexual harassment to gender, Gallop claims that she is putting feminism back into policies on sexual harassment. Yet, she can only claim this by advancing a retro-feminism which turns the clock back on the historically necessary development of feminist knowledges which connect gender to other forms of social oppression. By erasing her institutional privilege over others, it becomes quite clear that this "commitment" to ending violence against women is actually an opportunistic use of feminism to ideologically exempt herself—*as a powerful woman*—from her complicity in and perpetuation of violence against other women.   What she assumes is that institutionally powerful women, because they have experiences of "feeling powerful and sexy, smart and successful," are representative of the cutting edge of feminism. The entrepreneurial use of "successful" is the key concept here. Gallop obscures the fact that the "successful" is always successful *within the dominant social relations*. The "successful" is, in other words, the effect of working within the system—the very system that is structured on the social division of labor and marginalization of women. She does not question the social relations in which she and other women have become "powerful" and "successful" and thus ignores the reorganization of relations of production in the international division of labor in which capitalism is perfectly supportive of enabling *some* women to succeed within its ranks so as to more effectively manage the majority of women as free and cheap labor. Despite her objections to "identity politics," Gallop is quite all right with advancing an essentialized notion of "women" which erases the class differences between women who benefit from capitalist relations of production and those whose basic material needs can only be consistently and equally met through a fundamental abolition of the regime of profit and wage-labor. As long as this identification "as a woman" benefits her class interests it is perfectly fine, but insofar as it requires her, as a petit-bourgeois woman, to subordinate her "personal" desires and class privilege to the collective struggle to end the exploitation and oppression of all women, it is "essentialist." In the name of "feminism" and freedom of sexuality for all, Gallop's notion of desire is in actuality an insular one which is concerned with freedom of desires for some relatively privileged women.

Gallop is able to characterize those fighting against "hostile work environments" as "protectionist" because she erases the power relations and material inequalities that arise from class societies and presents "sexuality" and "desire" as if they are autonomous from larger social structures and material inequalities. Attempting to epistemologically debunk "protectionism" and an "essentialized" notion of women, and claiming to "deconstruct" a false opposition between the "personal" and "professional" in anti sexual harassment policy, Gallop rehearses the by now familiar ludic deconstruction of subjectivity. This ludic theory of subjectivity posits a self-inventing discourse divorced from the social relations of production as the condition of possibility for agency. However, as I will explain below, when agency, sexuality, desire and "choice" are abstracted from their social and material conditions of possibility, and represented as autonomous and "self-inventing" practices, it is then possible to represent struggles for basic material equality as calls for "special privileges" and "protection."

Gallop's theory of a self-inventing discourse is manifested most clearly in the theory of "impersonation" that she articulates in her introduction to *Pedagogy: The Question of Impersonation*, which serves as the basis for her subsequent analysis of gender and sexual harassment in "The Teacher's Breasts." Formally, Gallops theory of subjectivity appears to be quite different from the traditional theories of a "volitional" subject. Specifically, Gallop claims that "im-personation" calls into question "the traditional opposition between the personal as authentic and impersonation as false performance, . . . acknowledges the inadequacy of that opposition and moves beyond it" (*Pedagogy* 7). This "moving beyond" the opposition between the "constructed" and the "authentic" is articulated in Gallop through the notion of "in-voicing" (a concept presented in George Otte's contribution to the anthology): "Taking on someone else's voice is no longer just a restricted, specific practice but becomes 'a practice we all constantly enact'; not only the odd imitation but 'whatever is said is mostly borrowed'" (*Pedagogy* 17). In other words, impersonation is understood as a repetition of pre-existing discursive norms in which to posit a discursive "outside" to "impersonation" is at the same time to *construct* that "outside" as an "authentic identity" constituted in discourse (i.e., a "constitutive outside" that is an extension of the textuality of the "inside"). Consequently subjectivity is not a result of one's location within material relations (whether one owns the means of production or has only her labor-power to sell in order to survive) rather, it is an effect of one's location within discursive relations. For Gallop (like Butler and other post-al theoreticians) subjectivity *is* citation. To argue otherwise, according to Gallop, is to advance a "volitional misunderstanding" of performance which presupposes that subjects are autonomous from discourse and can choose to be "whatever [they] want" (*Pedagogy* 15).

Yet, if positing the possibility of a material "outside" to citationality always already assumes an "intentional" subject, on what material basis does ludic feminism account for a "radically different" impersonation? Gallop argues, "the way beyond the debilitating opposition between the personal and professional is to speak 'through a playful, *inventive*, eclectic use of preexisting genres'" (Karamcheti as quoted in Gallop 7; emphasis added). In short, "radically different" impersonations are a result of discursive *invention*. This mode of "invention," if not the product of a volitional subject is, on the terms of ludic politics, the product of what Butler (following Barthes and Derrida) calls "citationality": the imminent repetition of the structure of signification itself. In other words, discourse is the condition of possibility of its own "inventiveness"—the laws of motion of signification itself (*différance*) are what propel this repetition in "radically new" directions. Impersonation is defended as a *self-inventing* practice cut off from social, historical and economic conditions: cut off from the social relations of production.

Insofar as "im-personation" involves the *repetition* of already existing discursive norms, Gallop's ludic politics cannot account for the historical and material production of these discourses. If it cannot account for the occluded structures that give rise to the reproduction of discourses of gender, this form of politics cannot open up the possibility of intervening in these structures and transforming them in order to abolish the historical necessity for "gender." Ludic political intervention instead understands resignification and "discursive performance" as ends in themselves, as if a "redescription" or "re-metaphorization" of gender were tantamount to the revolutionary social transformation of material relations. It is not surprising that for Gallop what is most important as a signal of change for women is that they are *perceived* as freely desiring and freely consenting subjects. For Gallop, "the crucial question is whether women are treated as mere sex objects or whether we are *recognized* as desiring subjects" (*Feminist Accused* 37; emphasis added). Gallop "shares a preference for something like 'power feminism,'" a retro-feminist movement which "complain[s] that the feminist focus on phenomena like date rape and sexual harassment is reinforcing the notion that women are victims" (71). For Gallop, those forms of feminism that work to produce knowledges of the material conditions which oppress and exploit women are "victim feminisms," "stuck in an image of women's fragility," while "power feminism" focuses on the "need . . . to recognize, enjoy, and enhance our power" (71). Thus, Gallop opposes anti-sexual harassment policies which emphasize "hostile work environment" and unequal "power relations" on the idealist grounds that it is feminist discourses which critique the oppression of women, that are responsible for making women victims. This is idealist because it assumes that discourse theologically brings into being that which it names: *saying* and *perceiving* that women are oppressed and producing knowledges of the conditions of oppression, *causes* our oppression and, by contrast, *saying* and *perceiving* that we are "freely consenting" and "powerful" *causes* our "liberation." In doing so, this idealism blocks the production of the knowledges necessary to effectively intervene in and transform the conditions of women's oppression and exploitation, and moreover, reproduces the reactionary ruling class fantasy that people need only look within themselves and "recognize their power"—that is, pull themselves up by their own bootstraps—in order to be "powerful."

For Gallop, social change does not involve the fundamental transformation of the social relations of production in order to abolish exploitation—including the exploitation of women's paid and unpaid labor which economically compels them to go along with and "adjust" to harassment and "hostile work environments." Rather than struggling to produce a society in which all persons have material equality and collective ownership and control of social resources, social change and the power necessary for "self-determination" is to be found in parody, citation, pastiche, and quotation. On these terms, emancipation (which has itself been deconstructed by Laclau, Butler and others) is determined by access to discourse, not access to material resources. "Freedom" is tantamount to freedom of speech (and writing, citing, quoting . . .) not freedom from economic exploitation. Like Dobyns' notion of "creative expression," Gallop's so called "radical" politics is really a liberal whitewashing of the social and economic conditions which serve to block the exploited and oppressed masses from being "heard" and revolutionary positions from being produced. Moreover, it is a promotion of "liberty" (the liberation of desire) for those who already have access to the material means to fulfill their basic needs and the "excess" which allows them to control the livelihood of others. Such a whitewashing has little to do with social transformation for the benefit of all women and much more to do with preserving conditions of privilege for those few women who benefit from the existing social relations of production in capitalism.

This is the case because "discursive invention" promotes the understanding that there is no possibility of producing objective historical knowledges and effectively intervening in the material relations "outside" of discourse. In doing so it naturalizes these relations. The theory of representation that argues that there is no "outside" to discourse (or that we can never get to this "outside") assumes that all representations are always already misrepresentations—that there is an *undecidable* relation between "discursive" and "non-discursive" dimensions of reality which always already blurs our ability to explain the "non-discursive." Now, at the beginning of a new millennium, post-al theory has in fact reached a theoretical impasse because it is no longer able to "persuasively" ignore or mystify the "outside." Thus we are now witnessing a new wave of writing aimed at solving the problem of the outside pragmatically as in Cary Wolfe's *Critical Environment: Postmodern Theory and the Pragmatics of the "Outside"* (Minneapolis: University of Minnesota Press, 1998). Wolfe's book continues the bourgeois mystification of the "outside" by translating the more overtly idealist notion of discursive performativity into pragmatic systems theory's entrepreneurial notion of "operational truth." What Gallop, Wolfe and other post-al writers on "outside" erase, of course, is the question of class and property relations. As a result the "real" is either overtly replaced by the "text" (Gallop, Butler) or truncated and transformed by a violent reductionism (as in Wolfe) into the reality operational under capitalism, and the goal of radical political practice becomes the liberation of the subject of ironic or pragmatic interpretation. The pragmatic (as Rorty makes it clear) is always already ironic (of "principles"). Yet it is necessary to argue against the idea that there is no "outside" except as an operational outside. As Donald Morton and Mas'ud Zavarzadeh argue, this notion of representation,

> denies the alienation of the "real"—the fact that, as Marx has argued, there is, in class-based societies, always a distance between the "appearance" and the "real," between *what is* empirically and *what is* structurally. Through his notion of representation as always being misrepresentation (because the medium of representation—language—is itself subject to the laws of *différance*), Derrida posits this gap as ahistorical and eternal, as part of the human condition as such. (96).

The distance between the empirical and the structural is a historical and material distance produced through the process of exploitation in which the extraction of surplus-labor gives rise to the alienation of workers from the products of their own labor. The distance between representation and reality is not a transhistorical product of language itself. It is the effect of production practices of the ruling class and its legitimating ideology, which is produced to conceal the process of exploitation (the historical basis of alienation), rendering it fixed and unchangeable. It is precisely the seeming "staticness" of reality that capital promotes in order to prevent workers from understanding that it is through the exploitation of their collective labor that "what is" structurally exists and it is through their collective opposition to this exploitation that this reality can be transformed. The post-al deconstruction of the empirical, insofar as it replaces the "real" with the "text," and understands the distance between the two to be an inherent function of language, a transhistorical disparity (without accounting for the fact that language is itself produced under definite historical circumstances), contributes to the ideological legitimation of capitalist class relations by presenting the "play" of signification (and the corresponding difficulty in explaining reality) itself as a *natural given* not a product of the capitalist relations of production that rely on "misrepresentation" to justify exploitation.

Discursive "invention," then, is an ideological strategy of the ruling class deployed to conceal *material production* and the class contradictions and antagonisms on which it is based. It is not an epistemological succession of the inadequacies of prior theories as it claims but a mystification of material inequality and an erasure of the revolutionary struggle to abolish social relations of production based on the desires of some (i.e., profit) not the needs of all. This notion of discursive "invention" is the basis upon which post-Marxist apologists for wage-labor such as Laclau and Mouffe can claim that "the question about the conditions of possibility of the being of discourse is meaningless. It is equivalent to asking a materialist for the conditions of possibility of matter" ("Post-Marxism" 105). Not only do Laclau and Mouffe indicate that, in the name of "non-reductivism," they *reduce* social phenomenon to discourse, they also demonstrate that they have a complete lack of understanding of the historical and dialectical materialism that they reject. It is a "lack of understanding" based on their own complicity in and legitimation of ruling class interests. Indeed, historical materialism *does* investigate and account for the conditions of possibility of "matter" (Lacau and Mouffe's code word for "things") in the historical structures of the forces and relations of production. "Matter" as "thing," as Teresa Ebert has argued, is the product of the social relations of production—of labor practices and the class conflicts of which they are a part ("*Red* Feminism" 126). The "matter" in historical materialism is not a static, reified mass—a "thing"—it is an historical structure of social contradictions and antagonisms. The bracketing of an investigation of the conditions of possibility of such fundamental concepts as "discourse" (for textualists) or "matter" (for materialists) as "absurd" is really an alibi for ludic theorists not to account for their discursive practices on historical and material terms. Just as "intuition" in creative writing pedagogy is used to exempt the artist from accounting for her political practices, "invention" in ludic postmodern theory exempts the intellectual from having to account for her discursive practices on social, material, and historical terms. If discourse "invents" itself and its own repetition, if knowledge is not a product of material social practices but is rather the product of the inherent structure of language, then the intellectual cannot act on principles as they are always disrupted by the play of signification.

What then are the consequences of this theory of discursive "invention" for the struggle to emancipate women from exploitation, violence and harassment? Gallop and other ludic feminists endorse a "contemporary radicalization in feminist and queer theory that views all gender as performance" (*Pedagogy* 12). Yet, if gender *is* performance or impersonation (or citationality, or parody . . .), and there is nothing behind impersonation except the "impersonation" itself, Gallop ultimately argues that there is nothing behind gender except gender itself. "Gender" is itself the cause of "gender"! Gender becomes an immaterial, *self-inventing* practice—a ludic essentialism—which is cut off from the historical structures of the mode of production. Gender "rewrites" itself— it invents itself—and is discursively reversible. Such a notion of gender rips it out of historical and material relations and makes it flexible (like the "free play" of language) but unchangeable (like the presumed "inherentness" of this "free play").

It is this discursivist and self-inventing notion of gender that enables Gallop, in "The Teacher's Breasts," to read the sexual harassment of a female teacher by her male student as a "subversive" repetition of gendered norms. Reading Helene Keyssar's "Staging the

Feminist Classroom," Gallop purports to reject the identitarian terms upon which Keyssar has based her feminist pedagogy and a reading of an instance of sexual harassment in her classroom. However, Gallop does so by severing sexual harassment from a much broader system of the exploitation and oppression of women. During a scene in a play that Keyssar's class produced (Susan Miller's *Cross Country*), the heroine, a teacher, sexually harasses a male student who has been elected by his classmates to find out why she refuses to respond to their work for the course. When he goes into her office, rather than taking him seriously on an intellectual level (by producing an explanation that would publicly and openly account for her pedagogical practices), she instead kisses him (thus privileging the privatized "flow of desire" as an "uncontrollable urge" over public conceptual engagement). In Keyssar's class itself the situation is reversed with the person in the class who is playing the student in the scene and the person who is playing the teacher. While in the play the student leaves "but not without first touching her breasts" (Miller as quoted in Keyssar as quoted in Gallop, *Pedagogy* 83), the student in the class, growing hostile to the pressure exerted on his own gendered practices, "strode toward her and fiercely, with overt erotic impulse, grabbed and held each of her breasts" (Keyssar quoted in Gallop, *Pedagogy* 84). In the series of class discussions following this incident Keyssar finds herself having to contradict her own pedagogical principles of "undermining" her authority in the classroom by instead making use of her authority through providing a contesting interpretation of this scene. Meanwhile the student "insisted on the correctness of his initial interpretation, essentially on the grounds that 'no man would do otherwise'" (Keyssar as quoted in Gallop, *Pedagogy* 84).

In her re-reading of Keyssar's interpretation of this scene, Gallop affirms the student's reading by arguing that,

> I don't know what Keyssar's phrase "literally touching" literally means, but it suggests that when the script said "touching her breasts," the sense should be self-evident, "literal," not a matter of interpretation. And thus the interpretation by the so-called man playing the student would be particularly egregious. Keyssar tells it as if everyone else could see immediately how it should have been done, and the error thus could only be some sort of acting out. (*Pedagogy* 84).

Gallop can only say this because she presupposes an ahistorical undecidability between material relations and reading practices. **If there is an undecidable relation between the "text" and the "real," one cannot draw a conclusion about what is and what is not sexual harassment**. Yet to press charges for sexual harassment (to appeal to collective standards) one has to uphold principles that critique the objective conditions which (re)produce gender. If gender is the beginning and the end of itself, if gender is a trope that constantly re-writes itself; that is constantly re-written and recited through impersonation, then holding particular subjects accountable for their social and material practices (as when one is charged with sexual harassment), is seen as itself a participation in the reification and perpetuation of the regime of gender. Of course, this sort of maneuver (i.e., the "undecidability" of gender, property, etc.) is at the core of (post)structuralist jurisprudence (advanced by such ludic legal theorists as Fish, Derrida, Cornell . . .). A slippery law is useful for the ruling class since the ruled cannot prove its case against it. In the name of "subverting," "loosening" and "freeing up" gender, this preserves gender oppression by leaving those who are the targets of sexist violence with no recourse to do anything about it.

In the name of "undecidability" and discursive inventiveness, Gallop advances a reactionary determinate position while occluding the fact that she is doing so. Criticizing Keyssar's use of her authority as a pedagogue to intervene in sexist practices, Gallop argues that, "while feminist teaching based in appropriate feminine behavior has been implicitly defined by gender, feminist pedagogy can teach us to analyze effects of gender in our pedagogical practice rather than just acting them out" (*Pedagogy* 88). What Gallop is actually arguing is that it is not the male student who assumes that his desires are "given" ("no man would do otherwise") that is "acting out" rather, it is the feminist pedagogy which has attempted to intervene in this "self-evidency" by producing a counter-interpretation, that is "acting out." Here Gallop, like Dobyns, represents herself as the "rebel" against the "totalitarianism" of "political correctness" and, in arguing that the male student was simply "performing" desire, manifests the same nostalgia for a time without challenges to the so-called "self-evidency" of desire.

It is her reification of gender and desire that allows Gallop to argue that while the "woman-to-woman paradigm shows the teacher giving up her authority and its association with distantiation in favor of blurring the boundaries between teachers and students . . . [m]aleness in either teacher or student affects this paradigmatic blurring of authority" (*Pedagogy* 80). *By virtue of his identity*, the presence of a male student in the feminist classroom, according to Gallop, "poses a sexual question, if not a paradigmatic threat" (*Pedagogy* 81). What the male student (and particularly for Gallop, the "insubordinate" male student) disrupts and reveals in the traditional feminist classroom is its implicit gendering of teacher and students. On Gallop's terms, while the "all female" feminist classroom operates along the lines of a "hyper-feminine gendering of sexuality" and the male teacher/female student relation is, within this paradigm, "sexualized as harassment," the "male *students* . . . can neither be subsumed in the maternal desexualized erotic nor made to fit the sexual harassment case" (*Pedagogy* 81).

Engaging in a post-al diversion which appeals to the ludic notion of supplementarity—proposing that all identities are so fluidly invented and reinvented as to make it impossible to assign anyone a particular identity—Gallop contributes to the mystification of the difference between aggressor and victim, between oppressor and oppressed, and between exploiter and exploited. She does this by inventing a "split" between the "man" and the "student": is he the "man playing the student" or the "student playing the man"? Is he "really" engaging in practices of sexual harassment or is he performing? Can anyone "really" be engaged in any practices except performance? This follows the same logic as those defenders of Dobyns' practices of sexual harassment who would argue for the separation of "art" and "politics" and therefore exempt Dobyns from responsibility under the guise of "artistic freedom." The "man" in Dobyns is in no way connected to the "artist" in Dobyns since "art" and "politics" are entirely distinct and whoever attempts to relate them is engaged in political and theoretical totalitarianism. There is a "split" in the element called "Dobyns" and as such, we cannot find him guilty of any sexual harassment since we never know who Dobyns is: is he the MAN or the ARTIST? This logic makes it impossible to talk about Dobyns' sexist violence. Dobyns as an active bearer of social relations responsible for the social consequences of his practices disappears in the gap that his defenders invent. Just as the split between "art" and "politics" perpetuated in creative writing represents it as impossible to hold Dobyns accountable for his sexist violence (as we never know whether he is "performing" as a "man" or an "artist"), the split between "interpretation" (i.e., aesthetics) and "politics" as a material struggle that Gallop and others "invent" makes it impossible to find a male student guilty of sexual harassment, as we can never determine who he is: is he performing as a "man" or a "student"? Social principles disappear in the "gap" that post-al politics "invents" within "identity-as-difference" and the aggressors of oppressive practices are acquitted on the grounds of "incoherency" (and one that outdoes Dobyns' own defense of "incoherency" induced by alcohol!). However, the practices engaged in by the student in Keyssar's classroom were indeed an "acting out" of sexual harassment, although not as a result of the student's "innate" desires. Rather, in a time when putting a "human face" on capitalism is historically unconvincing; when capital literally cannot afford the "niceties" of social reform and as a result there is a backlash against all marginalized groups and a reprivatization of historical and material gains made by these groups, such a response on the part of a student to the critical pressure and intellectual ideas of his teacher is an instance of the backlash against feminism which is itself a manifestation of a global backlash against women under capitalism.

Keyssar's experientialist response to this incident, which ultimately argues that the student could not have known how to behave otherwise because he did not share experiences of oppression with women, is also limited. It is an inadequate response to sexual harassment because it assumes that understanding the "effects" of the oppression of women through descriptions of "experience" is enough to produce knowledges that can explain the historical material *causes* of this oppression. This promotes a reformist politics aimed at "making up" for the damages done to women and other marginalized subjects without a transformation of the conditions which give rise to these damages. However, Gallop's point of contention is ultimately not with this reformism (no matter what she "intends"), it is with the fact that Keyssar took a *decisive* position against sexual harassment. Gallop privileges objections to the "violence" of the closure of meaning over the struggle against the violence of sexual harassment and the global exploitation of which it is a part.

This notion of the "undecidability" (autonomy) of desire is in no small degree part of the elaborate strategies Gallop is deploying to explain away violence against women and to whitewash the sexual harassment charges against her, brought about by two of her own students. Her own practices which include "french kissing" a student in a bar and making public statements that refer to herself as "someone who might say her sexual preference is graduate students," she has publicly defended as "engaging in a 'performance', not acting on desire" (Talbot 34). Such performances, Gallop sees as a subversive resistance to the institutional codes that separate the "personal" and the "professional"—a resistance that she claims undermines her "authority" with students. Yet all of this really ends up being used as a pragmatic strategy by Gallop to protect her privilege to do "whatever she wants." Gallop purports, in an "academic" mode, to "problematize" the presumed naturalness of desire when she claims, for example, that she thinks of "flirting, theoretically, as a way of seducing students to learn" (Talbot 32). Yet, she has no difficulty renaturalizing the "flow of desire" in an "informal" mode when she states that: "Certainly part of who I've *always* been socially since I was an adult . . . is someone who makes sexual jokes with just about anybody, aside from strangers on a bus. I am someone who is sometimes flirtatious and who likes acting somewhat outrageous" (Talbot 29; emphasis added). By presenting herself as "always already" jocular and "always already" flirtatious (i.e., this is just the way "I AM"), Gallop erases the violence of sexual harassment and trivializes her practices by invoking the banal patriarchal cliché that she "was only joking." On these terms, holding Gallop accountable for her practices would be to impose limits on her "authentic" personality and "fun nature." This theoretical eclecticism between a notion of "authentic" individuality and "constructed" subjectivity reveals that her "commitment" to pedagogical principles that "challenge" institutional relations through "seduction" (as if students can only be challenged sexually) in the name of "bad girl" feminism and breaking down the naturalization of gender and desire, is really a pragmatic move to protect a petit-bourgeois lifestyle politics. Further, it *objectifies* students as if they can only be challenged sexually, *as static bodies*, and not intellectually and politically as members of a social collectivity.

Despite Gallop's denials, she herself is compelled to recognize the historical bankruptcy of her own "subversive revisionism" and its absolute ineffectivity in challenging the material conditions which reproduce gender. To this end Gallop states: "The sexual innuendo that functioned ten years ago to mark me as one of the girls with my students now marks me out as one of the guys" (Talbot, 30). What Gallop historically must recognize, but denies at every turn, is that her own pedagogical practices do not so much "subvert" or "reverse" gender as they do legitimate her own position of privilege in the academy in particular and her class privilege in general. This is further manifested in her statement that: "one of the reasons I can't undercut my authority with students by being shockingly informal is that my authority is based on an authorial persona that is itself shockingly informal—that's part of its authority. It seems like a terrible contradiction" (Talbot 30). While Gallop's analysis of her authority is itself an idealist one that occludes the fact that it is a product of her *class* position (not merely a projected persona) and the relative institutional status that she has as a commodifiable (and therefore money making) celebrity for the intellectual entertainment of others in her class, she is haunted by the contradiction that this class position produces for the "sometimes" radical professor: the contradiction between an expressed commitment to radical politics and a material interest in maintaining her relative privilege. Her "shocking persona," far from being the "progressive" position that she claims, is in actuality symptomatic of the violent managerial practices occurring all over the globe in which women are the targets of ruthless violence in order to legitimate the extraction of higher levels of surplus value from their labor.

Gallop attempts to deflect this charge by the "ethical" stance that her notion of "impersonation" is not a "depersonalizing strain that denies the connection between discourses and the bodies that produce them" (*Pedagogy* 15). Gallop "acknowledges" the existence of the material production of discourse, but she does so by redefining "materiality" itself as "matterism"—specifically the "matterism" of the body, sensations, and pleasures. For Gallop, as she makes clear in a nostalgic depiction of her "young feminist" undergraduate days, feminist solidarity is "symbolically enacted" in the heaping together of female bodies, in dancing bare-breasted, in the role-reversal of a lesbian teacher-student affair (*Feminist Accused* 12-16). In short, solidarity is in the commonality of women's bodies and their desires for one another, "a commonality that seemed to override the various social and institutional roles that separated us" (16). In this identitarian understanding of feminism, the female body and its desires "subvert" institutional relations. "The body" is the "excess" to the constraints of signification—it is a mass that "resists" signification and hence any form of theorization. Having excluded the possibility of explaining any set of relations other than discursive relations, in order to refer to "the body" as a material entity which produces discourse, Gallop and other post-al feminists must presuppose the existence of a "body" that lies in no relations whatsoever until it is inculcated into discursive relations.

Yet this is a violent suppression of the *material relations* in which "bodies" are inculcated: the relations of production in which the materiality of "the body" is a product of the praxis of labor—of practical activity and the class structures that determine this activity. In mystifying the relations of production—which in all class based societies are founded on exploitation—and reducing material relations to a transhistorical reified "body," these relations themselves are represented as fixed, ahistorical, and unchangeable. What is at stake in accepting such a theory is the abandonment of a project for emancipation from the exploitative social relations that are the economic basis of all hostile work environments—a project that can actually explain these relations in order to enable the collective intervention into and revolutionary transformation of them. This is a particularly damaging retreat for feminism in the era of transnational capitalism in which all over the globe women's unpaid and paid labor is increasingly subordinated to the capitalist relations of production and its regime of profit. Yet, in the proto-fascist imaginary of capitalism's consumer culture, those who argue for the necessity of critiquing material inequalities and producing a society in which all persons are free from exploitation are, as Gallop puts it, enforcing a "colorless egalitarian utopia where all women [are] the same" (16).

The class character of "discursive reversibility" of gender and its subsequent reification of material relations is thrown into sharp relief when we examine how this operates in the specific situation of Syracuse University. It is precisely the occlusion of material relations and its subsequent rejection of principled collective praxis that enabled the Women's Studies Program at Syracuse University from its Director Diane Murphy to its most casual associates to remain absolutely silent about Dobyns' sexual harassment in the public forum. Opportunistically claiming to be working "behind the scenes" along the "proper" institutional channels, Murphy is reported to have encouraged this "code of silence" while others pragmatically agreed. One professor offered her "personal support" rather than public commitment while another later suggested that if I (and members of the Revolutionary Marxist Collective) had not been so publicly critical in the past of the limits of the (bourgeois) feminist practices of the Women's Studies Program, then the Women's Studies faculty would have supported my case. In short, these so called "feminists" refused to come out publicly against the sexual harassment of a student who has an understanding of feminism (namely Marxist) different from their own and finds it historically urgent to publicly advance it.

This is because Syracuse University Women's Studies faculty operate not along the lines of principled solidarity and social commitment rather, they operate along Donna Haraway's liberal hegemonic coalitionism of "affinity" (155-157) or what Chela Sandoval has called "postmodern love": "a complex kind of love in the postmodern world where love is understood as affinity—alliance and affection across lines of difference" (413). In the absence of a materialist analysis and critique of the conditions that give rise to social inequality and exploitation, the post-al feminists of the Women's Studies Program concentrate on "compensating" for the effects of oppression through a mere "affirmation of differences." Thus, those who do not merely "celebrate differences" but advance a critique of the conditions of exploitation and material inequality that produce these differences, are considered to be too "dogmatic" and "authoritarian." But these practices of "affirmation" of "difference" are quite useful to relatively privileged women in the academy who do not want to subordinate their professionalist and personal interests (articulated as their own "particular differences") to the principles of the collective practice of critique. Acting just like Dobyns who makes use of "liberal ethics" to police radical practices (which he claims "bullies" those who aren't "converted"), these women can protect their petit-bourgeois privilege under the name of a tolerance for difference. Consequently, they privilege the privatized practices of affirmation, personal pleasure and reform not the world historical practices of critique, social emancipation, and revolutionary transformation. In the face of the praxis of critique these so called "feminists" retreat into the more comfortable and familiar domain of "friendship" and "experience." In short, they align themselves as Gallop does "for the feel of it all" (*Feminist Accused* 3). That is, when it feels good or is professionally advantageous to them.

The bankruptcy of the appeal to the so-called "dogmatism" of Marxist-Feminism as a way to protect the Women's Studies Program from public critique is made strikingly evident in subsequent sexual harassment cases at Syracuse University. In more recent cases other students (and their families) have found the University's sexual harassment policies, authored by Syracuse University Women's Studies Director Diane Murphy and Women's Studies Professor Marie Provine, to be inadequate. In a case against Syracuse University Tennis Coach Jesse Dwire for verbal and physical sexual harassment of female athletes, the University used these policies to minimize the reported sexual harassment to "verbal harassment" (giving Dwire only three months of suspension without pay during the summer of 1997). The students who were the targets of this harassment and their families (who are now suing Syracuse University for negligence in their ruling) "contend that the university's sexual harassment policy, developed by social work Director Diane Lydon Murphy, and political science professor Marie Provine, had failed them" (Goldstein 1). Rather than confront the inadequacies of their policies and practices in fighting sexual harassment and the oppression and exploitation of women, the Women's Studies faculty uphold a "code of silence" and participate in blame-the-victim strategies that find "fault" with the victim in order to justify their silence and non-action. On these terms, solidarity is replaced with "friendship" and professional "networking" so that when the critical pressure by radical students increases for a revolutionary understanding of sexual politics, the Syracuse University Women's Studies faculty withdraw their commitment to the emancipation of women and retreat into a petit-bourgeois *clique politics*. Yet sexual harassment, if it is to be opposed systematically, cannot be addressed on the "case by case" basis of clique politics (i.e., "Who is she?" "What does she think about us?") but must be *uncompromisingly opposed in every instance, on principle*, regardless of the ideas of the particular person subject to this harassment. Despite its activist rhetoric of "Your Silence Will Not Protect You" and "SILENCE=COMPLICITY" the Syracuse University Women's Studies Program has demonstrated in its practices that, *on principle*, it believes that it is perfectly all right for some (i.e., Marxist) women to be sexually harassed and for them to be silent: their silence indeed protects them and their institutional power.

At the same time that these so called "feminists" were protecting their relative privilege in the academy, the female and male staff workers at Syracuse University were risking what little resources that they have in a fledgling union campaign, to make the issue of sexual harassment in general and this case in particular a *public* issue. Proceeding from the systematic and principled understanding of sexual harassment as a way to devalue their labor, these workers refused to remain silent and treat sexual harassment as an "institutional negotiation" rather than a *conflict* and struggle over the control and use of their own labor power. Instead of remaining silent they published my formal grievance in their newspaper *Staff Infection*. As a response to this, **union officials demonstrated their own complicity by attempting to silence these workers through cutting the funding for their newspaper**. Their argument? Sexual harassment is not a "bread and butter issue" meaning: sexual harassment and gender cannot be understood on the terms of class and labor.

On the contrary, under capitalism "gender" and all other socially produced differences are ultimately deployed to serve one purpose: the extraction of higher rates of surplus-value from specific sectors of the proletariat (e.g. women) in order to increase the rate of profit. As Marx and Engels have written in the *Communist Manifesto*, as the structures of exploitation become more complex and capitalism becomes more sophisticated, what matters is the maintenance of a high rate of profit and questions of "gender," "sexuality," "age," "race" and so on are all subordinated to these same ends and interests: "All are instruments of labor, more or less expensive to use" (*Marx-Engels Reader* 479). All such "differences" help the capitalist extract higher amounts of surplus-value from the work force as a whole. The "subversive performance" of gender, its "flexibility," its inventive capacity to "re-write" itself is in actuality an ever changing strategy of capital to increase the rate of profit and legitimate wage-labor. Capital has an investment in maintaining "gender difference," and the subordination of women (and other forms of social inequality) so that it can extract higher amounts of surplus-value from the entire labor force. This works to increase the rate of exploitation not only of female workers but also of male workers. As the standard of living of male workers is pushed down in the process of bringing relatively cheap female labor to replace them, male workers are also pushed into the position of accepting less compensation and harsher working conditions for *more* of their labor time. In short, the working class *as a whole* has a material interest in ending the sexual division of labor and sexual harassment of women and the ruling class has a material interest in maintaining it. Convincing workers that sexual harassment is "not a bread and butter issue" is a divide and conquer tactic aimed at marginalizing female workers from male workers. Moreover it weaken the development of collective opposition to capitalism and the way it penetrates all aspects of social and so called "personal" life. **"Gender" is important precisely because it is *a site of class struggle* over the ownership and control of the means of production**.

Gallop and other ludic feminists would argue that my notion of gender is too rigid, too deterministic and cuts off the possibility of a "subversive" production of pleasure in the classroom. In fact, it is this argument for the "flexibility" of gender that is at the forefront of ruling class and petit-bourgeois appropriations of feminism—as transnational capitalism and those who benefit from it, need a "flexible" notion of gender that can be deployed and retracted, depending upon which is most enabling for the acquisition of profit. In response to Keyssar's interpretation of the scene in the play (i.e., that the historically accurate interpretation for the scene was that one breast should be touched), Gallop uses the difference between "Breast" and "breasts" (drawing from the Lacanian difference between Phallus and penis, and implicitly from the postmodern feminist difference between "Woman" and "women"), to draw a distinction between the monolithizing "good girl" pedagogy she rejects, and the plural, "more historical," "bad girl" feminism she is advancing. Gallop argues that: "The breast—singular, symbolic, and maternal—is precisely the imaginary organ of nurturance, what the good feminist teacher proffers to her daughter-students. Refusing to nurture . . . the bad, sexual teacher, brings into the discourse of feminist pedagogy not the breast, which is already appropriately there, but the breasts" (*Pedagogy* 87).

For Gallop the pedagogy of pleasure, or "bad girl" feminism, in which the teacher aims to please students by appealing to and producing "new" sites of pleasure, is liberatory because it "breaks" pedagogical rules (*Pedagogy* 85). She claims that unlike the situation where the student pleases the teacher for professional reasons, the reversal of this paradigm actually displaces professionalism because "a teacher trying to please students doesn't have that rational, pragmatic excuse" (*Pedagogy* 3). I leave aside here that in its negotiation of pleasure (which only *seems* avant-garde) Gallop's pedagogy does what the ruling class has always demanded from pedagogy: *not* to educate critique-al citizens with (conceptual) knowledge. Capitalism requires a skilled labor force which is pleasure seeking (consumerist) and, in its consumption "taste," too eclectic ever to be satisfied. This consumative eclecticism is the material base of the dominant pluralism. The ruling class has always encouraged such pluralism since the pluralist subject is too dispersed to be trusting of totalities (as in social totality). Gallop is an exemplary pedagogue of the ruling class. It is based on these ruling class assumptions that Gallop argues that the teacher pleasing the students "is a prime site where the personal tangles with impersonation" (*Pedagogy* 3). However, for all of her "high theoretical" rhetoric in which Gallop is careful to suggest that she is not positing a volitional subject free from discursive and institutional constraints, Gallop's notion of "pedagogy" and "student-teacher" relations assumes that they are determined by the "free choice" of the individuals involved, not the larger social structures in which knowledge practices are always involved. In the (by her own words) "sensationalist" mode of *Feminist Accused of Sexual Harassment*, she presents a completely dehistoricized and depoliticized notion of "desire" and the "student-teacher" relation as simply instances of "human relations" (48). On these terms, Gallop argues that, "Telling teachers and students that we must not engage each other sexually ultimately tells us that we must limit ourselves to the confines of some restricted professional transaction, that we should not treat each other as human beings" (*Feminist Accused* 51). But Gallop can only claim that her own pedagogical practices "please" students by erasing the objections of the two female students who filed formal grievances against her for sexual harassment, as well as several of their peers who engaged in a protest at the University of Wisconsin, Milwaukee, against the harassment engendered by Gallop's pedagogical practices. For these students,

Gallop's erotic pedagogy of desire is not at all "pleasing" or "humanizing." It is an instance of a violent reassertion of her power, a prioritization of her privilege, and an objectification of their bodies rather than a practice concerned with their intellectual development.

Not only is Gallop's ahistorical liberal humanist notion of teacher-student relations and desire not radical, it is reactionary because in the name of "blurring" boundaries it naturalizes the "desires" of those with relative privilege within existing social relations. Furthermore, it allows Gallop and others to mask their authority in order to abuse it and wield it more effectively.   This regressive notion of so-called "student centeredness" is exactly what enabled Dobyns to engage in a reversal relocating himself not at the aggressor of sexual harassment but as the victim of a rigid and "authoritarian" pedagogy.   To this end Dobyns states: "I have no economic reason for teaching . . . I teach because I love it, and if it becomes clear to me that teaching is impossible because one has to have a barrier between the students, then I'm not sure how I'll feel about that" (Buckley 10).   Dobyns' so-called "student centered" pedagogy and Gallop's "bad girl" pedagogy help legitimate reactionary practices such as sexual harassment in the name of "closeness" and breaking boundaries.

Gallop constructs an alibi for this harassment by dehistoricizing desire and presenting it as a "resistant" force autonomous from and opposed to institutional, social and economic relations.   Claiming to "subvert" the gendering of the classroom and break pedagogical authority, Gallop is not actually "displacing" gender, she is merely sexualizing it.   This sexualizing is understood as a progressive move enabled by the "branch of queer theory [which] has devoted itself to the defiant perversion of any norm, working toward a notion of the queer as the generalized case" (*Pedagogy* 12).   However, Gallop can only argue that this displaces the norm because she already, as has become increasingly popular with the emergence of post-al queer theory, presupposes a separation between sexuality and gender and a severing of each of these from the capitalist mode of production.

This "post-gender" and "post-class" theorization of desire is most notably introduced by Gayle Rubin in her article "Thinking Sex: Notes for a Radical Theory of the Politics of Sexuality" (for other ludic "performances" of this theory see: Grosz and Probyn, *Sexy Bodies*; and Meese, *(Sem)Erotics*). Dismissing Marxism as a "dismal exercise," as is popular on the post-al left, because it explains gender and other social inequalities on the materialist terms of class relations and the mode of production, Rubin goes on to claim that feminism as a theory of gender oppression is incapable of accounting for the "difference" of sexuality: "To assume automatically that this [i.e., the analysis of gender oppression] makes [feminism] the theory of sexual oppression is to fail to distinguish between gender, on the one hand, and erotic desire, on the other" (32). From this Rubin claims that "it is essential to separate gender and sexuality analytically to reflect more accurately their separate social existence" (33).

What this separation of gender and sexuality is a response to, on political terms (which even Rubin makes clear), is the historical pressure that feminist debates over the material status of sexist violence and the "limits of consent" have placed upon sexual practices. Rejecting as "revisionist celebrations of femininity," those feminist positions that attempt to account for gender and sexuality on the systemic terms of social structures, Rubin advances what she understands as a "pro-sex feminism" which "radically" moves beyond such revisionism by accounting for the "separate" but "intersecting" social processes of gender and desire (28-32). Yet this ends up being a "post-feminist" position, which does not so much intervene in the reproduction and naturalizing of gender as it simply ignores and elides it, thus endorsing the ludic essentialism (and revisionism) that gender will take care of itself. In fact, in the name of rejecting an "in between" position that attempts to find a "middle ground" within this debate, Rubin herself endorses, as the cutting edge of "radical sex," a simple reversal of "gender norms" through the practices of sadomasochism. Rubin's support for the reversal of gender roles (by putting women in the position of dominatrix), or the so-called "displacement" of gender (through same-sex sadomasochism), completely abstracts domination from the global conditions of exploitation that structure women's lives. In other words, this "reversal" treats gender as a "local" matter of intersubjective relations rather than a global strategy of capitalist exploitation to increase its capacity to extract surplus-value from the work force. In occluding capitalist exploitation which renders the majority of women on the planet propertyless (with only their own labor to sell) and therefore without control over the material resources necessary to determine their lives, Rubin's "post-gender," and "post-class" understanding of sexuality is itself merely a "immanent" revision of gender and class. Far from advancing the "autonomy" of sexuality from capitalism, her theory marks the increased subordination of sexuality to transnational capitalism and the state.

Rubin's text is a foundational attempt to relieve the crisis produced for the ludic left when the debates over material conditions become too historically burdensome and too personally constricting for petit-bourgeois "liberation." Yet, the historical existence of systemic violence and material exploitation comes back to haunt ludic postmodern feminists, such as Drucilla Cornell, who are compelled to point out, yet subsequently occlude through a series of discursive reversals: "the material suffering of women" (2). Consequently, the necessity for shifting political practice from gender to sexuality without accounting for them on historical and material terms, is for post-feminist politics to "move beyond" the historical burdens of debates in feminism over the question of the material dimensions of gender and violence against women. In short, it allows bourgeois feminists to gesture toward the material exploitation of women (to "troubleshoot" so as not to appear "unethical"), without a sustained commitment to combating this material exploitation— a commitment which requires the subordination of personal interests to collective principles. What this post-feminist politics actually serves to legitimate is the kind of lifestyle politics of the self that began to develop a new wave in the 1970s and reached new heights in the 1980s (aided by the revision of tax laws during the Reagan and Thatcher regimes to move unprecedented amounts of wealth from the working class to the— to use a sociological term—"upper-middle class"). In other words, like the dominant mode of creative writing pedagogy, this politics works to restore the petit-bourgeois retreat away from world historical battles over the material conditions of peoples lives to the more comfortable domain of the self and the body. It is, as Alex Callinicos points out about Foucault's "aesthetics of existence," "a way in which the sometime radical intellectual could learn to stop worrying and love late capitalist consumption" (98).

When sexuality is severed from gender (and gender is severed from class), sexuality serves as the escape valve from the pressure for closure in theorizing social differences as effects of systemic social relations. In post-al politics as a whole, sexuality is understood as the new discursive horizon—the supplement—that subverts any determinate (i.e., partisan) production of knowledge of exploitation and oppression and how to organize to abolish it. "The real" is constantly "disrupted" by sexuality, according to ludic queer theorists such as Joseph Litvak who claims that, "the sexual 'truth' about a person spreads out to suffuse everything he or she says and does, especially at the level of apparently nonsexual words and deeds and especially when he or she is unconscious of their 'true' significance" (20). However, this position lends its support to the notion that sexuality and desire are not simply the products of "specific" social practices as Rubin claims rather, sexuality is a pan-historical, eternally present, self-legitimating source of social meaning. What makes these arguments for the "specificity" and "autonomy" of sexuality useful for the post-al left is that it allows the possibility for sexuality to become another alibi for discursive invention and its occlusion of material production. Following this logic, one critic claims: "*sexuality originates in the projection of mobile, free-floating images* of the erogenous body on the physical map of the emerging self" (Chisholm 28; emphasis added). Consequently, for ludic feminists and queer theorists alternative sexualities are produced, like all social meanings, out of their local oppositions to one another within discourse.

This ahistorical theory of sexuality promoted by Rubin and others has been contested in John D'Emilio's materialist account of gay identity, which argues that it is the product of changes in capitalist labor relations, and subsequent re-organizations of such social *practices* as gender, sexuality, and the family. Specifically, D'Emilio points to the decline of "private" household production in which survival was organized around participation in a (heterosexual) family, and the rise of industrial production in which increasingly people could support themselves outside of a heterosexual family unit through wage-labor:

> As wage labor spread and production became socialized, then it became possible to release sexuality from the "'imperative" to procreate . . . In divesting the household of its economic independence and fostering the separation of sexuality from procreation, capitalism has created conditions that allow some men and women to organize a personal life around their erotic/emotional attraction to their own sex. It has made possible the formation of urban communities of lesbian and gay men and, more recently, of a politics based on sexual identity. (104).

In other words, shifts in the capitalist mode of production (the historical development of the forces of production and corresponding changes in the relations of production), not the "projection of mobile, free-floating images," are the historical causes of "gay identity" and shifts in sexuality. The development of concepts such as "homosexuality" and "heterosexuality" in the medical professions and other industries "were an ideological response to a new way of organizing one's personal life"— new ways which were themselves effects of the mode of production (D'Emilio 105). That is, the development of these terms as a focal point of identity is a product of changed material conditions in the development of capitalism.

As Donald Morton has argued multiple sexualities and the social contradictions and antagonisms over sexuality are produced not as a consequence of local discursive opposition but "from the gaps and strains created when the mode of production has moved to a new stage of development while the relations of production have lagged behind" (209-210). In short, it is the contradiction between the forces and relations of production that produces, on the one hand, the conservative New Right "family values" position which is aimed at restoring the social practices of gender and sexuality more useful for earlier stages of capitalism, and, on the other, a consumer culture in which the commodification of all sexual practices is affirmed in the name of profit. What this shows us is that capitalism is an opportunistic system: one which denies or promotes multiple sexualities depending on what is most profitable. In short it is a system in which some can have freedom of desire (insofar as it benefits the ruling class).

Freedom of sexuality for all, not some, requires basic material conditions that enable all people to be free from material need. In a society based on exploitation, in which the surplus-labor of the majority is appropriated for the profit of the ruling class the conditions are maintained in which the desires of some are privileged over the needs of the majority. The move to make sexuality autonomous from objective social totality—the capitalist mode of production, its class contradictions, and the corresponding social relations that these engender—is an ideological alibi to abstract the desire of the individual from the needs of the collective. In doing so, it appropriates struggles for freedom of sexuality and a reorganization of social relations of reproduction, in the interests of the ruling class. What is actually at stake in such theories is not freedom of sexuality for all but unregulated PROFIT for some. It is increased subordination of sexuality to commodity production and exchange. Naturalizing desire and then prioritizing desire over need is a way to legitimate the extraction of surplus-value and the maximization of profit and pleasure for the individual over the fulfillment of the basic needs of all citizens. In other words, the move to separate sexuality from social production *in the cultural imaginary* is a move to legitimate the "self-inventing" subject of capitalism who understands herself in terms of her presumed to be "unique" and "autonomous" desires. On these terms, "homosexuality" is not a transhistorical "identity" that is then repressed by a transhistorical "compulsory heterosexuality." Rather, as Donald Morton has argued, "capitalism's changing imperatives [have themselves] put pressure on an exclusive heterosexual structuring of desire . . . . the ultimate determinate structure [of all sexuality] is not one which promotes compulsory heterosexuality but one which promotes *compulsory consumption*" (Morton 192). In short, the ultimate determining structure is the regime of profit and wage-labor, which turns all sites of daily life, including sexuality, into occasions for the production of profit for the ruling class.

When the ideological abstraction of sexuality from the mode of production is understood as new and "progressive," what then does "effective" political practice come to mean but the free play of desire ("subversive pleasures") for those who "have," and continued oppression for those who "have not"? On these terms, solidarity is not based on collective interests it is based on pleasure. People work together as long as it is pleasurable—and what is pleasurable is what does not put pressure on the class interests of those who already have the relative privilege and leisure time to develop multiple pleasures. A "radical" subject on these terms is a subject who identifies with her own particular shifting differences, her multiple capacities for pleasure—she identifies, in other words, with what is available to her through sensory *experience*. Far from "disrupting" the logic of identity within mainstream feminist practices, this notion of sexuality merely reasserts it. This re-emergence of experience as the basis of knowledge within post-al queer politics can be seen in George Haggerty's article "'Promoting Homosexuality' in the Classroom," in which, despite his ludic "anti-essentialism," he argues: "it seems to me that the 'truth' of this 'experience' is too valuable to sacrifice to the ideal of theoretical unassailability . . . lesbian and gay students . . . cannot defer to others—by which I mean *any* others—who only imagine, however theoretically profoundly, how (homo)sexuality figures in their lives" (15). By this he means that the "experience" of gays and lesbians contains a knowledge that displaces the systematicity of the knowledge of theory—it disrupts its closure of meaning. Yet, for Haggerty and many queer theorists homosexuality is the condition of possibility for *all* sexuality—which means that the "truth" of *all* sexuality is found in this experience. Material reality becomes a matter of the desire of the body. Here one sees how two seemingly disparate sites (i.e., Dobyns' "anything goes" heterosexuality and Haggerty's "ethical" homosexuality) collapse into one strategy: the strategy of "experience" which is necessary for maintaining the self-inventing subject of capitalism.

This shift away from conceptual thinking toward the "experience" of desires of the body is a move *not* to theorize desire and account for the historical and material conditions of possibility for desire but to pragmatically *perform* desire. This ludic modality of desire can be seen in Dianne Chisholm's notion of a "cunning lingua" which is "not so much a signifier or signifying system which stands in, as linguistic or discursive representative, for the erogenous zone of partial body [sic] whose excitability/erectability is supposed to be the unmediated expression of desire . . . rather it is an efficient and efficacious simulacrum . . . a word-thing-act" (24). Following the Deleuzian notion of a "transgression of language by language," in which language has gone beyond representation and beyond conceptuality to produce a "gestural 'language' of the body," Chisholm collapses the conceptual explanation of the material conditions of desire into the rhetorical capacity of language to "imitate" or "mimic" the gestures of the body. Further, in doing so she claims to advanced a "de-idealized" notion of desire which "find[s] a way to talk about . . . bawdy 'linguality' in bodily terms, avoiding a critical reading which reduces writerly strategy and readerly responsivity to mere textuality" (19).

In other words, "materiality" for Chisholm (and Gallop, Butler, Cornell, Rubin, . . .) is the physicality of the "body" and its capacity for sensations. Chisholm's post-(post)structuralist theory of desire is in actuality a deconstruction of *différance* itself and a return to the pragmatism of mimesis. This neo-mimesis (which is also advanced in Cornell's *Beyond Accommodation*) understands language to reflect material reality insofar as it can produce multiple physical sensations within the body. Here, Chisholm merely performs the presupposed self-identical, self-generating practice of discursive invention by conflating textuality and "physicality" and replacing conceptuality with sensuality. Yet this ends up being a completely reactionary renaturalization of desire which sees it not as an historical and materialist social practice but in the ahistorical Deleuzian terms of "pure motion" or a post-conceptual *force* (33). For Chisholm "cunning lingua" is "radical" because it does not investigate the "cause of desire, but *acts* as outspoken cause" (29). As a theory of sexuality this rips the desiring subject out of history by occluding the structural causes of desire. As a result the subject becomes completely subordinated to his desire so that desire gets theorized as an uncontrollable force. Yet, to theorize desire in this way is to legitimate the unleashing of the *historically produced* desire to perpetuate violence against women and others, in the name of uncontrollable urges. This is most telling when Chisholm confirms that: "'all/ the delight in the world begins in access to a loving/ woman's loving body'" (Mary Fallon, *Working Hot* as quoted in Chisholm 38).

In the absence of access to, ownership of, and control over material resources, and the absence of access to the knowledges and analytical abilities necessary to intervene in these conditions (i.e., to the practices of critique), all that is needed is "access to a loving/woman's loving body." But this is exactly the kind of logic that helps legitimate the ruthless violence against women perpetuated by Dobyns and others. As I have argued earlier, if people are denied access to the collective practices of critique and social transformation and are, therefore, prevented from understanding and intervening in the social causes of their frustrations of oppression, they attempt to "relieve" these frustrations through *acting out* on the bodies of women, people of color, gays and lesbians, and others. It is the same objectification of the body—the same commodification of women as objects to be used and abused—that enabled Dobyns to say: "I was unhappy, I was drunk and she was there" (Dobyns, *The Syracuse Herald-Journal* 4/6/95: A-16).

In the trans-social space that post-al theories of desire invent, individuals need only "express themselves" and exercise their desires on others in order to exercise power in their own lives. But this reduces social change to the "care of the self" and (inter)personal relations. This strategy dehistoricizes personal relations by making them the center of social practices rather than the objective historical structures which make these relations possible. This brings the seemingly "radical" discourses of "pro-sex" queer theory and "bad girl" feminism quite close to the liberal "family values" feminism informing the 1995 U.N. Draft Platform for Women in Beijing. In a critique of the Platform, Makibaka (a collective of revolutionary women of the Philippines) explains that the Platform "assumes that women and men can exercise 'power' in their own terms." In doing so, other than disorienting women as to the real source and function of power (as one emanating from those who own and control the economic resources and political instruments of society), the root of women's oppression is ultimately situated at the personal or interpersonal level, in the realm of sexual politics, where class struggle and class contradictions are forced to take a back seat. (3).

For Makibaka, imperialism has viewed "gender," "sexuality" and other social practices as autonomous in order "to cover up its murderous tracks in the exploitation of women's labor and bodies . . . [and] has narrowed down the issue of women to the personal or subjective level, where imperialism and the class context are felt to be nonexistent" (13). The move to abstract sexuality from gender practices and both from the mode of production is a move to dehistoricize desire and gender as self-inventing practice that can only be addressed as a "negotiation" in individual relationships. If desire is a "self-inventing" practice beyond collective determination there is no possibility for collective revolutionary praxis as desire always disrupts principled praxis with strategies devised to increase desire. "Desire" becomes a site in which the bourgeois subject finds an unregulated space; a space of excessive practices. As an excessive practice "desire" is then used to legitimate the deregulation of ruling class interests. In other words, the "excess" of sexuality and desire is really an alibi for the excesses of the market which rejects principles for strategies in the interest of maximizing profit. The "deregulation" of desire by reprivatizing (taking back) sexuality from gender helps reprivatize the relative gains made by the working class in their struggle for control over the conditions of the working day. Post-al theorists assume that ending capitalism is not necessary for the emancipation of women and of gays and lesbians, and in so doing will argue that an emphasis on class struggle leads to an erasure and rejection of feminism and gay and lesbian liberation. On the contrary, a Marxist critique of sexual harassment marks a refusal to give up feminism and the struggle for gay and lesbian liberation to the interests of the ruling class.

Five

It is not surprising that in a time of a severe backlash against revolutionary Marxist politics committed to historical materialist critique and revolutionary social transformation, that the most progressive understandings of sexual harassment which situate it within a broader structure of exploitation and oppression and attempt to account for it in relation to a series of interrelated practices (of sexuality, invention, creativity, gender, class exploitation . . .), are also the most widely contested and often the first to be rejected. Nevertheless, it is precisely because of this backlash—which is actually a backlash against all exploited people—that Marxist explanations of social oppression including sexual harassment continue to be urgently necessary. Proceeding along this line, I and a small core of students (Adam Katz, Amrohini Sahay, Stephen Tumino, Mark Redding, Robert Young, and Brian Ganter) in the Revolutionary Marxist Collective at Syracuse University (1995) and on the editorial collective of a revolutionary Marxist student newspaper *The Alternative Orange*, struggled to advance revolutionary explanations of the sexual harassment perpetrated against myself and other students by Stephen Dobyns. In doing so our aim was to produce knowledges that could explain this seemingly "isolated" instance by connecting it up with the much larger pattern of sexist harassment and violence that Dobyns perpetrated against several of his students; the conditions within and the knowledge practices of the Syracuse University Creative Writing Program, the Department of English, and advanced capitalist universities in general that would enable the perpetuation and legitimation of these practices; and, finally, the global system of violence against women rooted in private property and the exploitation of human labor of which this instance is a symptom.

When it became clear, by the number of Creative Writing graduate students and the two Creative Writing faculty members who came forward to the University as a result of my public formal grievance, that the sexual harassment committed by Dobyns toward myself was not an "exception" but part of a long term pattern of intimidation and abuse of his graduate students, overlooked and shielded by the Syracuse University Creative Writing Program and Department of English, the main strategy deployed was to produce a "smoke screen" to discredit my charges and attempt to create a rift between the creative writers protesting against harassment by Dobyns and those of us who opposed this harassment from the standpoint of revolutionary Marxism. In a desperate attempt to shore up the Syracuse University Creative Writing Program and evade charges that it had contributed to producing a hostile work environment which remained silent about—and therefore complicit in—sexual harassment, Dobyns and his friends and colleagues embarked on a massive campaign to divert attention away from sexual harassment and present the Creative Writing Program as the "victim" of a Marxist "conspiracy." At the forefront of this diversion away from a rigorous critique of sexual harassment, Dobyns' friend and colleague Tobias Wolff claimed that: "It has been instructive, if not surprising to observe, as part of the response to Ms. Cotter's complaint, a venomous and wholesale denigration of the [Syracuse University] Creative Writing [P]rogram" (Nolan B-3). To further construct this narrative of the Creative Writing Program as "victim," Wolff claimed that "Since its inception, the student Marxist Collective has been attacking the creative writing program as elitist and anti-intellectual because the creative writers do not pursue the same interests as the student Marxist collective would like everyone else in the world to pursue" (Nolan B-3). The logic here, of course, is that Marxists are "aggressive" and "dogmatic" "suppressers" of "freedom of expression" so that by implication I (as a public Marxist) was an aggressor against the "free-expression" of Dobyns. According to this logic, I could not possibly be a victim of his sexist violence. Advancing this logic even more explicitly a student of Dobyns, Pam Greenberg, claimed that "Jennifer Cotter and her comrades . . . [in] the Marxist Collective [have] been virtually waiting for an issue such as this one to galvanize support for their larger aims" which she took to mean "attack[ing] the Creative Writing Program and creative writers as a whole" (Greenberg A-11).

Echoing the statements of Dobyns who said that "Cotter is being used as a pawn and as a way of attacking the creative writing program" (*The Daily Orange*, 4/7/95: 3), Dobyns' friends, protégés, and allies reassert a McCarthyist logic (i.e., that the Communists have come to "take over" Creative Writing and "get rid of" creative writers and "artists") in order to sidestep a systemic critique of sexual harassment (from any perspective) and whitewash the sexist actions of Dobyns and the continued existence of sexual harassment. In doing so they attempted to present a picture of the Creative Writing Program as fostering a "non-dogmatic" community "open" to criticism while those arguing for revolutionary social change were constructed as opposing open intellectual inquiry. In a December 1997 article for a Syracuse University student newspaper, *The Daily Orange*, Dobyns claimed that my case against him was "an attempt by the Marxist Collective to destroy the Creative Writing Program" because Marxists "don't believe that there is such a thing as a writer" and that Marxists believe "that there is no such thing as art" (Mehta, "For Dobyns and SU, a Debate Still Rages" 8). According to this narrative, Marxism is opposed to "art" and "writing" because it reads art and literature on the terms of social relations and thus denies "individual creativity." In addition, in a move to whitewash his sexual harassment and deflect "hostile work environment" charges, Dobyns claimed that holding a teacher accountable for the social consequences of his teaching practices is to suppress "necessary criticism of students' work" (Mehta, 10). In short, charges of "hostile work environment," according to Dobyns, abandon the project to improve students' writing by shutting off open critical engagement in favor of "celebrations" of all students work.

However, if the Creative Writing Program at Syracuse University was indeed such a "community" welcoming of "criticism" and an "open" exchange of ideas (as Dobyns and his allies claim), why were the 12 witnesses who testified against him—the majority of whom were students and faculty in the Creative Writing Program—afraid to come forward with their own grievances or supporting evidence until I made my case public? If the program was actually "open" to criticism, former Director of Creative Writing Michael Martone and Assistant Professor of Creative Writing Melanie Rae Thon, the only Creative Writing faculty to come forward to the university and take a stand against Dobyns' sexually harassing practices, would not have been so alienated and marginalized by Tobias Wolff, Mary Karr and other "celebrities" of the S.U. Creative Writing Program. But, because they spoke out against the hostile environment created by these practices and the failure of the Creative Writing Program to actively and openly address them, they were indeed so marginalized and alienated by other faculty in the program, that they were compelled to leave. In his responses to the stand taken by Thon and Martone, Dobyns merely reinforces their marginalization by reasserting crude sexist stereotypes that only "nervous" and "fragile" women (his construction of Thon) and "jealous" and "unsuccessful" men (his construction of Martone) accuse others of sexual harassment (Mehta, "Three Years" 9).

These sexist and authoritarian narratives are desperate maneuvers to block any open critique of and public stand against sexual harassment. In addition, by equating "creative writing" and "art itself" with one historically limited view (the bourgeois understanding of the "writer"/"artist" as "free" from historical and material conditions), Dobyns and his allies dogmatically block any open engagement over alternative conceptions of creativity and art. This entrepreneurial, free-market capitalist position is set on obscuring the structures of economic and social relations that cause sexual harassment and other manifestations of social oppression and exploitation rather than educating people so that they can make an informed decision on what perspectives they will hold in their words and actions on these social issues. The smokescreen of a "Marxist conspiracy" is thus an attempt to validate Dobyns' claims that: "I think this is exaggerated . . . the whole issue of sexual harassment has become a morass of uncertainty" (Weingast and Glor 1). Rather than promoting knowledge and undertaking a serious investigation into the conditions of the Creative Writing Program that could enable such practices to continue unchallenged, this logic is concerned with POLICING people from pursuing progressive social theory including the knowledges necessary to understand one instance of sexual harassment as part of a larger system of sexism.

Such practices were not only perpetuated by Dobyns and his friends and allies in the "local" context of Syracuse University, but also mainstream media such as *The New York Times Magazine* and *The Chronicle of Higher Education*, who were more concerned with rehabilitating the public image of Dobyns and the Syracuse University Creative Writing Program rather than opening up a serious investigation of sexual harassment in the workplace and inquiring substantively into all sides of the issue. *The New York Times Magazine*, which published an article by Francine Prose (discussed further below) who trivialized the case against Dobyns as "hilarious," evidently also finds serious opposition to sexual harassment (not to mention basic principles of "objective journalism") a "joke" since, despite the fact that they received several letters of protest to Prose's text from myself and others involved in the case, they refused to publish any of the letters that represented serious opposition to Dobyns (thus making it appear as if no opposition existed). Moreover, they had no problem whatsoever publishing letters of support from former students of Dobyns at the same time that they refused to publish letters of critique. Repeating the same move, *The Chronicle of Higher Education* and its reporter Robin Wilson, were more concerned with shoring up the S.U. Creative Writing Program by writing a "juicy" follow up story to my case against Dobyns focusing on the "controversy" between the "big named" authors of the Program rather than on producing knowledges of sexual harassment. Upon interviewing me, Wilson initially indicated that she was planning on preparing an article dealing with my sexual harassment by Dobyns. Yet, as I explained in my "Letter to the Editor" (*Chronicle* 4/4/97 B11), in the course of the interview it became clear that the purpose of the article was not to conduct an "objective" and "open" inquiry into a violent case of sexual harassment so as to investigate the larger system of violence against women and the resulting oppression of women in the academic workplace. Instead, Wilson had already decided that what was more important was Stephen Dobyns and the fate of the individuals in the Creative Writing Program at Syracuse. While Wilson was giving ally of Dobyns, Tobias Wolff, a 2 and 1/2 hour interview and allowing him to submit five pages of written notes on his reading of the case (which she mentions in the article itself), she asked myself and Professor Donald Morton (who, with uncompromising commitment to the struggle against sexual harassment, has written extensively on the case) perfunctory questions such as "what kind of alcohol was in the drink that Dobyns threw?"—the same questions she had asked me two years earlier when the event first occurred. Moreover, while the article gives publicity to the accusations by Dobyns' allies that this case was "manufactured" by the Revolutionary Marxist Collective, Wilson did not bother interviewing the RMC, and resisted my substantive explanations of the case, thus suppressing our oppositional analysis. As the Red Theory Collective at SUNY-Albany (a revolutionary Marxist collective then consisting of: Deb Kelsh, Laura Lane, Jennifer Mitchell, Tom Nespeco, Julie Torrant, and Rob Wilkie) made clear in their "Open Letter to the Community" (February 1997): in the guise of "objective journalism" this suppression of systemic revolutionary explanations and oppositional knowledges of sexual harassment by *The Chronicle of Higher Education* "serves the interests of the University-as-Industry, that is, the university as one site for manufacturing consent that serves business interests and reaps benefits from doing so."

In the time that has passed since the first series of events in this case took place, this policing of public opposition to sexual harassment has also taken the more overtly "personalizing" form of constructing me as one in search of "personal power." More recently Dobyns claims (in reference to me) that, "I think she used the whole thing as a pretext. It made her powerful" and goes on to circulate rumors that I was "signing autographs" at my workplace (Mehta, "For Dobyns" 8). In Dobyns' "new" terms, sexual harassment is in fact good for women since it advances their careers. This is how power distorts the very logic of daily life and social practices. On these terms, any of the backlash suffered as a result of taking a public stand is represented as a matter of "individual choice." But, as I made clear in my own "Letter to the Editor" of *The Daily Orange* (Jan. 13,1998), being the target of sexual harassment is not a "choice." One can keep the harassment to herself, internalize the violence, and blame herself (as so many of Dobyns' students felt compelled to do until I made my case public). Or one can take a stand against sexual harassment and not accept the sexist idea that it is a "personal problem" by instead situating it as a social problem. But doing so puts one at risk for public scrutiny and further harassment. Far from gaining "prestige" and "power" (or "signing autographs") for publicly opposing Dobyns' sexually harassing practices, I was subjected to further discrimination and harassment. During the period between inaugurating my formal grievance and the University hearing of it, I was actually denied a new job that I had been offered, on the last day of my two-week notice to my former employers, owing to publicity surrounding the case. In the wake of publicly taking a stand against Dobyns, I received harassing phone calls from members of the Syracuse community threatening kidnapping, gang rape and bodily mutilation.

Dobyns' "rumorology" is not a fluke nor is it merely a "local" practice. Rather, it is itself part of the violent practices in capitalist commodity culture deployed to create a "sensational" story line that cynically dismisses public opposition to sexual harassment as the result of those who are "power hungry" and in want of public attention. This ideological strategy is routinely deployed to discourage any public and thoughtful discussion of the issues that would break the silence around sexual harassment and open up the possibility of organizing for social change. Since this personalizing is such a pervasive part of commodity culture and the regime of private property and profit on which it is based, it is not surprising that these measures extend beyond those directly involved in the case.

Such practices can also be seen in the responses to the "Open Letter to the Community," circulated in February 1997 by the Red Theory

Collective (RTC) at SUNY-Albany protesting *The Chronicle of Higher Education*'s suppression of any systemic analysis and Marxist public critique of Dobyns' practices. As a result of the circulation of their text, the Red Theory Collective also became the targets of anti-Marxist and patriarchal attacks by other members of the SUNY-Albany community. One such attack, written by a graduate student at SUNY-Albany, Bob Black, is particularly symptomatic of the blame the victim strategy which accuses those who protest against sexual harassment of being power hungry. In a similar move to Dobyns, Black likens the Red Theory Collective to "Pol Pot" and accuses them of "authoritarianism," totalitarianism and support of the corporate university for addressing their protest letter against such practices to the academic community. For Black, those who argue for the production of knowledges that can explain sexual harassment in relation to social totality are only "impotent intellectuals . . . imposing revolution from above on an or-else basis" (August 5, 1997). According to Black, all rigorous knowledge practices are "authoritarian" and public critique is merely an opportunistic attempt to achieve personal power within an institution from which one has been excluded. This is the basis upon which Black (who, by his own admission had not read up on the case) reads me (for my public opposition to sexual harassment) as a "careerist" ("like Madonna") who has made a "business decision" by making my case public and is "much more interested in getting her systemic analysis of sexual harassment published than in redress for the sexual harassment she claims to have personally suffered." He accuses me, on the one hand, of using my "personal experience" as the basis of my systemic analysis (which is simply specious considering my extensive critique of experientialism in which I have explicitly argued that experience in general and "my experience" in particular cannot be understood as the basis of a critique of sexual harassment—rather, it is a symptom of a larger structure). On the other hand, he wants to delegitimate my case against sexual harassment because "in all probability Cotter's analysis preceded her victimization." For Black, I have trivialized the primacy of "experience" and merely used my "experience" in a secondary fashion—as "victim-credentials." Black repeats the same logic as Greenberg who suggests that I, and the Revolutionary Marxist Collective, were "just waiting" for an instance like this to occur in order to advance our political aims—as if a committed Marxist-Feminist who has a coherent theory and argument against sexual harassment could not possibly be the target of it!

This effort to localize and personalize sexual harassment on the terms of what Black calls the "singular features of one's unique experience," represents a branch of anarcho-activism in post-al capitalism which works to contain and limit collective revolutionary struggle—including opposition to systemic violence against women. For anarcho-activists such as Black and Greenberg, the "truth" of sexual harassment is the capitalist fantasy that people's "feelings," "pains," "interventions," "interests" BELONG to themselves. On these terms, when one does not ask for an "individual apology" but takes a PUBLIC stand against sexual harassment she is only working in "individual" interests to protect her "name" and acquire personal power. Moreover, for this logic, systemic analysis is really only a cover for the valorization of "personal experience" so that one's interventions into sexual harassment (whether informed by a systemic analyses or not) can only be understood on a case-by-case basis as an "individual's issue." But "feelings," "pains," "interventions," and "interests" are HISTORICAL and there is no way in which they can be "redressed" without a revolutionary transformation of the historical and material conditions that produce the "feelings" in the first place.

By representing the "experience" of sexual harassment as "non-generalizable" and only explainable on "individual terms" this strategy aims to block the production of "struggle-concepts" and explanations that can enable people to more effectively produce widespread social transformation. Moreover, it does so by representing collective struggles for social change which work to fundamentally transform existing social relations as "elitist" and "out of touch" with "the people." This is the effectivity of the strategies of anarcho-activists such as Black and Greenberg whose interests are to protect capitalism in new forms: they cynically represent themselves as on the side of "the people" and represent all attempts to promote and produce knowledges that will enable more effective revolutionary organization, as "elitist" and "dogmatic." But by blocking the production of knowledges and open critique-al contestation, this anarcho-activism merely replaces serious and thoughtful opposition to social oppression and material exploitation with pragmatism and "shocking effects."

This can be seen in the cynical dismissals of Dobyns' harassment as "salty language" meant to intellectually "disturb" and "provoke thought." Following this move to aestheticize the political, Greenberg casually dismissed a vast history of politically committed writing, not to mention several of her colleagues who opposed the hostile work environment created by Dobyns and his allies, by claiming that "it is a demonstrable fact that political correctness makes for bland and uninteresting writing" (Greenberg A-11). Like Wolff who defended the Syracuse University Creative Writing Program for not adhering to what he presumably understands to be a "dogmatic" Marxist agenda, Greenberg purported to be interested merely in learning "the craft of writing" and "not propagating a narrow social agenda." The politics of this statement, however, become evident when Greenberg dismissed my case against Dobyns, and my critique of sexual harassment, on the basis that I demonstrated "poor writing skills" in my public critique. Yet what is rejected here as "poor writing skills" are the boundary concepts and explanations necessary for pressuring the limits of the "common sense" with which Dobyns and others obscure their political positions. Far from not propagating a "narrow social agenda," Greenberg advanced the parochial understanding that "writing" can only be conceived in "one way" —dictated by the common sense of commodity culture which assumes art to be autonomous from social relations. Writing that mobilizes a critique of the dominant social order is often not immediately accessible on the terms of commodity culture because it is challenging to the cultural "commonsense" that conceals exploitation and oppression. It therefore requires effort, discipline, and commitment to understand and engage with. It is this discipline and social commitment that is rejected in the notion that "political correctness" makes for bland and uninteresting writing. In a culture of consumption and sensationalism, political principles are "bland" because they require thinking without "shocking" effects that appeal only to "immediate senses." For Greenberg, to overcome "blandness" it is necessary to mix oppression and harassment into writing. It is this privileging of aesthetic pleasure over progressive politics that enables Dobyns to write off the violence of his practices as an instance of democratic pedagogy: "I state my mind . . . I speak as I like to be spoken to. I make jokes" (Weingast and Glor 3). In short, it is perfectly all right for Dobyns to sexually harass, intimidate, and assault his female students as long as it is humorous and pleasurable to him. As a "good student" of Dobyns, Greenberg promoted a petit-bourgeois notion of "freedom" in which she could not be bothered to engage in the "uninteresting task" of social emancipation because it infringes on her "individual" ability to exercise her own "desires" and "pleasures" at the expense of those who have a relatively smaller degree of power and control over the conditions under which they live.

Turning sexual harassment into a joke is, of course, a very familiar patriarchal strategy to help delegitimate claims against and critiques of those who deploy sexually harassing practices. If the harasser was "only joking" then the victim is herself a "joke" for taking this harassment seriously. Nowhere is this logic more evident than in a "Hers" column of *The New York Times Magazine* (Nov. 6, 1995: 34-36), in which Francine Prose writes to erase the sexually harassing practices of her "friend Stephen Dobyns" by calling my formal grievance and the testimony of 12 witnesses in the Syracuse University hearing process (for which she was present as a "character witness" for Dobyns) a "hilarious" reassertion of "Victorian norms" (36). Like many "post-feminists" today who are dismissing contemporary feminism as a revival of Victorian norms and practices, Francine Prose's main point in her tirade defending Dobyns is that for a woman to put forward an accusation of sexual harassment against a teacher who has "merely" thrown scotch in her face, gazed at and made comments about her breasts, and shouted sexist remarks at her shows a very Victorian sense of morality. According to Prose, such actions on the part of Dobyns are not manifestations of sexual harassment but of "salty language" and at worst "only of bad behavior" (34). But what Prose dismisses as "salty language" and "bad behavior" is verbal and physical sexual harassment. Even in Prose's own version of the allegations made against Dobyns, this so called "bad behavior" includes making a sexual advance toward a graduate student (in Prose's terms: "one says he tried to kiss her"), circulating a "cruel sexual remark" about a professor, and stating (in what Prose characterizes as "salty" language but curiously still "edits" for public presentation--thus contradicting her own claims as to the "innocuousness" of this language) that another professor "might benefit from . . . a satisfactory sexual encounter" (34).

All of the acts which witnesses testified were made by Dobyns, are for Prose merely instances of "salty language" involving "attempts to be funny and to provoke" (34). Why are these acts not sexual harassment according to Prose? Because "no one suggests that he offered to trade good grades for sex . . . [and he] is not accused of sleeping with . . . students" (34). Since these sexually harassing acts do not directly involve sexual intercourse as barter for a grade, Prose (like Gallop) understands opposition to them as merely a Victorian quest for "protection" (36). In short, Prose denies that Dobyns' institutional authority over his graduate students combined with his repetitive sexually harassing remarks and deeds, and a much broader system of sexism of which they are a part, has anything to do with the production of an institutional environment that objectifies, dismisses, and abuses women and discourages anyone from speaking out against this violence. In fact, Prose dismisses altogether the possibility of a "hostile environment" and "patterns of intimidation" that enable the perpetuation of sexist harassment and violence, claiming that critiques of "hostile environments" advance a "smudged" logic (34).

Participating in the same logic as Prose, soon after I publicized my formal grievance Mary Karr, a member of the Syracuse University Creative Writing faculty suggested that she is "leery of using the 'university as parent'" (Buckley 10). Furthermore, she claimed that: "Sexism is inherent in the culture, but I don't think the university should be in the business of regulating behavior" (Buckley 10). In short, both Karr and Prose assume that sexual harassment (in the form of acts and expressions that do not involve intercourse) is a pervasive part of our culture, and *because* it is pervasive we should do nothing about it. The best way to deal with the widespread occurrence of sexism is for women to shut up and "get over it." Any attempt to address this widespread problem publicly and openly—any attempt to critique the knowledges in the university in particular and the culture at large that blur this widespread occurrence—in order to raise our understanding of the conditions which enable the perpetuation of sexism is seen by both

Prose and Karr as merely a quest for "protection" or regulating "behavior."

However, while Prose specifically evokes the Victorians to marginalize feminism, her fundamental premise is itself strictly Victorian (as is Karr's) and so by her own logic cannot be taken seriously. For both Prose and for the Victorians, sexuality (as in sexual harassment) is largely defined by genital contact so that sexual harassment involves only those *quid pro quo* cases in which a threat has been made for making such contact possible for the pleasure of the harasser. Yet, sexuality is not equivalent to sexual intercourse and sexual harassment is not primarily about genital contact: sexual harassment is about power and control over one's conditions of existence. Whether verbal, visual, physical or a combination these, sexual harassment is a manifestation of a much broader system of objectification and dehumanization of women in order to justify their exploitation. This is why charges concerning "the hostile workplace" and "patterns of intimidation" that Prose casually dismisses as "hilarious," and Karr dismisses as irrelevant to the University, are in fact the core of sexual harassment. Of course, both Prose and Karr claim to be feminists. According to Prose: "I think of myself as a feminist . . . I believed Anita Hill" (34); while Karr claims: "I would hope that women would be empowered enough to speak and act as Jennifer Cotter has done" (Buckley 10). Both Prose and Karr are, it must be kept in mind, powerful members of the literary esablishment. They hold and exercise power inside and outside of the academy. And, like all post-feminists who have to declare their feminist credentials while trying to suppress feminism, Prose and Karr are haunted by their own complicity in the very structures of power from which they formally distances themselves.

Ultimately, it is quite clear from this concealing of "hostile work environments," that what is most troubling to Dobyns and his allies is the kind of argument I and others have made: that sexual harassment is not just a result of the "bad" behavior on the part of a few "failed" individual men but is rather a practice systematically connected to and enabled by the larger structures of sexism within capitalism. It is exactly this kind of "thoughtfulness" that the liberal defenders of "free expression" and "self-invention" cannot tolerate because—even after the fall of the Berlin Wall when liberals of the world believe everything has been settled once and for all—it makes politics serious again by making systematic connections between the supposedly "isolated" and "autonomous" practices of gender, class, sexuality, discourse, creativity . . . . The liberal explanations of the pedagogy of pleasure at bottom imply that sexual harassment is a matter of personal character and individual choice, not historical and social determination. For them, democracy is a product of individuals "choosing" to be more "ethical" and "human." Yet, at a time when US capitalism has entered a new critical phase of post-war competition with other capitalist nations—a phase which has resulted in the largest gap in wealth in the last 70 years despite the so called "new prosperity"—the liberal agenda of trying to put a "human face" on capitalism is no longer viable. Liberalism, in short, is historically bankrupt in providing effective answers to the social misery that results from the ruthlessness of capitalist exploitation. A systematic and radical explanation of social relations makes the individualizing liberal explanations of sexual harassment (i.e., as "bad behavior," as "freedom of expression," as "creativity," etc.), advanced by Dobyns and his supporters, completely irrelevant and throws into sharp relief their own implication in the issues.

Those positions that reject the necessity for a critique of "hostile work environment" in the struggle against sexual harassment, suppress the fact that sexual harassment is not simply a "fluke" that occurs between individuals rather, it is a product of a larger power structure in which women and all working people are denied ownership of the means of production and access to the material means to determine their own lives. The economic system of capitalism, in order to maintain the reproduction and accumulation of capital, fundamentally relies upon and works to reproduce a division of labor and property relations in which the vast majority of people on the planet (those who are separated from ownership and control of the means of production and, as a result, have only their labor-power to sell in order to survive) are subject to the determination and control of those who privately own the means of production. This economic exploitation is the basis of the kind of hostile work environment in which women, under the threat of unemployment, starvation, homelessness, and destitution, are afraid to oppose sexual harassment and instead learn to "tolerate" and "accept" sexist abuse in the workplace. These "lessons" in the "toleration" of exploitation, oppression, and harassment are part of what Marx explains as a much broader "silent compulsion of economic relations" in which "the advance of capitalist production develops a working class which by education, tradition and habit looks upon the requirements of that mode of production as self-evident natural laws . . . [and] once [capitalist production] is fully developed, breaks down all resistance" (*Capital*, 899). Sexual harassment and other forms of violence against women in the workplace (whether the factory, the office, the home . . .) are part of this compulsion insofar as they reify gender and make use of it to ideologically reinforce the notion that exploitation and oppression are inevitable conditions that women should simply learn to "get used to." The repetitive and continual harassment and intimidation of women, and the institutional shielding of this harassment in which it goes on unacknowledged and protected, is a way to force women to accept, out of frustration and fear, the economic basis of their exploitation.

The promotion of "autonomous," "free-standing," and "self-inventing" subjects whether in the broader fields of creative writing and post-al feminist and queer theories, by practitioners of sexist violence like Dobyns, or their allies "locally" and in the popular media, is part of this "education" process driven by capitalist production. It is a means for resurrecting the transparency of consent. If women are "free standing" subjects then they "freely choose" to stay in particular situations, they "choose" to remain silent about the abuse leveled against them, and there is "nothing" coercing them not to actively oppose or leave abusive situations. In short, according to these anti-feminists, the power structures which produce hostile work environments do not exist and therefore, women are themselves responsible for the violence and abuse leveled against them! On these terms women are the self-inventing cause of their own oppression. The isolation and individualization of specific instances of sexual harassment is quite useful in shielding and maintaining sexual harassment because it prevents people from understanding it as part of a larger pattern of intimidation of women. When cases of sexual harassment get individualized, as Dobyns and his allies attempted to do, then the harasser is able, as an "autonomous" individual to appeal to an idealist notion of democracy in which he deserves "equal protection" to any other "isolated" individual. In other words, this "individualization" erases the fact that sexual harassment is systemic so that one who engages in practices of sexual harassment is acting as an agent of systemic inequality and against the very "principles" of "democracy" and "equality" appealed to for "protection." Instead the "individualizing" approach assumes, as Prose does, that sexual harassment can only be read in terms of "bad behavior." Yet this understanding of sexism cannot account for the oppression and exploitation of women on a global scale. It cannot account for the continued marginalization, harassment and oppression of women in the workplace and permeating into all aspects of social living. Sexual harassment does not simply occur because of the failures or "blunders" of a particular individual to live up to the standards of a democratic society. It is a manifestation of the fact that we do not live in a democratic society to begin with.

Because the "isolation" and "individualization" of sexual harassment cases is so useful in maintaining the oppression and exploitation of women, there is a historical necessity, as Stan Gray has argued, in framing "gender-specific" grievances on the broader terms of class struggle (90). Sexual harassment must be understood as part of a much broader managerial strategy of dividing, subordinating, containing and silencing workers' struggle against exploitation. It is a violent managerial practice used to "punish" women who struggle to end their exploitation and oppression, and prevent others from developing the means to do so. It is also a way to divide male and female workers by redirecting male workers' attention away from capitalist exploitation and toward women as the "source" of their frustration. In doing so sexual harassment serves to mystify the material source of power—ownership and control of the means of production—and replace it with the notion that power can be gained through the abuse of others. In short, sexual harassment is one of a series of strategies used to mute class consciousness, divert attention away from the abolition of private property, and naturalize workers' relative lack of control over the work process in which "wage workers are simply objects to be used and abused in the drive for greater production" (Gray 90-91).   These managerial practices and mystifications go on whether the harassment itself occurs in the workplace, in the home, in the bar, at a party . . . . Sexual harassment is part of the cultural practices that occur inside and outside of the workplace, enabled by the capitalist production process, that produce a working class that will accept and reproduce the conditions for its own exploitation.

Sexual harassment cannot be abolished through the "re-invention" of individuals or institutions, the "subversive" production of "pleasure" within existing social relations, or through the "creative" reversals of aggressor and victim or exploiter and exploited. It must be opposed through public and collective critique of the material conditions that enable its production and perpetuation. That is, it must be opposed through collective revolutionary praxis aimed at intervening in and transforming the material conditions of private property, which produce social relations in which desire is privileged over need, in which human beings are objects to be used for the production of profit, and in which the abuse of women is a "useful tool." Opposition to sexual harassment and the exploitation of women's lives and labor must be connected to the opposition to *all hostile work environments*—all work environments in which producers do not have collective ownership and control of the products of their own labor. This means bringing a revolutionary critique of capitalism back into the discourses of feminism and connecting the struggle to end violence against women to the revolutionary struggle against class exploitation and for international communism.

Acknowledgments

This text is the result of the collective labor and critique-al solidarity of others who have remained committed to this specific case in particular and the struggle to end sexist violence and capitalist exploitation in general. For their uncompromising commitment to revolutionary struggle and many of the ideas and arguments formulated in this text, I am indebted to the 1995 *Alternative Orange* editorial collective and the Revolutionary Marxist Collective at Syracuse

University (in 1995: Brian Ganter, Adam Katz, Mark Redding, Amrohini J. Sahay, Stephen Tumino, and Robert Young). I am furthermore indebted to David Keith for his public commitment to fighting sexual harassment. I also owe thanks to Scott Jones and Jennifer Cronin for their sustained support during the time of this case and their efforts to promote support among others. Lastly, I am indebted to my attorney Bonnie Strunk for her free labor in assisting me with this case.

Works Cited

Black, Bob. Unpublished Letter to Ms. Lane and Mr. Nespeco (as members of Red Theory Collective at SUNY-Albany). August 5, 1997.

Buckley, Bruce. "Writer's Block." *Syracuse New Times*. May 24-31, 1995: 9-10.

Butler, Judith. *Bodies That Matter: On the Discursive Limits of "Sex."* New York: Routledge, 1994.

Bishop, Wendy and Hans Ostrom, eds. *Colors of a Different Horse: Rethinking Creative Writing Theory and Pedagogy.* Urbana: National Council of Teachers of English, 1994.

Callinicos, Alex. "Wonders Taken for Signs: Homi Bhabha's Postcolonialism." *Transformation: Marxist Boundary Work in Theory, Economics, Politics, and Culture* 1 (Spring 1995): 98-112.

Chisholm, Dianne. "The 'Cunning Lingua' of Desire: Bodies-Language and Perverse Performativity." Grosz and Probyn: 19-41.

Cornell, Drucilla. *Beyond Accommodation: Ethical Feminism, Deconstruction and the Law.* New York: Routledge, 1991.

Cotter, Jennifer. "Letter to the Editor." *The Chronicle of Higher Education*, April 4, 1997: B11.

_____. "Letter to the Editor." *The Daily Orange*, January 13, 1998: 8.

D'Emilio, John. "Capitalism and Gay Identity." *Powers of Desire: The Politics of Sexuality*. Eds. Ann Snitow, Christine Stansell, and Sharon Thompson. New York: Monthly Review P, 1983.

Dobyns, Stephen. "Allegorical Matters." *The American Poetry Review* 24.2 (March-April 1995): 3.

_____. "The Voices One Listens To." *AWP Chronicle* 24.4 (February 1995): 19-24.

_____. "I Was Unhappy, I Was Drunk and She Was There." *The Syracuse Herald-Journal,* Thursday, April 6, 1995: A16.

Ebert, Teresa. "(Untimely) Critiques for a Red Feminism." *Transformation: Marxist Boundary Work in Theory, Economics, Politics, and Culture* 1 (Spring 1995): 113-149.

_____. *Ludic Feminism and After: Postmodernism, Desire, and Labor in Late Capitalism*. Ann Arbor: U of Michigan P, 1996.

Gallop, Jane, ed. *Pedagogy: the Question of Impersonation*. Bloomington: Indiana UP, 1995.

_____. *Feminist Accused of Sexual Harassment*. Durham: Duke UP, 1997.

Goldstein, Meredith. "S.U. Tennis Players File Suit v. Dwire." *The Summer Orange*, July 1, 1998: 1-2

Gray, Stan. "Fighting Sexual Harassment: A Collective Labour Obligation." *Color, Class and Country: Experiences of Gender*. Eds. Gay Young and Bette J. Dickerson. London: Zed Books, 1994.

Greenberg, Pam. "Students Want to Learn Writing, Not an Agenda." *The Syracuse Post-Standard*, Wednesday, April 12, 1995: A-11.

Grosz, Elizabeth and Elspeth Probyn, eds. *Sexy Bodies: The Strange Carnalities of Feminism*. London and New York: Routledge, 1995.

Haggerty, George. "'Promoting Homosexuality' in the Classroom." Haggerty and Zimmerman 11-18.

Haggerty, George and Bonnie Zimmerman, eds. *Professions of Desire*. New York: Modern Language Association, 1995.

Haraway, Donna. *Simians, Cyborgs, and Women: The Reinvention of Nature*. New York: Routledge, 1991.

Laclau, Ernesto and Chantal Mouffe. "Post-Marxism without Apologies." *New Reflections on the Revolution of Our Time*. Ed. Ernesto Laclau. London and New York: Verso, 1990: 97-130.

_____. *Hegemony and Socialist Strategy: Towards a Radical Democratic Politics*. New York: Verso, 1985.

Litvak, Joseph. "Pedagogy and Sexuality." Haggerty and Zimmerman 19-30.

Marx, Karl. *Capital, Vol. 1*. Trans., Ben Fowkes. London: Penguin Books, 1976.

Marx, Karl and Friedrich Engels. "Manifesto of the Communist Party." *The Marx-Engels Reader*, second edition. Ed. Robert Tucker. New York: W. W. Norton & Company, 1978.

McKeever, Jim. "Alcohol Woes Often Afflict the Creative, Says Prof." *The Syracuse Post-Standard*, April 7, 1995: C-4.

Meese, Elizabeth. *(Sem)Erotics: Theorizing Lesbian: Writing*. New York and London: New York UP, 1992.

Mehta, Seema. "For Dobyns and S.U., a Debate Still Rages." *The Daily Orange,* December 3, 1997: 8, 10.

_____. "Three Years Later, Program Sees Changes." *The Daily Orange*, December 3, 1997: 9-10.

Mies, Maria. *Patriarchy and Accumulation on a World Scale: Women in the International Division of Labor*. London: Zed Books, 1986.

Morrow, Kevin. "Dobyns Suspended; Sanctions Imposed." *The Syracuse Record*, July 24, 1995: 5, 14.

Morton, Donald. "Queerity and Ludic Sado-Masochism: Compulsory Consumption and the Emerging Post-al Queer." *Transformation: Marxist Boundary Work in Theory, Economics, Politics, and Culture* 1 (Spring 1995): 189-215.

Nolan, Maureen. "SU Writing Program Feels Under Siege." *The Syracuse Post-Standard*, Saturday, April 29, 1995: B1, B3

Ostrom, Hans. "Of Radishes and Shadows, Theory and Pedagogy." Bishop and Ostrom: xi-xxiii.

Prose, Francine. "Bad Behavior." *The New York Times Magazine*, November 26, 1995: 34-36.

Red Theory Collective at SUNY-Albany. "An Open Letter to the Community Regarding The Chronicle of Higher Education's Suppression of Jennifer Cotter's Analysis of the Sexual Harassment Committed Against Her by Stephen Dobyns." Publicly circulated letter. February 1997. Red Square, October 1997. The Red Collective, October 1997 (http://www.geocities.com/~redcritique.html)

Rubin, Gayle. (1984). "Thinking Sex: Notes for a Radical Theory of the Politics of Sexuality." *The Lesbian and Gay Studies Reader*. Eds. Henry Abelove, Michèle A ina Barale, and David Halperin. New York: Routledge, 1993.

Sandoval, Chela. "New Sciences: Cyborg Feminism and the Methodology of the Oppressed." *The Cyborg Handbook*. Eds. Chris Hables Gray, et al. London and New York: Routledge, 1995.

Syracuse University. *The Faculty Manual*. Edition 18, January 1995.

Talbot, Margaret. "A Most Dangerous Method." *Lingua Franca* (January-February 1994): 24-40.

Weingast, Jeffrey and Jeffrey Glor. "Suspended Professor Attributes Incident to Alcoholism." *The Daily Orange*, April 7, 1995: 1, 3.

Wolfe, Cary. *Critical Environment: Postmodern Theory and the Pragmatics of the "Outside."* Minneapolis: U of Minnesota P, 1998.

Wilson, Robin. "A Prestigious Writing Program and Its Big-Name Authors Face Charges of Harassment." *The Chronicle of Higher Education*. February 21, 1997: A8-A10.

Zavarzadeh, Mas'ud and Donald Morton. *Theory as Resistance: Politics and Culture After (Post)structuralism*. New York: Guilford P, 1994.

Huei-ju Wang

Women's "Oppression" and Property Relations:

From Sati and Bride-Burning to Late Capitalist

"Domestic Labor" Theories

This essay is a historical materialist investigation into the oppression of women in Indian feudal society as manifested in the various social practices such as sati as well as in advanced capitalist western societies. It will also critique-ally analyze the British intervention into the indigenous practices to justify its colonial rule. The investigation will also discuss the continued oppression of and violence against women in modern capitalist India as shown in the social practice of dowry demands by the husband and related bride-burning when such demands are not met. I will argue that these diverse and seemingly "autonomous" practices that existed in feudal India or continue to exist in modern India can be traced to the common feature of class/caste societies--private property. I will then focus on the "oppression" of women in advanced capitalist societies in the West and demonstrate that all modes of "oppression" are, in fact, "exploitation" of women and the effects of property relations.

Marxism, the "Material Base" and the Prodigal Sign

Given the marginalization of Marxism in the post-al[1] knowledge industry, however, it is necessary to say a few words on Marxist theory now. Historical materialism, which argues all social practices are historical and determined by the material conditions of production and class struggle, is marginalized at this historical moment in post-al theories. Long before the fall of the Stalinist Soviet Union[2], Foucault in the early 1970 wrote that "Marxism exists in nineteenth century thought like a fish in water" but is "unable to breathe anywhere else" (Order 262). The then archeologist Foucault thus consigned Marxism and its dialectic method to the museum of antiquity, though acknowledging it "may have stirred up a few waves and caused a few surface ripples" (262) in its own time--the early industrial capitalism when capital, having brutally expropriated millions of producers from their means of production, the feudal land, called into the existence of its "other," the proletariat, who have nothing but their own labor-power as a commodity to sell to survive, and some of whom fall even lower during each capitalist periodic crisis. But neither has Marx's materialist conception of history that posits "the history of all hitherto existing society is the history of class struggles" (The Communist Manifesto 55) become outdated because it is more than one hundred years old as Foucault seems to imply. Nor has his critique of bourgeois political economy, which mystifies capital as the source of profit, thereby occluding the exploitation of wage-labor. Foucault's attribution of "ageism" to Marxism only indicates his idealist understanding of history as the history of ideas. But ideas, as Marx and Engels argue in The German Ideology, do not have "an independent existence" and are conditioned by the development of forces of production (41; 47). In addition to exploitation of wage-labor, the continued existence of sweatshop slavery both in advanced capitalism and developing countries, where children and women workers are employed and exploited, proves that capitalism even at its epoch of decay has not renounced and will not renounce its exploitation of cheap labor because it is profitable and serves its own class interest. On the contrary, the exploitation of wage-labor is intensified to countervail the tendency of the rate of profit to fall resulting from individual capitalists' needs to constantly revolutionize the means of production to outperform other rival capitalists. Moreover, the extraction of surplus labor from the working class as a whole and gender division of labor are fundamental to accumulation of capital at the expense of the immediate producers. I have elaborated elsewhere Marx's contribution to the proletarian men and women by his scientific discovery of SURPLUS VALUE as the source of profit for capitalist accumulation in my discussion and critique of Gayatri Spivak's reading of Marx.

After the disintegration of the Soviet Union and that of other Stalinist states[3], Judith Butler confirmed the "so-called demise of Marxism" and "the loss of credibility that Marxist versions of history have recently endured" ("Poststructuralism" 3). Marx's materialist conception of history, which she misreads as the narrative of the belief in the progress of history rather than as the class struggle over the ownership of the means of production, for Butler "is now in permanent crisis" (3). Despite the marginalizing of Marxism by post-al theorists, Derrida called for a return to Marx, arguing "There will be no future without this [reading of Marx's works]. Not without Marx, no future without Marx" (Specters of Marx 13), yet only to "ghost" and "haunt," that is, deconstruct, Marxist knowledge, such as value and revolution. Here I would argue that the deconstructionist play with Marxist knowledge of value (exchange value), as in Spivak and Derrida, is not a "free play" but is class-interested to protect the interests of capitalist private property accumulated by the exploitation of the wage labor and unpaid domestic labor of women. Both post-al dismissal of and "engagement" with/deconstruction of

Marxist knowledge work to erase exploitation of surplus labor, upon which capitalist social relations, including bourgeois academy, are based, from the scene of theory and knowledge, and thus help protect the interests of the ruling class and capitalist private property.

Despite their theoretical differences on the surface, these post-al theorists as well as others including feminists, post-colonialists agree that the fundamental historical materialist premise that the material conditions of production--forces and relations of production--determine the superstructure (the political, the ideological, the philosophical...), and all social practices must be investigated systematically in a dialectical relation to the relations of production and class struggle is not only WRONG but TOTALIZING (read TOTALITARIAN). The classical Marxist model of base/superstructure, according to post-al logic of differance/supplementarity, not only establishes a hierarchal relation between the binary but is no longer attainable as the division between the two is unstable through the Derridean notion of supplementarity (Butler, "Merely Culture"). The notion of the supplement, according to Derrida, is dangerous, i.e., subversive in that:

> The supplement adds itself, it is a surplus..... It adds only to replace... The sign is always   the supplement of the thing itself... Its economy exposes and protects us at the same time according to the play of forces and of the differences of forces.... an infinite chain, ineluctably   multiplying   the supplementary mediations that produce the sense of the very thing they defer. (*Grammatology* 144-57)

But Butler's Derridean idealist critique of "mimetic representation" leaves out the function of ruling ideology, a Marxist concept largely displaced in post-al theories and replaced by Foucault's notion of discourse, as the mediation between the base and superstructure in Marxist theory to cover up the exploitation of surplus labor and unpaid domestic labor for capitalist accumulation. Butler takes the Derridean notion of "surplus" and "economy" as "given" in language/texuality, thus produces a new foundationalism while critiquing all foundationalisms.

To those who rejected the base/superstructure conception of the social and prioritized the superstructure over the mode of production, Marx has replied: "One thing is clear: the Middle Ages could not live on Catholicism, nor could the ancient world on politics. On the contrary, it is the manner in which they gained their livelihood which explains why in one case politics, in the other case Catholicism, played the chief part" (*Capital* 1 176). Contrary to Butler's claim that the base/superstructure is an "obsolete" concept, I would argue it provides an important frame for systematical investigations and analyses of all social practices in an integrated totality--a concept also displaced in post-al knowledge in favor of local, "subjugated" knowledge--while showing how they are reinforced through the mediation of ruling ideology to justify and secure the capitalist relations of production/exploitation/oppression.

The political effect of the displacement of the base/superstructure in post-al theories is that all social practices have their own raison d'etre, cut off from the global relations of production and class struggle. Thus, the play of the signifies, relations of power, women's oppression in class societies, women's unpaid domestic labor in capitalism, social construction of sex/gender/sexuality and other social practices are understood in post-al theories in their own specificity as if they were separable from the historically specific relations of production and class struggle. However, the concerted efforts in marginalizing Marxist revolutionary knowledges, which have scientifically demonstrated the relations of production and social divisions of labor as the basis of all social practices, are not simply the effect of "free-thinking" intellectuals "expressing" their "personal" political views but should be understood as one of the heightened forms of class struggle carried out in the arena of knowledge. The superstructure or the ideological forms, as Marx points out, is the site where antagonist classes become conscious of the existing material conflicts arising from the forces and relations of production and "fight it out" (*Contribution* 21).

One important issue that I take up in my engagement with and critique of various post-al theorists is the issue of "materiality" and the political effect of post-al/idealist and Marxist/materialist understanding of it on class struggle to transform global capitalism into international socialism. There are two major ways of understanding "materiality" in post-al theories. One follows Derrida and his "radicalizing" of the sign, and thus understanding "materiality" as the "material" part of the sign detached from the conceptual part, that is, as the free play of the signifier without a transcendental signified. The other follows Foucault and his notion of reversal of discourse/power, and thus understanding "materiality" as constituted in the reversal of discourse/power and the resistance of the body to discourse/power. Drawing on both Derrida and Foucault, Butler and other ludic feminists have articulated the body as a site of prodigal self-transformation without questioning the historical-objective conditions of labor in which the body is situated, regardless of its gender, sexuality and race. Against post-al ahistorical understanding of "materiality" as differance and as reversal of discourse/power, I argue for historical materialist understanding of materiality as praxis of labor, and as such it is the effect of the mode of production--forces and relations of production--and class struggle marked by antagonisms, conflicts and contradictions. Social change, thus, means transforming the material conditions of production, and not perpetually undoing binary terms (mind/body, nature/culture, revolution/reform, masculine/feminine, center/margin) as post-al theories argue. The class antagonism between capital/wage-labor, a material reality existing outside texuality and in capitalist relations of production, cannot simply be undermined in thinking without socialist revolution to expropriate the means of production from the exploiting class.

As Marx has noted,

> In the social production of their existence, men [and women] inevitably enter into definite relations, which are independent of their will, namely relations of production appropriate to a given stage in the development of their material forces of production. The totality of these relations of production constitutes the economic structure of society, the real foundation, on which arises a legal and political superstructure and to which correspond definite forms of social consciousness. (*Contribution* 20)

Thus, the final goal of social transformation is to transform the exploitative capitalist relations of production into international socialism, and does not confine itself to the superstructural change. The mode of my inquiry is materialist critique which posits there is a historical-objective outside from which to launch ideology critique in order to raise class consciousness to transform all the exploitative and oppressive practices of capitalism. The outside, as Zavarzadeh has argued (College Literature 98), is the WORKING DAY in capitalism where surplus value is extracted from the working class as a whole to accumulate capital for the owning class, thus producing the means of exploiting the working class anew. Since theory is a site of class struggle, throughout this essay I will persistently speak for the historical-objective interests of the working class and against the exploitative interests of the capitalist class, thus contesting Foucault's injunction against "the indignity of speaking for others" ("Intellectuals and Power" 209). In speaking for "others," by which I mean the exploited working class, I do not deny any worker's ability to speak for himself/herself, to speak out his/her exploitation/oppression in capitalism. Rather I argue that to end the exploitation and appropriation of the labor of "others," the working class "in itself" has to struggle "for itself" as a class, as "the ruling class" to full its historical mission to end all classes, which, to repeat, exist objectively in the material productions of life. To speak for the historical-objective interests of the working class is not a question of ethics, but rather one of class struggle. For the dictatorship of the proletariat.

Sati, Bride-Burning and Private Property

Each society, according to Foucault, has its own regime of truth ("Truth and Power" 131). In capitalism the reigning truth is "Freedom, Equality, Property and Bentham" for "all" (Capital I 280). However, this reigning truth is not merely an effect of discourse/power as Foucault might argue, but rather is the way the free market in/of capitalism operates. In it, as Marx explains:

> Freedom, because both buyer and seller of a commodity [labor power] are determined only by their own free will. They contract as free persons, who are equal before the law.... Equality, because each enters into relation with the other, as with a simple owner of commodities, and they exchange equivalent for equivalent. Property, because each disposes only of what is his [her] own. And Bentham, because each looks only to his [her] advantage. (*Capital* I 280)

In other words, the ideology of "Freedom, Equality, Property and Bentham" is rooted in the material base, in the capitalist mode of production and exchange, and is foisted upon the working class as "their own free will" to secure and justify the relations of production. Similarly, in rural villages in modern India the ideology for justifying the plight and impoverishment of the 33 million Hindu widows is karma--a Hindu belief that life's fortunes are dictated by good or evil deeds in former lives (Burns, "Once Widowed in India"). However, behind karma and free wage-labor, as I would argue, is the operation of private property which has worked against the interests of the working class and the poor. That is, the misery of the cast-out widows in India's rural areas in the 1990s and exploitation of the wage-labor and unpaid domestic labor in both advanced and developing countries are the effect of private property-- freedom of property for the owning class and thus freedom from property for the working class and the poor. As Marx and Engels write in *The Communist Manifesto*,

> It [wage-labor] creates capital, i.e., that kind of property which exploits wage-labor, and which cannot increase except upon condition of begetting a new supply of wage-labor for fresh exploitation. Property, in its present form, is based on the antagonism of capital and wage-labor. (68)

Since the post-al ahistorical understanding of the social and property as the free play of the signifier, as endless reversal of discourse/power--"materiality" understood in terms of the signifying chain and discourse/power--is unable to account for the material conditions of women in different modes of production, it is necessary to re-examine the value of historical materialism for being able to historicize and explain the situation of women, who, to emphasize, are not merely a category--a signifier open to resignification as Butler has argued--but are situated in the real, historical-objective relations of production outside of the discursive chain of signification. I thus argue for deploying the base/superstructure materialist frame, which I have already outlined, to investigate the conditions of women and the family in colonial and modern India and western capitalism as it allows for a materialist explanation of women's oppression in class society while attending to the historically specific forms of oppression. In so doing, I will try to demonstrate that the various social practices, especially the ones that oppress women both materially and ideologically,--from feudal sati and widow remarriage in colonial India, to dowry-related bride-burning, infanticide of new-born girls and abortion of female fetuses, and abandonment of propertyless widows especially among the rural poor in post-colonial India, to patriarchal gender division of labor and oppression of women in capitalism in the form of unpaid domestic labor,--have their common roots in private property. Thus, the oppression of women in both advanced and developing countries as well as the oppression of gay men and women and people of color in capitalism can be seen to be systematically produced by a mode of production that has historically relied on the heterosexual family and unpaid domestic labor to supply a sufficient labor force and has used differences among the working class such as race, gender and sexuality to divide and conquer the workers.

One of my goals here is to connect diverse social practices and relate them to private property and capitalism, which is enabled by the base/superstructure model that conceptualizes the society as a totality founded on the relations of production. This is, of course, understood in post-al discourse as an act of "totalization." However, it is precisely against the post-al logic of "fragmentation" and "autonomy" that I argue for historical materialist understanding of diverse social practices as arising from the material conditions of production and property relations determined by it in order that we can effectively eliminate unjust labor and other social practices through class struggle by transforming the material base that has given rise to the injustice in capitalism: the increasing poverty for the working class and the poor and wealth for the owning class.

To theorize and historicize the family, private property, women's oppression and colonialism/neo-colonialism, I argue, we need to situate these historical events in the mode of production in which they came into being and continue to be reconfigured as the effect of the increased productivity and contradictions of forces and relations of production. In doing so, we can show that the specific forms of family, private property and women's oppression are not "universal" institutions and practices from time immemorial, but have arisen at a certain stage of development of production because of the change in the mode of production. Colonialism, which came into being in the capitalist mode of production and continues to exist today in the form of neo-colonialism (mystified as "post-colonialism" in contemporary bourgeois theory) or globalization, can be shown to be the effect of globalization of capital. However, the attempts to explain these historical events in a dialectic relation to the material base as Engels did in his theorization of the family as the effect of the change in the mode of production, are often dismissed as "economic reductionism" (Barrett 28). To not take into account the material conditions of production as the base for various social practices is to posit these practices as having an "autonomous" existence outside this material history, understood as the historical process of development of productive forces through labor praxis and the outcome of class struggle. In fact, private property as the product of social labor not only indicates the existence of surplus over necessary means of consumption (Engels argued that the change in the mode of production--domestication of cattle--and subsequent increased level of productive force led to the surplus) but also presupposes unequal divisions of labor and thus unequal distribution of social wealth.

The capitalist mode of production is the material base for British colonial rule in India. The use of machinery in factory production and the need to expand the market globally for mass-produced, cheapened commodities in order to realize profits lay the ground for its colonial policy. As Amilcar Cabral has argued, imperialism, the last phase in the evolution of capitalism, has been a "historical necessity": the consequence of the capitalist productive forces and the search for profits, i.e., accumulation of surplus value, by monopoly financial capital. (Marxism 398). But it is a "necessity," as he goes on to say, like those of the national liberation of the colonized, the destruction of capital and the advent of socialism (398). In other words, imperialism is subject to the law of dialectics, the negation of the negation. However, British colonial ideology obscures the laws of history--development of the mode of production and class struggle over the productive forces and ownership of the means of production--from its subjugated Indian subjects, and justifies its rule on grounds of "moral superiority." The colonial ideology instead feminizes the "natives" as "a frail, cowardly, and soft bodied little people" (Recasting Women 36), thus unfit to rule themselves. It also connects the colonial situation to the degeneration of Hindu civilization, and argues that the abject position of Hindu women makes it necessary for the colonial state to intervene. In other words, the British colonizers produce an ideology on the fall of India as the outcome of the decline of Hindu culture and race, rather than as the effect of the capitalist productive forces and "free trade." While the British foregrounded the fall of Hindu culture and race to justify their colonial rule, the Hindu elites also believed a revival of their degenerated Hindu culture and race would regain the pre-colonial state. In this context, a racist/fascist ideology of the superiority of Hindu-Aryan race was popularized to forge a new "national" identity against the British rule. Moreover, this ideology worked to intensify the difference between Hindus and Muslims in colonial India. It is still deployed today by the Hindu ruling class to divide the workers as evidenced in the recent election of the Indian prime minister.

The Hindu cultural nationalists, as Uma Chakravarti points out, singled out the Muslim rule of India as the cause of the fall of India and the subjugation of Hindu women. According to M.C. Deb, a member of the Young Bengal group, the "ravages of Muslim rule" gave rise to the "sad and deplorable conditions" that "men in India looked upon women as household slaves" (37-8). The scapegoating of Muslims, popular among the Hindu nationalists, still does not answer the subjugation of women in colonial India, which was exacerbated by British rule. Segregation of women in separate individual households and their exclusion from public production and space, as manifested in the practice of purdah, is historical and material: it arose from the development of private property and the rise of class society. The oppression of women cannot be explained away by either religion or culture, but needs to be theorized in a dialectical relation to the material base that produces aspects of the superstructure, such as religion and culture.

But before offering my historical materialist analysis of these social practices, I would like to critique-ally engage with the discursive analysis of sati as offered by Lata Mani. In general, Mani argues that the public discourse of sati is largely manipulated by the British colonial power, but she treats this discourse and colonial power in isolation from the feudal, patriarchal mode of production increasingly invaded by monopoly capitalism. Therefore, she sets out to analyze the inner dynamics of signification in the discourse on sati, thus understanding it, to a large extent, as a discursive/religious practice. In so doing, she is unable to account for sati as a material practice enabled by private property, which I will further elaborate later from a historical materialist perspective.

Mani argues that the production of knowledge about sati, the privileging of brahmanic scriptures in interpreting the practice and reconstruction of Hindu "tradition" are specifically colonial. The "civilizing mission of colonization," for the British, says Mani, is not to impose a new Christian moral order but to restore the "truths of indigenous tradition," i.e., the "little read and less understood Shaster" ("Contentious Traditions" 95). Indeed, the colonial regime was able to accomplish this self-imposed mission because of its capitalist productive force, including the introduction of printing. As one Indian scholar Jadunath Sarkar wrote: "In the nineteenth century we recovered our long lost ancient literature, Vedic and Buddhistic,...The English printed these ancient scriptures of the Indo-Aryans and brought them to our doors" (qtd. in Chakravarti 29). The availability of printing also enabled the indigenous intelligentsia interpreting these ancient scriptures and reconstructing the past to popularize their work in pamphlets and journals, also products of printing (Chakravarti 32).

The colonial discourse on sati by both the British and the indigenous male elite, says Mani, is framed by the scriptural texts. Scripture in the colonial discourse is equated with religion, tradition, women and the law. A discursive shift occurred in the Hindu social reformer Rammohun Roy's discourse on sati as he increasingly relied more on the tradition of brahmanic scriptures than on conceptual analysis to interpret and argue against the practice. Such a discursive shift that privileged the brahmanic scriptures in interpreting sati, argues Mani, is the effect of the colonial rule (91). However, the framing of sati within the scriptural texts, argues Mani, not only marginalizes women in the debates but also determines the alterative to sati, which according to the scriptural text Manu is ascetic widowhood. Rather than attempting to address the issue of the oppression of women (imposed by the feudal patriarchal property relations), the discourse on sati becomes the site for colonial officials to justify their "civilizing" colonial mission to rescue Hindu women from their men and for indigenous elite males from both "progressive" and conservative sides to reconstruct their "tradition" as prescribed by the scriptures. Thus, it is "tradition" or scripture rather than women, argues Mani, that is locus of the debate on sati.

The official discourse on sati, says Mani, is based on three interdependent assumptions: the hegemony of religious texts, a complete indigenous submission to them and the religious basis of sati (95). However, Mani contests these assumptions and argues that there exists the "enormous regional variation in the mode of committing sati" (96). Although the colonial officials were aware of the differences and diversity in the modes of practicing sati, they continued, says Mani, to uphold the hegemony of scripture/religion. By portraying the widow either as victim of men or religion, the official discourse, argues Mani, denies the Hindu women both complex female subjectivity and agency in order to legitimate its intervention into the religious/scriptural practice on "the widow's behalf," hence its colonial rule. For example, one colonial official Walter Ewer argued that the widow is not at all a "free agent" in the performance of sati and she is "incapable of consenting and must therefore be protected from pundits and crowds alike" (93-4). "Women," concludes Mani, "are neither subjects nor objects, but rather the ground of the discourse on sati" (117).

The scriptural texts, argues Mani, were not homogenous but rather heterogeneous in their accounts of sati as they were written at different periods. The Hindu pundits as interpreters of the scriptures did not claim "truth" to their interpretations, but the British, according to Mani, manipulated the interpretations to serve their colonial interests. The "authority" of the scriptural texts, as she points out, is arbitrarily determined by the colonial officials: the older the text the greater was assumed its authority. For Mani, the colonial power can be seen at work in the manipulation of public discourse. However, I would argue that there is a material outside to power and discourse: the capitalist productive force, and that the crucial question is not that the British imposed the final meaning on the heterogeneity of the scriptural texts as Mani suggests, but that the scriptures are deployed to justify the oppression of women, and thus keeping the gender inequalities and patriarchal property relations in place as they are being challenged by capitalist imperialism. Even the "progressive" social reformer Rammohun argues against the practice of sati not so much because it oppresses women of high-caste as because it is not prescribed in the scriptures, and he argues for ascetic widowhood as an alternative because Manu prescribes it for women.

Mani's critique of the official discourse on sati, however, shows that she understands sati as an "autonomous" practice, independent of the material conditions of production and the property relations determined by it. Her Foucauldian critique which pays attention to differences, diversity and heterogeneity is no different from the official production of knowledge about sati in that both seek to record the practice in its details, and not to make a causal connection to the material base. The official eye, or the colonial power, ensures that not one single particular aspect of sati would escape the official observation. In contesting the official discourse, Mani also appeals to the subjective experience of the widow rather than to the historically objective condition of property relations. She writes that "we have no independent access to the mental or subjective states of widows outside of these overdetermined colonial representations of them" (97). Thus, she concludes that the complexity and inconsistence of the mental states of the widows makes it difficult to determine whether they were coerced or voluntary in performing sati. In doing so, she also understands sati as a personal experience rather than as the effect of the unequal socio-economic structure. Mani also states that the discourse on sati is "modern" in the sense that it shows "concern with individual will," although implicitly (116). However, I contest Mani's understanding of agency and modernity as "free individual will." What is at stake here is not so much whether or not sati is performed according to the widow's "will" as the feudal patriarchal property relations that justify women's oppression in the name of scriptural texts and severely circumscribe the very conditions of "choice," that is, lack of choice. The bourgeois notion of "individual free will" can be shown to have its limits when we situate it in the capitalist relations of production: it is a freedom in the market--to sell and buy--for the owning class, but a wage slavery and economic misery for the working class.

The framing of sati within the scriptures not only marginalizes women as Mani argues, but, more importantly, it presupposes sati is a religious/scriptural practice. The justificaiton for and the abolition of sati through interpretations of the scriptures does not so much explain the root cause of the practice as mystify it. It is more effective to theorize sati as a practice determined by labor relations and property rules. The historical and material conditions of possibility for sati, as I argue, is private property. In fact, we can find evidence of sati as a material practice in the colonial discourse on the women's question. Although Rammohun argues against sati as a "gross violation of the Shastras," he acknowledges it as "a material practice, relating its greater incidence in Bengal to women's property rights" (105). Bengal was a relatively wealthy region until British colonialism destroyed its advanced textile industry to protect its own and ruined its agricultural wealth by turning rich fields of rice and other grain into plantations of poppies for profits (Chomsky, World Orders 115). By connecting sati to private property, we can more easily understand why sati had a higher percentage among high-caste Hindus who were more likely to own property than the lower-castes. Of the 8,134 reported sati during the debate on the issue, most of them were committed by women of high-caste (Mani 88). The political economy of sati, thus, is to maintain the landed property within the male-line, that is, through father right. The material gains by the male relatives of the deceased husband and the pundits performing the ritual were well recognized by the colonial officials. Walter Ewer pointed out that upon committing sati, the widow relinquishes "her legal right over the family estate" and that the pundits were rewarded for officiating the ritual (93). Behind the myth that the Hindu widow mounts the pyre of her deceased husband cheerfully in her devotion to him is the economic and its consequent sexual oppression of Hindu women and the ongoing primitive accumulation of capital. The political economy of sati has resonance in the burning of witches in the Europe in the seventeenth century and in the US in the nineteen century in that both practices were enabled by private property and involved struggle over private property and appropriation of it away from women. While the "witches" were burned the church officials confiscated their properties to pay for the war conquest (Mies 85). The witch trials not only provided employment for the legal professionals such as lawyers, judges and the councils but also were "a lucrative source of money and wealth" (Mies 84-5).

The practice and concentration of sati among high-caste Hindus foregrounds the role of the family in the feudal mode of production as the institution of transmitting landed property to male descendants. It also shows that the material condition of possibility for patriarchy--men's control over women's labor, sexuality and fertility--is, contrary to the dominant feminist views, private property. The material condition of possibility for the single (heterosexual) family and confining of women in individual separate households, as Engels argues in The Origin of the Family, is the development of private property and rise of class society. Engels' historical materialist explanation that the form of the family changes as the effect of the change in the mode of production, as I mentioned earlier, has been subject to critique from feminists, who regard it as being "economic reductionism" (Barrett 28). Also, these feminists have pointed out that Engels fails to give attention to the role of the family in forming one's gender, sexuality through ideology. In other words, they tend to see the family as part of the superstructural. Barrett, for example, states that Engels "explains the development of the monogamous family as the consequence of the amassing of private property, classically relating the explanation of a 'superstructural' phenomenon (the family) to its economic 'base' " (27). However, Barrett here misstates Engels' view on the family, which is not merely part of the superstructural in the sense that in the family one learns to form one's gender, sexual identity through familial ideology, but is itself part of the social relations of production because it produces the next generation of labor force. In her introduction to the 1988 edition of her early work, *Women's Oppression Today*, Barrett questions the family as a "primary site" of the oppression of women (xx). Instead she argues that we should investigate women's oppression in terms of work (outside the family) and the state, which she regards not as the organ of exploitation of one class by another to safeguard private property (Origins 23). The effect of glossing over the family as one site of women's oppression is that it naturalizes the privatized domestic labor, which is unpaid, and thus helps perpetuate women's exploitation in capitalism. I will return to the issue of domestic labor in advanced capitalist societies in the second part of this essay. In sum, the inequalities between the sexes as well as between the social classes are historical and increase with the development of production founded on private property. As Engels concludes:

> Since civilization is founded on the exploitation of one class by another class, its whole development proceeds in a constant contradiction. Every step forward in production is at the same time a step backward in the position of the oppressed class, that is, of the great majority. (*Origin* 215-16)

It can be argued that a class analysis of women's oppression may not apply to the ancient Hindu caste system which is determined by birth and not by the social relations of production and private ownership of the means of production. However, the Hindu caste society is not an egalitarian society as is the "primitive society" based on communal property because of the extremely low level of productivity, and rather that it is an exploitative society founded on private property and exploitation of labor of lower-castes by the upper caste. In other words, like class, caste is not a "natural" social relation, but developed historically in the mode of production. In fact, the division of Hindu feudal society into four major castes--the priests, the soldiers, the farmers and merchants and the laborers--indicates the forms of production in the Hindu society, and its social divisions of labor are such that the upper castes were freed from the direct production process and specialized in their social functions whereas the lower castes were engaging in the production of necessities to meet the needs of the whole society. The caste system, as Evelyn Reed argues, is "inherently and at birth a class system" (Problems 97). Reed also argues that while the caste system reached its fullest development only in certain regions of the world, such as India, the class system evolved far beyond it to become a world system which engulfed the caste system. In India today, where the ancient caste system survives in decaying forms, capitalist/class relations and power, she writes, prevail over all the inherited pre-capitalist institutions, including the caste relics (97).

Although one of the prime agents of the British colonial regime, the East India Company, banned the practice of sati in 1829, the change at the level of law did not resolve the fundamental social contradictions, arising from private property, in Indian society, nor protect Hindu widows from the male-dominated society. As Hindu feminist Ramabai commented on the British justice: "the British were hardly going to bother about the rights of women if British profit and rule in India might be endangered thereby" (Chakravarti 74). In fact, as defender of "property, family, religion, order," the East India Company had more interest in keeping the existing social inequality in place than in eradicating it, and instead instituted laws that reinforced the existing social conflicts to secure its material gain in the colony. For example, the Permanent Settlement of 1793 first introduced in Bengal and later expanded to other Indian regions not only re-empowers the existing landholding groups but turns them into "individual property owners" along with the former tax collectors, thus creating a new class who owned and controlled the means of production, the land. The privatization of land, as Chomsky writes quoting a comment from a British enquiry commission, "yields wealth to local clients and the British rulers while 'the settlement fashioned with great care and deliberation has to our painful knowledge subjected almost the whole of the lower classes to most grievous oppression'" (*World Orders* 116). The peasantry, expropriated from the land, were forced to become either "tenants-at-will" leasing a lot of land from the owning class with money borrowed from the money-lenders or agricultural laborers. The privatization of the land, a historical and material practice that Marx says "could only arise in a bourgeois society, and one which was already well developed" (*Capital* I 183), was being implemented in the colony as well and thus turned the land into a source of profit for both the land-owners and money-lenders as well as the colonial regime at the expense of the laboring classes.

On the other hand, the "individual property rights" extended to the colonial subjects, as Kumkum Sangari and Sudesh Vaid point out, were "vested primarily in the hands of men, and women generally had only ancillary rights accruing from their subordinate relationships with men" (6). Despite the patriarchal nature of the "individual property rights," the new land-owning class included women as well. To secure their class interests, the women landlords, says Kapil Kumar who argues for "a gender-class approach to the 'history of feminism'" ("Rural Women" 338), were no less oppressive and exploitative than their male counterparts. Sangari and Vaid also argue that the Widow Remarriage Act of 1856 is "virtually a paper legislation" because it contains clauses that deny the widow the right to her husband's property upon remarriage (16). For the widow, the act is more a reminder of what material loss she will incur by her remarriage than an encouragement for her to exercise her legal right. Here we can see the mystification class interests in bourgeois law: what is given in the law is undermined by the economic considerations.

The colonial regime, Sangari and Vaid argue, was reactionary toward the Married Women's Property Act which was written into law in 1882 after a long struggle by British feminists in England. However, the property reform in England, which was made historically possible because of the capitalist mode of production and the property relations determined by it, had little effect on the lives of the working-class women in Britain, whose position in the capitalist relations of production made them part of the exploited class producing social wealth. It is a law based on the protection of private property and leaves intact the social relations of production that allows the accumulation of private property in the hands of the few owing class, though giving the bourgeois women the right to "individual property." Private property, as Marx argues, is a social relation, a historical-objective condition of labor. In capitalism, as I have pointed out earlier, private property has become the means of exploitation of wage-labor. The freedom of property, on the one hand, for the owning class is the freedom from property, on the other, for the working class and the poor. A property right reform like the Married Women Property Act will not eliminate the exiting social inequality in one nation if the existing exploitative class/labor relations on the global scale remains unchanged.

If the reification of the scriptural texts helps conceal sati as a material practice, in karewa (widow remarriage) we can more easily see how this practice is connected to private property, to the preservation of landed property in the family. The popularity of karewa among the majority of landowning classes, as Prem Chowdhry argues, grew out of the need to retain landed property in the family ("Customs" 315). Karewa, although allowing widows to remarry, is in essence an oppressive practice prescribed for widows to ensure the transfer of landed property from the deceased husband to his brothers or other male relatives. Upon remarriage, the widow is denied the right to inherit property from her deceased husband. It is a remarriage restricted to the male relatives of the deceased husband. The colonial regime supported this seemingly "progressive" practice because it recognized that karewa is a class practice that keeps the landed property in the family. The attempts by widows to alienate the family property is regarded as tearing the economic unit of the Hindu society apart, and thus discouraged. The need for the family for the land-owning class and economic and sexual oppression of women within the land-owning class are the effect of the class/caste society founded on private property.

The abolition of sati by the British, although leaving the patriarchal property relations unexamined and giving attention to "women's rights" in name and not in practice, nevertheless is an important event in the history of women in modern India. But has the oppression of and violence against women disappeared in India with the abolition of sati? The continued migration since early this century by widows to Vrindavan--a Hindu pilgrimage city in central India that has become a "refuge" for cast-out widows, who believe by dying in such a holy town they can break the cycle of birth and re-birth (Borah, "State of Widows")--proves that private property continues to be the material source of Indian widows' oppression in particular and women's oppression in class societies in general. Some, as both Borah and Burns wrote, fled to Vrindavan to escape hardship as unpaid domestic servants or dasi at in-laws' home after the death of their husbands. Others were brought and abandoned there by their relatives, who believed that widows bring them "bad luck" and thus tried to get rid of them. Just as the sati performed by widows is not a question of "free choice" but rather one of lack of choice, so too the post-sati poor widows have few options than migrating or being sent to Vrindavan. To be a Hindu widow without any means of self-support in the 1990s, wrote Burns quoting Uma Chakravarty, is still to "suffer 'social death.'" That is, unless the widow controls "property," she is treated shabbily and even ostracized (Borah). Most of all, some of the widows at Vrindavan are still in their teens, married off by parents as "unwanted burden" and widowed in their teens. At the same time, the modernized India has witnessed some of its "luckier" women "fly air force jets, head million-dollar corporations and sit in Parliament" (Borah). How does one explain this contradictory and uneven development for Indian women? Certainly, it is not the working of karma as most of the widows at Vrindavan seem to believe. Rather it is the effect of class-divided society and its unequal social divisions of labor, thus unequal distribution of social wealth.

On the other hand, the reported cases of bride-burning related to excessive dowry demands also suggest that the oppression of women and violence against them have not ceased to occur. While the feudal sati is performed in the public in the name of religion/scripture and/or "devotion" to the deceased husband, the modern bride-burning is a private, secret event, a female murder committed when the exorbitant dowry demands are not met. In some cases, the mother-in-law, along with her son and husband, is also found guilty of murdering her daughter-in-law whose family has failed to meet the dowry demands. According to an Indian Government report, about 5,000 young, newly married brides were killed over dowry extortions in India every year between 1987 and 1994, although unofficial numbers are much higher and are increasing at an alarming rate. Based on these figures, the International Society Against Dowry and Bride-Burning in India, Inc. estimated that by the year 2,000, 25,000 brides will lose their lives in India over dowry extortions unless an effective measure is adopted to save them from this heinous crime (Thakur, "Practical Steps").

How are we to understand this violence against women over dowry demands in modern India? I disagree with one of Thakur's efforts to analyze bride-burning through a "correct" reading and interpretation of the ancient Hindu scriptures. In doing so, he repeats the colonial debate on sati in that the scriptural texts ("discourse") are invoked to explain a material practice that arose from private property and has been exploited by capitalism to expand its consumer market. Maria Mies argues that dowry, a patriarchal feudal practice, not only does not disappear with the replacement of feudal production relations with capitalist commodity production, but is exploited by the capitalist logic to create a market for commodity production. The dowry, says Mies, has become a source of wealth extracted by coercion and violence from the bride's family and a source of ready money for consumption, and it is increasingly consumed by the groom himself rather than by his family to buy expensive commodities such as a car or to start a business of his own. Mies goes on to argue that "the command over dowry gives all men the chance to get hold of money ... and to have access to modern consumer items" (162). In other words, Mies seems to suggest that it is patriarchy per se that gives all men material privileges over women in capitalist India. However, I would like to argue that it is the capitalist mode of production and its social relations of production that encourages the "residual" patriarchal practices to survive. As Mies has argued, dowry does not disappear with the advent of capitalism in India, but is exploited by capitalism to increase a market for consumption. The dowry, as she writes, "pays the way for the spread of market-values and market-commodities, even among the poor" (162). Dowry as a social practice, as Evelyn Reed argues, is enabled by the development of private property, and as such it spells out the downfall of women in history, who are now devalued as dependent housewives and have to pay for the "honor" for being made a wife whereas in the earlier practice, bride-price, which is a compensation by the groom for the loss of labor of his bride to her family after her marriage, women's labor is recognized and appreciated (Woman's Evolution 411-32).

The excessive dowry demand not only directly endangers the lives of young women in cases of failure to meet the demand, which may be renewed or increased after marriage, it also has a far-reaching impact on the life and death of the female foetuses. The excessive dowry demand, says Mies, has encouraged the rural peasants in India to abort the female foetus in order to avoid paying exorbitant dowry in the future. The father of the future bride in the "dowry infested areas" certainly not only does not benefit from such a patriarchal practice, but is oppressed and exploited by it, which is an indication that it is class and not gender that is at work here. If we follow Mies' argument that dowry is a gender issue and that therefore all men benefit from dowry demand, then it cannot explain why the father because of his class position in the capitalist social relations of production now finds it a financial burden to pay for the dowry which he was able to command when he himself was a groom. The dowry is a class issue: the extraction of surplus labor by the transnational capital. The bride's family has no "free will" not to conform to this patriarchal-capitalist practice. The "need" to pay for the bride's dowry is not the need of the bride and her family but the "need" of increased consumption by global capital to accumulate, though the practice benefits the groom who gets to consume the labor of others, which in the last instance is performed to facilitate the interests of global capitalism and its "free market." Behind the freedom to sell and to buy is the exploitation/oppression of women, wage-laborers and the poor. The sex-determination tests and abortion of female foetuses, Mies also points out, have become one more lucrative business in India, one more example of deployment of modern technology to make profits. Although India has enacted laws to prohibit dowry demand and female infanticide, these laws apparently are unable to effectively address the social practices that arose from private property and have become aggravated in capitalist India. Violence against young women and female foetuses can end only by a revolutionary solution: overthrowing the capitalist mode of production and transforming capitalist private property into social property. The socialist revolution can only be achieved when the exploited classes recognize that their common exploiter and oppressor is the regime of transnational capital and wage labor and that the oppression of women is mediated through patriarchal practices to naturalize and thus facilitate accumulation of capital.

The Family, Domestic Labor and Capitalism

In my discussion of sati and karewa as material practices, I have tried to show that Indian women's subjugation in colonial India arose from the feudal/patriarchal mode of production and property relations, which were increasingly challenged by imperialist capitalism to suit capital's own interest, and that the feudal family largely served as the institution of property inheritance. Now I want to shift my focus to the advanced capitalist societies. In capitalism, married working class women not only spend their working days as wage-laborers but have to spend their few "free hours" doing housework and/or child care, which is not paid for. In addition, capitalism with its commodity production and exchange, has rendered women's domestic labor valueless. In household production, women had contributed to producing goods for immediate consumption for their family, and the surplus was exchanged for other goods. Now in capitalism, women's labor as well as men's, if not exchanged against capital, is valueless in that it does not produce surplus value, the source of capital. I will also examine the ways in which the heterosexual monogamous family has undergone a structural change as the result of the rise of capitalism: it has ceased to be a production unit and has become a consumption unit on the one hand, it has developed as a realm of the "private sphere" seemingly (ideologically) distinct from the relations of production on the other.

The materialist concept of mode of production, as opposed to Fredric Jameson's non-productionist and non-totalizing concept, a "mode of production" which is a rewriting of Derrida's notion of *différance*[4] (*Postmodernism* 406), can demonstrate the historical emergence of the heterosexual monogamous family and account for its continual transformations as the effect of the change in the mode of production. That is, the nuclear family as we know it today is not a transhistorical nor an autonomous unit of any society, but needs to be situated in the capitalist mode of production and analyzed accordingly. According to Engels, increased productivity and wealth, brought about by the domestication of cattle, development of private property and rise of class society, gave rise to the institution of the privatized family. The existence of the single family, as Engels argues, is the victory of private property over communal property. The privatization of the household management, segregation of women in individual separate monogamous family and their exclusion from public social production is historical and material: it is the effect of the development of private property and the rise of class society. However, feminists, while recognizing Engels' contribution to challenging the myth of "universal nuclear family," have critiqued Engels for a tendency to "hypostatize" the family and thus attribute an "imaginary unity" to "the family" (Barrett 29). In response to this critique, I would argue that Engels' materialist conceptualization of the family as the effect of the change in the mode of production does not attribute a "sameness" to the privatized institution but rather provides a materialist framework through which we can historicize and explain its specific emergence and transformations. In effect, the family is not a "static," unchanging entity but has undergone transformations brought about by the change in the mode of production. "Social relations," as Marx has argued, "are closely bound up with productive forces" (*Poverty* 80). *As he goes on to explain:*

> In acquiring new productive forces men [and women] change their mode of production; and in changing their mode of production, in changing the way of earning their living, they change all their social relations. (80-1)

In contestation with the arguments made against the Marxist theory of the family for being "productionist" or "economistic," I would argue that without conceptualizing the family as part of the mode of production, that is, as an integral part of the social relations of production, we will not be able to account for the transformations of the family at a certain stage of development of production and only at such a stage and not at others. The crucial question here is not to focus on the differences between each individual family but to foreground the historical objective socio-economic structure that produces the differences between the forms of families. My discussion of the family below, however, is restricted to the family in advanced capitalism where because of the change in the mode of production the traditional family in this part of the world underwent a structural change as early as the 19th century.

The ideological understanding of the family and the economy as separate realms, as Eli Zaretsky points out in his analysis of the American family under industrial capitalism, is specific to capitalist society (*Capitalism* 23). Before the rise of industrial capitalism the farm family, because of the effect of the division of labor between town and country, was primarily a unit of production of necessary goods for immediate consumption based on private productive property, hence it was also the patriarchal institution for transmitting private property; it also reproduced its own condition of production by reproducing the next generation of the labor force. The effect of commodity production and exchange is the concentration and centralization of private property in the hands of the capitalist class, which is an ongoing process as manifested in the mergers of big corporations. Capitalist private property, which is, in effect, the congealed surplus labor of the working class, is the private ownership of the means of production, whereas "private property" for the working class is "objects of consumption" such as food, clothing, domestic articles and, for the better-paid sectors of the working class, a home (Zaretsky 62). Reification, on the other hand, requires that the society should learn to satisfy all its needs in terms of commodity exchange and that its members acquire reified consciousness (Lukács, *History* 91). It is indeed as Marx and Engels have argued in *The German Ideology*: "Life is not determined by consciousness but consciousness by life" (47).

By drawing most members of the proletarian family into the factory as wage laborers, industrial capitalism as it developed in Britain severely destablized the family. The employment of children and women in factories, made possible by the advent of machinery, the use of which is to extract surplus labor, led Engels to predict the "dissolution of the family" (*Condition* 154). Proletarianization turned the family into a "support system" for those members who could not sell their labor power because of youth, old age, disability or ill health (*German* 52). Proletarianization, as Zaretsky argues, created for the working class a new form of the family--one that is perceived as separated off from the sphere of commodity production but in reality is dominated by capitalist development. In addition, the alienation of labor--the separation of the producer from the means of production and means of subsistence, the transformation of social relations between the producers as that of between things, and the separation of the producer from the product of his/her labor--in commodity production and exchange created the need for the family as a "utopian retreat" from the social division of labor. By "dividing" society between work and life, capitalism created the material conditions for men and women to "look to themselves, outside the division of labor, for meaning and purpose" (66). Proletarianization gave rise to new forms of subjectivity; and the family in capitalism, as Zaretsky has argued, has gradually developed as a realm for the development of "personal" life in which men and women seek "love, personal happiness, domestic felicity" (61; 64).

Despite the emotional need for the family, intensified by the alienation of labor, the proletarian family in late capitalism is an integral part of the social relations of production, as it survives on wage-labor and produces the new generation of the labor force for the regime of capital. The family, as Lindsey German argues, plays a central economic role for the capitalist class: the reproduction of labor power (50) in addition to its ideological construction of gender and sexuality. The reproduction of labor power, although necessary in any form of society, is privatized and subsidized by the unpaid labor of women (and, to some extent, men as well) at home and the wage labor of men and women outside the home. The political economy of the reproduction of labor power is the reproduction of the capitalist social relations of production: capital on one side and wage labor on the other side. The privatized domestic labor shows that the working class family in capitalism functions not so much to meet the needs of its members but to meet the needs of capital at the expense of the needs of the working class. In contrast, under the cloak of love, the family for the bourgeoisie still has the function of transmitting capitalist private property within the family. Capitalism, which employs the labor of women for private accumulation, does not free women of the working class from domestic labor but requires them to continue to provide domestic service free for capital while working as exploited wage-workers because they have nothing but labor power to sell to survive.

The domestic labor debate in the West not only foregrounds one aspect of women's oppression in capitalism through unpaid labor at home but also demonstrates the fact that the gendered division of labor is profitable to capitalism. At the core of the debate, which started in the late 1960s and lasted into the 1970s, is whether or not domestic labor is productive labor[5], i.e., producing surplus value. Mariarosa Dalla Costa and Selma James in *The Power of Women and the Subversion of the Community* argued that domestic labor is productive of surplus value because it produces the commodity, labor power. Thus, women, argued Dalla Costa and James, should demand wages for housework. However, critics of Dalla Costa and James have pointed out that the wage demand for housework not only reinforces the existing gender division of labor but also legitimizes privatized domestic labor, thus undermining class struggle for international socialism as the material condition for collectivizing housework[6] (Buechler, note 3, 30). Angela Davis, for example, argues that the "wages for housework" strategy does not relieve the "housewives" from the drudgery nature of the housework[7]-- cooking, washing dishes, doing laundry, sweeping, shopping, etc. (*Women, Race, and Class* 222-44). The existing paid houseworkers, such as cleaning women and domestic workers, as she points out, are receiving a wage for their work but are subject to the same unpleasant working conditions. In the United States, a large number of black working class women, until clerical jobs become more accessible to them, have been doing housework for a paycheck, but at the expense of neglecting their own households. Davis also critiques Dalla Costa and James' call for women to refute "the myth of liberation through work" because, for them, "slavery to an assembly line is not liberation from slavery to a kitchen sink" (*Materialist Feminism* 51; 48). Instead Davis argues that it is more effective that women leave the home not to protest their housework but in search of jobs so that they can "challenge the capitalists at the point of production" with working men (241). Once on the job, women can fully participate in the struggle for equal pay for equal work. The demand for equal pay for equal jobs, as Alexandra

Kollontai has argued, should not be considered as simply a "women's issue," but rather as a class issue, that is, as part of class struggle against capital. As she explains,

> The class-conscious worker must understand that the value of male labor is dependent on the value of female labor and that, by threatening to replace male workers with cheaper female workers the capitalists can put pressure on men's wages, lowering them to the level of women's wages. (*Selected Writing* 126)

However, the struggle for equal pay for equal work should not be an end in itself, but rather a strategy to consolidate the working class as a whole to overthrow the wage-labor system and reorganize the labor of the whole society to meet the needs of the producers rather than the needs of capital. Revolutionaries, as Rosa Luxembourg has put it, are the best fighters for reforms precisely because they have the goal of revolution (German 231).

Like Dalla Costa and James, other feminists such as Maria Mies have rejected Engels' argument that "the first condition for the liberation of the wife is to bring the whole female sex back into public industry" (*Origin* 105). Mies has argued that "women's introduction into socially productive labor" has failed to liberate them from "patriarchal oppression, exploitation and violence" (160). Both Mies' and Dalla Costa and James' arguments have summed up the working conditions for the low-paid women producers and the sexism they are subject to in the workplace, but they have failed to show that it is capitalism, in its drive for profit and the accompanying divisions of labor in the factory, that has turned labor, which is "part of one's life," into "a sacrifice of one's life" (*Wage-labor and Capital* 19). Capitalism benefits from sexism to maximize the rate of profit. Dalla Costa and James' argument for "wages for housework," on the other hand, implicitly accepts the exploitation of surplus labor by capital. The wage form, as Marx has demonstrated, misleads the workers to believe their work is fully compensated, but in reality, their working day is divided into necessary labor, for which they are only compensated enough to reproduce their labor power, and surplus labor during which they work free for capital.

Paul Smith has offered one of the most rigorous critiques of domestic labor as productive labor. His critique, following Marx's theory of value, grasped the "inner, necessary connection" between value form, substance of value and magnitude of value in the capitalist mode of production (208). More importantly, Smith's critique demonstrates that it is not Marx's critique of capitalism, as some feminists have argued, but rather the capitalist mode of production and exchange that devalues and marginalizes women's domestic labor. In fact, as Engels has argued, the devaluation of domestic labor is historical. The development of commodity production created the material condition that privileges public social production over private domestic labor as the former is productive of surplus value in a commodity exchange system and the latter is not. However, domestic labor has a higher value in household production than in capitalism because it produces useful goods for immediate consumption by members of the family.

Smith argued that from the standpoint of capital not all forms of concrete labor produce value and only those "performed within the social relations of commodity production which takes the form of socially necessary, abstract and social labor" can be said to be producing surplus value (201). As he explains, domestic labor, a private, concrete, useful labor, cannot become "abstract labor" (substance of value) or "socially necessary labor" (magnitude of value) because it is "performed independently of the regulation of labor through the value of its product," that is, it does not follow the law of value (205; 207; 210). As he argues, "there is no mechanism whereby individual domestic labor can be expressed as socially necessary labor; there is no competition between 'domestic units' to minimize the labor time embodied in their products; inefficient households do not fail to sell their commodity" (208). The arguments for domestic labor as productive labor, I would add, fail to take into account the law of competition in capitalist production and wrongly presuppose an equivalence of the productiveness of labor in capitalist production and housework. As Smith points out, "the relative technological backwardness of the domestic labor process" (214) indicates that it does not constitute a branch of social production in capitalist production, which is constantly revolutionized because of competition between individual capitalists. The fact that domestic labor cannot achieve either qualitative or quantitative equivalence with other forms of concrete labor, as Smith argues, lies in the nature of capitalist commodity production and exchange. The value of labor power, according to Marx, is determined, as in the case of every other commodity, by the labor time socially necessary for the production of the means of subsistence of the laborer. In capitalist production, various concrete forms of labor are reduced to their common quality as abstract labor through exchange. As Marx writes, "by equating their different products to each other in exchange as values, they equate their different kinds of labor as human labor. They do this without being aware of it" (*Capital* I 166-67).

For Smith, domestic labor is not productive labor because it falls outside the capitalist mode of production. To argue thus, however, does not mean that domestic labor is autonomous from the capitalist mode of production. Rather, Smith argues that it is the capitalist mode of production, the production of commodities for exchange, that precludes domestic labor from becoming "socially necessary labor," thus productive. Domestic labor, which "takes place outside the capitalist mode of production" (214) and is "one of its external conditions of existence" (211), argues Smith, is one of the labors that is necessary for the reproduction of capitalism without being productive of surplus value[8]. By working on the wage-purchased goods in a useful way, domestic labor, as he argues, "transfers their value to the replenished labor power but does not add to that value" (211). In sum, to be productive in the capitalist relations of production, labor has to be sold to or exchanged against capital. As Marx has argued, "the same labor can be productive," when bought by capital to make a profit out of it, "and unproductive" when bought to consume its use value (*Theories of Surplus Value* 162). To repeat, the fact that domestic labor is not productive labor for capital is not the result of Marx's marginalization of domestic labor but the effect of the separation of the producers from the means of production. That is, individual consumption, which, as Marx writes, is at the same time the reproduction of labor power, falls outside the capitalist labor process during which by working on the means of production, the laborer not only transfers the value of the raw materials to the product but adds new value to it through his/her new labor.

Although not participating in the domestic debate, Mies critiqued Marx's formulation of productive labor as production of surplus value because she thought it contributed to making invisible women's subsistence, non-wage labor. She argued that wage labor cannot be productive without tapping, extracting or appropriating "labor which is spent in the production of life, or subsistence production" and largely done by women for the satisfaction of human needs (47). She considered Marx's concept of productive labor as limiting in understanding women's labor both under capitalism and actually existing socialism. For Mies, productive labor is expanded to include women's non-wage labor as well as other non-wage labor by slaves, contract workers and peasants in the colonies and upon which capitalist productive labor can be built, exploited and extracted (48). As she writes:

> In contrast to Marx, I consider the capitalist production process as one which comprises both: the superexploitation of non-wage laborers (women, colonies, peasants) upon which wage labor exploitation then is possible. . . This is the main reason for the growing poverty and starvation of the Third World producers. (48)

Mies defines the exploitation of non-wage laborers as "superexploitation" because it is based on the appropriation of the time and labor necessary for people's own survival, not just wage-labor exploitation. Mies' expansion of productive labor allows for the theorization of "primitive" accumulation of capital to include colonization and women's forgotten labor. However, in expanding the concept, Mies not only renders it a-historical but dissolves Marx's concept of mode of production (Omvedt 41). "The concept of a productive worker," as Marx explains, "implies not merely a relation between the activity of work and its useful effect, between the worker and the product of his [her] work, but also a specifically social relation of production, a relation with a historical origin which stamps the worker as capital's direct means of valorization" (*Capital* I 644). By rejecting the concept of mode of production and replacing it with "a world systems approach," as Omvedt points out, the feminists of the German School to which Mies belongs had difficulty theorizing pre-capitalist history (41).

While Mies critiques Marx for helping render women's non-wage labor invisible, when it is the capitalist mode of production and exchange that has done so as I have argued, Donna Haraway finds the Marxist category labor both an "ontological" and "pre-eminently privileged one" (*Simians* 158). Haraway critiques other socialist feminists' efforts to accommodate the Marxian category of labor to include all women's activity for attributing a "unity" among women relying on an epistemology based on the "ontological structure of 'labor'" (158). Such an essentializing move, in her view, not only demonstrates Marxism's humanism but also "erase[s] or police[s] difference" (158). However, Haraway's rejection of classical Marxism because of what she regards to be "essentialism" and "humanism" is based on a misreading of Marx. As Marx notes,

> Labor is, first of all, a process between man and nature, a process by which man, through his own actions, mediates, regulates and controls the metabolism between himself and nature .... he acts upon external nature and changes it, and in this way he simultaneously changes his own nature. (*Capital* I 283)

In other words, labor is not ontological but rather historical.

Haraway's charge that Marxism is both a "humanism" and an "essentialism" is misleading. Her understanding of Marxism as "rationalism" is also incorrect. In critiqing Feuerbach who "resolves the religious essence into the human essence," Marx has argued that what was understood as "the human essence" in Feuerbach is, in effect, "the ensemble of the social relations" (T*he German Ideology* 122). This "ensemble of the social relations" is not merely "the [logical] movement of pure reason," says Marx, but rather is the effect of the "historical movement of production relations." As he writes: "Economists explain how production takes place in [bourgeois] relations, but what they do not explain is how theses relations themselves are produced..." (*Poverty* 77; emphasis added). Haraway's story of the cyborg, which is post-labor, post-humanism/essentialism, post-hunger, post-communication, etc, becomes fallacious each time one conducts one's daily material practice in eating, drinking, speaking, etc. In short, for her as well as for most of post-al theorists, theory and praxis are two different matters, whereas knowledges are in actuality derived from labor praxis and theory is the guide for action. Haraway's dismissal of labor, and thereby the exploitation of surplus labor in capitalism, in the name of epistemology helps serve the interests of capital.

The domestic labor debate also posed the fundamental question: "who benefits" from women's domestic labor? For some feminists the answer is that men/husbands benefit. Heidi Hartmann, for example, argues that men, regardless of their class position, have vested interests in relegating domestic labor to women. Underlying her argument is that patriarchy and capitalism are two distinct and autonomous systems and that patriarchy is the cause of women's oppression in capitalism. I have argued that it is capital that benefits from women's unpaid domestic labor. Capitalism benefits most when women undertake both a wage-labor job and housework. Hartmann's critique of Dalla Costa's argument for "Wages for Housework" is that by focusing on the relation of the housework to capital Dalla Costa fails to pay attention to the relation between men and women as exemplified in housework (7-9). In Hartmann's view, by doing so Dalla Costa subsumes the feminist struggle, i.e., the struggle between men and women, under the struggle against capital. For Hartmann, the "earlier Marxists" have failed to recognize "the vested interests men had in women's continued subordination" (5). Thus, she concludes that "since capital and private property do not cause the oppression of women as women, their end alone will not result in the end of women's oppression" (5). Hartmann's unwillingness and inability to acknowledge that women's oppression and other forms of oppression around race and sexuality are rooted in class society only indicates her version of socialist feminism is actually bourgeois which, as Kollontai points out in her critique of bourgeois feminism in general, "unconsciously takes its starting point from the interests of its own class, which gives a specific class coloring to the targets and tasks it sets for itself . . ." (59). As Kollontai explains:

> The feminists seek equality in the framework of the existing class society; in no way do they attack the basis of this society . . . The feminists see men as the main enemy, for men have unjustly seized all rights and privileges for themselves, . . . For them a victory is won when a prerogative previously enjoyed exclusively by the male sex is conceded to the 'fair sex.' (59-60)

Hartmann's theory of patriarchy, though conceptualized from a quasi-materialist approach, is what Lindsey German calls a "male conspiracy" theory against women. Patriarchy, as defined by Hartmann, is "a set of social relations between men, which have a material basis [men's control over women's labor power], and which, though hierarchical, establish or create interdependence and solidarity among men that enable them to dominate women" (14). In other words, by exercising control over women's access to socially productive labor/resources and by restricting women's sexuality, men, according to Hartmann, are rewarded with personal services from women, and thus with "feeling powerful and being powerful" despite their hierarchal rank in patriarchy (18). However, German has contested the ideology that men benefit from women's subordination. "The working class as a whole," as she argues, is "characterized not by its power, but its powerlessness (*Sex* 76; emphasis original). It is denied the means of production and has only the labor power as a commodity to sell for survival. Once workers are too old to sell their labor power, they are worthless to the capitalist class and dependent on their family for survival. Hartmann's dual-system theory, which sees patriarchy and capitalism as two distinct and separate systems each with its own "laws of motion," is a theory aimed at analyzing women's oppression from the view point of gender, and thus a theory advocating the struggle between men and women. But her theory, which sees patriarchy not as "a universal, unchanging phenomenon" as Juliet Mitchell does in her psychological articulation of patriarchy, has difficulty, as she herself acknowledges, identifying the mechanism of patriarchy. As Iris Young argues in her critique of the dual-system theory, it is more effective to theorize patriarchy and capitalism as one unified system and pay attention to the gender division of labor as the core of the socio-economic structure.

From feudal sati, to modern dowry-related bride-burning, neglected and impoverished widows, female infanticides and the abortion of female fetuses, to colonialism/neo-colonialism, to the emergence and transformations of the family, to women's oppression/exploitation in capitalism via wage-labor and unpaid domestic labor, to oppression of people of color and gays and lesbians, to commodification of racial/ethnic/sexual identities to make profits,..etc, these diverse practices, institutions and events across time and nations arise not from the ideas of the mind but from the material conditions of production and the property relations determined by it. As Marx and Engels note:

> people won freedom for themselves each time to the extent
> that was dictated and permitted not by their ideal of man, but
> by the existing productive forces. All emancipation carried

through hitherto has been based, however, on restricted productive forces. (*Collected Works* V 431)

Late capitalism, however, has developed sufficient forces of production to meet the needs of all people, laying the material foundation for international socialism. But because of the private ownership of the means of production, human needs are denied and exploitation/ oppression is reinforced to stave off the falling rate of profit. On the one hand, the overproduced food stuff is locked away in warehousez or destroyed for the sake of profits; on the other, millions of people, especially, children, go hungry without food. This fundamental class contradiction explains the "inhuman" ways in which the working class and the poor around the globe satisfy their needs. The interests of capital and wage-labor are diametrically opposed to each other (*Wage-Labor* 39). Class struggle is the only way out of the barbarism of capitalism. It is the only revolutionary weapon to emancipate the workers and their families the world over and to build a new society in which production is to meet people's needs and from which to combat all the exploitations and oppressions arising from class and capitalist society.

Notes

[1] Mas'ud Zavarzadeh has theorized "post-ality" as "the ensemble of all practices that, as a totality, obscure the production practices of capitalism--which is based on the extraction of surplus labor," as "a regime of class struggle against the and material contradictions of capitalism caused by the social division of labor" ("Post-ality" 1).

[2] For a dialectic materialist explanation of Stalinism as counter-revolution and workers that posits a structural change, a rupture, in capitalism," and as "attempts to solve--in the theoretical imaginary--the historical betrayal of the workers' state," see Leon Trotsky's writings. Trotsky also demystified the bourgeois ideology which equates Stalinism with socialism and thus mystifies them as "twins" of evils while there exists a fundamental difference between the two: the former serves the interests of the Stalinist bureaucracy whereas the latter strives to emancipate the working class from the exploitation of surplus labor.

[3] Butler wrote in the following words, "the dissolution of Marxist states" (3; emphasis added), apparently equating Stalinism with Marxism, which is the very opposite of it.

⁴ Jameson describes it as follows: "it includes a variety of counterforces and new tendencies within itself, of 'residual' as well as 'emergent' forces, which it must attempt to manage or control (Gramsci's conception of hegemony) . . . . Thus, differences are presupposed by the model" (406). Jameson's "mode of production" turns out to be a hybrid of ideas: composed of the Nietzschean notion of multiple forces that destroy and re-generate themselves and the post-al understanding of the social as the articulation of differences and pluralism, i.e., Gramsci's class hegemony reunderstood as signification. In so doing, Jameson erases labor and production from the Marxist concept of the mode of production, which is historically determined by the forces of production and the level of class struggle.

⁵ In a footnote in *Grundrisse*, Marx defines a productive laborer in capitalism as the one that "directly augments capital" (305-6; emphasis added). Marx argues that a piano maker is a productive worker but a piano player is not. The difference lies in the fact that the piano maker reproduces capital whereas the pianist only exchanges his/her labor for revenue. The pianist, as Marx goes on to explain, may indeed stimulate production via his/her performance but such a labor that is not spent on material production, no matter how useful it may be, is not productive labor. Marx also points out that some economists have allowed "the so-called unproductive worker to be productive indirectly" (305). Despite Marx's emphasis that labor is productive only when directly exchanged against capital, this emphasis on the historical, objective conditions of labor has been largely ignored by some of the domestic labor theorists who argue domestic labor is productive labor as it indirectly reproduces labor-power as a commodity.

⁶ The collective organization of domestic work and child care, as Alexandra Kollontai argues in "Communism and the Family," liberates the working woman from "domestic slavery" and allows her to devote her evenings to readings, attending meetings and participating in other social activities (255-6). International socialism is the only solution to women's exploitation/oppression (Lenin, *Collected Works* 23: 301). In fact, in capitalism, the basic housework, such as cleaning, cooking, doing the laundry, has been socialized only to make profits and not to meet people's needs. Only those who have money, behind which stands class/labor relation, can afford to eat at restaurants, to dry-clean their clothing, to hire the cleaning company to do the cleaning..., and so on. The passing of the education of the young from the parents to the communist collective does not mean to take the child away from the parents as bourgeois propaganda would have it but rather mean to have better trained educators to supervise the young so that all children, born within or out of marriage, can get equal and quality education. In

bourgeois society, only the bourgeois children get sufficient attention, not necessarily from their parents, but from their paid nannies and tutors. Class, as Lindsey German argues, to a large extent, plays an important role in what kind of life a child might have even before his/her entry to the world and his/her chance of "success" in the future (*A Question of Class* 7-20).

   [7] Some materialist feminists, however, have pointed out that many women work at home, not to tend their household, but as piece workers and domestic workers to make both ends meet.

   [8] In *Grundrisse*, Marx notes that "There are works and investments which may be necessary without being productive in the capitalist sense, i.e. without the realization of the surplus labor contained in them through circulation, through exchange, as surplus value" (531). Like domestic labor, public school education and public hospitals are one of the "external conditions" of reproduction of capitalism. They are unproductive but necessary for the education and health of the future wage-workers from the standpoint of capital. Moreover, they are paid out of the collective surplus value produced by the working class. In other words, in capitalism there are wage-workers, such as public school teachers, nurses, the police and the army, without being productive of surplus value, because of capitalism as a system of production for commodity exchange that measures things as productive in terms of surplus labor and frequently marginalizes socially useful labor because while it may meet Needs but does not produce Capital. The increasing privatization of education and health care in advanced capitalism indicates, as Marx notes, "the degree to which the real community has constituted itself in the form of capital" (531).

Works Cited

Barrett, Michele. *Women's Oppression Today: The Marxist/Feminist Encounter.* Rev. ed. London: Verso, 1988.

Borah, Santanu. "State of Windows in India."   http://csf.colorado. edu/mail/ecofem/aug96/0010.html.

Buechler, Steve. "Sex and Class: A Critical Overview of Some Recent Theoretical Work and Some Modest Proposals." *Insurgent Sociologist* 12, no.3 (1984): 19-32.

Burns, John F. "Once Windowed in India, Twice Scorned." *New York Times* March 29, 1998.

Butler, Judith.   "Pos-structuralism and Postmarxism." *diacritics* 23.4 (Winter 1993): 3-11.

——. "Merely Culture." Social Text 52/53 (Fall/Winter 1997): 265-77.

Cabral, Amilcar. "Class and Revolution in Africa." In *Marxism: Essential Writings.* Ed. David McLellan. New York: Oxford UP, 1988. 392-409.

Chakravarti, Uma. "What Happened to the Vedic Dasi? Orientalism, Nationalism and a Script for the Past." In *Recasting Women.* Ed. Kumkum Sangari and Sudesh Vaid, 27-87.

Chomsky, Noam. *World Orders: Old and New.* New York: Colombia UP, 1994.

Chowdhry, Prem. "Customs in a Peasant Economy: Women in Colonial Haryana." In *Recasting Women,* eds. Kumkum Sangari and Sudesh Vaid, 302-336.

Dalla Costa, Mariarosa, and Selma James. "Women and the Subversion of the Community." In *Materialist Feminism.* Ed. Rosemary Hennessy and Chrys Ingraham, 40-53.

Davis, Angela. *Women, Race, and Class.* New York: Random House, 1981.

Derriida, Jacques. *Of Grammatology.* Trans. Gayari Spivak. Baltimore, Maryland: The Johns Hopkins UP, 1976.

——. *Specters of Marx: The State of the Debt, the Work of Mourning and the New International.* Trans. Peggy Kamuf. New York: Routledge, 1994.

Engels, Friedrich. *The Origin of the Family, Private Property and the State.* Introd. Michele Barrett. New York: Penguin, 1986.

——. *The Condition of the Working Class in England.* Ed. David McLellan. New York: Oxford UP, 1993.

Foucault, Michel. *The Order of Things: An Archaeology of the Human Sciences.* New York: Vintage, 1970.

——. "Intellectuals and Power" *in Language, Counter-memory, Practice.* Ed. Donald Bouchard. Ithaca, New York: Cornell UP, 1977.

——. "Truth and Power" in *Power/Knowledge: Selected Interviews and Other Writings 1972-1977.* Ed. Colin Gordon. New York: Pantheon Books, 1980.

German, Lindsey. *Sex, Class,and Socialism.* London: Bookmarks, 1989.

——. A Question of Class. London: Bookmarks, 1996.

Haraway, Donna. *Simians, Cyborg, and Women: The Reinvention of Nature.* New York: Routledge, 1991.

Hartmann, Heidi. "The Unhappy Marriage of Marxism and Feminism: Towards a More Progressive Union." In *Women and Revolution,* ed. Lydia Sargent, 1-42.

Jameson, Fredric. *Postmodernism; or, The Cultural Logic of Late Capitalism.* Durham, N.C.: Duke UP, 1991.

Kollontai, Alexandra. *Selected Writing.* Trans. Alix. Holt. New York: Norton, 1980.

Kumar, Kapil. "Rural Women in Oudh 1917-1949: Baba Ram Chandra and the Women's Question" in *Reacting Women*. Ed. Kumkum Sangari and Sudesh Vaid, 337-69.

Lenin, V.I. *Collected Works*, Vol. XXIII. New York: International P, 1945.

Lukács, Georg. *History and Class Consciousness: Studies in Marxist Dialectics*. Cambridge, Massachusetts: The MIT P, 1994.

Mani, Lata. "Contentious Traditions: The Debate on Sati in Colonial India." In *Recasting Women: Essays in Indian Colonial History*, eds Kumkum Sangari and Sudesh Vaid, 88-126.

Marx, Karl. Capital: *A Critique of Political Economy*, Volume One. Trans. Ben Fowkes. New York: Vintage, 1977.

———. *A Contribution to the Critique of Political Economy*. Ed. Maurice Dobb. New York: International P, 1970.

———. *The Communist Manifesto*. Ed. Frederic Bender. New York: Norton, 1988.

———. *The Poverty of Philosophy*. New York: Internaitonal P, 1992.

———. *Wage-labor and Capital and Value, Price, and Profit*. New York: Internaitonal P, 1976.

———. *Theories of Surplus Value*. New York: International P, 1976.

———. *Grundrisse*. Trans. Martin Nicolaus. New York: Penguin Books, 1973.

Marx, Karl and Friedrich Engels. *Collected Works* Vol.5. New York: International P, 1976.

———. *The German Ideology*. Ed. C.J. Arthur. New York: International P, 1970.

Mies, Maria. *Patriarchy and Accumulation on a World Scale: Women in the International Division of Labor*. London: Zed Books, 1986.

Omvedt, Gail. "'Patriarchy': The Analysis of Women's Oppression." *Insurgent Sociologist* 13, no.3, (Spring 1986): 30-50.

Reed, Evelyn. Problems of Women's Liberation. New York: Pathfinder P, 1969.

———. *Women's Evolution: From Matriarchal Clan to Patriarchal Family*. New York: Pathfinder P, 1975.

Sangari, Kumkum and Sudesh Vaid, eds. *Recasting Women: Essays in India Colonial History*. New Jersey: Rutgers UP, 1990.

Smith, Paul. "Domestic Labor and Marx's Theory of Value." In *Feminism and Materialism*, eds. Annette Kuhn and AnnMarie Wolpe, 198-219.

Thakur, Himendra B. "Practical Steps Toward Saving the Lives of 25,000 Potential Victims of Dowry and Bride-Burning in India in the Next Four Years." *Journal of South Asia Women Studies*. No.2, Vol. 2 (May 1996).

Zaretsky, Eli. *Capitalism, the Family, and Personal Life*. New York: Harper and Row, 1976.

Zavarzadeh, Mas'ud. "Post-ality: The (Dis)Simulations of Cyber-capitalism" in *Transformation I: Post-ality: Marxism and Post-modernism.* Washington, D.C.: Maisonneuve P, 1995.

——. "'The Stupidity That Consumption is Just as Productive as Production": In the Shopping Mall of the Post-al Left." *College Literature* 21.3 (Oct. 1994): 92-118.

Rob Wilkie

CYBERPEDAGOGY AND CLASS-AS-LIFESTYLE

WITH AN EPILOGUE ON

THE CLASS POLITICS OF EDITING

IN (CORPORATE) LEFT JOURNALS

"For us and especially for our successors…it is just as important to arm ourselves with knowledge as to arm ourselves with steel in order to beat off our enemies."
                          –Maxim Gorky, "We Must Know The Past"

The Return of Class (To Pedagogy) as "Lifestyle"

From those on the "right," who deploy the rhetoric of "political correctness," to the "liberal left" clerks who are now rallying behind the new class slogan of "Left Conservatism," the aim of the petty-bourgeois intelligentsia is to substitute for a pedagogy of critique based on conceptual explanation of the social aimed at educating the critique-al citizen, a post-al[1] "rhizomatic" education in which the social relations of production are studied not conceptually, but analogously and topologically. Critique and critique-al citizenship are thus rejected as "molar" knowing while the sensual, the pleasureful and the performative are canonized as "molecular".

Such is the work of the pedagogue Henry Giroux who argues that the "failure" of radical education has been the abandonment of "the language of possibility for the language of critique" (120). Like their friends on the right, the "progressive" pedagogues such as Giroux now tailor their educational "strategies" – the "progressive" pedagogue has nothing but "strategies" since they have jettisoned theory for pragmatics –to blur the historical (*class*) relations of production through performance of the analogical. Giroux is not alone in his rejection of critique-al pedagogy. In the introduction of *Between Borders: Pedagogy and The Politics of Cultural Studies*, "Bringin' It All Back Home – Pedagogy and Cultural Studies," Lawrence Grossberg argues that this "new" kind of pedagogy, one of "articulation and risk," which refuses "the traditional forms of intellectual authority" and the ability to "assume that either theory or politics, theoretical or political correctness, can be known in advance" (18) is now necessary in this, the post-al "aporia" of history. Of course, this is not a "new" pedagogy but is symptomatic of the continued efforts of the petty-bourgeois clerks to render illegible the "contradictions of material life, from the conflict existing between the social forces of production and the relations of production" (Marx *Contribution* 21) while simultaneously representing, as for example in the work of Judith Butler, the "traditional grounds" of "solidarity," in other words the solidarity of labor, as in "crisis" (Butler 59).   The representation, in the petty-bourgeois political imaginary, of a social "crisis" resulting not from the social division of labor but from divisive ideas is a dissimulation that, in actuality, by providing the "answer" to the "crisis" in a rhetorical "unification" of political ideologies, legitimates the rising tide of fascist practices.

   As Marx and Engels explained in the *Manifesto of the Communist Party*, the bourgeoisie can not exist without "constantly revolutionizing the instruments of production" (487).   It is within this "revolutionizing" that the historical contradiction of class society between the forces of production (those of technology and labor) and the relations of production (the relations between those who own the means of production and those who only own their labor power) arises. In so far as the role of education under capitalism has been the production of an ideological "suturing" over this contradiction – rendering as "natural" that which is historical and transformable – it is therefore no surprise that at this historical moment when the international bourgeoisie are coming face-to-face with "the biggest financial challenge facing the world in a half century" (Sanger, online), when it has become nearly impossible to ignore the increasing level of class contradiction surrounding the system of private property and exploitation without being seen as a "henchman" of capitalism, that a formerly "post-foundationalist" petty-bourgeois intelligentsia suddenly is converted to a class-foundationalism and returns to a "class" analysis . Appropriating the concept of "class" as a way of ideologically containing the "crisis," the pedagogues of the ruling class have tried to normalize it by turning it into sociological jargon rather than a concept in social struggle. It is a mark of this rush to recuperate "class" by sociologicalizing it that, for example, *PMLA* (the organ of the humanities establishment) has published a special issue on class and books with titles like *Rethinking Class* are suddenly everywhere. The *PMLA*, the editors of *Rethinking Class*, and their allies are normalizing "class" by turning it, following the recent trends in bourgeois sociology, into a "lifestyle" which is supported by "income" regardless of whether the income is for "wages" or "profit."   It is a "class" that, thus, blurs the concept of class, a "class" that has nothing to do with the place of the subject of labor in production but is a function of consumption. Within this frame of the recuperation of "class" as a "naturalized" category the petty-bourgeois intelligentsia draw upon the emptiest understandings of materiality, mere "matterist" discourses, in an attempt to produce solutions to the crisis that cover up social contradictions and leave present structures intact. That is, the very concept of social contradiction itself, in the last instance the historical contradiction between the forces and relations of production, is displaced with rhetorical notions of play and simultaneity in regards to the "fluidity" of the post-al society.

The "Cyber," Class, and the Pedagogy of the "Post"

"Cyber-theory," one of the "thousand and first" shades of idealism, has become the latest pseudo-materialism to mystify the (immediate) "sensation" of "experience" as the "Real" of social relations. The political imaginary of a millennial utopia pervading the discourses of such "disparate" theorists as politicians Newt Gingrich and Al Gore and "high theorists" George Landow and Donna Haraway marks not the "reality" of a "cyber-utopian" future, but the attempts to ideologically legitimate as "natural" the class struggle in communication technology. Presenting an image of the future devoid of "spatial" and "temporal" distances, this bourgeois hallucination of the new millennium, in which telephone lines and fiber optic cable reify class struggle as the result of "outdated technology," has become the new social logic for petty-bourgeois intellectuals who cannot quickly enough gorge themselves on the latest technological advancement.

In what has become in a short time a canonic text in bourgeois "cyber"-pedagogy, *imagologies: Media Philosophy* by Mark C. Taylor and Esa Saarinen combines the rhetoric of the capitalist financial czars – such as Alan Greenspan, who in a speech before the joint economic committee on 10 June 1998 reiterated the belated bourgeois hope that capitalism has put crisis cycles (of boom and bust) behind itself and thus finally moved "beyond history" and, in turn, "beyond" class struggle – with the post-al renewal of Hegelian idealism. The theory of imagologies, marked by Taylor and Saarinen's claim that Marx's analysis of capital is "not directly applicable to post-industrial society" and that it is necessary to revert to Hegel's "speculative philosophy" (which they read via Baudrillard) in order to be able to effectively anticipate what DeBord termed the "society of the spectacle" of the Twenty-first Century in which the "the real is the idea" ("Simcult" 3), posits dialogue as freed from author(itarian) constraints and as "free-flowing" as the electronic data that pulsates throughout the internet. Here dialogue, marked by the "wiring" of transnational classrooms, becomes the ideological panacea to the educational "crisis" – the introduction of cable wire as a substitute for the production of critique-al knowledge. In other words, the logic of the argument that the inability of contemporary educational strategies to mask the contradictions of material life is the direct result of "techno-lack"

– positing the equation that "more computers" equals "better learning" – is "founded" upon an attempt to legitimate the use of technological advancement for the exploitation of the working class: "class struggle ends with an Apple in every classroom!" Of course, for bourgeois theoreticians such as Taylor and Saarinen, the "overcoming" of class struggle is not even a question for the coming cyber-utopia. Privileging a performative understanding of social relations based upon the possibility of access to the images of a ludic consumer society, *imagologies* represents contradiction as "gap" and, in turn, "celebrating" the social "gaps" as the "natural" outcome of an excess of social codes.

      The rise of the rhetoric of "techno-scientific" development within capitalist production, evident for bourgeois economists in the almost instantaneous manner in which "currency" travels at the speed of "current," has for post-al theorists necessitated a "re-theorization" of capitalism in order to understand what, for those in the North, has signaled the "end" of production (history), namely reproduction. This is evident in a recent essay by Fredric Jameson, "Culture and Finance Capital," in which he rewrites Deleuze and Guattari's rewriting of capitalist relations of production from twenty-five years prior–"production is immediately consumption" (4)–arguing that "finance capital brings into being: a play of monetary entities that need neither production (as Capital does) nor consumption (as money does)" ("Finance" 256). Jameson's capitalism, which now has as its inspiration the "spirit"-uality of the Heideggerian "Being" – finance capital is the "dwelling" from which arise "monetary entities," without origin, that simply "exist" – "collapses" the social levels between production and consumption ("Finance" 265) and, in doing so, erases the fundamental concepts of Marxism. For Jameson, the collapse of social levels, such that there is an "instant reflex" from consumption to production ("Finance" 264) goes hand in hand with what he previously termed "a kind of flatness or depthlessness" (*Postmodernism* 10) that, he now argues, "supersedes" alienation. ("Finance" 264). In other words, the necessity of knowledge of the object is subsumed into the object itself, rendering the object a (neo-Kantian) "thing-in-itself" and, in turn, eliminating the possibility of an objective knowledge of the object, from the outside and beyond the immediacy of the "experience" this bourgeois positivism with a vengeance represents as some kind of neo-materialism. Jameson's dissimulative rewriting of the capitalist mode of production as a "spirit"-ed realization of being (of "things-in-themselves"), beyond tailing the actual events of the recent global "finance" crisis – which have proven that "financial" capital is not "immaterial" but, in fact, marks an attempt to "artificially" regulate the cycles of production and thus, as with all aspects of the capitalist mode of production, at its core, an issue of labor – is symptomatic of the attempts by the pundits of "techno-science" to "normalize" crisis through the celebration of "contradiction." Jameson can do nothing at the end of his essay except proclaim, full of rearguard bravado, that financial capital "steers unwittingly towards a crash" ("Finance" 265).

The post-al re-theorization of capitalism, in which the relations of production are blurred through the ludic play of the analogy, is at the core of Taylor and Saarinen's project. The philosophy of *imagologies* is that "the word is never simply a word but is always also an image" ("Styles" 3). This argument has as its matrix the post-structuralist idealism of the "absolute relativism" of "knowledge"/"concepts" (Deleuze et. al, *What is Philosophy?* 21) that is a staple of the discursive sociology of the post-al. Troping on the deconstruction trope of the "transcendental signifier," Taylor and Saarinen argue that "The return of figure disfigures the disfiguration of concepts by reinscribing the imago in the midst of the logos" ("Communicative Practices" 13). Their "negation" of the logos, however, does not amount to a theoretical "return" to a "originary" logocentrism. With the "reinscription" of the imago into logos (the "folding" of image into language) comes a renewed importance upon "superficiality" since the "foundation" – the point of "origin" – is "writing". The "figure" which has come to "disfigure" the "disfiguration" – to return "meaning" to "logos" – is itself the product of "writing" (reinscription) and, as such, bound by the relativism of (post-al) language theory. In their words, "It is time to move beyond the institutional practices of triviledge [sic], toward networks and surfaces, toward the play of superficiality, toward interstanding [sic]" ("Communicative Practices" 8). Reducing conceptual knowledge (the "institutional") to that of "triviledge" and setting it up in opposition to the notion of a "superficial" "interstanding" the core of this move to the superficial is what forms the basis of their argument about the potentially "liberatory" aspect of imagology, namely the rejection of an outside in favor of an ever regressive "inter" knowledge of negation. Like other post-al theorists—such as Deleuze and Guattari—who substitute the "scientific concept" with the "relative concept" produced from an ever expanding rhizome, Taylor's and Saarinen's understanding of "access," a term to which they continually return, is one in which the systemic relations between objects that determines their meaning—in other words, the social relations of production—are rendered opaque through a focus on immanence and locality. Of course, what is at the core in the rejection of the scientific concept is not the "liberatory" – since relativism can "liberate" only in so far as it reduces the line of vision from the historical to the immediate, rendering the subject "ideologically blind" – but precisely its opposite: the suppression of systemic knowledge.

Marking the intellectual depravity of the theory of imagology is the design of the text itself. The type-face, which is as far as the theoretical program of *imagologies* can reach, is "dismantled" in diagonals, shapes, font changes, and fragments. The jettisoning of the material in favor of (ludic) matterism, "With the inexorable expansion of the mediascape, all reality is mediaized and thus becomes virtual" ("Virtuality" 6), leaves the "superficiality" of typeset as the most "material" for Taylor and Saarinen (and their bourgeois editors). The text, with its motto/slogan of "If you read books, justify it", is the another in a series of attempts to remove critique from the realm of "cyberspace". Taylor and Saarinen turn science and theory, through their troping of all "modernist" knowledges as the "book," into a criminal act which, like the "terroristic narratives" within Lyotardian language games, must be "justified". It is precisely a mark of the importance of post-al theory to the bourgeois publishing industry that a text as conceptually and intellectually empty as Taylor and Saarinen's not only is published, and is obviously given a significant design budget, but in so far as they are willing to take on the policing role of keeping the "simcult" cosmopolitan free from critique that it has taken on such significance in the burgeoning field of "cyber-pedagogy". I leave aside here the fact that in spite of its claims of "connectedness" (of individuals in a "knowledge network") that "cyber-pedagogy" is ultimately a mode of legitimating cost-cutting and downsizing in adult education – "distance learning". It is, in other words, an economic strategy to increase the rate of profit for the corporate university and a political device to give the "adult" (mostly working) people who can not attend a regular classroom a "cheap" (intellectually as well as financially) education.

What the "theory" of *imagologies* amounts to is an anti-theory theory that reproduces the "necessity" of "creativity" over "critique" argument that has become a crucial site of restructuring in the humanities. By substituting "participation" and "performance" – code words deployed by so-called "progressive pedagogues" such as Henry Giroux or Jane Tompkins and avant-garde teachers such as Judith Butler and Gregory Ulmer for the exchange of "sensations" – for the practice of critique, Taylor and Saarinen signal "interaction" – the guiding "principle" of cyber-pedagogy – on specific terms, ones that do not call into question the framework from which imagologies itself was constructed. It is on these grounds that it becomes clear that what constitutes "interaction" here is the bourgeois myth of the "free market" and the "free individual". In other words, the knowledges now being privileged in the U.S. academy and the rest of the advanced capitalist economies are those which displace a systemic theorization of capitalism by replacing "globality" with "locality," scientific/objective knowledge with experiential knowledge, and collective praxis with coalitional pragmatism. These "new" categories, while not "new," appear as such precisely because of their ability to replicate the notion of the "freely" producing individual who "freely" reproduces these transcendental ideas of "knowledge" and the "individual". It is because these post-al knowledges are in contradiction with even their limited stated objectives, those of increased democratization through mere "vocal" participation, that they have become so attractive to the corporate world of late capitalism. Those students/workers whom post-al theory supposedly "liberates," those who have been rendered "voice-less" by the "grand narratives" of the modernist epoch, are denied access to those knowledges which would enable them to push beyond the experiential politics of the "local" into theorizations of a historical materialist frame, and thus into truly effective social action, that of a socialist revolution. Of course, this is what makes post-al theory so desirable to the transnational ruling class. It is with this understanding of "interaction" as "performativity" that Taylor and Saarinen make the claim, "America is at its most exciting when it does not theorize, articulate, or conceptualize, but when it acts" ("Philosophy" 17). But for whom is America's "unthinking action" exciting? Was America at its "inarticulate" best during the recent bombings of Afghanistan, Sudan, and Yugoslavia or during the "Third Way" liberals' retrenchment of welfare programs and educational privatization?[2]

Science and the Politics of Relativism

It is the contradictory fetishization of techno-scientific develop-ment and, in the same moment, the vilification of scientific knowledge (objective truth) that marks the theoretical bankruptcy of "cyber-theory". One finds this tension between the development of the means of production and the attempt to understand that development from within the immanent logic of a "performative" materialist analysis in the work of "cyborg" theorist Donna Haraway. Like other representatives of the post-al left, Haraway collapses history into individuatized interpretations of events in relation to what is perceived as a "shift" or "break" in the historical relations of capitalism. She argues in her latest text, *Modest Witness*, that "for the oppositional critical theorists, both the facts and the witnesses are constituted in the encounters that are technoscientific practice" (35). Positing no outside to discourse, Haraway claims that she is "invested in continuing the need for stabilizing contingent matters of fact to ground serious claims on each other" (33) and, on the basis of this "investment" – a level of "participation" based upon her "personal" interest in performing radical politics – argues that the Scientific Revolution does have "practical inheritances" but, at the same time, has "set up a narrative about 'objectivity' that continues to get away of a more adequate, self-critical technoscience committed to situated knowledges" (33). Haraway advances here a relativized "materialism" that, like the trace of Derridian différance, only ever refers back to itself in a perpetual re-narrativization. This is clearly articulated in her argument of the material, rearticulated as "materialized figuration" (23) or the linking of "stories, desires, reasons, and material worlds" (64). "History" and "identity" and "language" here, like the imago/logos of Taylor and Saarinen, are re-written as the "implosion" (the continual "negation" of "presence" by "absence" and "lack") of all into "language". Any "object," she continues, must be "teased open" to show the "threads that make up its tissues" (68). The articulation of history as the "linking," displacing contradiction for continuance, of "tissues" is then used to displace class conflict as a "permanently contingent" "promiscuous commingling" between "the fantastic and the ordinary" (68-69). Class division is rewritten here as a desiring relationship between two incompletes of an impossible whole.

Drawing upon the logic of a "performative" materialism, while Haraway can recognize the development of "new" forces of production, she can articulate no way of theorizing the historical necessity of social transformation, only mark its inevitability[3]. She argues that "the conclusion that the technoscientific agenda for everybody is set by the economically dominant powers, especially the United States, is inescapable" (57) and yet can only state, before descending into the appreciation of bourgeois reforms that is symptomatic of her historical class position (as petty-bourgeois intellectual) that "the end of the Second Millennium threatens to be much more than a narrative device" (55). This is an empty "prediction" masquerading as the truth of historical progression that not only says absolutely nothing, but undermines her entire project of "continual construction through historically located practice" (68). This is an opportunistic "reversal" to an vacuous "matterism" that marks a desperate attempt to re-write that which her "relativism" can not account for: the "outside" existence of class struggle. Haraway, instead, looks superficially at the relations of transnational capital and states that the "work processes" of technoscience are heterogeneously distributed between humans and non-humans (machines) such that production can occur "independently of human manufacture" (142). In attempting to calm bourgeois anxiety, Haraway (like all post-al theorists) here removes labor, which is fundamental to any production process within capital (even the automated machine is a condensation of dead labor), from her narrative as if that alone will forestall the aging of the bourgeoisie.

It is within this rejection of materiality and science that the "play" of the "performative" materialists becomes the foundation of "interstanding" [sic]. The contradictory logic of the love/hate relationship between the petty-bourgeoisie and the machinery that hurls them into the proletariat[4] informs Taylor and Saarinen who, having displaced the material relations of production in favor of the "matterism" of the "linked" network, argue that "In simcult, we have no intellectually secure foundation for anything" ("Superficiality" 10). In order to maintain their worth to the ruling class, they pronounce that "imagination" is the only way to measure value. "The register of the imaginary is anarchic. Images proliferate, the net spreads, the volume rises, no one is in control" ("Simcult" 9). The idea that "no one is in control" and that there is no "intellectually secure foundation for anything" marks an attempt to "paradoxically" isolate the individual while, in the same moment, arguing that the individual is constantly "networking". This, however, is not "new" but is symptomatic of a move to maintain/update the bourgeois "individual" and the myth of the "free market". The subject here, who has "lost" all foundation, is thus "free" to "produce" ("proliferate images") divorced from the question of the relations of that production.

The project of *imagologies*, like all ideological attempts to render the individual "without foundation," dismisses the historicity and materiality of "ideas" and "knowledge." Statements like "Expert language is a prison for knowledge and understanding", ("Communicative Practices" 8) "Brilliance is stupidity if it cannot communicate" ("Communicative Practices" 10) and "Media philosophy is philosophy for children...You must, therefore, dare to be naive and superficial by talking their language and not trying to impose your concepts in them" ("Naivete" 3) are symptomatic of the argument that "theory" is "too dense" for the general public, and that to theorize is a totalizing practice that can not understand the "unique" individual. What Taylor and Saarinen set up here as a "dare" – the "dare" to be ignorant – is, in fact a (standard) bourgeois articulation of education which situates the revolutionary proletariat both as "children" and as "confined" by the "prison" of expert language. Of course, Taylor and Saarinen, like all "avant-garde" teachers, do not dismiss all "expert" knowledge – the "expert" knowledges necessary to understand the technology of their project seem to be O.K. – but only those knowledges which call into question the politics of their project. In other words, for Taylor and Saarinen the "prison" is not "expert language" but the knowledge of the exploitative relations of production. Such a "dare" (to be ignorant) is symptomatic of only the ignorance of the petty-bourgeois intellectual who assumes that the working class is not inherently as intellectually "privileged" as himself and thus will never be able to comprehend anything but the most basic issues of their existence – something they are not only already "aware" of, but have already gone well beyond![5] It is only the "superficial" reader who would see such anti-intellectual (non critique-al, non conceptual) rhetoric as "groundbreaking" instead of the same interested misreadings that the trade-unionist left and the far right have been using to represent the development of ever more complex theorizations of the social relations of late capital "unintelligible" and "useless" to the working class.

By reducing ideology critique (the "dense") to local criticism (the "naive") *imagologies* updates the historical function of education as prescribed by the ruling classes – what Lenin calls "an instrument of the class rule of the bourgeoisie" (86). When Taylor and Saarinen argue that

"Expert language is a prison for knowledge and understanding" they are making the argument for "practical" knowledge. This is the same position that has been deployed, as Teresa Ebert argues, in the attack on the critique-al humanities by the allied forces of transnational capital (5). The "imagological reader," having been denied access to the "dense" critiques of historical materialism, is, instead, provided with representations of the contradiction of the forces and relations of production – the introduction of "new" technology and the reduction of the cost of labor power – that render this historical contradiction as "natural" and "inevitable". Thus while students may be technologically "connected" to the global classroom, this connection amounts to nothing more than an ideological adherence to a transhistorical and "naturalized" conception of capitalist development. This is manifest in Taylor and Saarinen's (lack of) theorization of their turn towards "networking" business connections as a response to a university system that they no longer see as being fit for their needs; that is, as long as the theories that work to critique the theoretico-political foundations of their project are allowed. In other words, while they claim that "The imagination must be undisciplined. That is why the university cannot bear it" ("Ending the Academy" 5) what they can not "bare" is not only a "disciplined" "imagination" (critique) but the threat that the critique-al humanities pose to the development of transnational capitalism and thus to the "safety" of the new "network".

Not "Technological Revolution" But Technology and Revolution!

In the beginning of their endeavor Taylor writes in an email to Saarinen regarding the feasibility/difficulties of the global classroom, "But I don't think it is money we need. It seems to me that this idea is interesting enough to attract corporate sponsorship" ("Communicative Practices" 7). Because *imagologies* displaces the possibility of locating the attack on critique-al knowledges in anything but a "naturalized" history of capitalism, the imagological reader is thus hailed to "celebrate the benefits," with no way to make sense of the material costs: shrinking monetary resources, higher tuition, increased class size, etc. Later on, Taylor even remarks that the president of the Williams College admits that "the college is in the midst of a major capital campaign," and that "he did not have time for a limited undertaking" ("Simcult" 5). Instead of looking at it as a "lack of time" – a pragmatic response based on localized bureaucratic concerns – we can see the privatization of the academy that has been on going for the past two decades. The attack on the critique-al humanities – ideologically sutured as a "standards revolution" by the ruling class (Healy A21) – is part of a systemic initiative to rid the system of what Lenin calls "a weapon" in the struggle for emancipation (87): theoretical knowledges which produce a critique-al, and ultimately revolutionary, citizenry. Around the world attacks on education, under the guise of the IMF/World Bank's "structural adjustment" program, are leaving the world's population with little or no access to critique-al knowledges. We must understand these attacks as connected and as the result of increasingly aggressive capitalist policies. Without such an understanding, we are trapped within the immanent critique of individual States and yearly budgetary battles of the "trade-unionist" radicals.

It is in direct relationship to this "standards revolution" that the "traditional" humanities have had to defend themselves against the criticism that they are "outdated," that they provide little use for an increasingly "cyber" culture that, in so far as it is understood that "any" information is immediately available via the internet, no longer "needs" the sort of "exposure" to culture that marked the traditional humanities. While often the work done in the sciences results in the production of a visibly marketable commodity (the patent-able "discovery") research done in the "old" humanities is not seen as having "marketable value". As a result, the humanities have either taken a defensive stance, as in we teach "Literary Literacy" (Perloff B4) or have attempted to make use of technology in order to "perform" the image of being "cutting edge"[6]. At the same time however, they are not "only" inviting technology into the classroom, but a particular understanding of technology that is necessary in assisting capitalism's increasingly aggressive expansion. In other words, regardless of whether the stance taken against the "privatization" of education – whether it is a "return to the traditional" or a "cutting-edge" façade – these pragmatic responses do not question the institutional imperative to "justify" the humanities as a site of "skills" pedagogy, but instead merely capitulate to the will of the ruling class. We can see that Saarinen – because his "fame" as a capitalist reformist has made him an advisor to the Finnish bourgeoisie – has no problem with the privatization of the academy when he says in an email to Taylor, "The big news, however, is that the Finnish Telecom guys will donate the use of the phone lines. I may have to do some lectures for them but that's OK, *I like these guys* [emphasis mine]" ("Media Philosophy" 7). It seems that privatization of the academy is "OK" as long as it is "personally beneficial." This again illustrates the reductivist function of imagology. One is no longer able to connect corporate interests with the attacks on higher education, but instead one can only focus on the limited "local" benefits of corporate sponsorship.

Saarinen and Taylor's "appreciation" of privatization is possible precisely because they take as their "foundation" that "consumer culture," divorced from the fundamental concept of labor, is liberatory. Thus, like Haraway they see the computer as "liberating" the consumer and the producer alike:

With the emergence of sophisticated analysis of consumption made possible by advanced electronic technology, the manufacturing process becomes considerably more flexible and diversified. Instead of the manufacturer simply imposing standardized patterns of consumption on seemingly passive consumers, consumers play a more active role in determining what is produced ("Electronomics" 3).

Taylor and Saarinen, in order to "justify" their vision of the "simcult" cosmopolitan merely reiterate the banalities of the "freedom" of "post-Fordism". Thus, what they "promise" as "cutting-edge" is ultimately nothing but what produces a higher rate of profit for the owning class and a more intense degree of exploitation of the workers. Instead of the promise of "togetherness" and "bridging the gaps," communication technology has continued the widespread povertization of the world through its function as a tool for the increase in profit through the decrease of global wages. From the free export zones in Asia and Africa, to the Maquiladoras in Mexico, the international bourgeoisie has turned the "promise" of the techno-scientific cosmopolitan into a curtain behind which they consolidate their wealth at the expense of the overwhelming majority of the world's population . In Southeast Asia, one area where the technological revolution is being "built," workers are forced to work day and night building microchips while working with chemicals and pollution deemed too dangerous for American workers until they are physically disabled, usually after a period of only six years[7]. These are the objective social relations that Taylor and Saarinen cannot risk articulating. They argue instead that, "In hypertext, all the border guards have been assassinated. The entire world of knowledge becomes a free-trade zone. In this common market, currency is current" ("Interstanding" 6). As Grant Kester argues in his essay, "Access Denied: Information Policy and the Limits of Liberalism," this understanding of technology as a "free trade zone" is based upon "the nomadic, bourgeois individual who floats free of institutional and social constraints" (Kester, online). Since their philosophy of imagology can not account for the material divisions between those who own the means of production and those who own nothing but their labor power, to do so would be "too dense," it can only work to ideologically displace this contradiction, removing it from the possibility of critique, and subsequently the appearance of transformation.

As Marx demonstrates in *Capital*, "the starting point of modern industry is...the revolution in the instruments of labour" (397); that is, the development of the technology of production to correspond with the necessity of lowering the costs of commodity production: "like every other increase in the productiveness of labour, machinery is intended to cheapen commodities" (374) and that "in so far as machinery dispenses with muscular power, it becomes a means of employing labourers of slight muscular strength" (398).   The "machine" is not the onto-theological "becoming" that is the cyber-theorist's hallucinatory dream for the millennial utopia but, instead, represents the level of development of production at the historical moment. It is a tool, an extension of labor itself produced by labor, for producing the meeting of needs that, under capital, is employed only in favor of the bourgeoisie. Fully within the logic of techno-determinism of our time that represents both "conservative" and "leftist" political positions supportive of the bourgeoisie – for example Newt Gingrich has stated "In 21st-century America...every American will have a cellular phone, which will probably be a fax, which will probably be a modem, which will probably in some way tie them into a world." (NYTIMES 11 December 1994) while Al Gore dreams of a time when technology will usher in a "new Athenian age of Democracy" (1994) – Taylor and Saarinen's prediction for the future of cyber-capitalist relations can not explain the relation between the revolutionizing of the means of production, the increasing contradictions between the forces and relations of production, and the inability of the "benefits" of technology to "reach out" to the working class. Instead, theirs becomes an argument for the liberation from within capitalist relations.

Imagologies: Media Philosophy is part of a much broader "offensive" aimed at rendering revolutionary theories "useless" and while providing reformist answers to the rising international crisis of production. By inviting a "naturalized" capitalist logic into the classroom, Taylor and Saarinen's philosophy of imagology is nothing more than the updating of the dominant model of education, working to secure the adherence of the next generation of the labor force to the brutality of the capitalist system. We must then see the global classroom, as it has been constructed for us by Taylor and Saarinen, not as a learning tool, not as a closing of the gap, but instead as widening the gap between the classes, and as an affirmation of the policies of oppression and exploitation of late capital. Erasing the possibility of a socialist revolution, Taylor and Saarinen provide their bourgeois patrons with a utopian re-representation of social inequality, where the images of class division are removed as quickly as the click of a mouse.

Epilogue: The Corporate Left, Class, and Censorship

And along come well-dressed, enlightened and educated gentlemen, mouthing phrases about liberalism, democracy and Socialism...gentlemen who possess a virtual monopoly of the legal opposition in the press, in the leagues, and at meetings and elections . . ."

> – Lenin "In Memory of Count Heyden"

A new "Western 'marxism'" is emerging in Europe and in the United States – a "Western 'marxism'" that is an annex of corporate culture and, like global capital, itself deploys the myths of "difference" and the rhetoric of cosmopolitanism only to suppress universality and internationalism. In place of universality – and its critique-al politics – it manufactures (under "the silent compulsion of economic relations") an imperialist consensus and by the ruse of cosmopolitanism squashes all struggles for internationalism. This is a corporate left, in short, that has no use for "class," "revolution," "critique," "contestation," or even "diversity": it is the violent articulation of bourgeois totalitarianism and is resistant to any "ideas" other than the ones that advance the interests of the North Atlantic ruling classes.

It is a mark of the political and theoretical bankruptcy of this corporate left that the left editors – including those who, like yourself[8], at least in "opportune situations" (MLA cash bars, "Rethinking" conferences) call themselves "Marxist" or "marxist" – are now competing with the bourgeois liberals to out-mediate the crisis of global capitalism by marginalizing the contesting practices of revolutionary Marxism. These contestations, which are the articulations of class struggles in the arena of politics, are now routinely represented as matters of (aggressive) "style," (intransigent) "tone," and (shrill) "rhetoric" by the left editors and then quietly "edited" out of the left publications so as not to be offensive to the liberal sensibility. The left publications, in short, have become little more than the echo chambers of the liberal press and their pragmatic politics.

Recently, I wrote a review of a book (*imagologies: Media Philosophy*) that has, in a very short time, become a canonical text of the bourgeois knowledge industry. In my review, I attempted to demonstrate not only the reasons for this "popularity" but the active ways in which the book "mediates" the crisis of global capitalism into issues of "mode," "taste," "mood," "manner," and "form" in general.   In other words, my review put in full display the practices by which the contradictions of contemporary bourgeois knowledges are "mediated" by substitution of the "cognitive" for the "political," the "aesthetic" for the "economic," and the "pedagogical" for "class conflict". I made it clear that the goal of revolutionary (or even "progressive") pedagogy is not to "delight" or even "enlighten" – as the book in question claimed – but to produce class consciousness because "pedagogy" is not simply a witness, but a participant in history.

I sent my review to *Mediations*, which advertises itself as a "Marxist" journal. The editors of *Mediations* accepted the review for publication, but when it was actually published, I could barely recognize what was published as my text. Obviously what I had to say about these issues had hit a nerve in the editorial "collective" of Mediations which collectively had, throughout the editing process, attempted to normalize my text. Specifically, one of the editors, Amitava Kumar – whose own recent collection of essays, *Class Issues: Pedagogy, Cultural Studies, and The Public Sphere* is, like imagologies , a white wash of the liberal establishment and its pedagogies[9] – attempted, in an email forwarded to me on 9 September 1997, to cross out the sections of my review that engaged "class issues" and put in their place politically innocuous "safe issues" that currently are "hot" in liberal pedagogy. (Why Amitava Kumar, who is basically a photojournalist and writer of memoirs and personal essays, is in charge of editing "theory" essays for a Marxist or even "marxist" journal remains a puzzle to me – but that is another issue and has to be discussed in another text.)[10] By deploying aesthetics as a tool of pedagogical and class crisis management, his post argued for the erasure of the word (of course he means the entire practice of) "critique" and, instead of hard-hitting questions about the role of the "cyber" in class contestation, for providing "provocative" questions that can simply titillate the desire of the reader.

"Stimulation," "entertainment" and "delighting" of the reader – rather than theoretical "explanation" of the issues – is, evidently, for him, the goal of writing. I am focusing on Amitava Kumar's editing practices not in order to single one "person" out. Rather, my focus on his practices is because while Ron Strickland and other editors have – at least in this particular case – played the role of passive bureaucrats, Amitava Kumar has with unusual aggressiveness put into words the "silent ideology" of corporatist editing that underlies editorial practices at *Mediations*. I am reading his remarks symptomatically: not as an "expression" of his views, but as the articulation of a historical position in the corporate left editing practices now.

To be clear, I am not surprised at Amitava Kumar's attempts to censor and suppress my text. After all, it is by such acts of political and institutional accommodation that he – without having published a single book written by him ("theory" or otherwise) and by sheer left networking – sits on the editorial boards not only of *Mediations* but also of *Rethinking Marxism*, *Cultural Logic* and other "left" journals. What I am surprised at is that the other editors of a putatively Marxist (or is it "marxist"?) journal have passively sat by and allowed one single person – who is quickly becoming the in-house editor and pedagogue of the ruling class – to censor a partisan text arguing for the necessity of international proletarian revolution and produce a politically "mild" text from it.

I am writing to protest the censoring of my text by *Mediations* and demand that in your next issue you publish my full text as I submitted it to you in January 1998 and that you agreed to publish on 9

February 1998[11]. If you fail to do so, I will have no choice but to republish the essay in another Marxist publication.

Edited without my knowledge, the version of the essay that appears within the pages of *Mediations* in no way reflects the manuscript that I sent you in January 1998 and that you agreed to publish (as indicated in your post to me on 9 February 1998). This act of censorship, as I have already hinted, is not an act of "neglect" or "oversight" but is symptomatic of the ways in which left editors have joined the bourgeois liberal editors in suppressing revolutionary ideas and practices. It seems that when faced with maintaining even the most basic of the reformist principles to which they aspire, following the ideals of bourgeois democracy, "left" editors cannot come up with enough "reasons" to suppress and block – by censoring – revolutionary Marxist texts.

In "An Interview with Barbara Foley," editor Ron Strickland (opportunistically?) sides with Marxist theory and practices and calls the post-al practices "self-imposed quietism" (64). It is therefore all the more ideologically revealing that he has participated in the censoring of my text and the (re)production from my manuscript of a text which is, in its current construction, to a large extent "quietist." Why "formally" denounce "quietism" and actually practice it? Is this not the purest form of political "opportunism"? An act of class betrayal? What is the place of such counter-revolutionary "opportunism" in a Marxist (or even "marxist") journal? Although in the same interview with Barbara Foley he asks about "strategies" for "reviving" the best of the "old left" while "advancing the struggle in the current moment" (61) the brutal censoring of my text is representative of the rising anxiety among the petty-bourgeois intelligentsia who, in the face of the failing rate of profit around the globe, are abandoning their "left" principles and circling their academic publishing wagons. Such bourgeois "leftists" as Judith Butler and Paul Bove are now given free reign at academic conferences and in the pages of *The Nation* (11 May 1998) to conduct their neo-McCarthyite witchhunts against revolutionary Marxists (under the guise of "Left Conservatism") in the interests of their ruling class bosses. "Left Conservatism" is now doing for the bourgeois left what "political correctness" has done/is doing for the financiers on the right and their allies in the bourgeois knowledge industry. The convergence of the two is a demonstration of historical solidarity of all the supporters of global capitalism – the bankers of the right and the academics of the left. Their relentless all-out assaults on the revolutionary left, while shouting the battle cries of "political correctness" or "left conservatism," are in actuality the informing "principles" of Amitava Kumar's editing guidelines. Given the fact that "editing" is the control of what actually gets to the public, one can see how Amitava Kumar and *Mediations* are rewarded by the entrenched institutions for their editorial policing of the revolutionary left. To be concrete, Judith Butler also has a plan for "reviving" the best of the "old left," and, in striking similarity to the editors of *Mediations*, it too simply "edits out" those who refuse to "mediate" Marxism with reformist liberal politics and millennial (re)"interpretations" of bourgeois ideals[12].

The interests of the editors of *Mediations* can be clearly seen, as I have already outlined, in relation to comments made by Amitava Kumar in response to my essay. While arguing that the use of the word "critique" in the essay was "mechanical," and that one could "escape" such "formulaic" prose with an increase in the number of "provocative questions" (9 Sept. 1997), it is apparent (judging from the censored version of my text actually published by *Mediations*) that by "provocative questions" Amitava Kumar meant entertaining and delighting remarks about side-issues that were non-offensive to the elite in the academy.

It is also politically interesting that while Amitava Kumar (and, as their "silence" towards his corporate editing practices show, all the editors of *Mediations*) regards my prose to be "formulaic," he has no problem whatsoever with his own prose or, to take the other extreme, the "prose" of such contemporary critics (who are part of the corporate left network) as Gayatri Spivak. Amitava Kumar's prose is nothing but "formulaic." The fact that its "formulaic" character is invisible, because its formula is the formula of the bourgeois commonsense and its cadences are the cadences of the exchanges on the market, does not mean that the prose is not "formulaic." Gayatri Spivak's "prose" is the very embodiment of the "formulaic" – it follows lexia by lexia, clause by clause – the formula of a spectral writing that the bourgeois philosophy has inherited from Left Hegelians. It is, therefore, not the "formulaic" which is bothering Amitava Kumar – if the issue is the "formulaic" then his prose as well as the prose of his co-networkers are both formulaic. It is, rather, what the "formulaic" is doing in my writing which has caused my manuscript to be heavily censored. While the "formula" in Kumar's and Spivak's prose hides the contradictions of capitalism in the cadences of commonsense or in the folds of (subtle) theosophical "medi(t)ations," mine puts them in the public space and draws attention to them. My prose displays the contradictions in order to mark their political economy and thus produce class consciousness in the reader. It is the clash of these two paths – " mediation" or "confrontation" – that has caused my text – by a violent use of petty-bourgeois editorial power – to become what it has: a maimed text.

In the same manner it is now clear that "provocative questions" were a cognitive ruse for Amitava Kumar and *Mediations* to increase the indeterminacy of the essay by reducing "accurate charges" (i.e. revolutionary Marxist critiques) to "more pedagogically useful" questions in order to provide "cool," non-offensive, intellectually pleasing, politically safe, and easily consumable summer reading material for the members of the Marxist Literary Group at their annual picnic, the "Institute on Culture and Society" –so named "for those of you who are worried about using the term 'marxist' on your vita" (GSC-SC list serve, 17 March 1998). By turning "provocative" questions into statements of historical materialist critique, my essay evidently has offended Amitava Kumar's aesthetic sensibilities! My revised offending essay, which you agreed to publish, was "scrapped"–so that Amitava Kumar and the "aesthetic marxists" who circle around him can keep their credentials with the rulers of the academy by maintaining a "pleasing" tone to their "marxist" journal.

Although the subtitle of the current issue of *Mediations* is "Teaching Marxism" it again is no surprise when one looks at the state of academic publishing as a whole, and Mediations as a part of that bourgeois institution, that sections of my essay which situate the project of Taylor and Saarinen in relation to the current movement against revolutionary Marxism in academia, a move representative of the very actions of this editorial board, was removed entirely. Perhaps instead of "Teaching Marxism" as the subtitle–an egregious political overstatement for a forum that advocated teaching *Marx: The Video*, "enjoying what we know not" and coming up with a "good hook" for students – you should have chosen a more accurate subtitle such as "How to Have Fun with Marxism: Baudrillard Reads Marx and Afterward We All Go To Disneyland." When understood in the context of increasing class antagonism the suppression of my essay becomes symptomatic of the attempts by (corporate) left editors who, in a moment of rising unrest by the proletariat, sit back as the managerial clerks of the international bourgeoisie showing off their latest aesthetic "tag." (All the "cool" "marxists" are wearing "post" again this year.)

In their collective attempt to marginalize revolutionary Marxism, the editors of Mediations have once again declared their allegiance to the interests of global capital against

THE ORGANIZATION OF THE PROLETARIAT

FOR INTERNATIONAL COMMUNISM!

Notes

[1] Mas'ud Zavarzadeh's revolutionary concept for the class of intellectuals who argue that there has been a "shift" in capitalist relations of production such that we are "post-history": "Post-ality is the ensemble of practices that, as a totality, obscure the production practices of capitalism – which is based on the extraction of surplus labor (the source of accumulation of capital) – by announcing the arrival of a new society

which is post-production, post-labor, post-ideology, post-white, and post-capitalist" (1).

[2] The bourgeois political imaginary of the "third way", situated between right-wing neo-liberalism and leftist "trade-union" politics as the "post-historical", "post-ideological" and "post-political", has become the standard class slogan of the "New Left/Labor" parties of the North Atlantic and is symptomatic of the moralization of the political and, in turn, the mystification of State power behind a rhetoric of "rights" and/only with "responsibilities."

[3] More recent examples of this performative science are texts collected in Barbara Herrnstein Smith and Arkady Plotnisky, ed. *Mathematics, Science, and Postclassical Theory* (Durham, Duke UP, 1998). The underlying ideology of this post-al "science" becomes more clear in "Reading Animals: Zoographics" a "session" organized with participation of Herrnstein-Smith by Thomas Cohen for the MLA Convention in 1998. The preoccupation with zoographics is symptomatic of the advanced stage of commodification and alienation of labor under capitalism. The more the relations among people is reduced to relations among things, the more "animals" perform the imaginary transcendence from this regime of reification.

[4] The constant introduction of new technology, necessitated historically by the development of the social relations of production and itself a product of labor, into the labor process consolidates the wealth of the owning class while, in the same instance, increases the antagonism between labor and capital and, thus, sets the foundation for social revolution. The petty-bourgeoisie, while historically "fluctuating" between the bourgeoisie and the proletariat, support the private ownership of the means of production and in turn celebrate the introduction of technology without question in an attempt to renew their position as "a supplementary part of bourgeois society" (Marx). They are, however, a class with no historical power. As the "mediators" of the class struggle, caught between the two great social classes, the very developments of technology they support, and the resultant consolidation of wealth in the hands of the ruling class, forces them into the ranks of the proletariat. To be clear, this is not an argument against "progress" but instead a mark of the contradiction that arises, between the forces and relations of production, as the result of the introduction of technology under capitalism – what represents the emancipation of the working class becomes, when used by the bourgeoisie, an apparatus of repression and exploitation. One has to look no further than the petty-bourgeois mis-leaders of the recent GM strike who gave up the right to strike on the local level – the UAW had already given up the right to strike on the national level in the settlement to a previous strike – as well as the

commitment not to contest the continuing lay-offs at the plant in exchange for a (time) limited return of the factory's casting dies and training, only for themselves, in the latest production technologies.

[5] For example, what does the recent Saturn strike represent but the recognition of the working class that the managerial strategies of the "dialogic" – the "sharing" of "power" through "dialog" – at which Saturn was at the forefront, does not interpellate workers against their material interests as it cannot erase the fact of the historical contradiction of the relations of private property. In other words, the supposedly "ignorant" workers have already determined Taylor and Saarinen's "network" to be theoretically and politically bankrupt.

[6] To be clear, this is not an argument against the "cutting edge" – the production of boundary knowledges of social relations – but the status that "cutting edge" has for the ruling class. In other words, what stands in as "cutting edge" – the brute introduction of computers and "hypertextual" educational programs – is an ideological cover for the class interests of owners. Truly progressive ("cutting edge") pedagogy, as Lenin argues, provides the working class with the theoretical knowledges necessary to critique the contradictions of material life and, in turn, produce the most advanced theoretical knowledges.

[7] The absurd lengths to which the petty-bourgeoisie will go to justify the practices of their bourgeois patrons and to "feel good" about their disregard for the working class is apparent in Donna Haraway's reactionary notion that the "techno-science" industry, particularly in the factories in Southeast Asia, enable a "liberation" from capitalist relations. She argues that in the "simcult" cosmopolitan factory, the "intense pleasure in skill, ceases to be a sin, but an aspect of embodiment" ("Manifesto" 222) and that the women of Southeast Asia are "actively rewriting the texts of their bodies and societies" ("Manifesto" 219). Haraway's liberatory notion of "pleasure," far from being liberatory, posits no outside, no future beyond the exploitative relations of capitalist production.

[8] This epilogue is a text in several voices: part an "open letter," part a critique, part a history of publication of my text. Although in order to be "specific," I have named names of specific persons and outlined their practices, the referent of my "you" throughout this text is plural. It, therefore, marks the position of all (corporate) left editors and not only the editors of the "marxist" journal *Mediations* who are addressed here in the first instance.

[9] For a rigorous Marxist critique of Kumar's *Class Issues* see Stephen Tumino's review in the Spring 1999 issue of *Textual Practice*. Similar to the manner in which my *Mediations* essay was "edited," Stephen Tumino's essay was also subject to the interests of "corporate"

left publishing and censored. Peter Nicholls, the review editor of *Textual Practice*, sent an e-mail to Mr. Tumino indicating that he thought that his critique of Gayatri Spivak's stated wish in that volume to "break our vanguardism" as an instance of "linguistic fascism" was a "trifle extreme and under-argued" and asked if he would be willing to "change the wording" (27 Oct. 98). Mr. Tumino's reply was that: "linguistic fascism". . . might in fact sound a "trifle extreme" but it is a concept used in more or less the same situations by other scholars and critics. My point is not to "sensationalize" the issues but to tease out from Spivak's knot of assumptions what I regard to be their very politically dangerous consequences. It is all the more necessary to use the concept here because of the way Spivak's writings are "naturalized" as part of the Western Leftist canon. I would like to suggest that instead of changing it, we simply "document" the use of the concept and if you wish I can re-write this note and add it to the review (19 Sept. 1998).

Mr. Nicholls responded that this "seems a good idea" and requested that the note expanding on the concept "linguistic fascism" be submitted but that it be "brief" because "Routledge don't like large editions at proof stage" (29 Sept. 1998). When Mr. Tumino received the proofs (24 Nov. 1998) the note was not included and the text was as he originally wrote it. When the text was finally published, however, it contained no mention of "linguistic fascism" at all and neither has there been any acknowledgement by the editors of *Textual Practice* of their extreme form of censorship of ideas or their cynical exploitation of the labor of others. The editors of *Textual Practice* have resorted to simply "editing out" that which might offend their political allies and corporate patrons under the guise of a commitment to scholarly neutrality and tone--the very practice that the concept linguistic fascism is meant to explain. To be clear, what is at stake in these examples is not whether the editors of *Mediations* or *Textual Practice* are "negligent" as editors, but rather to foreground the fact that despite the appearance of editing as a series of self-enclosed "private" practices, that *all* editorial decisions are, in fact, socially and historically determined: under the guise of scholarly neutrality and technical-managerial concerns they always support the interests of the ruling class and suppress the red critique which is committed to "comprehensive political exposure" of "all manner of sophisms by which each class and each stratum *camouflages* its selfish strivings and its real 'inner-workings'," of "every manifestation of tyranny and oppression, no matter where it appears, no matter what stratum or class of people it affects. . . , of every event, however small" in order to "clarify for absolutely everyone the world-historical significance of the struggle for the emancipation of the proletariat" (Lenin).

[10] The reason I raise the issue of "qualifications" is not because I think "experts" would do a more self-reflexive editing. Rather it is because the liberal knowledge industry always conceals its ideological work, which is aimed at protecting the interests of the ruling class, as the advanced work of advanced and highly qualified scholars, critics, and theorists. In other words, the liberal academy has used credentials to give the impression of "neutrality' and "objectivity" to its textwares. Therefore, I think it is necessary to raise the question of qualifications/credentials and make managers-editors (gatekeepers of ideas on behalf of the ruling class) accountable in the very terms that they use to legitimate their textwares and silence the "other" as "unqualified". They cannot have it both ways: either credentials and qualifications matter or they do not. If they do, what is that makes the "qualified", "qualified"?

[11] From: Ron Strickland
To: Rob Wilkie
Date: Monday, February 09, 1998 3:19 PM
Subject: review   Rob,
I got the review of Imagologies... thanks! Plan to publish it in the next issue of Mediations, due out in May.
Ron Strickland

[12] See Judith Butler on "Left Conservatism" in *Theory and Event* (Vol. 2, No. 2 and No. 3) and *The Nation* (11 May 1998) as well as her exchange with Ernesto Laclau in *Diacritics* (Spring 1997. Vol. 27, No. 1).

Works Cited

Butler, Judith. Letter. *The Nation*. 11 May 1998: 2, 59.

Deleuze, Gilles and Felix Guattari. *Anti-Oedipus: Capitalism and Schizophrenia*. Trans. Robert Hurley, Mark Seem, and Helen R. Lane. Minneapolis: University of Minnesota Press, 1983.

Deleuze, Gilles and Felix Guattari. *What is Philosophy?*. 1991. Trans. Hugh Tomlin and Graham Burchell. New York: Columbia University Press, 1994.

Dimock, Wai Chee, and M.T. Gilmore, eds. *Rethinking Class*. New York: Columbia University Press, 1994.

Ebert, Teresa L. "Quango-ing the University: The End(s) of Critique-al Humanities." *The Alternative Orange*. 5.2 (1997): 5-47.

Giroux, Henry A. *Pedagogy and the Politics of Hope: Theory, Culture and Schooling*. Boulder, CO: Westview Press, 1997.

Gore, Vice-President Al. "Remarks as Delivered to the International Telecommunications Union." Buenos Aires: March 21, 1994.

Greenspan, Alan. "Testimony of Chairman Alan Greenspan Before the Joint Economic Committee, U.S. Congress." June 10, 1998. Online. http://www.bog.frb.fed.us/oarddocs/testimony/9980610. htm

Grossberg, Lawrence. Introduction: "Bringin' It All Back Home – Pedagogy and Cultural Studies." *Between Borders: Pedagogy and the Politics of Cultural Studies*. Ed. Henry A. Giroux and Peter McLaren. New York: Routledge, 1-25.

Haraway, Donna "A Manifesto for Cyborgs: Science, Technology, and Socialist Feminism in the 1980s" *Feminism/Postmodernism* Ed. by Linda J. Nicholson. New York: Routledge, 1990. 190-233.

_____. Modest *Witness@ Second_ Millennium .FemaleMan_ Meets_ OncoMouse*. New York: Routledge, 1997.

Healy, Patrick and Peter Schmidt. "In New York, a 'Standards Revolution' or the Gutting of Public Colleges?" *The Chronicle of Higher Education.* 7 July 1998, Sec. A: 21-22.

Jameson, Fredric. *Postmodernism or The Cultural Logic of Late Capitalism*. Durham, NC: Duke University Press, 1991.

_____. "Culture and Finance Capital." *Critical Inquiry.* Vol. 24, No. 1 (Autumn 1997). 246-265.

Kester, Grant. "Access Denied: Information Policy and the Limits of Liberalism." *Afterimage* January 1994: 26.1. www.cc.Rochester. edu/college/FS/Publications/Kester/Access.html

Lenin, V.I. "Speech at the First All-Russia Congress on Education, August 28, 1918." *Lenin Collected Works.* Vol. 28. 1965. Moscow: Progress Publishers. 1977.

Marx, Karl. Capital: Volume One. *Marx-Engels Collected Works*. Vol. 35. New York: International Publishers, 1996.

_____. *A Contribution to the Critique of Political Economy.* Ed. Maurice Dobb. New York: International Publishers, 1970.

_____. *Wage-Labour and Capital & Value, Price and Profit.*. 1976. New York: International Publishers, 1990.

Marx, Karl and Fredrick Engels. "Manifesto of the Communist Party." *Marx-Engels Collected Works.* Vol. 6. New York: International Publishers, 1976. 476-519

Perloff, Marjorie. "Restoring 'Literary Literacy' to the English Curriculum." *The Chronicle of Higher Education.* 9 May 1997, Sec. Opinion: B4.

"Rereading Class" *PMLA.* 113 (March 1998): 198.

Rosenbaum, David E. "Republicans Like Both Previews and Returns." *NY Times.* 11 Dec. 1994, Sec. 4: p.1, 16.

Sanger, David E. "One Year Later, Asian Economic Crisis is Worsening." *NY Times.* 6 July 1998. Online.

Strickland, Ron. "An Interview with Barbara Foley." *Mediations*, Vol. 21
    (Spring 1998). 58-66.
Taylor, Mark C. and Esa Saarinen. *Imagologies: Media Philosophy*.
    New York: Routledge. 1994.
Zavarzadeh, Mas'ud.   "Post-ality: The (Dis)Simulations of Cyber-
    capitalism." *Transformation 1*. Ed by M. Zavarzadeh, T. Ebert,
    D. Morton. Washington, D.C.: Maisonneuve Press, 1995. 1-75

Teresa L. Ebert

The Spectral Concrete:

Bodies, Sex Work and (some notes on) Citizenship

One

Contemporary cultural critique distinguishes itself from the so-called "modernist" cultural analysis by its intense focus on what it calls the "concrete." As my marking, "what it calls," implies, the "concrete" is a contested category: it is neither the particular of the commonsense, nor is it the bodily sensuous, the epistemologically empirical or the textually referential. The "concrete," as I will argue, is itself a highly complex and complicating notion that cannot act, without sustained theorizing, as the foundation of a post-foundationalist cultural critique. In this essay I will engage the "concrete" in contemporary (by which I mostly mean poststructuralist and post-poststructuralist) cultural critique, beginning with the notion of citizenship, which has itself become a theoretical zone for the return of the concrete, and then work my way towards the concrete in sex work and matters of transnational desires.

Culture, one can argue, is the apparatus by which the "individual" is transformed into a "subject" and given the necessary consciousness skills to become a fully instituted person. Citizenship is the resituating of the cultural subject into the political sphere: the individual who successfully becomes a subject, in other words, is then endowed with "rights" ("human rights") and given a certain social and political space.

I want to begin the discussion of citizenship—which has now returned to cultural studies after a long period of marginalization—by "complicating" it through posing the question: How effective is the concept of citizenship for the emancipation of women? In working toward an answer, I will be taking as my test case the global struggles of sex workers. In doing so, I will be demonstrating some of the consequences of my theorizing the concrete in cultural critique, what I call "Red cultural studies" and how it provides an explanatory, materialist knowledge that contributes to an emancipatory praxis.

Feminism and contemporary cultural studies have long criticized the dominant, Enlightenment notions of citizenship for being too abstract and masculinist and neglecting the concrete embodied sexed, gendered subject--to the real detriment of women's struggles to achieve equality and freedom. But efforts to provide alternative theories are proving, in many ways, to be just as problematic, for first we have to resolve the issues of how to theorize difference and the sexed, gendered body and what is the concrete if we are to have an effective materialist feminist cultural studies. Even the seemingly self-evident principle of freedom has its own limits, and feminists and cultural critics alike have to engage the question Marx posed in the "Jewish Question": It is "by no means sufficient to investigate: Who is to emancipate? Who is to be emancipated? Criticism had to investigate a third point. It had to inquire: What kind of emancipation is in question?" (149).

Let me first review one of the most recent efforts to articulate a feminist theory of citizenship and justice--Drucilla Cornell's attempt at a postmodern rewriting of sexed subjects into a liberal rights-based theory of freedom. In her book, *At the Heart of Freedom: Feminism, Sex and Equality* (1999), Cornell turns from her earlier poststructuralist and post-Enlightenmnet work to embrace the liberal individualism of Kant and John Rawls. "Something is missing," Cornell claims, "in both the limited formal equality for women found in the United States and in the social equality provided women in the socialist states....What has been missing is the protection of each person's imaginary domain, that psychic and moral space in which we as sexed creatures who care deeply about matters of the heart, are allowed to evaluate and represent who we are" (x). Protection of this "imaginary domain" is, for Cornell, the basis of equality and the guarantee of freedom. This is because "freedom," according to Cornell, means a "person's freedom to pursue her own happiness in her own way" (18) or, as she also says, "the freedom to be ourselves" (x). This "freedom," she says, "must be understood as a right that cannot be displaced...the right of each person to represent his or her sexuality, or what...[she calls] sexuate being" (x-xi).

This right is at the core of the problem of "inclusion" in theories of justice and citizenship for Cornell. Equality, she claims, is based on the "right to be included in the moral community of persons as an initial matter" (20). But the "conditions of inclusion," Cornell argues, "have failed to address the relationship between the ideal of the free person and the project all human beings have of orienting themselves as to their sexuate being." Any fair and distributive justice, according to Cornell, must "ensure the right to self-representation of each person's sexuate being" (26) These rights are "grounded" in the "protection of the imaginary domain" because, Cornell claims, "the imaginary domain gives to the individual person, and to her only, the right to claim who she is through her own representation of her sexuate being. Such a right necessarily makes her the morally and legally recognized source of narration and resymbolization of what the meaning of her sexual difference is for her..." (10). The equal protection of this right, for Cornell, is basically the protection of personhood, identity and "freedom of personality" from the state. The "protection of the imaginary domain," according to Cornell, "seeks to get the state out of the business of giving 'form' to our intimate lives" (26). Following this emphasis on the state, she defines "patriarchy" as "the state-enforced and culturally supported norm of heterosexual monogamy as the only appropriate organization of family life" (22). "Sexual freedom" is thus the right to sexual self-representation "freed from state-imposed sexual choices that limit all of us" (xi).

Cornell's understanding of freedom here is basically an elaboration of traditional 18th century rights of civil citizenship--the protection of the "private" individual from the state. Civil citizenship, as T. H. Marshall outlined in his now classic text "Class, Citizenship and Social Development," is: "composed of the rights necessary for individual freedom--liberty of the person, freedom of speech, thought and faith, the right to own property and to conclude valid contracts, and the right to justice" (71). Cornell is not questioning these priorities, rather she is simply extending the notion of "personhood" to encompass the sexed subject--not as a stable subjectivity but as a process of symbolic performances and self-representations--which she marks by her notion of the "imaginary domain."

It is quite telling that Cornell's notion of the "imaginary domain" of "a self-authenticating sexuate being" is, itself, a rather contradictory and eclectic reappropriation of Enlightenment views of the rational, egoistic individual mixed in with poststructuralist discourses on the decentered subject. On the one hand, the imaginary domain is the transcendental, utopian and thus idealist "moral space" of the "conscience as the sanctuary of personality" as well as a "heuristic device" (15). On the other hand, it is the arena of the Freudian "bodily ego" and the Lacanian imaginary as the nonconscious realm of fantasy and the imperative of desire. Cornell is especially concerned with the function of the "bodily ego" and the way it shapes our representations of ourselves as "corporeal beings." Her articulation of this notion demonstrates the way 18th century bourgeois notions of the individual in terms of property relations are surreptitiously brought back into her postmodern feminism. The "sense of ourselves" furnished by the bodily ego, is based, she says (quoting Oliver Sacks at some length), on the perception of "our bodies [as] proper to us, as our 'property,' as our own...the owning...of our own physical selves . . . " (34). Cornell's uncritical reiteration of civil citizenship--both in her theory of rights and in her formulation of the self-possessing "sanctuary" of individual personality" is especially problematic for feminism. As Nancy Fraser and Linda Gordon have argued, "civil citizenship ...was a property conception of rights" that "made property rights the model for all other rights" and thereby "excluded from civil citizenship...those who did not own property, either because they were unable to get their resources defined as property (for example women, tenants, workers) or because they were property (slaves)" (55).

The "property model" not only determines who has access to rights, it also, as Marx argues in "the Jewish Question," determines what counts as freedom. In her book, *At the Heart of Freedom*, Cornell emphasizes that her "central argument" is that "a person's freedom to pursue her own happiness in her own way is crucial for any person's ability to share in life's glories" (18). What kind of liberty or freedom is involved here? According to Marx, "the right of man to liberty," that is, liberty as a right of the person in civil society,

> is based not on the association of man with man, but on the separation of man from man. It is the right of this separation, the right of the *restricted* individual, withdrawn into himself.
> The practical application of man's right to liberty is man's right to *private property*....The right to private property is, therefore, the right to enjoy one's property and to dispose of it at one's discretion,...without regard to other men, independently of society, the right of self-interest. This individual liberty and its application form the basis of civil society. It makes every man see in other men not the *realization* of his own freedom, but the *barrier* to it....the whole of society exists only in order to guarantee to each of its members the preservation of his person, his rights, and his property. ("On the Jewish Question" 162-63)

The citizen of civil society is the exemplary bourgeois--the isolated, "possessing individual," what I call the citizen of desire, who places her own self-interest above any collective good or social need. In civil society, the term "equality," Marx notes, is "non-political." It "is nothing but the equality of the *liberte* described above, namely: each man is to the same extent regarded as such a self-sufficient monad" (163).

The disturbing extent to which Cornell subscribes to this as the model of freedom for feminism is suggested by her declaration: "We do not want sexual freedom to replace social equality; we want social equality redefined so as to serve freedom" (xii). But this freedom is the freedom of the "self-sufficient monad" to represent her desires without any real attention to the social needs of others--others who act as a (potential) imposition or limitation on the "sanctuary" of her "sexual self-actualization." It is a freedom, that as T. H. Marshall demonstrates, has long been quite consistent "with the inequalities of capitalist society," and is, in fact, "necessary to the maintenance of...inequality" (87). There is no room in Cornell's "imaginary domain" of symbolic freedoms for the real material economic demands of "social citizenship," which Marshall and others have articulated as "the whole range from the right to a modicum of economic welfare and security to the right to share to the full in the social heritage and to live the life of a civilized being according to the standards prevailing in the society" (72). Cornell's protected rights of the "imaginary domain" entirely obscure the realities of class inequalities in capitalism--they are simply idealist exercises in desire situated in the realm of discursive representations. In fact, Cornell goes so far as to declare that "freedom of personality as a political ideal need not be rooted in a truth about the human condition" (39). Cornell, in short, is offering us an idealist, illusory freedom accompanied by a spectral equality that has no ground in the real material conditions of need and labor that shape human sexuality and gender differences.

Cornell's individualist theory of symbolic freedoms is a defeatist, fatalist retreat for feminism and left cultural studies from the pressing social issues confronting us. When Cornell's argument for the "protected rights of the imaginary domain" is put to the test--as I will do later in this essay by examining how she deals with the problem of the emancipation of sex workers--we are left with little more than a localist identity politics. We are witnessing, today, the almost complete dismantling (especially in the United States and Great Britain) of "social citizenship" as it was articulated even in the liberal "welfare state," and the increasing gap between the rich and poor--between the transnational bourgeoisie and the international proletariat--is growing at a staggering rate. We find capitalism today waging an intensive war against "social citizenship"--against the rights of economic security and social well being for all--and it is doing so by reviving the property relations and possessive individualism of civil society as the hegemonic realm of freedom. Feminism and cultural studies need to be extremely wary of joining this new tyranny of the neoliberalism of the market. Questions of freedom cannot simply become exercises in the rights of desire for the bourgeoisie, instead we must engage the fundamental issues of the rights of all people to have their needs meet, and to live a life of economic security, social well being and emancipation from exploitation. Sexuality and sexed, gender differences are not simply the embodied representations of the imaginary, they are fundamental effects of the social division of labor and it is only with emancipation from the exploitation of our labor that we can begun to construct true sexual freedom.

Two

The first step in building a theory and praxis of sexual emancipation as part of an inclusive citizenship is to break with the empty idealism we find in theories such as Cornell's and articulate a materialist theory. But materialism, itself, has become even more of a contested category in the wake of poststructuralism, and historical materialism is widely dismissed today as an anachronism in the age of triumphalist capitalism and post-communism. What I call a post-al logic-- postmodern, post-class, post-labor, post-production--has come to dominate cultural studies largely because it claims to have superseded the seemingly abstract, reductive and totalizing logic of classic Marxism by offering an apparently "up to date," flexible accounting of the specificity, differences, and singularity of the concrete. Its focus on the concrete enables critics to "complicate" their articulations of culture and power. Materialism in post-al discourses has been rearticulated in the desire of *the bourgeoisie to mean not the materiality of class struggles but a delectable materialism* of the sensuous, of concrete pleasures. Delectable materialism delights in the tactile sensualities, erotics and sublimity of the concrete—especially of concrete bodies and embodied significations. We have a profusion of post-al stories of the specific, the particular and the concrete--from the now "classic" tales of Foucauldian "events" and Lyotardian "differends" to the most recent textual pleasures of Sedgwick's "queer reading...attune," as she says, "to the heartbeat of contingency" (25) and now canonized in such extravagances of reading as Thomas Pepper's *Singularities. Delectable materialism* is the theory of the material put forth in late capitalism to displace *dialectical materialism* --which, conveniently and to the delight of the culture industry, is now routinely assumed to be abstract, reductive, and, of course, totalizing. One of the paradoxes of delectable materialism is that, while it critiques historical materialism for "reductiveness," it itself reduces the "concrete" to the merely "empirical." In fact, it assumes, without any argument, that it always already "knows" the concrete. The question, of course, is what is the concrete? The bodily sensual, the epistemologically empirical, the textually referential?

The almost reflexive invocation of the concrete in post-al discourses has become so pervasive that even such a thoughtful Marxist as Fredric Jameson takes it up. In a recent essay on Marxism and Deleuze, he begins his rhapsody on the "greatness" of Deleuze—in particular Deleuze's "transcodings" of Marxism---by invoking Marx on the concrete. "Marx," Jameson writes, "had a better formula: bourgeois thought, he said (which we may also read as Greek philosophy), sought to rise from the particular to the universal, our task is not to rise (note the persistence of the verb)—to rise from the universal to the concrete" ("Marxism and Dualism," 394).

Jameson, in short, is invoking Marx as a benediction in the pursuit of the concrete over the universal. However, Marx never proclaimed our task is "to rise from the universal to the concrete" as Jameson claims. Jameson seems to be referring here to the passage on the "concrete" in the Grundrisse (he cites the *Collected Works* of Marx and Engels.) Not only is this not a careful paraphrase, it is, in fact, a rather astounding misinterpretation of Marx for such a sophisticated reader and knowledgeable Marxist—a reading that is particularly telling of the "post" condition. In representing Marx's text the way he does, Jameson reifies a binary (concrete/universal) that Marx, himself, subjects to a materialist critique and dialectical overturning. The binary, however, is central to both the old bourgeois and the new post-al distortions of Marx and Marxism—it is the binary between concrete particularities and reified, abstract universals. By attributing such a binary to Marx's theorization of the concrete and the abstract, Jameson is turning Marx's materialist intervention into the ideology of the abstract and abstraction quite upside down. What is even more telling is that Jameson does so in order to fit Marx into an analogy to Hegel—a gesture to re-Hegelize Marx. It is not insignificant that Jameson also instructs us to "read" "bourgeois thought" in a quite ahistorical way as "Greek philosophy" in order to make his analogy to Hegel when the "bourgeois thought" Marx is critiquing is political economy, Adam Smith not Aristotle. (I put aside here another misrepresentation of Marx's notion of Greek art which seems to propel Jameson's reference.) Marx turned Hegel's dialectic on its head to render it materialist, but we now have Jameson overturning Marx's materialist notion of the concrete, occluding it and turning it into an idealist theory.

The "concrete" in Marx, is not the "self-evidence" of the commonsense nor is it, as I have already hinted, the bodily sensual, the epistemologically empirical or the textually referential. The concrete, in other words, is not the particular, sensuous singularities celebrated in post-al theories—especially the specificities of the body. However, the concrete body has become the exemplary instance of the concrete in post-al theories and one of the main ways to secure both knowledge and practice, as Elizabeth Grosz demonstrates: "Bodies," she says,

> have all the explanatory power of minds. Indeed…the focus on bodies, bodies in their concrete specificities, has the added bonus of inevitably raising the question of sexual difference…Questions of sexual specificity," she continues, "questions of which kinds of bodies, what their differences are,

and what their products and consequences might be
can...more readily demonstrate, problematize, and transform
women's social subordination to men (vii-viii).

This focus leads her to propose a new materialism, what she
calls "corporeal feminism." For Grosz, such a feminism, which grounds
its theory of subjectivity on the body's concrete corporeal surface, is
"nondualist" and "committed to both a....nonphysicalist materialism and
an acknowledgment of sexual difference" (viii). Not just Grosz, but nearly
all post-al cultural critics—from feminists and queer theorists to post-
colonialists--take the concrete to be the sensuous, sensible specificity
that resists abstraction and exceeds conceptuality, and is embodied, one
way or the other, in the sexed, racially marked body.

For Marx and other historical materialists, and thus for Red
cultural studies, however, the concrete is not   a resistance to
"abstractions"—it is itself an abstraction! Marx makes this quite clear in
his "Introduction" to the *Grundrisse* when he writes:

It seems to be correct to begin with the real and the concrete,
with the real precondition, thus to begin, in economics, with [for
example] the population, which is the foundation and the
subject of the entire social act of production. However, on
closer examination this proves false. The population is an
abstraction if I leave out, for example, the classes of which it is
composed. These classes in turn are an empty phrase if I am
not familiar with the elements on which they rest. [For instance]
wage labour, capital, etc. These latter in turn presuppose
exchange, division of labour, prices, etc. For example, capital is
nothing without wage labour, without value, money, price etc.
Thus, if I were to begin with the population, this would be a
chaotic conception [*Vorstellung*] of the whole, and I would then,
by means of further determination, move analytically towards
ever more simple concepts [*Begriff*], from the imagined
concrete towards [less and less complex] abstractions until I
had arrived at the simplest determinations. From there the
journey would have to be retraced until I had finally arrived at
the population again, but this time not as the chaotic
conception of a whole, but as a rich totality of many
determinations and relations....The concrete is concrete
because it is the concentration of many determinations, hence
unity of the diverse. (100-101)

Marx is turning the concrete on its head—just as he has done
with the idealist Hegelian dialectic. While the bourgeois common sense
regularly considers the concrete to be a tangible particularity, a

"singularity" and thus the "real" basis of knowledge, Marx shows how misleading such a notion is. Its seeming immediacy, ready intelligibility, and coherence is imaginary. The concrete, as Marx demonstrates, is an abstraction. It is a complex—even chaotic—conjunction of diverse relations and determinations that can only be grasped through conceptualization. As Marx demonstrates, the process of knowing the concrete is not an immediate perception of the sensible and sensuousness but an analysis or unpacking of the layered components, moving to ever more simple, that is, ever more fundamental concepts to articulate these root relations. Having "arrived," Marx says, "at the simplest determinations"—that is, at these root relations—we "retrace" these various relations, their connections and determinations, arriving back at the concrete. Only now, we are able to conceptualize the concrete—not as a simple sensible object—but as the complex "concentration of many determinations,...a unity of the diverse."

Three

How does such a reading hold up against the concrete of the "body"? Is the specificity of the body an "imagined concrete"—one that occludes the "reality" of the body as a complex concentration of determinations? If the concrete is not the particular but a historical "totality" of diverse relations, how does this call into question the anti-totality logic of theories of the local? How we answer these questions have a number of implications for how we theorize materiality and articulate the knowledges necessary for a socially transformative cultural studies--for a Red cultural studies.

To address these questions, I want to return to a closer analysis of Elizabeth Grosz's "corporeal feminism" and examine it in relation to citizenship. Grosz's text is in many ways exemplary of the kind of delectable materialism that now dominates post-al cultural studies. As I have already indicated, Grosz puts forth her focus on the "body's concrete corporeal surface" as the basis for a "non-reductive," "nonphysicalist materialism"--one especially able to articulate a theory of the subject in terms of the specificities of the sexed body. But how does Grosz actually theorize this concrete materiality? Early on, Grosz identifies one of the key issues when she asserts that "the specificity of bodies must be understood in its historical rather than simply its biological concreteness" (19). Indeed, the effectivity of any materialist theory depends on how it articulates the historical relations and determinations constituting the concrete. However, this is precisely the basic aporia of Grosz's own theory--its ahistorical mystification of the concrete. The body in Grosz's analysis is almost entirely isolated from all historical relations; she does have a limited discussion and summary of a Foucauldian analytics of power which is incorporated with his genealogy of discursive practices. But even this limited historical approach is largely absent from her own specific analysis of sexed bodies.

This omission is especially important because the subtext of Grosz's work is a substitution of an idealism articulated as corporeal materialism for a historical materialism. Since she is writing within a postmodern frame, the elision of Marxist historical materialism literally "goes without saying." In other words, within post-al and much feminist discourses today, the marginalization of Marxist and historical materialist assumptions is so widely accepted, it does not have to be argued, it need only be marked in passing as Grosz does. Grosz, like Judith Butler in her widely circulated text, "Merely Cultural," dismisses or declares obsolete Marxist theories of "base and superstructure" and dialectics for their deficiencies by reasserting quite common misrepresentations of Marxism--these amount to a caricature of Marxism instead of a serious engagement with it.

Grosz claims, for example, that the "base/superstructure model," is one "in which biology provides a self-contained 'natural' base and ideology provides a dependent parasitic 'second story'" (17). Such a simplistic representation of highly complex issues, which have been the subject of theoretical work among generations of Marxists and feminists alike, borders on the comical. But the politics of knowledge in the academy now is such that the comical is (mis)taken as a "deep" analysis of the issues at hand. Few are even willing to raise questions about Grosz's analysis since raising such questions puts the credibility of the questioner in questions. The postmodern rules, as do all ruling practices, through its hegemonic power and not by the complexity of its argument for the truth of the matter.

Grosz's comments show a nearly total ignorance of the historical materialist understanding of the dialectical relations of base/superstructure, which are a complex, dynamic process. It is important to again stress that the base in Marxism is never biology but the historical relations of production--including the practical activity of labor as it transforms nature and mediates biology/body. The accuracy of Grosz's dismissal, however, is beside the point. What is recognized here by many of her readers is the comforting recirculation of a reassuringly familiar story--the imagined inadequacy of Marxism.

Similarly she dismisses the dialectic as "the possibility of a supersession of the binary terms" (21). This might be said to bear upon the Hegelian version of the dialectic, but the dialectic in historical materialism is a complex and productive way of understanding the historical relations determining the concrete. The Marxist dialectic is not a simple Hegelian formalist/logicist operation aimed at the supersession of binaries, but rather it is an intensification of the existing contradictions at a higher level. "Dialectical logic," according to Lenin,

> demands that...in order to really to know an object we must embrace, study, all its sides, all connections and 'mediations'....Secondly, dialectical logic demands that we take an object in its development, its 'self-movement'...in its changes. In relation to a glass this is not clear at once, but even a glass does not remain unchanged, particularly the purpose of the glass, its uses, its connections with the surrounding world. Thirdly, the whole of human experience should enter the full 'definition' of an object as a criterion of the truth and as a practical index of the object's connection with what [humans] require. Fourthly, dialectical logic teaches that 'there is no abstract truth, truth is always concrete'." ("Once Again on the Trade Unions," 94)

I will return to the question of the dialectic later, but here I want to note what Grosz offers in its place. "Nature," she argues, " may be understood not as an origin...but as materiality in its most general sense, as destination..." and the relation of nature and culture "is neither a dialectic....nor a relation of identity but is marked by the interval, by pure difference" (21). In other words, the basis for what she calls "a nondichotomous understanding of the body" is the notion of a "pure difference." Thus in place of a dynamic dialectic of changing historical relations we are offered a mystified "pure difference," and in place of historical materialism we find a "materiality" of nature, biology articulated as "destination" or as she says later, "a set of (possibly infinite) tendencies and potentialities" (191).

This concept of "pure difference" is the core of Grosz's theory of sexual specificity and concrete materiality and centers her idealism. She concludes her work, by calling for a "subject [that] is no longer seen as an entity--whether psychical or corporeal--but fundamentally as an effect of the pure difference that constitutes all modes of materiality" (208). Grosz develops this notion in direct analogy to Saussure's and Derrida's notion of linguistic difference and a Deleuzian notion of desire. However, she goes even further and posits the notion of sexual difference as 'a difference that is originary and constitutive" and which "occupies a preontological--certainly a preepistemological--terrain insofar as it makes possible what things or entities, what beings, exist...and insofar as it must prexist and condition what we can know..." (209).

I put aside here the rhetoric and movement of ideas that sound very much like the Left Hegelian idealism that Marx and Engels critiqued in The German Ideology. *This originary sexual difference that is the condition* of possibility of all that exists, all knowledge is quite clearly an ahistorical, universal principle--an abstract, mystified "pure difference" produced by an eclectic reappropriation of linguistic difference and borrowing from Derrida's indeterminate trope of *"différance"*; Deleuze and Guattari's "body without organs," and Lacan's idealist notion of the "real" now widely popularized by Zizek. As Grosz goes on to assert, the principle of "pure difference" or "alterity" is the very possibility and process of embodiment: "it conditions but is also a product of the...plasticity of bodies which makes them other than themselves, other than their 'nature,' their functions and identities" (209). In short, the enabling condition, the root relation of the specificities of sexed bodies, of the concreteness of corporeality, is an unspecified, abstract, ahistorical difference that is also as she says a "remainder, an indigestible residue," in short, an excess in any relation (208). Grosz is turning sexual difference into a mystified essentialism--that she declares, "irreducible" and "irradicable." Thus we find that feminism's long struggle to demonstrate the historical construction and transformability of sexual difference is now rendered an irradicable, irreducible, mystified "terrain," that, Grosz claims,

> "entails . . . simultaneous recognition and effacement of the spacings, the intervals, the irreducible if unspecifiable positioning, the fissures and ruptures, that bind each 'thing' to every other and to the whole of existence without, however, linking them into an organic or metaphysical wholeness or unity . . . (209)

Grosz, in short, has substituted an unspecifiable difference that mystically binds all things, and all existence for the historical realities of sexual difference. Her corporeal feminism of concrete specifities becomes nothing more than the latest "grandiose abstraction" positing an "absolute," universal, ideal at its core--only this one is not holistic but a mystified difference of unspecifiable intervals, spacings and ruptures. She is, of course, articulating here the post-al litany of gaps, fissures, incommensurabilities constituting difference in the discourses ranging from Derrida to Foucault to Lyotard.

The concrete, the specific is not a resistance to conceptualization rather it is only intelligible through conceptualization. The question is HOW we conceptualize it; what is an effective conceptualization? The imagined concreteness of what Lenin calls an "objective idealism" based on such "sublime" (to use a term popularized by Lyotard) abstractions as "pure difference" and the "immemorial" (to use another of Lyotard's terms)? Or a dialectical analysis of the matrix of actual existing historical relations constituting the multiple determinations of the concrete as a complex conjunction?

In the name of the concrete and specific, Grosz has given us what Lenin, in his reading of Berkeley, calls an "objective idealism" (*Materialism and Empirio-Criticism*, 32). Instead of an effective series of conceptualizations articulating the complex historical relations constituting the concrete of "lived bodies," we are left with yet another metaphysics--a corporeal metaphysics, but a metaphysics all the same. The fact that this is also a metaphysics of difference rather than a metaphysics of identity does not takes us far in knowing and transforming the contradictory relations and intense struggles around social differences in the historical realities of living bodies. Grosz's corporeal feminism, I would argue, is an evasion of these complex real historical relations that constitute bodies and determine subjectivities in the lived realities of social inequities; of privilege and oppression; of pleasure and pain; of exploitation and struggles for emancipation.

Grosz claims that her corporeal feminism provides a non-dualist mode of knowing that overcomes the limits of dialectics. But what she substitutes for dialectics is an eclecticism that raises serious problems for a politically effective feminist materialism and cultural studies. Within a post-al frame, eclecticism may seem an open, nonclosural indeterminacy or a form of "overdetermination." But such indeterminacy or overdetermination cannot provide the grounds for transformative knowledge--it simply leaves the status quo unchallenged as it oscillates between the indecisive logic of "on the one hand" and "on the other hand." Thus Grosz does not so much avoid dualism as simply oscillate between two poles: the binary of cultural inscription and a resistant corporeality. As she describes her position in her concluding chapter:

> I am reluctant to claim that sexual difference is purely a matter of the inscription and codification of somehow uncoded, absolutely raw material as if these materials exert no resistance . . . to the process of cultural inscription. This is to deny a materiality or a material specificity and determinateness to bodies. On the other hand, the opposite extreme also seems untenable. Bodies are not fixed, inert, purely genetically or biologically programmed entities that function in their particular ways and in their determinate forms independent of their cultural milieu and value . . . (190)

It is not that there is anything objectionable here in itself, but that she simply belabors the obvious. Grosz has not been able to theorize or explain the relation between cultural inscription and the body, she simply oscillates between its two poles. In place of an explanation of their relations, she offers a description of their duality, even as she denies that she is engaged in a dualistic practice. Certainly she has some richly detailed and engaging descriptions, but we never get beyond description and an oscillating dualism. For the most part we are confined to a series of familiar discussions of discursive representations, codifications and inscriptions of the body. For all her claims for understanding bodies in their historical concreteness and material specificity, she deals almost entirely with bodies as largely autonomous corporeal surfaces isolated from nearly every social series and historical relation except discursive and cultural inscriptions. We are left with irreducible, irradicable differences that cannot be changed, although their particular form may be, Grosz claims, infinitely pliable within the bounds of this pure binary difference.

In contrast to these eclectic oscillations and distortions, the purpose of a dialectical logic, as Lenin made clear, is to analyze concrete specificities in relation to the entire complex matrix of historical relations-- in so far as possible--not to simply reify an oscillating dualism of cultural inscription and biological/corporeal determination, to use Grosz's example. The point of a materialist analysis--if it is to go beyond the empiricism that Grosz calls "physicalism"--is not to fetishize some biological or "preontological" determining "pure difference" but to be able to articulate the diverse range of social and historical determinants producing social differences of gender, sex and race in order to transform them.

What is missing from Grosz's feminist materialism, as well as from various other forms of post-al materialisms, is the entire complex of historical and social relations we mark by the concept "labor." But right here I meet up against the resistance of the hegemonic post-al logic that has made a commonplace truism of the idea that sexuality, gender difference and labor are incommensurable. The division of labor and class struggle have little to tell us about desire, sexual difference and gender oppression, or so we are told repeatedly--with a repetition compulsion that, in itself, should give us pause

Four

It is possible, I think, to generalize the aim of all materialisms as the effort to base any knowledge of the real on the concrete sensuous. But how do we understand the sensuous? Grosz's corporeality has not been much help--it has simply led us back to the sublime abstractions of a metaphysics of difference.

I want to engage here one other feminist reading of the sensuous concrete of women's sexed bodies--Iris Young's phenomenology of "Breasted Experience," which follows Irigaray's "metaphorics of fluidity" (as opposed to a "mechanics of solids") and also served as a basis for Gros'z own focus on corporeal flows and fluids of gendered bodies.

Young is especially important to our discussion of left cultural studies and feminist materialism, because in the early 1980's she wrote several essays that helped articulate a productive basis for a feminist historical materialism. She argued for feminism to "regard the social relations of production of a particular historical social formation as one system in which gender differentiation is a core attribute" ("Socialist Feminism" 181). The ground of such a gender-differentiating materialism is the social division of labor which she put forth as "more fundamental than that of class" ("Beyond" 50). The basic principles she articulated for a feminist historical materialism still hold today. Feminist historical materialism, she argued,

> should remain Marxist in the sense that it takes the structure of laboring activity, and the relations arising from laboring activity, broadly defined, as a crucial determinant of social phenomena...[I]t must also find a way of analyzing social relations arising from laboring activity in gender-differentiated terms. ("Socialist Feminism" 186).

Here in 1980 we have a very useful articulation of the core dialectic of an effective feminist historical materialism, but it also, I think, provides a productive basis for all cultural politics—to analyze the specificity of cultural practices in relation to laboring activity and the social relations that arise from them, and particularly to analyze the ways in which these social relations of labor are differentiated by gender, race, sexuality and nation. However, the necessity of this analysis has been largely abandoned by nearly all feminists and cultural critics with the notable exception of a few committed socialist feminists and classic Marxist cultural critics. The primary analysis of laboring activity has been abandoned not because it is not historically necessary and politically effective--unquestionably it is both. But because this line of theorizing was abruptly cut off and marginalized by a class struggle in theory. A class struggle asserting the hegemony of those ideas and modes of knowing--under the banner of a new radical postmodernism--that occluded the underlying structures of capitalism, leaving them largely unexamined and unquestioned, while it shifted the focus of critique elsewhere--to the play of signification; to the local exercise of power in discursive practices; to the corporeality of the body, and the performativity of gender. In doing so, it took materiality to be simply a resistance to conceptuality and any closural meaning.

Iris Young, has herself followed the postmodern turn, and recently has stated that "I have come to feel that socialism, as a politics for the United States, is terribly abstract . . . It is not false, but nevertheless it is too abstract to say that [the] enemy is capitalism" (5) Is capitalism too abstract to be an effective object of a transformative theory and practice--is the site of struggle really elsewhere? Or have we lost the knowledges to understand and explain how the production and exploitation of differences according to gender, race and sexuality are fundamentally integrated into capitalist exploitation, into the divisions of labor and class struggle, here and globally?

Unfortunately, Young has herself contributed to this loss of politically transformative knowledges and the displacement of an effective feminist historical materialism. She has substituted an existential phenomenology for laboring practices in understanding the concrete reality of "breasts," for example. She now stresses that "no experience of reality is unmediated by language and symbols," while arguing that still "there are aspects of perception, action and response that are not linguistically constructed" (*Throwing Like a Girl* 13). These have to do, she says, with "the lived body--the tactile, motile, weighted, painful, and pleasurable experience of an embodied subject; and how this subject feels about its embodiment" (14). She points out that the "description of this embodied existence is important because, while laden with culture and significance, the meaning embodied in habit, feeling, and perceptual orientation is usually nondiscursive" (14). But she is not so much concerned with the complex historical relations and laboring activities determining the reality of breasts as she is with the "women-centered experience of breasts" (192). She acknowledges that this is "conceptualization...a construction, an imagining" (192).

So again we are left with the question of how to conceptualize the sensuous and what is an effective way of knowing the concrete? What Young has substituted for a dialectical analysis of gender-differentiating through laboring practices, is a series of "affective" descriptions: that is, how breasts, lactation, breast feeding feel--the affectivity, the feelings, produced both by male-dominated representations and fetishized gaze and by women-centered perspectives. She thus writes a series of descriptions of the sight, touch and feel of the concrete sensuousness of breasts ranging from the "male gaze in which woman is the Other, the object, solid and definite, to imagine the woman's point of view, the breasted body becomes blurry, mushy, indefinite, multiple and without clear identity" (192-93). The site of subversive intervention is no longer laboring practices. Instead she focuses on the affectivity, the feel of breasts, of nipples. She writes that

Breasts are a scandal because they shatter the border between motherhood and sexuality. Nipples are taboo because they are quite literally, physically, functionally undecidable in the split between motherhood and sexuality. One of the most subversive things feminism can do is affirm this undecidability of motherhood and sexuality. (199)

I think we have lost a great deal by Young's substitution of phenomenology for historical materialism and her abandonment of a rigorous dialectical analysis of how the complex concreteness of breasts are determined by the multiple historical relations arising out of laboring practices and the relations of production of capitalism.

Young writes in seductive detail about the sensuous feeling of breast feeding her child. Yes. breast feeding can be pleasurable. But what are the conditions that enable a woman to breast feed in the first place, that provide her with enough sustenance to be able to lactate, and enough resources to have the sense of comfort, well-being and freedom from dire necessity to be able to luxuriate in the practice. Or even to have to time to do so. All these conditions are linked fundamentally to gender differentiated laboring practices. Why have feminists found it so necessary to erase the impact of labor and class differences on our bodies. To occlude the class privileges involved in the affective pleasures we celebrate?

The sensuousness of breasts, the contested borderline of motherhood and sexuality are fundamentally linked to labor practices, and for nearly all women today, the international division of labor of global capitalism. Young may now find capitalism too "abstract" to be the enemy since she has the freedom to have adequate food, a decent house and nurse a baby with access to the best health care. But what about other mothers, impoverished ones suffering under the increasing expansion of the capitalist wage labor and commodity production in rural Brazil or Guatemala. Many of these mothers are not able to breast feed because the complex concreteness of their breasts, of their relation to their infants and the daily survival of themselves and their children are being multiply determined by the relations of production of capitalism. As Nancy Scheper-Hughes has described in her *Death Without Weeping*, for the impoverished women of the Alto region of Northeastern Brazil, the borderline of motherhood and sexuality, of life and death is labor and the commodity relations of capitalism.

The sensuousness of these women's breasts are not only inscribed and encoded by the discursive representations of male dominated culture. Even more important their very function and nature have been fundamentally altered by the intervention of commodity production. The breasts and breast-feeding practices of "third world" women are being intensively commodified as new sources of profit, and new markets for Western companies such as Nestle who intensively promote powdered milk and baby formulas. A common practice, as Penny Van Esterik notes in her study *Beyond the Breast-Bottle Controversy*, is for infant food companies to market their products "directly through the health care system" (138). In Thailand, for example, where there is a high percentage of hospital births, "The hospital is the locus of industry-medical interaction." Not only were infants "bottle feed by nurses with infant formula in the hospital," but "health professionals directly promote commercial infant feeding products...recommend specific brands, give samples personally, or offer discounts or incentives to patients to purchase certain brands from them or from their institutions." In one hospital, "nurses make a commission of between 5 percent and 6 percent on each can of infant formula" (136-137).

The extensive promotion of bottle-feeding has lead to a substantial ideological change in the representations, inscriptions and encoding of women's breasts and their relation to nurturing their infants. Baby formulas are represented as rich, strong and healthy while women's breast milk is re-coded as diseased and dangerous to the health of their infants. Scheper-Hughes reports that many of the poor, malnourished women of the Alto region, described their breast milk "as salty, watery, bitter, sour, infected, dirty, and diseased...as 'unfit' for the infant" (326). The affectivity of breasts for these women is not the erotic pleasures of nursing but the pain and suffering of being unable to feed a starving baby for fear one's own seemingly diseased milk will harm the baby while not having the money (the wages) to buy the seemingly more healthy baby formula, or if one has formula, diluting it so with only water available--often highly polluted and contaminated water--that it does indeed harm the child. The objective reality of these women's working day under capitalism means they must sell their labor power as commodities in order to earn the money to feed themselves and their children. But as Scheper-Hughes notes, "wage labor and the work available to women," especially in urban areas, are, "incompatible with breast-feeding" (316-317). Currently "only 44 percent of infants in the developing world are exclusively breast-fed," according to Sharon Lerner, who points out that "a dangerous combination of poverty and unsanitary conditions makes baby formula a deadly alternative to breast milk. The lives of an estimated 1.5 million infants would be saved worldwide every year if all children were exclusively breast-fed in the first six months of life" (14-15).

The negative encoding of breast milk is also beginning to acquire a very different material reality with the global spread of AIDS--one that again points to the necessity of engaging the dialectical relations of capitalism and the concreteness of women's breasts. According to

Lerner, "developing countries are home to 90 percent of the world's AIDS cases, and...an HIV-positive mother who also breast-feeds has a 10 to 20 percent change of passing the virus through her milk. That means at least 300 infants per day are being infected through breast-feeding" (15). The prediction for AIDS as the main cause of infant mortality is as high as "58 percent of infant deaths in Zimbabwe and 61 percent in Botswana by the year 2010" (15). Given the unsanitary conditions of most women living in poverty, however, breast-feeding may still be preferable. Richard Marlink of the Harvard AIDS Institute argues, according to Lerner, for a "'balancing act,' in which the risk of AIDS must be balanced against the risk of death and disease associated with formula" (15). However, one decides the breast-bottle feeding controversy in AIDS cases, what the African situation make especially clear is the basic economic relations of health and breast-feeding under global capitalism--there are few if any resources for combating AIDS and improving the health of lactating mothers in nearly every sub-Saharan African country.

This situation is a direct outcome of the continuing imperialist exploitation of Africa's labor and social and natural resources. According to a special report in *The New York Times, "Eighteen of the world's 20 poorest countries are in* Africa, and 30 or the poorest 40" (Darnton A8). Their debt burden is so high ($180 billion) that "Just servicing it costs the countries $10 billion every year--four times more than they all spend on health and education" (A8). The global inequity of resources and production is even more desperate when we note that "Africa's share of world trade has fallen below 4 percent and is now closer to 2 percent...Direct foreign investment in Africa is so paltry it is not even measured in the latest World Bank study" (A8). Africa continues to be "under the thumb of outside powers" but this time the "external superpowers are the International Monetary Fund and World Bank" (A1) who are dictating the economic, political and social policies in a number of African countries. According to former president Julius Nyerere, "when we reject I.M.F. conditions we hear the threatening whisper: 'Without accepting our conditions you will not get any money and you will get no other money'" (A9). The external debt of Mozambique is 426 percent of its GNP, the highest debt load, whereas the lowest Botswana is 16 percent of its GNP (A8). One "lawyer, writer and ardent feminist" in Burkina Faso, Monique Ilboudo, describes thinking "of the World Bank as some kind of monster...It sits on top of Africa like an octopus sucking us dry" (A8).

The sensuousness, the affectivity of breasts is not an immanent affect but a dialectical relation to the material conditions of the global inequities of wealth, resources and labor. Breast feeding has a very intimate connection to IMF and World Bank policies through the resources available to meet the health needs of mother and child, particularly under conditions of an epidemic like AIDS and the dearth of resources to fight it in the impoverished countries of Africa. Red cultural studies moves beyond affective theories concerned with "feeling" the pain, oppression, and pleasures of ourselves and others to develop effective theories and praxis for working to transform the international division of labor and global inequities. To do so, Red cultural studies puts forth a labor theory of culture that enables it to articulate the political economy of cultural practices--specifically the relation of cultural practices to global capitalism.

The "abstractness" of capitalism is an ideological blindness that prevents us from seeing the way its relations of production; division of labor; inequities of wealth distribution, and commodification shape and effect the concrete reality of our breasts, our bodies and our daily lives. This "abstractness," however, is itself an effect of the historical relations of capitalism--specifically the reifications that arise from commodity exchange so clearly articulated by Marx in the first chapter of Capital. The answer to such abstractness is not to turn to ever more autonomous, individualized, local sites of inquiry which further reify the particular as delectable cultural studies seeks to do. Instead we need to more rigorously articulate a complex dialectics mapping the full complexity of laboring practices, relations of production, commodity exchange, class conflicts and the ways these both shape and are in turn acted upon by specific aspects of our daily lives, our sexual and racial differences, our bodies, and our other practices. In short, an effective cultural studies needs to critique the abstract relations of capitalism, studying them in their concrete historical specificity so we can understand how the economic, social and cultural forms, organized on behalf of profit, neglect need and produce social differences that constitute the basis for extreme inequalities of class, gender, race, sexuality, age and (dis)ability.

At the root of such a cultural studies is again the issue of an effective materialism and the problem of how we can know the sensuous. Marx, in *The German Ideology*, outlines the nucleus of such a historical materialist theory. Critiquing the idealist materialism of Feuerbach, which has much in common with the delectable materialisms I discussed earlier, Marx writes:

> He does not see how the sensuous world around him is not a thing given direct from all eternity, remaining ever the same, but the product of industry and of the state of society; and indeed, in the sense that it is an historical product, the result of the activity of a whole succession of generations, each standing on the shoulders of the preceding one, developing its industry and its intercourse, modifying its social system

according to the changed needs. Even the objects of the simplest 'sensuous certainty' are only given him through social development, industry and commercial intercourse. (39)

Each sensuous object, in other words, whether a glass, a cherry-tree, or our bodies, are the consolidations and effects of the history of relations that have gone into producing them and the conditions in which they arise--these determinations, for historical materialists, are ultimately, but not solely, the relations of production and laboring activities. The sensuous then is not a fixed, stable object, nor is it simply the resistant tactile or corporeal surface on which discourse inscribes itself. The sensuous, Marx argues, is the "sensuous activity" of people; it is "unceasing sensuous labour and creation [and]...production" (40). Feuerbach, Marx argues, is unable to see the "object of the senses" as "sensuous activity" because he remains in the realm of ideas, or in post-al terms, we can say the realm of discourse, and "conceives of [people] not in their full social connection, not under their existing conditions of life, which have made them what they are, he never arrives at the really existing active [people] but stops at the abstraction ['human'] and gets no further than recognizing 'the true, individual, corporeal [human]'." in terms of emotions (41). For post-al feminism and delectable cultural studies, as we have seen, they stop at the abstraction of the "body." They get no further than recognizing "the true, individual, corporeal body" in terms of signification and cultural inscription and rarely go beyond the limits of discursive practices to engage the full range of human activities and labor which have historically constructed what we know and recognize as sensible, that is intelligible to our senses. In short, like Feuerbach, they "never manage," as Marx says, "to conceive the sensuous world as the total living sensuous activity of the individuals composing it" (41)-- it is at most the world of their discursive practices.

Why this concerted erasure of labor and production from human practices, from our analysis of the sensuous, material world? In doing so we not only blind ourselves to the most basic principle of human life but we also abandon the first premise of historical materialism--a materialism not of matter and things, but a materialism of human "sensuous activities," a materialism of human subjects and society in the totality of their complex, concrete interactions with nature and with their own multiple relations and determinations. Engels sums up this fundamental dialectical principle in his "Speech at the Graveside of Karl Marx" when he says Marx discovered the simple fact, hitherto concealed by an overgrowth of ideology, that mankind must first of all eat and drink, have shelter and clothing, before it can pursue politics, science, religion, art, etc. and that therefore the production of the immediate material means of subsistence and consequently the degree of economic development attained by a given people or during a given epoch, form the foundation upon which the state institutions, the legal conceptions, the art and even the religious ideas of the people concerned have been evolved, and in the light of which these things must therefore be explained, instead of vice versa as had hitherto been the case. (39)

Red cultural studies is the insistence on never losing sight of the materiality of people's needs and the "sensuous" laboring activity and productive relations involved in meeting those needs. It is a concern for understanding the multitude of ways that these relations of production are imbricated in and shape every aspect of the organization and construction of the social, the cultural and the everyday—not in any simple, unidirectional way, but in a complex, changing dialectical process. But many of those working on the scene of left cultural studies today have largely forgotten this fundamental truth or perhaps it is more accurate to say, largely evade it.

Five

What is the "concrete" of sex work and how can cultural studies effectively know it? The concrete here is especially a case of what Marx has called a complex "concentration," "a rich totality of many determinations and relations." The solution to the problem of the emancipation of sex workers depends on the complexity of our analysis-- our ability to not settle on particular, localist perceptions of the tangible, but to develop a dialectical understanding of the relation of sex work to the totality of human interconnections and socio-economic relations in capitalism. For how we understand the complex "totality" of the problem determines, in large part, our ability to act on the existing social relations to transform them.

Feminists and sex workers are all bitterly divided over the politics of pornography, prostitution and sexual pleasures but this division, I would argue, is largely a result of a too narrow and localist focus on particularities. One side of the debate views pornography and prostitution as sites of male sexual oppression and violence against women, and as such must be banned through various strategies of regulation, even criminalization--some of the most well known proponents of this position are, of course, Catharine MacKinnon and Andrea Dworkin and such former sex workers as "Linda Lovelace." The other side defends against this position as a violation of sex workers' identity, freedom of choice, self-representation and civil rights, as well as an unwarranted restriction on the rights of all to the free pursuit of pleasure and sexual freedom-- examples of this position include not only organizations for sex workers' rights but also such post-al feminists as Laura Kipnis' defense of *Hustler* magazine and Constance Penley's texts on the subversive pleasures of pornography.

In trying to resolve this dilemma, Drucilla Cornell's logic of the imaginary domain leads her into a very conflicted and ad hoc position. The "question to be addressed" in "the terminology developed in this book" she says is: "by selling their sex, have prostitutes excluded themselves from the moral community of persons?" (53)   The ethical dilemma Cornell posits is between, on the one hand, "an abstract ideal of the person, with its insistence on the space to orient oneself as a sexuate being, would have a presumption against state-enforced sexual morality, including state regulation of prostitutes," and on the other hand, the position that "if the state is called on to give equal protection to bodily integrity as instant in the imaginary domain and as a minimum condition of individuation, can't we make the argument that someone who has violated her own bodily integrity no longer has a self to represent?" (53).

"Following this argument," she says:

> It would seem that the state should prohibit this kind of self-objectification in the name of the minimum conditions of individuation that I have defended...By prohibiting prostitution, the state is protecting prostitutes' chances to become the persons they now are not, since they have reduced themselves to property. (53).

Cornell goes on to point out that "prostitutes' organizations" have strongly objected to this argument, and she herself cannot accept the consequences of her own logic--she cannot accept any state intervention in the individual's self-representations, even if it is to protect the very "bodily integrity" she has been defending. Instead she ends up advocating an ad hoc position in support of, as she says, prostitute's "right to the self-representation of her sexuate being" and "the collective effort of prostitutes to claim themselves" through "unionization" (56-57). Such a position is a common activist position to provide some local amelioration of the worst conditions that sex workers face, but it contributes little to the larger struggle for the emancipation of sex workers and largely discards much of its own logic. It becomes little more than an idealist exercise that makes little if any contribution to our understanding and intervention in the real material conditions of sex workers.

A historical materialist and dialectical analysis, on the other hand, can provide us with a radical reunderstanding of the situation on which to act. Such a materialist analysis will begin by conceptualizing the subject in the sex industry as a "sex worker." It is not insignificant that Cornell retained use of the "identity" marker of "prostitute." The concept "sex worker," according to Kamala Kempadoo, "suggests we view prostitution not as an identity--a social or psychological characteristic of women, often indicated by 'whore'--but as an income-generating activity or form of labor for women and men. The definition stresses the social location of those engaged in sex industries as working people" (3). The concept "sex worker," in other words, is a social marker indicating a labor relation in the system of commodity exchange in capitalism--it points to a dialectical relation to all other forms of labor relations in capitalism.

In describing her "first job in the sex industry" as a nude dancer in a peep show, Vicky Funari observes that:

> It could also be seen as not too different from jobs I've held in the past. I have waitressed, and been sexually harassed by bosses and customers...I have worked in an office, and been stuck in a cubicle with a coworker who just could not grasp the hard fact that I preferred my woman lover over him. I have worked in the film industry, and felt myself a cog in a multimillion dollar machine that markets "entertainment" around the sex-value of its stars. These all look like sex industries to me. I wondered: What is the difference between jobs within work systems that hypocritically deny the importance of sex to their smooth operation as opposed to those that exploit it as their very reason for operating? If capitalism was structuring my work experiences, and if sexism was structuring roles within capitalism, what had I to lose by facing overt rather than covert realities? I certainly had a choice of not doing this particular work, but I never had a choice of not dealing with its existence" (19-20).

The more common analysis of sex work, however, is not a dialectical one but yet another localist analysis that isolates it as special case and represents it as a practice of choice and desire, of self-ownership, in order to legitimate sex work within the discourse of civil society and to gain the status "citizen"--that is of persons with rights of property and self-determination--for sex workers. To do so feminists and sex-worker activists create a binary between legitimate and illegitimate sex work -- between "free" and "coerced" work. Jill Nagle, who identifies herself as one of the "sex worker feminists" who "speak not as guests, nor as disgruntled exiles, but as insiders to feminism" (3), argues that

> Sex workers activists around the globe have been laboring for more than two decades to improve conditions for those who choose the profession, and to oppose all forms of coercion, in the process calling attention to the larger economic context that severely circumscribes the range of options for all women (and most men). A small group of such activists recently helped ensure that the Platform for Action that emerged out of the United Nations' Beijing Women's Conference in October 1995 clearly differentiated between forced and voluntary prostitution, condemning only the forced variety" (2)

The "voluntary" kind is valorized while forced sex work is condemned. This dichotomy does not in anyway solve the dilemma. As was the case with Cornell, it does support some local amelioration of the harsh conditions of sex work, but at a cost that greatly facilitates further exploitation of sex work and all workers in capitalism. For it legitimates, quite simply the selling of bodies and sexual labor. The sex workers' rights movement requires the legitimatization of sex work, and this is based on the normalization of the commodity exchange of sex, of sexual labor, of bodies. Some would argue that it is simply a recognition of how widespread an economic activity sex work already is--how many women, children and some men find it necessary to use sex work to supplement the inadequate wages they are paid for "other forms of income-generating work," described by Kempadoo, as "domestic service, informal commercial trading, market-vending, shoeshining or office work" (3) in order, as she says, for their "family well-being or survival" (4). But recognition too often and too quickly becomes acceptance and legitimization of the commodifyng relations in the everyday economic reality in global capitalism.

What is emancipation of sex workers? Is it the normalization, legitimization and decriminalization of sex work so that workers can gain the same rights of fair wages and safe working conditions as other workers? The same rights to self representation, choice and property as any civil citizen? Or is emancipation the end of exploitation and freeing people from the necessity of having to sell one's body--not as a moral issue, but as a fundamental social right to have one's economic needs met and to well-being?

The first position involves an acceptance--willingly or not--of the exploitation, commodification, exchange and selling of human bodies and human labor. At best it can attempt local reforms to improve the conditions under which these transactions occur. But it is inescapably an acceptance of the exploitative economic relations of capitalism and subscription to the dominant bourgeois ideology of individualism and civil society that represents the economic exchange of human labor and human bodies as "free choice" and the free pursuit of individual desire. It is an acceptance that is itself blind to the "real" material economic relations of capitalism and is an act of "false consciousness." Of course, I am fully aware that the notion of "false consciousness" is a widely contested one--in large part because it is seen, on the one hand, as a denial of the right of self-representation, through the binary of "true" or "false," and, on the other, as having been displaced by kind of "cynical reason"--an "enlightened false consciousness"-- that "knows" but acts anyway. Both views, however, are based on the isolated individualism of the autonomous monad. However, if we understand not only the individual, but also the economic exchanges in which she is involved, in a dialectical relation to the overall social relations of production in capitalism, we arrive at a very different knowledge for which "false consciousness" is an effective "struggle concept" to use Maria Mies' term.

In *Capital*, Marx explains the process by which the worker exchanges her labor-power for wages. This exchange he notes is represented in bourgeois ideology as a free, unfettered and equal exchange between two self-possessing individuals when it is, he says, the theft of the workers' unpaid or surplus labor. It is anything but an equal exchange--it leaves the worker, Marx says, "like someone who has brought his own hide to market and now has nothing else to expect but a tanning." Nor is it a free exchange for it takes place, as Marx says, under "the silent compulsion of economic relations"--a compulsion that "sets the seal on the domination of the capitalist over the worker." False consciousness is not an epistemological construct of true or false. Rather it is the absence of class consciousness; an absence that misrecognizes the compulsion of economic relations as free and therefore accepts the exchange of wages for labor power, of wages for sexual labor as free and equal. All sexual labor, just as all wage labor, takes place under the "silent compulsion of economic relations" and involves the exploitation of the worker. As Vicky Funari explains, "a long period of unemployment and an empty bank account got me into that mirrored room" of the peep show (23).

Sex work, in short, is the selling of sexual labor that is very much part of a continuum of the commodification of people in capitalism through the everyday buying and selling of their labor power. We need to critique both the false consciousness that blinds us to the coercion involved in all these exchanges and break down the distinctions not only between voluntary and coereced sex work, but between sexual labor and all other forms of wage labor. We need to especially critique the bourgeois ideology that represents sexual labor as degrading while valorizing wage labor as a natural and fair exchange--both are highly exploitative, alienating relations. And we need to critique the dichotomy between paid sex work and seemingly "free" sexual intimacy in our daily interpersonal relations. As the Bolshevik revolutionary, Alexandra Kollontai, has argued, all sexual and marital relations in bourgeois society are grounded on property relations and have extended "the concept of property rights to include the right to the other person's whole spiritual and emotional world" (242). As a result, Kollontai argues, "healthy sexual instinct has been turned by monstrous social and economic relations...into unhealthy carnality. The sexual act has become an aim in itself--just another way of obtaining pleasure, through lust sharpened with excesses and through distorted, harmful titillation's of the flesh...Prostitution is the organized expression of this distortion of the sex drive..."(286). In other words, the pursuit of pleasure as a performance of freedom, is a very specific historical practice of the owning classes and not the basis for egalitarian, sharing relations of mutual sexual pleasure and personal regard among people. The valorization of excessive sexual stimulation and excitation as ends in themselves, distorts human relations and capabilities and is a direct reflection of the alienating commodification and exploitation of human relations that arises with capitalism.

A historical materialist and dialectical understanding of sex work put forth by Red cultural studies recognizes the exploitation of the sex worker--not as a moral issue--but as an exemplary instance of the commodification of all human labor under capitalism. The struggle to end the exploitation of sex workers is not a special case of the privileged seeking to "rescue" the victims--as has often been the charge against feminist reforms of sex workers. Rather it is a matter of people breaking with their class positions--through a knowledge of social totality--and acting on it by joining in solidarity with the struggles of the oppressed to end the exploitation of all people in capitalism. It involves the struggle to show how the seemingly "free" choices offered us by capitalism are, in fact, exploitative relations. The emancipation of the sex worker requires the emancipation of all from exploitation of their labor--from the appropriation of their surplus labor. It involves an end to the buying and selling of all human bodies and their labor--whether sexual labor or not. It is, as Kollontai calls for, "an end to all relations based on financial or economic considerations" (230) whether we are considering marriage, sexual relations or work. It is, in short, the end of property relations as the measure of human relations. It means the struggle to build a new socialist society organized not around profit but on meeting peoples needs. As Marx described it in the *Critique of the Gotha Program*: from each according to her ability to each according to her needs!

Works Cited

Butler, Judith. "Merely Cultural." *Social Text* 52/53, Vol. 15. 3-4, Fall/Winter 1997: 265-89.

Ebert, Teresa. *Ludic Feminism and After: Postmodenrism, Desire, and Labor in Late Capitalism*. Ann Arbor: U of Michigan Press, 1996.

Cornell, Drucilla. *At the Heart of Freedom: Feminism, Sex and Equality*. Princeton: Princeton UP, 1998.

Darnton, John. "In Poor, Decolonized Africa Bankers Are New Overlords." *The New York Times* (20 June 1994): A1, A8-A9.

Deleuze, Gilles and Felix Guattari. *Anti-Oedipus: Capitalism and Schizophrenia*. Trans. R. Hurley et al. Minneapolis: University of Minnesota Press, 1983.

Engels, F. "The Funeral of Karl Marx." *When Karl Marx Died: Comments in 1883* Ed. Philip Foner, ed. New York: International Pub., 1973. 38-43.

Fraser, Nancy and Linda Gordon. "Contract versus Charity: Why is There No Social Citizenship in the United States?" *Socialist Review* 92/3, v. 22 n. 3 (1992): 45-67.

Funari, Vicky. "Naked, Naughty, Nasty: Peep Show Reflections." *Whores and Other Feminists*. Ed. Jill Nagle. New York: Routledge, 1997. 19-35.

Grosz, Elizabeth. *Volatile Bodies: Towards a Corporeal Feminism*. Bloomington: Indiana UP, 1994.

Irigaray, Luce. *Sexes and Genealogies*. Trans. G. Gill. New York: Columbia UP, 1993.

Jameson, Fredric. "Marxism and Dualism in Deleuze." *The South Atlantic Quarterly* 96.3 (1997): 393-416.

Kempadoo, Kamala and Jo Doezema, eds. *Global Sex Workers: Rights, Resistance, and Redefinition*. New York: Routledge, 1998.

Kollontai, Alexandra. *Selected Writings*. Trans. And Intro. Alix Holt. New York: Norton, 1977.

Lerner, Sharon. "Striking a Balance as AIDS Enters the Formula Fray." *Ms.* March/April 1998: 14-19.

Lenin, V. I. *Materialism and Empirio-Criticism, Collected Works* 14. Moscow: Progress, 1965. 17-388.

Lenin, V. I. "Once Again on the Trade Unions." *Collected Works*, v. 32. Moscow: Progress , 1965. 70-107.

Marshall, T. H. *Class, Citizenship, and Social Development*. 1964. Westport, CT: Greenwood P, 1973.

Marx, Karl. *Capital* v. 1. Moscow: Progress, 1954.

---. *Grundrisse: Foundations of the Critique of Political Economy.* Trans. M. Nicolaus. New York: Penguin, 1993.

---. "On the Jewish Question." *Collected Works* v. 3. New York: International Publishers, 1975. 146-74.

Marx, Karl and Frederick Engels. *The German Ideology. Collected Works* v. 5. 19-539.

Nagle, Jill. *Whores and Other Feminists.* New York: Routledge, 1997

Pepper, Thomas. *Singularities.* New York: Cambridge UP, 1997.

Ranes, Barbara. *From Baba to Tovarishch: The Bolshevik Revolution and Soviet Women's Struggle for Liberation.* Chicago: Marxist-Leninist Books and Periodicals, 1994

Scheper-Hughes, Nancy. *Death without Weeping: The Violence of Everyday Life in Brazil.* Berkeley and Los Angeles: U of California P, 1992.

Sedgwick, Eve Kosofsky. "Paranoid Reading and Reparative Reading; or, You're So Paranoid, You Probably Think this Introduction Is about You." *Novel Gazing: Queer Readings in Fiction.* Ed. E. Sedgwick. Durham: Duke UP, 1997. 1-37.

Van Esterik, Penny. *Beyond the Breast-Bottle Controversy.* New Brunswick: Rutgers UP, 1989.

Woolfson, Charles. *The Labour Theory of Culture.* London: Routledge, Kegan Paul, 1982.

Young, Iris. "Beyond the Unhappy Marriage: A Critique of the Dual Systems Theory." *Women and Revolution.* Ed. Lydia Sargent. Boston: South End Press, 1981. 43-70.

---. "Socialist Feminism and the Limits of Dual Systems Theory." *Socialist Review* n. 50-51 (1980): 169-88.

---. *Throwing Like a Girl and Other Essays in Feminist Philosophy and Social Theory.* Bloomington: Indiana UP, 1990.

Books Received

Agamben, Giorgio. *Means without End: Notes on Politics.* Minneapolis: U of Minnesota P, 2000.

Badiou, Alain. *Deleuze: The Clamor of Being.* Minneapolis: U of Minnesota P, 2000

Bamyeh, Mohammed A. *The Ends of Globalization.* Minneapolis, U of Minnesota P, 2000.

Beynon, Robert, ed. *Critical Dictionary of Global Economics.* New York: Routledge, 1999.

Braverman, Harry. *Labor and Monopoly Capital.* 25th Anniversary Ed. New York: Monthly Review P, 1998.

Burton-Jones, Alan. *Knowledge Capitalism: Business, Work and Learning in the New Economy.* Oxford: Oxford UP, 2000.

Cohen, Thomas, et al., eds. *Material Events: Paul de Man and the Afterlife of Theory.* Minneapolis: U of Minnesota P, 2001.

Critchley, Simon and William R. Schroeder, ed. *A Companion to Continental Philosophy.* Malden, MA, and Oxford: Blackwell, 1999.

Cuklanz, Lisa M. *Rape on Prime Time: Television, Masculinity, and Sexual Violence.* Philadelphia: U of Pennsylvania P, 1999.

Ebert, Teresa L. *Globalization, Class and Cynical Reason: A Forum on Contemporary Theory and Transcultural Critique.* Working Papers in Cultural Studies. Pullman: Washington State U, 2000.

Eagleton, Terry. *The Idea of Culture.* Malden, MA, and Oxford: Blackwell, 2000.

Friedman, Thomas L. *The Lexus and the Olive Tree: Understanding Globalization.* New York: Farrar, Strauss , Giroux, 1999.

Gates, Bill. *Business @ the Speed of Thought.* New York: Warner, 1999.

Gregory, Frank, ed. *Speaking of George Gilder.* Seattle: Discovery Institute, 1999.

Gribbin, John with Mary Gribbin. *Almost Everyone's Guide to Science: The Universe, Life and Everything.* New Haven: Yale UP, 1999.

Hahnel, Robin. *Panic Rules: Everything You Need to Know about the Global Economy.* Cambridge, MA: South End P, 1999.

Harvey, David. *The Limits to Capital.* 1982. New Intro. London and New York: Verso, 1999.

Hennessy, Rosemary. *Profit and Pleasure : Sexual Identities in Late Capitalism.* New York: Routledge, 2000.

Hitchock, Peter. *Oscillating Wildly: Space, Body, and Spirit of Millennial Materialism.* Minnesota: U of Minnesota P, 1999.

Hughes, Jonathan. *Ecology and Historical Materialism.* Cambridge: Cambridge UP, 2000.

Kumar, Amitava. *Passport Photos.* Berkeley: U of California P, 2000.

Landry, Bart. *Black Working Wives: Pioneers of the American Family Revolution.* Berkeley: U of California P, 2000.

Law, Lisa. *Sex Work in Southeast Asia: The Place of Desire in a Time of HIV/AIDS.* New York: Routledge, 2000.

Lehman, Peter, ed. *Masculinity: Bodies, Movies, Culture.* New York: Routledge, 2000.

Negri, Antonio. *The Savage Anomaly: The Power of Spinoza's Metaphysics and Politics.* Minneapolis, U of Minnesota P, 2001.

Phillips, Richard, Diane Watt and David Shuttleton, eds.. *De-Centering Sexualities: Politics and Representations Beyond the Metropolis.* New York: Routledge, 2000.

Rifkin, Jeremy. *The Age of Access.* New York: Penguin Putnam, 2000.

Robinson, Cedric J. *Black Marxism.* 1983. Introd. Robin Kelley. Chapel Hill: U of North Carolina, 2000.

Rorty, Richard. *Philosophy and Social Hope.* New York: Penguin, 1999.

Rosen, Michael, and Jonathan Wolff, ed. *Political Thought.* New York: Oxford UP, 1999.

Sprinker, Michael, ed. *Ghostly Demarcations: A Symposium on Jacques Derrida's "Specters of Marx."* London and New York: Verso, 1999.

Wartenberg, Thomas E. *Unlikely Couples: Movie Romances as Social Criticism.* Boulder: Westview P, 2000.

Weber, Cynthia. *Faking It: U.S. Hegemony in a "Post-Phallic" Era.* Minneapolis, U of Minnesota P. 1999.

Žižek, Slavoj. *The Ticklish Subject.* London and New York: Verso, 1999.

Journals from **Lawrence & Wishart**

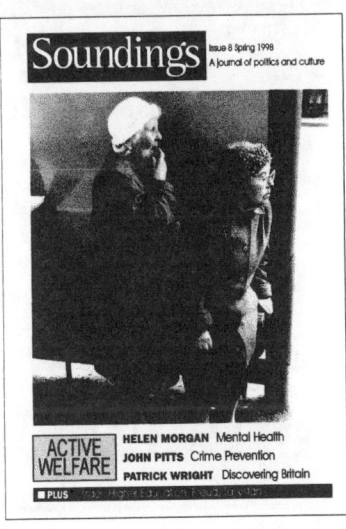

THE MATERIAL QUEER

A LESBIGAY CULTURAL STUDIES READER

"This smart materialist critique of postmodern theory is challenging, original, and provocative. In the best sense it is the 'Western Civ' reader of gay lesbian queer studies."--John D'Emilio, "Donald Morton has always been a voice warning against the secondary impotence of academic discourse . . . [but] these wide-ranging essays will surely come to something—a politics at once explosive, productive, and vitally queer."—David Bergman. "Morton's historically wide-ranging anthology makes for a powerful intervention in the current course of queer studies." —Gary C. Thomas

EDITED BY

DONALD MORTON

Westview Press
5500 Central Avenue
Boulder, Colorado 80301-2877

Cultural Studies

EDITORS

Lawrence Grossberg and Della Pollock,
Both at University of North Carolina at Chapel Hill, USA

SCOPE

Cultural Studies, like the field itself, is in constant motion as it
reinvents critical traditions. Each issue brings to light important
new perspectives on cultural expression and cultural practices in all
their manifestations - from Shakespeare to the X-Files, at pop
festivals and in living rooms, in the workplace, within academia, in
cyberspace and beyond - as they engage with the politics and
economics of race and ethnicity, gender and sexuality, and other
issues of identity, community and change.

Whether it publishes seminal papers on new questions and
discourses such as whiteness studies, or pursues debates on long-
standing issues, *Cultural Studies* is a powerful influence on this
constantly expanding field and on students and specialists in
disciplines such as literary studies, womenís and gender studies,
philosophy, history, ethnic studies and political science.

SUBSCRIPTION RATES

1999 - Volume 13 (4 issues)
Print ISSN 0950-2386
Institutional rate: £135.00; US$195.00
Personal rate: £30.00; US$46.00

ORDER FORM   rcus

PLEASE COMPLETE IN BLOCK CAPITALS AND RETURN TO THE ADDRESS BELOW

Please invoice me at the ☐ **institutional rate** ☐ **personal rate**

☐ Please send me an inspection copy

Name _____

Address _____

_____

_____

E-mail _____

Routledge • PO Box 25 • Abingdon • Oxfordshire • OX14 3UE • UK
Visit the Taylor & Francis Home Page at http://www.tandf.co.uk

The **RED CRITIQUE**

An Electronic Journal of Revolutionary Marxism

". . . nothing less than 'radical' transformations will satisfy [them]."
— Cary Nelson and Stephen Watt, denouncing THE RED CRITIQUE in their
Academic Key Words: A Devil's Dictionary For Higher Education.

THE RED CRITIQUE aims at red-ing social and cultural theory
for new revolutionary praxis.

The first issue of THE RED CRITIQUE is focused
on:

Knowledge, Inc.: Labor, Intellectuals, and Global Capitalism

The issue discusses, among other things, the
political economy of knowledges; the claims made
that knowledge and not labor is now the source of
value in the "new capitalism"; the myth of the
death of the proletariat . . . as well as the role of
intellectuals in social transformation and their own
incorporation into the knowledge industry and the
neoliberal economic order.

Texts by Julie Torrant, Rob Wilkie, Kimberly
DeFazio, Deb Kelsh and others.

THE RED CRITIQUE will publish biannually
theoretical essays engaging issues from labor to
sexuality; from (cyber)colonialism to emerging forms
of fascism; from health care and the welfare-state to
"globalization"; as well as short essays providing
Marxist analysis of the "daily" and current cultural and
political events.

THE RED CRITIQUE
P.O. Box 4254
Stony Brook, New York, 11790-0905
USA

redcritique.org

college
Literature

Kostas Myrsiades, Editor

CL is published in Winter, Spring, and Fall. Regular rates, USA: institutions $48 per year; individuals $24 per year. Other countries add $10.

A triannual journal of scholarly criticism serving the needs of college/university teachers by providing access to innovative ways of studying and teaching new bodies of literature and experiencing old literatures in new ways.

The journal provides usable, readable, and timely material designed to keep its readers abreast of new developments and shifts in the theory and practice of literature by covering the full range of what is presently being read and taught as well as what should be read and taught in the college literature classroom.

CL accepts papers that deal with textual analysis, literary theory, and pedagogy for today's changing college classrooms. Manuscripts should between 8000 to 10000 words.

Address all correspondence to

COLLEGE LITERATURE
210 E. Rosedale Avenue
West Chester University
West Chester, PA 19383
610-436-2901/2275
Fax 610-436-3212
collit@wcupa.edu

Forthcoming issues

Cultural Violence
Teaching Literature at the End of the Millennium
Beat Poets
Medieval Culture
Literature and Art
Working Class Literature

and a General issue every Spring

CAPITAL & CLASS

SPRING 2000 JOURNAL OF THE CONFERENCE OF SOCIALIST ECONOMISTS

#70

Michael Neary
Hyundai Motors 1998–1999: The Anatomy of a Strike

Massimo De Angelis
Globalization, New Internationalism and the Zapatistas

James White McAuley
Mobilising Ulster Unionism: New Directions or Old?

Martin Upchurch
The Crisis of Labour Relations in Germany

Lesley Hoggart
Socialist Feminism, Reproductive Rights and Political Action

Peter Hudis
The Dialectical Structure of Marx's Concept of 'Revolution in Permanence'

BOOK REVIEWS

LUDIC FEMINISM

AND AFTER

POSTMODERNISM, DESIRE, AND LABOR IN LATE CAPITALISM

Teresa L. Ebert

"Ebert keeps in view the political consequences of what she sees as the middle-class individualism and privilege that inform 'ludic feminism.' She is a first-rate scholar whose work deserves favorable comparison with that of many of the figures she engages—Butler, Cornell and Gallop in the field of feminist theory; Harvey and Callinicos in the field of Marxist theory."—**Barbara Foley**.

The University of Michigan Press

Ann Arbor

FS | FEMINIST STUDIES

Three Issues Annually

	1 YEAR	2 YEARS	3 YEARS	BACK/SINGLE ISSUES
Individuals	$30	$55	$80	$15
Institutions	$95	$170	$265	$35
Students*	$20			

* Note: A photocopy of a dated
proof of current student status is
required to subscribe at this rate

Foreign Orders
Add Postage
Surface: $12/year
Airmail: $40/year

Mail Orders to:
FEMINIST STUDIES
0103 Taliaferro
University of Maryland
College Park, MD 20742

volume 26, 2000

number 1
The journal proudly presents the three winners of the Feminist Studies Graduate Student Award for the best article submitted during the1998 contest. Other articles draw from the past: one explores makeup as an indicator of female agency, sexuality, and citizenship during World War II while another argues that the upsurge of women opera composers during the late 18th century was an ironic consequence of Rousseau's musical work and aesthetic theorizing. We have two review essays: one analyzing recent Black feminist criticism, and the second reviewing feminist interventions in the culture of images; as well as a commentary that looks at the lives of writers and sisters, Katherine Du Pre Lumpkin and Grace Lumpkin in an effort to understand how identities emerge and change over time; and a cluster of poetry and fiction by Filapina women writers.

number 2:
A Special Issue on Women and Health
Articles include two examinations of obstetrics: one historical and the other an ethnographic study of obstetrical ultrasound. Other articles examine the problems facing feminist demographers as they explore the gendered dimensions of maternal education and child health; the female orgasm in Second Wave feminism; and the creation of a feminist health agency in the 1960s that helped US women obtain abortions in Mexico. One review essay looks at medical practice and women's access to abortion before and after Roe v. Wade; and the second explores the reappraisals of psychoanalytic theory and practice by lesbian and gay theoreticians. Three commentaries share first-hand accounts of living with long-term illness: the effects of crippling arthritis; the struggle to regain memory after the removal of a brain tumor; and a teenage girl's grappling with her mother's diagnosis of cancer. Fiction, poetry, and art complement the issue.

number 3
A Special Issue: Women of the Indian Subcontinent
Articles explore the age of consent debate in colonial Bengal as a liminal moment in the discourse of the "woman question"; how domestic servants in contemporary India negotiate their identities as men and women; the locations and dislocations of traveling in the Himalayan region of India; while a reexamination of the work of Kamal Das emphasizes the locational politics of textual reading practices. Review essays analyze sexuality, law and the colonial state; gender and the South Asia diaspora; gender, violence, and partition; and the woman's movement in India today. The issue also contains an art essay that looks at South Asian quilt makers and their work; as well as contemporary fiction and poetry.

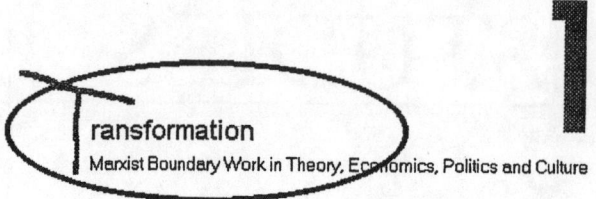

Transformation
Marxist Boundary Work in Theory, Economics, Politics and Culture

POST-ALITY:

Marxism and Postmodernism

mas'ud zavarzadeh
robert albritton
alex callinicos
teresa ebert
greg dawes
donald morton
a. sears & c. mooers
colin hay
bob hodge
jorge larrain
paul le blanc
jennifer cotter

POST-ALITY
DE(CON)STRUCTION OF MARX'S *CAPITAL*
HOMI BHABHA'S POSTCOLONIALISM
RED FEMINISM
MARXIST CRITIQUE OF THE SUBJECT
QUEERITY AND LUDIC SADO-MASOCHISM
HEGEMONY, CLASS, AND SOCIAL MOVEMENTS
META-NARRATIVE AND POLITICAL EFFACEMENT
LABOR THEORY OF LANGUAGE
IDENTITY, THE OTHER, AND POSTMODERNISM
CULTURE, IDENTITY, CLASS STRUGGLE
"LEFT" JOURNALS AFTER THE "POST"

JOURNAL OF THE HISTORY OF SEXUALITY

Barbara Loomis and William Bonds, Editors

Established in 1990, **JHS** illuminates the history of sexuality in all its expressions, recognizing various differences of class, culture, gender, race, and sexual orientation. Its cross-cultural and cross-disciplinary character brings together original articles and critical reviews from historians, social scientists, and humanities scholars worldwide.

January/April 2000, Volume 9, Number 1/2

Self-Pollution, Moral Reform and the Venereal Trade: Notes on the Sources and Historical Context of the *Onania* (1716)
Micheal Stolberg

"Strong Animal Passions" in the Gilded Age: Race, Sex and a Senator on Trial
Lynn Hudson

Bathhouses, Hustlers and a Sex Club: The Reception of Mikhail Kuzmin's *Wings*
John E. Malmstad

Nakedness, Non-Violence and *Brahmacharya*: Gandhi's Experiments in Celibate Sexuality
Vinay Lal

Subscription Rates:
Individuals $41, Institutions $115, Canada/Mexico $12, Other foreign add $22.
Single Copy Rates:
Individuals $15, Institutions $32, Mexico/Canada $3, Other foreign, add $5.50.

University of Texas Press, Journals Division, Box 7819, Austin, Texas 78713-7819

Mediations

The Journal of the Marxist Literary Group

In Recent and Forthcoming Issues of Mediations

Spring, 1999

Neil Larsen on Postcolonialismand Imperialism
Bill Mullen on Displacement and Diaspora
Chris Kamrath on John Sayles' Border Cinema
Plus a Special Section on Chile after Pinochet,
Featuring Ariel Dorfman, Sophia McClennen, and More

Spring, 1998

Lauren Berlant on Cultural Studies
Shawn Miklaucic on Jameson and Form
Forum on Teaching Marxism With Michael Sprinker,
Neil Larsen, Avery Gordon, John Mowitt, Alan Wald,
Kenny Mostern, and Peter Hitchcock
An Interview with Barbara Foley
Artwork by Tseng Kwong Chi, Robert Flynt, Karen Baldner,
Robert Farber, John Ford and Carol Irving

Spring, 1997

John Barberet on Utopian Discourse
Crystal Bartolovich on the New World Order
Mary Layoun on "Wedding in Galilee"
June Deery on Cyber-fiction
Simone Osthoff on Michael Jackson and Orson Welles
Photographs by Alan Sekula, Alison Sky, Sergei Skyratov,
and Debra Risberg

Subscriptions are $20 annually, which includes membership in the
Marxist Literary Group. To subcribe or for a sample copy contact:

Mediations
English Department
Illinois State University
Normal, IL 61790-4240

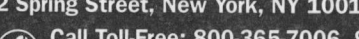

MARXIST | THEORY CRITIQUE PEDAGOGY

The Newsletter of The Red Collective (http://www.redcritique.org)

Available from:

The Red Collective
P.O. Box 4254
Stony Brook, NY 11790-0905

Published by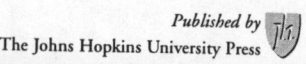
The Johns Hopkins University Press

LISA BRAWLEY and
STUART MOULTHROP, Editors

EYAL AMIRAN and **JOHN UNSWORTH,**
Founding Editors

POSTMODERN culture

As the first peer-reviewed electronic journal in the humanities, *Postmodern Culture* is a groundbreaking experiment in scholarly publishing. Not just the first publication of its kind, it is also the longest-surviving electronic journal, the first electronic journal published by a university press, the first peer-reviewed journal to appear on the World Wide Web, and the first academic journal to publish networked multimedia. More than any other journal in recent history, it has helped create its medium, its audience, and its methods. Now in its eighth year of publication and its second with The Johns Hopkins University Press, *Postmodern Culture* offers a forum for commentary, criticism, theory, and debate on subjects ranging from identity politics to the economics of information, from readers in the text to writers at the mall. *Postmodern Culture* consistently delivers serious analysis of important ideas, along with reviews, cultural observations, and experiments in media and genre.

Published online three times a year in September, January, and June. Vol. 8 (1997–1998).

http://www.press.jhu.edu/journals/postmodern_culture/
http://www.iath.virginia.edu/pmc/

ANNUAL ELECTRONIC SUBSCRIPTIONS
$20, individuals; $50, institutions

Prepayment is required.
☐ **INDIVIDUAL ACCESS**
($20, annual subscription)
· Unique user name and password
· Tables of contents emailed to you
· Hypertextual links between all issues
· Ability to search full-text
· Comprehensive new World Wide Web interface designed for most browsers

To order online:
http://www.press.jhu.edu/access/
indiv_form.html

☐ **Institutional/campus-Wide Access**
($50, annual subscription, or as part of a full-resource subscription to Project MUSE™)
· Hypertextual links between all issues
· Full campus/educational usage including printing/downloading
· Archival rights, ILL (facsimile image only), electronic reserves
· Ability to search full-text
· Comprehensive new World Wide Web interface designed for many browsers
To order online:
http://muse.jhu.edu/ordering/
subscription_form.html

Send orders to: The Johns Hopkins University Press, P.O. Box 19966, Baltimore, MD 21211-0966 USA. To place an order using Visa or MasterCard, **call toll-free 1-800-548-1784,** or (outside the USA) call 1-410-516-6987, or FAX us at (410) 516-6968, or email: esubs@jhupress.jhu.edu

Alternative Orange

Electronic Archives

(http://www.crosswinds.net/~altorange/

RADICAL TEACHER

A Socialist and Feminist Journal
on the Theory and Practice of Teaching

Radical Teacher, P.O. Box 383316
Cambridge, MA 02238

Subscription Rates (three issues per year)

☐ $14   Regular

☐ $35   Sustaining

☐ $ 8   Part Time/Unemployed/Retired

☐ $30   Library/Institution

☐ $ 5   Single Issue (current)

Add: $10 for airmail delivery overseas

       $ 5 for surface delivery overseas

       $ 5 for Canada or Latin America

Because of increased bank charges for foreign exchange all checks (including Canadian) must be in U.S. dollars.

Radical Teacher is an independent magazine for educational workers at all levels and in every kind of institution. The magazine focuses on critical teaching practice, the political economy of education, and institutional struggles.

The South Atlantic Quarterly
Edited by Fredric Jameson

Past issues include

Derek Walcott: An Intertextual Perspective
N. Gregson Davis

German (Dis)Continuities
Martin J. Morris

Friendship
Peter Murphy

Psycho-Marxism: Marxism and Psychoanalysis Late in the Twentieth Century
Robert Miklitsch

Bakhtin/"Bakhtin": Studies in the Archive and Beyond
Peter Hitchcock

Diaspora and Immigration
V. Y. Mudimbe, with Sabine Engel

Domestic/Tragedy
Julie A. Carlson

Future issues include

After the Garden?
Michael Crozier

Michel de Certeau—in the Plural
Ian Buchanan

Harbin and Manchuria: Place, Space, and Identity
Thomas Lahusen

Mysterious Actions: New American Drama
Jody McAuliffe

Single issue: $12
Individual subscription: $32
Duke University Press
Box 90660
Durham, NC 27708-0660
Subscriptions: 919-687-3602
Fax: 919-688-2615
Email: subscriptions@dukeupress.edu

Notes to Contributors

Manuscripts should be typed and double-spaced throughout, including "Notes" and "Works Cited," and have one-inch margins on all sides of the page. Explanatory notes should be compiled under the heading "Notes" and placed at the end of the essay (not at the bottom of the page), following the text and before the list of "Works Cited," which make up the final pages of the essay. Do not indent references in the works cited. Italicize book titles if possible; otherwise underlining is acceptable. Please send one hard copy of the manuscript as well as a copy on diskette, and use IBM-compatible software. Please clearly identify on the diskette the title of your article, the file name(s), and what software was used (i. e., MicroSoft Word 2000, WorkPerfect 7.0, etc.). Your name and address should appear at the top of the first page of the essay and the pages should be numbered. Please keep formatting (i. e., boldface, different size fonts, etc.) to a minimum; do not use soft-hyphens at the end of lines, or place extra spaces between paragraphs, quotations or endnotes--however, you may use extra spaces to indicate section breaks.

Transformation follows the style conventions of *Webster's Third International Dictionary* in such matters as spelling, hyphenation, and the Modern Language Association's recommendations in bibliographical notation and documentation (*MLA Handbook*, 5th edition). References to works should be included in the text along the lines of the following models:

She then writes: "I would like nevertheless to suggest that, far from having exhausted itself, the great ideology debate of the 1960s and 1970s was broken off prematurely, before a series of crucial issues could be addressed" (Silverman 15).

or

Kaja Silverman writes, "I would like nevertheless to suggest . . . " (15).

The parenthetical documentation (Silverman 15) refers the reader to the "Works Cited," which lists all the texts that you have referred to in your essay. If necessary to avoid confusion when two or more works by the same author are under discussion, give a shortened title in the sentence or the parentheses. Please notice that there is no "p." or "," after the name of the author.

Sample Works Cited

Books by one author

Silverman, Kaja. *Male Subjectivity at the Margins*. New York: Routledge, 1992.

Books in Several volumes (and translations)

Marx, Karl. *Capital*. Vol. 1. Trans. Ben Fowkes. New York: Vintage Books, 1976.

Books by two authors

Deleuze, Gilles, and Felix Guattari. *Anti-Oedipus: Capitalism and Schizophrenia*. Trans. Robert Hurley, Mark Seem, and Helen R. Lane. Minneapolis: U of Minnesota P, 1983.

Books edited

Kamuf, Peggy, ed. *A Derrida Reader*. New York: Columbia UP, 1991.

A work in an anthology/edited collection

Said, Edward. "An Ideology of Difference." *"Race," Writing, and Difference*. Ed. Henry Louis Gates, Jr. Chicago and London: U of Chicago P, 1986. 38-58.

Essays in journals

Barrett, Michele. "Feminism's `Turn to Culture.'" *Women: A Cultural Review* 1.1 (1990):22-24. [note: 1.1 refers to volume number followed by issue number]

Entries for a republished book

Hocquenghem, Guy. *Homosexual Desire*. 1978. Trans. Daniella Dangoor. Durham, NC: Duke U P, 1994.

Notes on Contributors

Dana L. Cloud is Associate Professor of Communication Studies at the University of Texas, Austin. Her teaching and research focus on the rhetoric of social movements, critique of American political culture, and contemporary theories of discourse and society. She has published one book, *Consolation and Control in American Politics and Culture: Rhetorics of Therapy*, along with a number of articles in journals and edited anthologies. Currently she is working on a second book, this one documenting the voices and dilemmas of union democracy activists. She is an activist in a range of social movements and is a longtime member of the International Socialist Organization

Jennifer M. Cotter is a Ph.D. candidate in English at the University of Pittsburgh. She has written extensively in feminism, Marxism, materialism, sexuality, cultural studies, globalization, transnationalism, and pedagogy. She is currently writing a book that advances a historical materialist critique of dominant feminisms in the wake of "transnationalism." She is a co-founder and co-editor of *The Red Critique: An Electronic Journal of Revolutionary Marxism.*

Teresa L. Ebert has written *Ludic Feminism and After: Postmodernism, Desire and Labor in Late Capitalism* (University of Michigan Press) and *Culture and Its Other: Sexuality, Class and the Flaneur* (forthcoming). Her cybertext, *Quango-ing the University: The Ends of Critique-al Humanities* is in *Cultural Logic* (http://eserver.org/clogic/1-1/ebert.htm).

Donald Morton's writings on critical theory and cultural studies have appeared not only in such books as *The Material Queer: A LesBiGay Cultural Studies Reader*, but also in such journals as *Cultural Critique*, *PMLA*, *College English*, *diacritics*, *Social Text*, *Textual Practice*, . . . He is now completing a book (*Red-ing the Queer*) on the class politics of sexualities.

Bob Nowlan is assistant professor of critical theory and cinema studies with the Department of English at the University of Wisconsin-Eau Claire. Besides completing *Queer Theory and the Politics of Radical Social Change: A Marxist Critique*, he is also at work on *Fear and Frenzy, Repression and Resistance, State Terrorism, Sexual Conflict, and Class Struggle: Film Noir and the (Post)Modern American Political Imaginary*.

Huei-ju Wang's writing and research focus on critical theory, transnational cultural studies and materialist feminism and philosophy. Currently she is completing work on Hegel, Marxism, and contemporary theory.

Rob Wilkie is a member of the Red Collective and a co-editor of *The Red Critique: An Electronic Journal of Revolutionary Marxism* (http://www.redcritique. org).   A Ph. D. student in English at the University of Albany, SUNY, his other publications include "Privatization of The Academy: Technology in Service of The Bourgeois Intellectual" (Mediations*) and "Postmodernism as Usual: 'Theory' in the American Academy* Today" (*Postmodern Culture*).

Transformation 3

Class

And

...

The next issue of Transformation is on class—the theory of class, class critique and class analysis—as well as questions of class and global capitalism, race, sexuality, ethnicity, nationality, gender, knowledge, taste, division of labor, writing ...